RENOIR

RENOIR

A RETROSPECTIVE

Edited by Nicholas Wadley

BEAUX
ARTS
EDITIONS

ISBN 0-88363-962-9

This book was designed and produced by
JOHN CALMANN AND KING LTD, LONDON

Designer Robert Updegraff
Typeset by Composing Operations Ltd, England
Printed in China

The excerpts in this book are reproduced by kind permission of the
copyright owners, as follows:

Jean Renoir, *Renoir, My Father* (translated by Randolph and Dorothy Weaver). © 1962 by Jean Renoir. Reprinted by permission of A.D. Peters & Co Ltd. and Little, Brown and Company.

Renoir: An Intimate Record, by Ambroise Vollard, translated by Harold L. Van Doren and Rudolph T. Weaver. © 1925 and renewed 1953 by Alfred A. Knopf Inc. Reprinted by permission of the publisher.

Paul Valéry, *The Collected Works,* edited by Jackson Matthews, Vol. 12: *Degas, Manet, Morisot,* translated by David Paul, Bollingen Series 45. © 1960 Princeton University Press. Excerpts reprinted with permission of Princeton University Press and Routledge, Kegan Paul, London.

John Rewald, *Studies in Impressionism.* Reproduced by permission of Thames & Hudson Ltd, London.

Translations from Charles S. Moffett et al., *The New Painting,* © 1985 by The Fine Arts Museum of San Francisco. All rights reserved.

The History of Impressionism, 4th revised edition 1973, by John Rewald. Copyright © 1946, The Museum of Modern Art, New York. All rights reserved. Reprinted by permission.

A. Tabarant, *Pissarro.* Reproduced by permission of The Bodley Head, London.

Jacques-Emile Blanche, *La Pêche aux Souvenirs,* © Flammarion, Paris, 1949.

Gerd Muehsam, *French Painters & Paintings from the Fourteenth Century to Post-Impressionism: A Library of Art Criticism,* © The Frederick Ungar Publishing Company.

Camille Pissarro, *Letters to his son, Lucien,* edited by John Rewald with the assistance of Lucien Pissarro. Translated by Lionel Abel. Copyright © 1943 by Pantheon Books Incorporated. Reprinted by permission of the publisher.

Teodor de Wyzewa, *Peintres de jadis et d'aujourd'hui.* © Librairie Perrin, Paris.

Maurice Denis, *Theories, 1890–1910.* © Editions Lanore, H. Laurens L.T.

Octave Mirbeau, *Renoir,* © Bernheim Jeune, Editor, 1913.

Gustave Geffroy, *La Vie Artistique,* E. Dentu, Paris, 1894. © Editions Fayard, Paris.

Julie Manet, *Journal (1893–1899).* © Klincksieck, Paris, 1979.

Léonce Bénédite, *Madame Charpentier and her Children* from The Burlington Magazine, Vol. XII, December, 1907.

Walter Pach, *Queer Thing, Painting.* © Harper & Row, New York, 1938. Reprinted by permission of the publisher.

Cassatt & her Circle, Selected Letters, edited by Nancy M. Mathews. Courtesy of Abbeville Press, New York.

Matisse: His Art and His Public by Alfred H. Barr, Jr. English translation copyright © 1951, The Museum of Modern Art, New York. All rights reserved. Reprinted by permission.

Françoise Gilot and Carleton Lake, *Life with Picasso.* © McGraw-Hill, New York and Thomas Nelson & Sons, London. Reprinted by permission.

Clive Bell, *Since Cézanne,* © the author's estate and Chatto & Windus: The Hogarth Press Ltd.

Extract from Maurice Denis, *Du symbolisme au classicisme. Théories,* © Hermann, Paris, 1964.

André Lhote, 'Renoir et l'Impressionisme' (1920), in *Parlons Peinture,* Paris 1936. © Editions Denoël, Paris.

Extract reprinted by permission of Faber and Faber Ltd from *The Life and Opinions of Walter Richard Sickert* edited by Robert Emmons.

Clive Bell, *Landmarks in Nineteenth Century Painting,* © the author's estate and Chatto & Windus: The Hogarth Press Ltd.

Charles Fogdal, *Essais critiques sur l'Art Moderne,* Librairie Stock, Paris 1927. © Editions Stock.

Christian Zervos, *Le retour au sujet est-il probable?* © Editions "Cahiers d'Art", 1931.

Extract reprinted by permission of Faber and Faber Ltd from *The Meaning of Art* by Herbert Read.

P. Heron, *The Changing Forms of Art.* Reproduced by permission of Routledge, Kegan Paul, London.

Art and Culture: Critical Essays by Clement Greenberg. Copyright © 1961 by Clement Greenberg. Reprinted by permission of Beacon Press, Boston and Thames and Hudson Ltd, London.

Keith Vaughan, catalogue for retrospective exhibition. Permission Whitechapel Art Gallery.

Kenneth Clark, *The Nude: A Study in Ideal Form.* No. 2 in the A.W. Mellon Lectures in the Fine Arts, Bollingen Series XXXV. © 1956, 1984 renewed by the Trustees of the National Gallery of Art. Excerpts reprinted with permission of Princeton University Press and John Murray Ltd, London.

John Berger, *Permanent Red.* Reprinted by permission of the author and Methuen Ltd, London.

Philip James, *Henry Moore on Sculpture.* Copyright © 1966, 1971, by Philip James and Henry Moore. Reprinted by permission of Viking Penguin, New York and Macdonald, London.

Kenneth Clark, *Civilisation.* Reprinted by permission of John Murray Ltd, London, and Harper & Row, New York.

Joel Isaacson, *The Crisis of Impressionism 1878–1882* Reprinted by permission of the University of Michigan Museum of Art.

Old Mistresses: Women, Art and Ideology by Roszika Parker and Griselda Pollock. Copyright © 1981, Roszika Parker and Griselda Pollock. Reprinted by Pantheon Books, a division of Random House Incorporated.

Tamar Garb, 'Renoir and the natural woman', The Oxford Art Journal, Volume 8, 1985. Reprinted by permission of Oxford University Press.

Professor Lawrence Gowing, *Renoir,* ACGB catalogue, 1985. Extract reprinted by permission of Professor Gowing and the Arts Council.

Fred Orton, 'Reactions to Renoir keep changing', The Oxford Art Journal, Volume 8, 1985. Reprinted by permission of Oxford University Press.

Excerpts transcribed from 'Renoir, What is Painting for, anyway?' Reproduced by permission of the British Broadcasting Corporation, Howard Hodgkin, Bridget Riley and David Sylvester.

Full information for each excerpt is given in the Bibliographical Index, pp.10-11.

Jacket: Detail of *Dance at Bougival*, 1883. Museum of Fine Arts, Boston (Picture Fund). See colorplate 84

CONTENTS

Bibliographical Index

Full details of each source book are listed at the first reference, and in an abbreviated form of author and date thereafter. Where a later edition has been used, the original date of publication is given first in parentheses. Translations are by Paula Clifford, Judith Landry or Nicholas Wadley unless otherwise indicated.

References in the margin notes on the texts to "Daulte" followed by a number are to Françoise Daulte, *Auguste Renoir, Catalogue raisonné, I, Figures 1860–1890*, Durand-Ruel, Lausanne 1971.

p. 49 Georges Rivière, *Renoir et ses Amis*, Floury, Paris, 1921, pp. 3–6.

p. 51 Théodore Duret, *Manet and the Impressionists*, Grant Richards, London, 1910, pp. 159–60.

p. 51 Jean Renoir, *Renoir, My Father*, (1958), Collins, London, 1962, pp. 57–67.

p. 55 Ambroise Vollard, *Renoir, An Intimate Record*, Knopf, New York, 1925, pp. 24–29.

p. 57 Albert André, *Renoir*, (1919), Crés, Paris, 1928, pp. 54–55.

p. 57 Vollard 1925, pp. 30–31.

p. 59 Lionello Venturi, *Les Archives de l'Impressionisme*, Durand-Ruel, Paris, New York, 1939. I, p. 30.

p. 59 *Cahiers d'Aujourd'hui*, Paris, No. 2, January 1921.

p. 60 Venturi 1939, II, p. 276.

p. 60 *L'Opinion Nationale*, Paris, June 20, 1868.

p. 60 *La Presse*, Paris, June 23 1868.

p. 61 Venturi 1939, II, pp. 281–82.

p. 61 Trans. Paul Valéry, *Degas, Manet, Morisot*, Routledge & Kegan Paul, London, 1960, pp. 129–33.

p. 63 Venturi 1939, II, p. 283.

p. 64 Rivière 1921, pp. 14–20.

p. 74 Rewald, *Studies in Impressionism*, Thames & Hudson, London, 1985, pp. 9–25.

p. 75 Rivière 1921, pp. 61, 68–71.

p. 77 Venturi 1939, II, pp. 288 ff.

p. 78 Trans. Charles S. Moffett et al., *The New Painting, Impressionism 1874–1886*, Fine Arts Museums of San Francisco, 1986, p. 141.

p. 80 Vollard 1925, pp. 62–63.

p. 80 Ambroise Vollard, *Recollections of a Picture Dealer*, Constable, London, 1936, p. 169.

p. 80 Rivière 1921, pp. 121–26.

p. 84 Venturi 1939, II, pp. 286–87.

p. 84 Trans. John Rewald, *History of Impressionism*, (1946), Museum of Modern Art, New York, 1973, pp. 368–70.

p. 85 Trans. Charles S. Moffett et al., 1986, pp. 184–85.

p. 86 Rivière 1921, pp. 65–68.

p. 88 Rivière 1921, pp. 77–78.

p. 105 Rivière 1921, pp. 89–91.

p. 106 Venturi 1939, II, pp. 308 ff. Trans. B.E. White (ed.), *Impressionism in Perspective*, Prentice Hall, New Jersey, 1978, pp. 8–9 and Judith Landry.

p. 108 *Chronique des Arts et de la Curiosité*, Paris. April 14 1877.

p. 108 Venturi 1939, II, p. 322.

p. 109 Venturi 1939, II, pp. 291–92.

p. 110 Trans. Charles S. Moffett et al., 1986, pp. 234–36.

p. 112 Venturi 1939, II, pp. 326 ff.

p. 114 Rivière 1921, pp. 167–76.

p. 118 A. Tabarant, *Pissarro*, John Lane & Bodley Head, London 1925, pp. 39–40.

p. 119 Philippe Burty, *La République Française*, Paris, May 27 1879.

p. 119 Castagnary, *Le Siècle*, Paris, June 1879.

p. 120 J.K. Huysmans, *L'Art Moderne*, Charpentier, Paris, 1883, pp. 58–59.

p. 120 Reprinted in Théodore Duret, *Histoire des Peintres Impressionistes*, Floury, Paris 1922, pp. 27–28.

p. 129 Venturi 1939, II, pp. 334–38.

p. 132 *L'Impressionnisme*, Galerie Braun, Paris, p. 11.

p. 132 Renoir 1962, pp. 187–90.

p. 136 Paul Gachet, *Deux Amis des Impressionistes*, Musées Nationaux, Paris, 1956, pp. 166–67.

p. 136 Venturi 1939, II, p. 277.

p. 137 Renoir 1962, pp. 128–29.

p. 137 Jacques-Emile Blanche, *La Pêche aux Souvenirs*, Flammarion, Paris, 1949, pp. 443–45.

p. 138 M. Florisoone, "Renoir et la famille Charpentier: lettres inédites", *l'Amour de l'Art 19*, Paris, 1938, p. 36.

p. 139 Venturi 1939, I, pp. 116–17.

p. 140 M. Schneider, "Renoir: lettres sur l'Italie", *L'age d'or – etudes I*, 1945, p. 97 ff.

p. 141 M. Drucker, *Renoir*, Tisné, Paris, (1944), 1945, pp. 103–4.

p. 143 Venturi 1939, I, pp. 115–22.

p. 156 Rewald 1973, pp. 469–70.

p. 156 J.K. Huysmans, 1883, pp. 256–66.

p. 157 Trans. Charles S. Moffett et al. 1986, pp. 411–17.

p. 158 Venturi 1939, I, pp. 64–65.

p. 159 Venturi 1939, I, pp. 125–26.

p. 159 Venturi 1939, I, pp. 126–27; 267–68.

p. 160 Rivière 1921, pp. 197–201.

p. 163 Vollard 1925, pp. 118–23.

p. 164 Venturi 1939, I, pp. 127–29. Trans. from L. Nochlin (ed.), *Impressionism and Post-Impressionism 1874–1904* . . . New Jersey, 1966, pp. 45–47.

p. 165 *La France*, Paris, December 8 1884.

p. 165 Renoir 1962, p. 224.

p. 166 Trans. Gerd Muehsam (ed.), *French Painters and Paintings from the Fourteenth Century to Post-Impressionism: A Library of Art Criticism*, Frederick Ungar Pub., N.Y. 1970, pp. 511–12.

p. 167 Venturi 1939, I, pp. 131–32.

p. 167 D. Rouart (ed.), *The Correspondence of Berthe Morisot*, Lund Humphries, London, 1957, p. 130.

p. 168 Camille Pissarro, *Letters to his son Lucien*, Kegan Paul, Trench, Trubner, London, 1943, pp. 107–8, 120.

p. 168 *Vincent Van Gogh: The Complete Letters*, Thames & Hudson, London, 1958, Vol II, pp. 556–59, 566–67.

p. 169 François Daulte, *Renoir I*, Durand-Ruel, Lausanne 1977, p. 53.

p. 170 D. Rouart (ed.), 1957, pp. 144–45.

p. 179 Rivière 1921, pp. 202–3.

p. 180 Gustave Geffroy, *Claude Monet, sa Vie, son Oeuvre*, (1924), Macula, Paris, 1980, pp. 261–62.

p. 181 Téodor de Wyzewa, *Peintres de jadis et d'Aujourd'hui*, Perrin, Paris, 1903, pp. 371–76.

p. 183 Arsène Alexandre, "Renoir", Durand-Ruel, Paris, May–June, 1892.

p. 183 Maurice Denis, *Théories*, Rouart & Watelin, Paris, 1920, p. 19.

p. 184 Octave Mirbeau, *Renoir*, Bernheim-Jeune, Paris, 1913, p. 10.

p. 184 D. Rouart (ed.), 1957, p. 172.

p. 185 Renoir 1962, pp. 279–80.

p. 186 Renoir 1962, pp. 236–38.

p. 187 Gustave Geffroy, *La Vie Artistique*, 3rd series, E. Dentu, Paris, 1894, pp. 111–26.

p. 192 Renoir 1962, pp. 255–57.

p. 193 Renoir 1962, pp. 268–70.

p. 209 Julie Manet, *Journal (1893–1899)*, Klincksieck, Paris, 1979.

p. 212 Manet 1979.

p. 213 Jeanne Baudot, *Renoir*, Editions Littéraires, Paris, 1949, pp. 11–30.

p. 215 Thadée Natanson, *Peints à leur Tour*, Albin Michel, Paris, 1948, pp. 28–32.

p. 216 Baudot 1949, pp. 40–43.

p. 217 Renoir 1962, pp. 301–12.

p. 219 Baudot 1949, pp. 49–50.

p. 220 Venturi 1939, I, pp. 169–96.

p. 222 Wyzewa 1903, pp. 376–87.

p. 234 E.L. Duval, *Téodor de Wyzewa, Critic Without a Country*, Librairie Droz, Geneva, 1961, pp. 139–40.

p. 234 Venturi 1939, I, p. 182.

p. 235 Trans. White (ed.), 1978, pp. 21–24.

p. 237 *The Burlington Magazine*, vol XII, December 1907, pp. 130–35.

p. 241 Renoir 1962, pp. 388–90.

p. 243 Walter Pach, *Queer Thing, Painting*, New York, 1938, pp. 104–6.

p. 246 Venturi 1939, I p. 107.

p. 247 J. Meier-Graefe, "Auguste Renoir", Floury, Paris, 1912.

p. 257 Mirbeau 1913, n.p.

p. 258 N.M. Mathews (ed.), *Cassatt and her Circle, Selected Letters*, N.Y. 1984, pp. 308, 313, 315.

p. 259 Vollard 1925, pp. 148–52.

p. 260 Alfred Barr, *Matisse, his Art and his Public*, Museum of Modern Art, New York, 1951, p. 196.

p. 261 Françoise Gilot/Carleton Lake, *Life with Picasso*, Penguin, London, 1966, p. 260.

p. 262 Albert André (1919) 1928.

p. 276 Baudot 1949, pp. 96–99.

p. 278 Clive Bell, *Since Cézanne*, Chatto & Windus, London, 1922, pp. 66–73.

p. 280 Roger Fry, *Vision and Design*, (1920), Pelican, London, 1961, pp. 209–13.

p. 282 Maurice Denis, *Théories du Symbolisme au Classicisme*, Hermann, Paris, 1964, p. 124 ff.

p. 284 André Lhote, *Parlons Peinture*, Denoël A. Steele, Paris, 1936, pp. 164–70.

p. 288 Trans. Gerd Muehsam (ed.), 1970, pp. 514–15.

p. 288 Geffroy (1924) 1980, pp. 279–82.

p. 301 W.R. Sickert, *The Life and Opinions of W.R.S.*, Faber, London, 1941.

p. 301 Clive Bell, *Landmarks in Nineteenth Century Painting*, Chatto & Windus, London 1927, pp. 174–82.

p. 304 W.R. Sickert, *A Free House!* Macmillan, London, 1947, p. 158.

p. 304 Vollard 1925.

p. 308 C. Fogdal, *Essais critiques sur l'Art Moderne*, Librairie Stock, Paris, 1927, pp. 175–84.

p. 311 *Cahiers d'Art*, 3, Paris, 1931, pp. 117–26.

p. 313 Herbert Read, *The Meaning of Art*, Faber, London, 1931, pp. 127–29.

p. 314 Robert Rey, *La Renaissance du Sentiment Classique*, Les Beaux Arts, Paris, 1931.

p. 339 Albert C. Barnes & Violette de Mazia, *The Art of Renoir*, Barnes Foundation, Merion, Pa., 1935, pp. 39–40.

p. 340 John Rewald, *Renoir Drawings*, (1946), Thomas Yoseloff, New York, 1958, pp. 8–13.

p. 341 P. Heron, *The Changing Forms of Art*, Routledge & Kegan Paul, London, 1955, pp. 121–22.

p. 342 Clement Greenberg, *Art and Culture*, Beacon Press, Boston, 1950, pp. 46–49.

p. 344 *Keith Vaughan, Retrospective Exhibition*, catalogue, Whitechapel Art Gallery, London, March–April 1962, p. 30.

p. 345 Kenneth Clark, *The Nude*, (1956), Penguin, London, 1960, pp. 154–61.

p. 348 Renoir 1962.

p. 358 John Berger, *Permanent Red*, Methuen, London, 1960, pp. 199–200.

p. 359 Philip James (ed.), *Henry Moore on Sculpture*, Viking Press, New York, 1966, pp. 195–97.

p. 360 Kenneth Clark, *Civilisation*, John Murray/B.B.C., London, 1969, pp. 342–43.

p. 360 *The Crisis of Impressionism 1878–1882*, catalogue, University of Michigan Museum of Art, 1979–80, pp. 32–39.

p. 371 Rozsika Parker and Griselda Pollock, *Old Mistresses; Women, Art and Ideology*, Routledge & Kegan Paul, London, 1981, pp. 121–23.

p. 372 *The Oxford Art Journal*, Oxford, Vol. 8, No. 2, 1985, pp. 4–14.

p. 373 *Renoir*, catalogue, Arts Council of Great Britain, Hayward Gallery, London, 1985, pp. 30–33.

p. 375 *The Oxford Art Journal*, Oxford, Vol. 8, No. 2, 1985, pp. 28–33.

p. 377 B.B.C. Television, London, 1985.

ACKNOWLEDGEMENTS

I am very grateful to those friends and colleagues who have given me suggestions and advice in compiling the texts: to Martha Kapos, Jasia Reichardt, Stefan Themerson, David Thompson, Gerard Wilson, Christopher Yetton and particularly to Steven Bury, senior librarian at Chelsea School of Art, London, for his unfailing and freely-given help; to Paula Clifford and, especially, Judith Landry for all their work on the translations, as well as to Barbara Wright, Blanche Bronstein and Anita Seal for their guidance; finally, to Elisabeth Ingles, Susan Dixon, Annabel Hood and Robert Updegraff for their editorial, research and design skills in putting the book together with me.

As far as the sources are concerned, I and the publishers are grateful to all those publishers and authors who have given permission for their texts and translations to be reprinted here and to all those museums and private collectors who have allowed works to be reproduced. I am particularly indebted to the research in two recent publications: Barbara E. White's *Renoir, his Life, Art and Letters* (Abrams, New York, 1984 and Flammarion, Paris, 1985) and *Renoir,* the exhibition catalog by John House and his colleagues (Arts Council of Great Britain, 1985). Like all writers on Impressionist painting, I also owe an important debt to John Rewald for his founding work on the subject.

NICHOLAS WADLEY

PUBLISHER'S NOTE

Inconsistencies of spelling, punctuation and style occur in some excerpts because we have reproduced the originals exactly. Where translations have been made specially for this book, normal American spelling and punctuation have been used.

CHRONOLOGY

1841

FEBRUARY 25. Renoir is born at Limoges, the sixth of seven children of Léonard and Marguerite (née Merlet) Renoir (respectively tailor and dressmaker). He is baptized Pierre-Auguste the same day.

1844–54

His family moves to Paris. Renoir is educated at a Catholic school, sings in the choir of St. Eustache. He receives voice training from the young Gounod, is introduced to opera and, for a while, professional training as a singer is considered.

1854–59

Is apprenticed for four years to a porcelain painter and subsequently works as a jobbing decorator for a manufacturer of blinds, as a painter of fans and as a mural-painter of café-bars.

Takes drawing lessons from the sculptor Callouette at a school of drawing and decorative arts.

1860–64

Is registered to copy paintings in the Louvre and prints in the Bibliothèque Impériale.

Enters the studio of Charles Gleyre, Ecole des Beaux Arts, in 1861; fellow student there from 1862 of Monet, Sisley, Bazille. Draws from the antique, master prints, paintings and the model. His examination record is mostly undistinguished, his best being fifth (out of 27) in a perspective examination; 10th (out of 106) and 20th (out of 80) in drawing examinations.

Visits the Louvre with Fantin-Latour.

Meets Pissarro and Cézanne at this time and – during summer painting trips to Fontainebleau – Diaz, Courbet, Corot, Daubigny. Is befriended by the painter Jules Le Coeur.

Sends two paintings to the Salon: *A Nymph with a Faun* is rejected in 1863, *La Esmerelda* is accepted in 1864. (Both were subsequently destroyed.)

1865

SPRING. His parents move to the suburbs (Ville d'Avray).

He stays frequently with Sisley in Paris and with Jules Le Coeur in Marlotte, where he meets Lise Tréhot, subsequently his mistress and model.

Shows a portrait of Sisley's father and *Summer Evening* at the Salon.

1866

Stays frequently with Sisley and the Le Coeur family.

JANUARY. Exhibits three paintings in Pau.

SPRING. Submits two paintings to the Salon: *Landscape with Two Figures* is rejected (despite interventions by Corot and Daubigny); a sketch made at Marlotte is accepted, but withdrawn.

JULY. Shares a studio with Bazille (until 1870), joined there briefly by Monet.

1867

SPRING. *Diana* is rejected at the Salon. Signs an (unsuccessful) petition calling for a Salon for the rejected works.

JULY–AUGUST. Spends summer in Chantilly.

1868

JANUARY. With Bazille, moves to a studio near the Café Guerbois, meeting place of Manet and his circle, which they frequent; also meets Degas, Duret, Zola, Burty, Silvestre, etc.

MARCH? Commissioned, via Charles Le Coeur (architect, brother of Jules), to decorate the Paris house of Prince Bibesco (decoration destroyed 1911.)

SPRING. *Lise* is accepted at the Salon and well reviewed.

SUMMER. Stays at Ville d'Avray.

1869 ·

SPRING. *Summer* is accepted at the Salon.

JULY–SEPTEMBER. Works with Monet at Bougival during the summer; they paint *La Grenouillère* together.

AUTUMN. Shows two paintings at Galerie Carpentier, Paris.

1870

SPRING. *Bather* and *Woman of Algiers* are accepted at the Salon.

OCTOBER. Is drafted into the cavalry following the outbreak of the Franco-Prussian war; posted to Tarbes, Libourne (where he falls ill) and then to Bordeaux.

NOVEMBER 28. Bazille is killed in action.

1871

SPRING. By April has returned to Paris. During Commune spends time between Paris and Louveciennes, his parents' home.

AUGUST. Stays in Marlotte with Jules Le Coeur.

AUTUMN. Rents a studio and apartment in Rue Notre-Dame-des-Champs, Paris; renews contact with Monet.

1872

MARCH. Is introduced by Monet to Durand-Ruel, who purchases a flower still life and *Pont des Arts*, exhibited later in the year in London.

SPRING. *Parisian Women Dressed as Algériennes* is rejected at the Salon. Signs a petition to the Fine Arts Minister requesting a *Salon des Refusés*.

APRIL. His model Lise marries.

SUMMER. Works with Monet at Argenteuil; they visit Caillebotte.

1873

SPRING. *Ride in the Bois de Boulogne* and a portrait are shown in a *Salon des Refusés*.

MARCH? Through Degas meets Théodore Duret, who purchases *Summer* and *Lise*.

SUMMER. Stays with Monet in Argenteuil.

AUTUMN. Moves apartment to Rue Saint-Georges, where his circle includes Georges Rivière.

1874

APRIL–MAY. Exhibits six paintings in the first show of the *Société anonyme coopérative des artistes peintres, sculpteurs, graveurs, etc* (the first "Impressionist" Exhibition), Boulevard des Capucines, Paris, including *La Loge* and *Parisienne*.

JUNE. Durand-Ruel shows two Renoir paintings in London. His friendship with the Le Coeur family is broken off.

JULY. Stays with the Monet family in Argenteuil, as does Manet.

DECEMBER 22. Death of Renoir's father at Louveciennes.

1875

MARCH. Sells 20 paintings for modest prices at an auction of Impressionist paintings, Hôtel Drouot, Paris. Meets the collector Victor Choquet and the publisher Georges Charpentier. Makes new contacts with critics, writers and patrons through the salons of Mme Charpentier.

Bazille, *The Studio of Bazille, Rue de la Condamine.*
1870. Musée d'Orsay, Paris.

SPRING. Probably is rejected at the Salon.

Is commissioned to copy Delacroix's *Jewish Wedding in Morocco.*

1876

FEBRUARY. Shows two paintings, Société des Amis des Arts, Pau.

APRIL. Shows 15 paintings in the second Impressionist exhibition, Rue le Peletier, Paris, including *Study (Nude in Sunlight),* a painting of his model Margot.

SUMMER. Working on paintings of Montmartre.

SEPTEMBER. Stays with Alphonse Daudet at Champrosay.

Commissions from the Charpentier family, including a mural.

1877

APRIL. Shows 21 paintings in the third Impressionist exhibition, Rue le Peletier, Paris.

Is instrumental in the founding of the journal *L'Impressioniste,* to which he contributes two articles on the decorative arts.

MAY. Sells 16 works in an auction at the Hôtel Drouot, Paris.

OCTOBER. Meets Gambetta; requests curatorship of a provincial museum.

Friendship with the pastry cook Eugène Murer; attends the Wednesday dinners at his restaurant in the late 1870s.

1878

MAY. *The Cup of Chocolate* is accepted at the Salon.

MAY-JUNE. His illustrations are published in Duret's *Les Peintres Impressionistes* and Zola's *L'Assommoir.*

JUNE. Three Renoir paintings are sold for only 157 francs at the auction of Hoschedé's collection, Hôtel Drouot, Paris.

1879

FEBRUARY. Margot (Alma-Henriette Leboeuf), his model (and maybe mistress) since 1875, dies of smallpox.

APRIL. Does not contribute to the fourth Impressionist exhibition.

MAY-JUNE. *Portrait of Madame Charpentier and her Children, Portrait of Jeanne Samary* and two pastel portraits accepted at the Salon. The Charpentier portrait is well hung and well reviewed in the press.

JUNE-JULY. Paintings and/or pastels and then drawings shown in two exhibitions at the gallery of Georges Charpentier's newly founded journal *La Vie Moderne,* in which Edmond Renoir writes a supportive article.

COLORPLATE 1. *Return of a Boating Party.* 1862. 20 × 24″ (51 × 61 cm).
Collection Mr. and Mrs. Maxwell Cummings, Montreal.

COLORPLATE 2. *Jules le Coeur in the Forest of Fontainebleau.* 1866. 41½ × 31½″ (106 × 80.5 cm).
Museu de Arte, São Paulo (Assis Chateaubriand), Brazil (Photo Luiz Hossaka).

COLORPLATE 7. *Lise.* 1867. 71½ × 44½″ (181.6 × 113 cm).
Folkwang Museum, Essen.

23

COLORPLATE 8. *Alfred Sisley and his Wife.* 1868. 41½ × 29″ (106 × 74 cm).
Wallraf-Richartz Museum, Cologne.

SUMMER. Stays with the Bérard family, whom he met through the Charpentiers, at Wargemont, near Dieppe. Visits and agrees to tutor Jacques-Emile Blanche, Dieppe; executes decorations for Mme Blanche.

1880

JANUARY. Breaks right arm in a bicycle accident.

APRIL. Does not contribute to the fifth Impressionist exhibition.

MAY–JUNE. *Mussel-fishers at Berneval, Young Girl Asleep* and two pastel portraits are accepted at the Salon. Like Monet, Renoir protests at the bad hanging of his work; he canvases Zola's support and proposes a new structure for the Salon.

SUMMER. Stays with Bérards, Wargemont.

AUTUMN. Starts *Luncheon of the Boating Party* at Chatou. Aline Charigot, his future wife, poses for him.

1881

JANUARY. Durand-Ruel begins regular purchasing of Renoir's work.

MARCH–APRIL. Travels in Algeria.

APRIL. Does not contribute to the sixth Impressionist exhibition. Painting at Chatou, is visited by Whistler.

MAY–JUNE. Two portraits are accepted at the Salon.

JULY. Stays with Bérards at Wargemont and Blanches at Dieppe.

OCTOBER. Leaves Paris for Italian trip, probably with Aline. Visits Venice, Rome, Naples, Calabria, Sorrento, Capri.

1882

JANUARY. Visits Wagner at Palermo, paints his portrait. Returns to France via Naples and Marseilles. Stays at L'Estaque, works with Cézanne.

FEBRUARY. Contracts pneumonia; is taken seriously ill and his respiratory system is permanently impaired.

MARCH. After his refusal to take part in the seventh Impressionist exhibition, Durand-Ruel arranges a retrospective contribution of 25 Renoir paintings from his holding.

MARCH–APRIL. Six weeks' convalescence in Algeria; returns to Paris early May.

MAY–JUNE. A portrait is accepted at the Salon.

SUMMER. Visits to Bérards at Wargemont; Monet at Pourville; Blanche at Dieppe.

1883

APRIL. First major one-man exhibition (70 works), Durand-Ruel, Boulevard de la Madeleine, Paris. Ten works subsequently shown by the dealer in London and three in Boston.

MAY–JUNE. *Portrait of Madame Clapisson* accepted at the Salon.

SUMMER. Visits Caillebotte near Argenteuil.

SEPTEMBER/OCTOBER. Trip to Jersey and Guernsey.

AUTUMN. Paintings included in an Impressionist exhibition in Berlin.

DECEMBER. Makes a trip with Monet, prospecting possible motifs along the Riviera. They visit Cézanne.

1884

MAY. Drafts a proposal for the "Society of Irregularists", an association of artists, craftsmen and designers.

SUMMER. Stays with Bérards, Wargemont.
Visits La Rochelle.

DECEMBER. Monet proposes regular monthly dinner gatherings of the Impressionist painters. Octave Mirbeau emerges as a strong supporter in *La France*.

1885

MARCH. Renoir's first son Pierre born to Aline. Caillebotte is his godfather.

JUNE. Exhibits 32 paintings, Hôtel du Grand Miroir, Brussels; well reviewed by Verhaeren.

SUMMER. With Aline and Pierre, shares a house with the Cézanne family in La Roche-Guyon, visiting Wargemont in July.

AUTUMN. Visits his wife's family home at Essoyes.

NOVEMBER. Stays with the Bérards, Wargemont.
His Paris studio is now in the Rue Laval.

WINTER 85/86. Berthe Morisot starts her Thursday soirées, at which Renoir, Mallarmé and Degas are among the regulars.

1886

JANUARY. Morisot sees his new work in his studio.

FEBRUARY. Eight paintings are shown at *Le Cercle des XX*, Brussels.

APRIL. 38 Renoirs are included in an Impressionist show organized by Durand-Ruel in New York.

MAY. Declines to contribute to the final (eighth) Impressionist exhibition.

JUNE–JULY. Five paintings are included in an international exhibition at Georges Petit, Paris.

JULY. Stays at La Roche-Guyon, with Aline and Pierre.

AUGUST–SEPTEMBER. Two months in Brittany.

DECEMBER. Spends Christmas *en famille* at Essoyes.
Friendship with Téodor de Wyzewa begins at around this time.

1887

MAY. Durand-Ruel sends five paintings to a New York auction; includes five others in a mixed exhibition there.

MAY–JUNE. Six paintings (including the 1884/87 *Bathers*) are included in mixed exhibition, Georges Petit, Paris.

AUGUST–SEPTEMBER. Visits to Le Vésinet and Louveciennes.

SEPTEMBER–OCTOBER. Stays with Murer in Auvers, visited by Pissarro.

1888

FEBRUARY. Stays with Cézanne family, Jas de Bouffan, Aix; then in Martigues.

MAY–JUNE. 24 works are included, in a mixed exhibition, with Sisley and Pissarro, at Durand-Ruel's Gallery, Paris.

SUMMER. Working at Argenteuil.

SEPTEMBER. Stays with Caillebotte, near Argenteuil.

AUTUMN. Goes to Essoyes for the rest of the year.

DECEMBER. His face is partially paralysed after a chill. Undergoes electrical treatment.

1889

JULY. Declines to exhibit at the Exposition Universelle, Paris, because his work is unsatisfactory.

SUMMER. Staying in Provence.

1890

JANUARY. Agrees to send five works to *Le Cercle des XX* in Brussels.
Contributes to the fund to buy Manet's *Olympia* for the nation.

APRIL 14. Marries Aline Charigot in Paris.

MAY. Refuses an offer of official decoration.

MAY–JUNE. *Daughters of Catulle Mendès* accepted at the Salon, his last submission there.
Visits La Rochelle.

SEPTEMBER. Stays with Berthe Morisot in Mézy.

AUTUMN. Aline loses a child in a miscarriage.

1891

FEBRUARY–APRIL. Stays in South of France, at Tamaris-sur-Mer with Téodor de Wyzewa (who publishes a supportive essay on Renoir) and at Le Lavandou, returning to Paris via Nîmes.

APRIL 7. Death of Victor Choquet.

JULY. Paintings of 1890–91 shown at Durand-Ruel, Paris.

SUMMER. Visits to Morisot, introduces her to Aline.

1892

APRIL. *Young Girls at the Piano* (Musée d'Orsay, Paris) is purchased by the state, at the instigation of Mallarmé.

MAY. Retrospective exhibition of 110 works at Durand-Ruel, Paris.

MAY–JUNE. Visits Spain, Madrid and Seville with Paul Gallimard, a patron.

AUGUST–OCTOBER. With family visits Brittany: Pornic and Pont-Aven. Meets Emile Bernard and Séguin.

1893

APRIL. Stays with his family at Beaulieu, near Nice.

JUNE–AUGUST. Visits Gallimard, Deauville; then goes to Essoyes; to Saint-Marcouf in Normandy and to Pont-Aven.

1894

FEBRUARY–MARCH. Two works are included in *La Libre Esthétique* exhibition, Brussels.

FEBRUARY 21. Death of Caillebotte; Renoir, as executor, oversees the bequest to the state of his collection.

AUGUST. Stays with Gallimard, Bénerville.

Gabrielle Renard, cousin of Aline, joins Renoir household as a nursemaid and subsequently a model.

SEPTEMBER 15. Birth of Jean Renoir; godparents are Georges Durand-Ruel and Jeanne Baudot.

SEPTEMBER–OCTOBER. Paints at Versailles. Further rheumatic attacks.

1894/95

At around this time meets Ambroise Vollard and the painter Albert André, both to be his biographers and André to become a close companion of his last years.

1895

JANUARY. With his pupil, Jeanne Baudot, near Martigues.

MARCH 3. Death of Berthe Morisot; Renoir becomes a guardian of her orphaned daughter Julie Manet.

AUGUST. Traveling in Brittany, partly with Julie Manet and her cousins, partly with Aline and their children: visiting Quimper, Pont-Aven, Tréboul.

AUTUMN. Visits Jacques-Emile Blanche at Dieppe.

DECEMBER. Buys a house in Essoyes.

1896

MARCH. Helps organize a Morisot retrospective exhibition, Durand-Ruel, Paris. Hangs it with Monet and Degas.

MAY–JUNE. His work is exhibited in Rouen [30 paintings in Eugène Murer's Hôtel du Dauphin et d'Espargne] and in Paris [42 works at Durand-Ruel].

JULY–AUGUST. Visits Bayreuth for a performance of *The Ring*, but finds little sympathy with either Wagner's music or opera at large. Rather than sit out the festival, he moves on to Dresden, where he visits museums.

OCTOBER. Rents a studio in Rue de la Rochefoucauld, Paris.

NOVEMBER 11. Death of his mother, aged 89, at Louveciennes.

1897

FEBRUARY. Renoir paintings enter the Luxembourg Museum in Paris as part of the Caillebotte Bequest.

SUMMER–AUTUMN. Stays with family in Essoyes. Breaks his right arm again in another bicycling accident. Julie Manet, Paule and Jeannie Gobillard, stay with the Renoirs in Essoyes: Julie's tuition by Renoir begins. It continues back in Paris, where he also starts to advise Jeanne Baudot on her painting.

Desboutins, *Renoir*. Drypoint. 6 × 4¼″ (16 × 11 cm). S. P. Avery Collection, Miriam and Ira D. Wallach Division of Art, Prints and Photographs, The New York Public Library (Astor, Lenox and Tilden Foundations). © DACS 1987.

1898

FEBRUARY. Visits Cagnes [maybe for the first time].

MAY–JUNE. Shares an exhibition with Monet, Pissarro, Sisley at Durand-Ruel, Paris.

JULY. Rents a chalet at Berneval for the summer; is visited there by Julie Manet and the Gobillard girls.

SEPTEMBER. In Essoyes.

SEPTEMBER 9. Death of Mallarmé; Renoir attends his funeral at Valvins with Julie Manet two days later.

OCTOBER. Travels in Holland, with Georges Durand-Ruel, Bérard and others. Visits The Hague, Amsterdam.

DECEMBER. Quarrels with Degas over sale of a painting to Durand-Ruel.

1899

JANUARY 29. Death of Sisley.

FEBRUARY. Leaves for Cagnes, where he undergoes treatment for his rheumatism. Jeanne Baudot there for two weeks.

APRIL. 42 Renoir paintings are shown in an exhibition shared with Monet, Pissarro, Sisley at Durand-Ruel, Paris.

MAY. Contributes a painting to an auction (organized by Monet) raising funds for Sisley's children.

Ten Renoirs sold in auction of Count Armand Doria's collection.

JUNE. Ten paintings, a pastel and a drawing by Renoir sold in the auction of Victor Choquet's collection.

JUNE–AUGUST. Stays at Saint-Cloud; visited there by Julie Manet, the Gobillard girls, Téodor de Wyzewa.

AUGUST. Visits Aix-les Bains for treatment.

DECEMBER 22. Leaves Paris to spend winter in the south. Stays first at Grasse, then (with Aline) at nearby Magagnosc. Renoir donates *Portrait of Jean Renoir as a Child* to the Museum of Limoges.

1900

JANUARY–FEBRUARY. 68 works are shown in a Renoir exhibition at Bernheim-Jeune, Paris.

APRIL. 21 works by Renoir are in a Monet and Renoir exhibition at Durand-Ruel, New York.

MAY–JUNE. Goes, via Avignon, for treatment at Saint-Laurent-les-Bains, Provence.

11 Renoir paintings are included in the Exposition Universelle, Paris.

AUGUST. Stays at Louveciennes.

Decides, after some deliberation, to accept the order of *Chevalier de la Légion d'Honneur*.

NOVEMBER. Winters (until April) at Magagnosc, near Grasse.

1901

JANUARY. Renoir's *Woman Playing a Guitar* bought by the Museum of Lyon.

APRIL–MAY. Visits Grasse and then Aix-les-Bains, for further treatment.

MAY 6. Six Renoirs sold in an auction of the Abbé Gaugain's collection, Hôtel Drouot, Paris.

JUNE. Returns to Essoyes, where his son Claude (Coco) is born, August 4.

SEPTEMBER. Visit to Fontainebleau; paints portraits of the Adler sisters, future daughters-in-law of Alexandre Bernheim.

OCTOBER. 23 works by Renoir are included in a mixed show at Paul Cassirer, Berlin.

1902

JANUARY–APRIL. In Le Cannet, where Albert André works with him.

JUNE. 40 works are shown in a Renoir exhibition, Durand-Ruel, Paris.

Renoir enlarges the family property at Essoyes by purchasing and incorporating the adjoining house.

1903

FEBRUARY–MAY. Spends winter at Le Cannet and Cagnes.

MAY. Stays with André at Laudun en route for Paris.

AUGUST–OCTOBER. At Essoyes.

NOVEMBER 13. Death of Pissarro.

Spends winter at Cagnes, until the following spring.

Photograph of Renoir with Adèle Besson and Albert André at dinner, Les Collettes, Cagnes. © BBC Hulton Picture Library.

27

1904

JANUARY. Considers legal action over suspected forgeries of his work.

FEBRUARY. 12 works exhibited with *La Libre Aesthétique*, Brussels.

SPRING. Leaves for summer at Essoyes.

AUGUST–SEPTEMBER. At Bourbonne-les-Bains for treatment, then returns to Essoyes.

OCTOBER–NOVEMBER. 35 paintings are exhibited in a "Renoir room" at the *Salon d'Automne*, Paris.

1905

WINTER. At Cagnes.

JANUARY–FEBRUARY. 59 works are included in a Durand-Ruel exhibition of Impressionism at the Grafton Galleries, London.

MAY. About 18 Renoirs sold as part of the Bérard collection, at Georges Petit, Paris.

SUMMER. Has a new studio built at Essoyes.

OCTOBER–NOVEMBER. Nine works are shown at the *Salon d'Automne*, of which he is Honorary President.

1906

WINTER. In Cagnes, where Maurice Denis visits him.

SUMMER. In Essoyes, apart from a visit to Bourbonne-les-Bains for treatment.

OCTOBER. In Paris, until November when he returns to Cagnes. Five paintings are shown at the *Salon d'Automne*.

OCTOBER 22. Death of Cézanne.

1907

WINTER. In Cagnes, where he spends most of the year.

MAY. At the sale of the collection of Georges Charpentier, who had died in 1905, *Portrait of Madame Charpentier and her Children* is bought by the Metropolitan Museum, New York.

JUNE. Buys the hillside estate known as "Les Collettes" in Cagnes, spends the winter nearby while his house is being built there (1907–8).

1908

APRIL–MAY. 42 works are included in an exhibition of still life paintings at Durand-Ruel, Paris.

(MAY?). Vollard encourages him to make sculptures.

MAY–JUNE. 37 works are shown in an exhibition of landscape paintings by Monet and Renoir at Durand-Ruel, Paris.

AUTUMN. Moves into his new house in Les Collettes, where he is to spend most of the rest of his life.

NOVEMBER–DECEMBER. 41 works are shown in a Renoir exhibition at Durand-Ruel, New York.

DECEMBER. Monet visits him in Cagnes.

1909

In Cagnes for most of the year, where he is visited by André, Jacques-Emile Blanche, Paul Durand-Ruel, among others, possibly visiting Essoyes in the summer.

c. 1909–10

Writes a preface for a new edition of Cennino Cennini's *Libro dell'Arte*, advised by Maurice Denis, who visits him in Cagnes. It is published by Henri Mottez, as the preface to a new edition of his father, the painter Victor Mottez's translation of Cennini, Paris 1910.

1910

APRIL. 37 works are shown in a Renoir retrospective, Venice Biennale.

JUNE. 35 works by Renoir are shown in an exhibition of Monet, Renoir, Pissarro, Sisley at Durand-Ruel, Paris.

SUMMER. Visits Germany with his family and sees Rubens' paintings in Munich. Returns to Cagnes via Paris.

OCTOBER. One painting is included in the *Salon d'Automne*.

1911

JANUARY. Renoir is visited in Cagnes by Mme Cézanne and her son.

MARCH. Approves the draft of an article by Walter Pach, based on interviews with him over several summers. (It is published, New York, May 1912.)

Approached by a Munich Museum about purchase of work. Contributes 500 francs to a memorial fund for Sisley.

JUNE–JULY. In Paris, visits the Ballets Russes.

OCTOBER. Rents a studio in Paris, Boulevard Rochechouart. Promoted to *Officier de la Légion d'Honneur*.

NOVEMBER. Returns to Cagnes.

1911–12

Meier-Graefe's monograph, the first on Renoir, is published in German and French.

1912

28 works are shown in a mixed exhibition at Manzi-Joyant, Paris.

JANUARY. Rents an apartment in Nice for health reasons: rheumatism prevents him using his Cagnes studio. From around this time can only paint with brushes fastened to his hand.

JANUARY–FEBRUARY. An exhibition of 41 works is shown in Munich (Galerie Thannhauser) and Berlin (Paul Cassirer).

FEBRUARY–MARCH. 21 works are shown at Durand-Ruel, New York.

SPRING. 24 works are included in a centennial exhibition of French art, Institut Français, St Petersburg, Russia.

APRIL–MAY. 74 works are shown at Durand-Ruel, Paris.

JUNE. 58 Renoir portraits are shown at Durand-Ruel, Paris.

AUGUST. After a paralysing stroke in June, he undergoes an operation. He is no longer able to walk and convalesces at Chaville.

AUTUMN. Returns to the south of France (until the following spring).

OCTOBER–NOVEMBER. Two paintings are shown in the *Salon d'Automne*.

DECEMBER. Auction of the Henri Rouart collection includes Renoir's *Parisienne* and *A Morning Ride in the Bois de Boulogne*, the latter purchased by Paul Cassirer for 95,000 francs.

1913

JANUARY–FEBRUARY. 41 works are exhibited at Galerie Thannhauser, Munich.

FEBRUARY. Is visited by Maurice Denis.

Five works by Renoir are included in the Armory Show, New York. His son Jean enlists in the army.

MARCH. 52 works are shown at Bernheim Jeune, Paris, who publish a catalog-cum-book with a preface by Octave Mirbeau.

SPRING–SUMMER. At Vollard's instigation, Renoir collaborates with Richard Guino in producing sculptures.

WINTER. Divides time between Cagnes, Grasse and Nice.

1914

JANUARY. Gabrielle Renard leaves Renoir's household to marry.

FEBRUARY. Is visited by Mary Cassatt.

30 works are shown at Durand-Ruel, New York.

MARCH. Renoir works on a tapestry cartoon for the Gobelins factory and on a portrait of Rodin, who visits Cagnes.

APRIL. Is visited by Jacques-Emile Blanche.

JUNE. In the estate of Count Isaac de Camondo, three Renoir paintings enter the Louvre.

Self-Portrait. 1915. Crayon. Formerly Vollard Collection.

AUGUST. Germany declares war on France. Renoir leaves Paris for Cagnes.

OCTOBER. Both his sons are wounded in active service; Aline leaves to visit Pierre at Carcassonne and Jean at Luçon.

1915

APRIL. Jean Renoir, returning to the front, is seriously wounded again, in the leg. Aline visits him in Gérardmer.

JUNE 27. Death of Aline Renoir. She is buried at Essoyes.

JULY. Renoir goes to Paris, where he is visited by his son Jean, released from hospital. At this period, start the conversations between them which became the basis for Jean's biography, *Renoir, My Father*.

NOVEMBER. Returns to Cagnes, asks Durand-Ruel to make an inventory (with Vollard) of his work in Paris.

1916

WINTER. In Cagnes.

MARCH. Renoir's bronze *Venus Victorious* is shown at the Triennale, Paris.

JUNE. Visits Paris.

Presents a painting to the Musée Municipale of Limoges.

SUMMER. In Essoyes.

AUTUMN. Returns to Cagnes.

OCTOBER. 26 works are included in an exhibition of French art at Winterthur, Switzerland.

1917

JANUARY. 18 works are shown at Durand-Ruel, Paris.

Albert André and his wife stay with Renoir at Cagnes, as does Jean Renoir, on leave.

JUNE–JULY. 16 works are included in an exhibition on behalf of the war wounded at Paul Rosenberg, Paris.

JULY. Visits Paris, returning to Cagnes via Essoyes in August.

SUMMER. A group of English artists and collectors write in tribute to him, on the occasion of *Les Parapluies* being exhibited in London.

SEPTEMBER 26. Death of Degas.

OCTOBER–NOVEMBER. 60 works are included in an exhibition of modern French art, Kunsthaus, Zurich.

DECEMBER. His collaboration with the sculptor Guino ends. Matisse makes the first of several visits to Renoir in Cagnes.

1918

FEBRUARY. André sends to Renoir the text of his monograph for approval.

FEBRUARY–MARCH. 28 works are shown at Durand-Ruel, Paris.

MARCH. Vollard sends to Renoir the 667 illustrations to the first volume of *Tableaux, Pastels & Dessins de Pierre-Auguste Renoir*, which he approves and signs. (It is published later in the year.)

Renoir is visited in Cagnes by Mary Cassatt and, later in the month at Nice, by René Gimpel.

Divides time between Cagnes and Nice, health deteriorating.

NOVEMBER 11. Armistice is declared, to end the War.

1919

FEBRUARY. Renoir is appointed *Commandeur de la Legion d'Honneur*.

APRIL. 35 works are shown at Durand-Ruel, Paris.

MAY. Albert André's monograph *Renoir* is published.

AUGUST. Makes his last visit to Paris, via Essoyes. Invited by Paul Léon, the Director of the Beaux Arts, he is carried around the Louvre for a private viewing.

SEPTEMBER. In Essoyes, en route for Cagnes.

DECEMBER 3. Renoir dies in Cagnes, of congestion of the lungs.

He is buried three days later at Essoyes.

Photograph of Renoir, Adèle Besson and Albert André. 1917. Collection Jacqueline Besson-André.

INTRODUCTION

There never has been a shortage of books on Renoir. Only six years after his death, the author of one of eight monographs published in Paris in the 1920s, Gustave Coquiot, felt obliged to pen the following *"Avant-Propos."*

– Another attempt at a book on Renoir?
– But of course!
– There's no call for that triumphant air!
– I'm not assuming one.
– This is at least the 365th attempt.
– The 366th exactly.
– And what will it say that's new?
– Oh! Not a great deal!
– So?
– Only perhaps to correct a few mistakes.
– And this 366th will contain no more than that?
– That is so.
– So this could go on indefinitely?
– Of course.
– I no longer understand!
– Don't try to understand!
– So . . . what's it all for?
– Well, this 366th attempt will secure for me, above all else, the great pleasure of spending more time with Renoir.
– Ah! Well if that's the case. . . .

And so it has gone on: at least three monographs in each decade since then and the total now around forty. The selection presented here from the vast literature on Renoir reveals, particularly in the first fifty years or so, a remarkable consensus. As Coquiot suggested in 1925, most writers express their pleasure in Renoir's frankly celebratory imagery and propose a largely homogeneous view of the man and his art. The same half-dozen or so paintings are cited repeatedly as his masterpieces. That this homogeneous view corresponds closely to Renoir's view of himself is not so surprising when we recognize how many of the pioneer writings were based on long conversations between the artist and his biographers, some of them intimate friends. The tradition was reinforced in the 1950s with the publication of his son Jean's book, *Renoir, My Father,* a biography fundamentally shaped by the artist's own words and personality. In face of an unceasing tide of affirmation, the bluntness of Mary Cassatt (1913/14) or the caustic impatience of Keith Vaughan (1953) come as something of a relief.

We are left wondering whether this rounded endorsement of the artist is not rather indiscriminate, and if so why? It certainly contrasts with writing about his contemporaries, even though Renoir probably acquired more personal fame in his own lifetime than any of them. This disparity may also be linked with a recurrent suspicion that his painting is not really relevant to later values and practices. This is clearly evident, for instance, from a comparison with the type of attention and intellectual level of analysis focused upon Cézanne. Renoir is a more "popular" artist, we may argue? But Gauguin or Van Gogh, both of whom command an enormous "popular" following and readership, are the subjects of a serious literature of much greater substance, leaving no doubt either of their "greatness" or of their unshakable historical importance.

For all the hymns of praise to this "lover of life," this natural and sensual painter, untroubled by dogma or guilt, there occur in the later writings – particularly of the last thirty years – lingering doubts that maybe these qualities are not enough, or that only occasionally is the magic strong enough to carry such instinctive art onto the highest level. A London critic wrote in 1905 that "the most unequal of the great

Impressionists excels in painting living, palpitating flesh, but his most enthusiastic admirers cannot defend certain phases of his art in which he sinks far below the level even of mediocrity." Eighty years later, the organizer of a major Renoir exhibition in London told a press conference that "actually over 90% is rubbish. . . . We don't want to anaesthetize his work, but I hope we have disguised the boredoms."

This book sets out, through a survey of the writings on Renoir over the last century and a quarter, to clarify the cumulative picture that history has left us of the man and the artist. The texts have been selected to include the best of the most characteristic and the most frank writings (whether supportive or hostile), as well as some of the more unusual personal views of Renoir. Together they compose an original and complete monograph.

What of Renoir the man? Pissarro described him in 1887 as "that most variable of men" and, throughout, we encounter very different sides of his personality. On the one hand there is his indecisive shyness, as boy and man: a modesty that gave rise to his view of himself as "a cork" floating on the stream of circumstance. "I have always accepted things as they came along," he told Ambroise Vollard, and the evidence supports this. As a young apprentice, he was tempted to go into partnership with the proprietor of the blind-painting workshop. It was his young friend Henri Laporte who talked him out of it, persuading him instead to enroll at the École des Beaux Arts. Renoir appears to have enjoyed working for someone else and he behaved towards his dealer, Paul Durand-Ruel, as to a paternalistic employer. Similarly, it was at Vollard's initiative that Renoir started making sculpture. Other friends described his restlessness and hesitancy. Renoir wrote to Théodore Duret in 1881: "What a misfortune always to hesitate. But that is the basis of my character and as I get older, I'm afraid I won't be able to change." In 1892, a critic defined him as "an artist basically too undecided . . . for him to be properly ranked among the masters."

We see other sides to Renoir, as well. He appeared charming and accessible, a vivacious social personality in the café life of the artists and in the *beau monde* of Madame Charpentier's *soirées*. He mixed easily with his patrons. If his reticence showed in his passive acceptance of fate and of the inevitability of change in his personal life, his attitude to change in the outside world revealed an outspoken reactionary fervor. He railed against electricity, dentistry, sulphur-matches, sewage pipes, banks, all-night stores, education, railways and corsets. He was a cautiously practical man, prudish and thrifty, his son tells us. He advised Durand-Ruel that "the only wise thing is to expect the worst" and – compared to his peers – his attitudes to officialdom had a thrifty pragmatism, uncomplicated by too much ideology. For all his joking to Durand-Ruel about deserving an honorary *commode* to celebrate his *Légion d'Honneur* appointment, he accepted honors as legitimate means to an end.

He deplored the excesses of Romanticism, extravagance in architecture and melodrama in theater, literature or music. "He avoided coarse words as much as possible," Jean Renoir writes, "reserving them for a limited number of personal enemies." His nationalism and his attitudes towards women were prejudices tantamount to chauvinism. Although he finds something positive to say about almost all cultures that he encounters (except English painting), he invariably affirms the lasting value of French painting, French furniture, French music, French literature and Parisian women.

He bemoaned the loss of eighteenth-century values, the lack of proper professional training for artists and the demise of individual craftsmanship in an increasingly commercial world. For all his outward modesty and shyness – and Maurice Denis still spoke of these in the 1890s – these private beliefs were dogmatic and confident enough to generate several public pronouncements about art at large. There is also that faintly sanctimonious tone that occasionally creeps into his advice to the teenage diarist Julie Manet, and even into the more subjective records of conversations with his son, Jean.

At worst, then, Renoir comes through with a reactionary view of the world that was formed early and that remained content with its own blinkers. At best, he appears thoughtful, humane, generous and entertaining; and, so long as he was painting, uncomplaining about the frustration and debilitating pain of his later years. The picture is not simple. Renoir's image of himself as a shy "cork" is always somewhat at odds with accounts of the witnesses, to whichever extreme their evidence gravitates.

Jean Renoir discusses the important change in Renoir's life brought about by the birth of a first son, Pierre, in 1885 and by his subsequent marriage. Georges Rivière goes so far as to suggest that it may have precipitated the crisis in Renoir's painting of the 1880s. Whatever its secret character, Renoir was deeply affected by the change from an unattached painter (a free agent who could move at will between different parts of the country and could take professional success or failure as they came) to a position of domestic responsibility. We may guess how difficult it was for him to assimilate his new status from the fact that he wished to appear to friends as if no change had taken place. He told no one of Aline's presence on his trip to Italy in 1881. It seems that his close friend Berthe Morisot was unaware of the existence of Aline or Pierre in 1886, and this despite the fact that she discussed and admired Renoir's mother-and-child drawings in his studio. She did not meet Aline until 1891, when she wrote to Mallarmé: "I shall never succeed in describing to you my astonishment at the sight of this ungainly woman whom, I don't know why, I had imagined to be like her husband's paintings." This may say something about the distance between Renoir's idealized images and the "reality" they represented, but it also underwrites Julie Manet's innocent amusement at Aline's recollection of being a slim 22-year-old. Julie also gives affectionate glimpses of Renoir being "led by the nose" and buying a house [in Essoyes] that he didn't want to buy.

Mostly, Aline emerges as a simple woman, absorbed in chickens, rabbits, *bouillabaisse* and her husband's well-being: precisely the sort of uncomplicated woman that Renoir sought to surround himself by. During the last two decades of his life, the house of this increasingly frail and dependent man was full of large, accommodating women who spent their time sewing, singing, cooking and posing for him. Aline's sole aim in life had been "to surround her husband with an atmosphere of calm." Husband and wife were of one mind. Renoir advised his son: "Why teach women such boring things as law, medicine, science and journalism, which men excel in, when women are so fitted for a task which men can never dream of attempting, and that is to make life bearable." Jean Renoir writes of 1915 that "the death of my mother had completely crushed him" and a little later, "not enough time had yet elapsed for him to be able to overcome the confusion in his mind caused by my mother's death."

Considering that his brush painted more women than anything else, it is no surprise that Renoir's women form the central focus of all writing about him, ever since his early success with *Lise* in 1867. Rivière (1877) encourages the ladies to have their portraits painted by Renoir and the following year Duret promises the gentlemen who commission such portraits: "Renoir's women are enchantresses. . . . You will have a mistress, but what a mistress!" This sort of context makes clear that in his chauvinism and his obsessive sensuality, Renoir was a child of his time. His boast that "I loved women even before I learned to walk" and his novelettish anecdotes about Mme Lévy's attempts to seduce him in the porcelain factory, are very much of their time. So, too, is what seems to us as the boorish insensitivity of his pronouncements upon women. "Women don't question anything," Renoir said. "You feel reassured when you're with them. . . . I like women best when they don't know how to read. . . .

She even makes mistakes in spelling and in my opinion that's essential in a woman," and so on. Yet his son assures us: "His respectful attitude towards women was often described to me by his friends . . . as chivalrous."

In the 1870s, the actress Jeanne Samary concluded: "Renoir is not the marrying kind. He marries all the women he paints, but with his brush." Vollard remembered Renoir explaining a still life of roses to him as "an experiment I'm making in flesh tones for a nude." As Walter Sickert put it: "He is better at women than flowers. They interest him more," and critics have long recognized that he did not want this interest diluted by anything else. In 1899 François Thiébault-Sisson saw the Renoir model as "a passive being of instinct . . . her expression reflecting no inner light . . . a decorative motif." For Julius Meier-Graefe (1912): "Renoir puts before us a divine celebration of flesh, still innocent of desire, not yet tainted by passion; still idyllic and yet brimming with powerful sensuality." An equation of painting with sexuality was real enough for Renoir. There is his notorious reply to a journalist who had asked how he could paint when his hands were so crippled: "With my prick." Renoir also said, to his son: "I am afraid that future generations won't know how to make love well, and that would be most unfortunate for those who haven't got painting." It is only in such a context that we can make sense of a remark in a letter to Albert André about "happy painting which, very late in life, still gives you illusions and sometimes joy."

The sensual male celebration in Renoir's painting of women as animals to be enjoyed has been acclaimed and sustained for over a century by writers, collectors, dealers, museum-goers. It comes as no surprise that this hierarchy of values has been confronted and dismantled by a generation of art historians whose thinking is enlightened by late twentieth-century feminist values. Writers such as Roszika Parker and Griselda Pollock (1981) and Tamar Garb (1985) have re-seen Renoir's unthinking women as "an evasion of reality," as "oppressive" and as "palpable flesh displayed for the viewer's pleasure." In the terms of this retrospective anthology, the polarity between these views and those, for instance, of Lawrence Gowing (1985) – no less passionate and eloquent in their subscription to more traditional, sensual joys in life and the practice of painting – reveals a confrontation in contemporary thinking about Renoir not encountered since the 1860s.

What do we learn of Renoir the artist? Usually, that he was the simplest of artists, the self-professed maker of an untroubled and untroubling art. Roger Fry (1920), among others, identifies Renoir as an artist characterized by a common, unpretentious touch. There is much support for this image in Renoir's own recorded views. He believed that the Folies-Bergères should receive state subsidy before the Comédie Française; he mixed most readily with men who are "interested only in horses, women and boats." He appears on the face of it as the most non-intellectual and anti-theoretical of artists of his or almost any other generation, as a chap rather than a god, as David Sylvester (1985) puts it. But to settle for that view would be to disregard the lasting and hypnotic extraordinariness of his imagery and the evolving theory of art that accumulates from all his first- or second-hand statements. This is reflected as much in the fluctuating evaluation of his art, as in the changing appearance of the paintings themselves.

Renoir was a thoroughly professional artist. His prodigious manual dexterity was recognized from the outset. "Such skill isn't natural" was the comment of the man who employed him as a teenager to paint blinds. As a student, he applied himself more earnestly than his peers to harness this ability to the practices of drawing and painting. "Be a good workman first and foremost," Rivière remembers him saying. As a painter, he took a highly practical attitude to finding the best available means of using his natural abilities to earn a living. We see this in his pursuit of a market and reputation in portraiture. We see it in his policy of pursuing the official Salon as a market place; we see it in his attitude to official recognition and honors. He took critics seriously and was more disturbed by lack of comment than by hostility. Barbara E. White has suggested convincingly that the paintings he chose to exhibit each year were in some measure a considered response to the previous round of critical reaction. He wanted his painting to be liked so that he could paint on, untroubled. "I can't paint if it doesn't amuse me," he told Jean. "And how can you be amused when you're wondering if what you're doing is making people grind their teeth." It distressed him that charming and "joyous" painting (like Fragonard's for example) was never taken seriously. The same thought underlies his much-quoted comment: "When Pissarro painted views of Paris, he always put in a funeral, whereas I would have put in a wedding." Such thoughts, however deeply rooted in his attitude, his craftsmanship or his passionate sense of a French tradition, have only served to compound the view of Renoir as the archetypal anti-intellectual painter, the Renoir who says "what goes on inside my head doesn't interest me. I want to touch . . . or at least to see." Most later writers have followed this line. "Renoir paints as you or I breathe," Octave Mirbeau writes. To Arsène Alexandre (1892): "His felicity is that of a witty child." Even Meier-Graefe, whose first monograph (1912) remains one of the best we have, subscribes: "He paints as the bird sings, as the sun shines, as buds blossom. Never has anyone created with less artifice. His is the movement of the infant towards its mother's breast."

By the time of Renoir's death, this view was an established tradition. André Lhôte (1920), in his obituary article, sought to deflate it, suggesting that Renoir spread the "legend of the nightingale painter" deliberately to mislead the hordes of journalists who pestered him. He proposes that Renoir was laughing up his sleeve, that he was an ideologist whose frivolous remarks masked the underlying seriousness of the man. He stresses the Renoir who says both "painting is a craft like joinery" and "even the most adept hand is only the servant of the mind."

This serious Renoir is at his most visible during the 1880s, the decade which saw both his increased responsibilities as a man and the well-documented "crisis" in his painting. He saw a lot of Renaissance and Classical art for the first time on his trip to Italy and subsequently became involved with a type of figure painting that was more timeless in its subject matter and less spontaneous in its execution. He wiped paint off and re-started, over and over again. His mode of drawing was transformed. While he still admired facility in painters – in Velasquez, for example, and in Monet – this is the period when he lamented most bitterly the lack of a proper training. He complained to Vollard that those who invented the "new" painting had not taught him about oil paint. "I knew neither how to paint nor to draw." He worked hard to change his art and learned great respect for Cézanne, whose "imperfections," he said, "are only refinements obtained by enormous learning."

While Renoir valued his great *Bathers* of 1885-87 as one of his best paintings, he was still in doubt about what he had significantly achieved from his long period of experiment. At the end of the decade, he declined to show in a major exhibition of French art of 1889, because "I think that everything I have done is bad and it would cause me a great deal of pain to see it exhibited." That decade appears to us now as the most self-conscious, considered and in some ways most radical phase of Renoir's art. The divided opinion of others on this period is one of the recurrent themes of the writing since then. It is the moment that separates his path from that of Impressionist painting. He always discussed his decision to exhibit at the Salon rather than with the Impressionists in economic terms, but maybe this is another example of the difference between Renoir's public and unspoken thoughts. The distancing from the dazzling and seductive qualities of his earlier painting was immediately apparent.

Pissarro wrote to his son in 1888: "I had a long talk with Renoir. He told me that everyone, from Durand-Ruel to his old collectors, is criticizing him and attacking his attempts to break with his romantic period."

On the positive side, Maurice Denis wrote warmly in 1905: "Instead of those transient impressions, where light flickered and fluttered, softening forms which were exquisite but frail, we now see him constructing sober, solid figures, steeped in classical serenity. . . ." For Clive Bell (1919), after some stilted paintings that lacked "the old inevitability," the great *Bathers* put Renoir "a good head above all his contemporaries save Cézanne." John Rewald (1946) writes a sterling defence of Renoir's gains from the "crisis" and Albert Barnes (1935) and Kenneth Clark (1956) endorse this. Charles Fogdal (1927) recalls Renoir telling visitors: "If I hadn't survived beyond 70, I wouldn't exist."

In the wake of this recognition of the mature Renoir as a composer of considered images, some historians have re-examined his Impressionist paintings. Joel Isaacson (1979) identified radical Degas-like innovations in the odd relationships of Renoir's figures to their context. Again, this proposes a painter quite at odds with the Renoir who confided in Albert André (1919) that every composition he painted involved doing violence to his natural predilections. In the end, we must decide each time whose predilections we are reading about: Renoir's or those of the writer.

Apart from the natural attention given to Renoir as the great figure-painter of Impressionism, he is frequently singled out among his peers as the "romantic Impressionist," descended from French eighteenth-century painting. This romantic quality was first identified by Philippe Burty (1877) and other contemporaries contrasted it with the relatively cool objectivity of Monet's eye. Pissarro used the term in the 1880s about Renoir *and* Monet in contrast to the "scientific" Impressionism that he saw spreading in the wake of Seurat. Renoir is subsequently written of as the poet among Impressionists by Téodor de Wyzewa (1903) and Robert Rey (1931). Rey, like Lhôte and Albert Barnes & Violette de Mazia (1935), also seeks to separate Renoir from Monet and to align him more with Cézanne and Seurat as a major post-Impressionist, who redirected the undisciplined sensuality of early Impressionism with a re-awakened classical sensibility. Increasingly we find Renoir's name linked not with Monet, but with Manet or Cézanne. As early as 1912, Maurice Raynal, friend of the Cubists, could write "no one would think of treating Renoir and Cézanne as Impressionists."

Roger Shattuck, in *The Banquet Years* (1955), saw Renoir in a family group with Ravel and Proust: "Their rich, beautifully orchestrated masterpieces portray *la belle époque* at its ripest and never lose control of its sensuous plenitude. But all three gaze fondly backwards towards the waning century and tell us not so much what has changed since 1885 as what can be made to survive." John Berger (1960) calls Renoir's art "the dreamy aftermath of a secure culture of material comfort and private prosperity that he represents historically." Gowing has discussed the issue of Renoir's irrelevance to serious consideration by later artists because "his work offered no sign of what was to come." Here a similar conclusion is reached from three significantly different vantage points. And it is beyond question that, considering how seminal was the art of Renoir's time for subsequent painting, relatively few important twentieth-century artists have so far left us their thoughts on Renoir. Redon loved Renoir's landscapes. Bonnard was an admirer, but Léger, rather surprisingly, said next to nothing about him. Matisse spoke about him as the master of thin paint and as a portrait painter with a gift for life like Goya. Picasso had a Renoir on his wall in 1918. Sickert admired Renoir's consummate craftsmanship. Rouault wrote in his 1926 *Souvenirs Intimes:* "Glory to you, Renoir, for having often been drunk with color when so many others sought only a mediocre success and withered away," a rare tribute to the exposed risks that Renoir's natural art involved.

Much twentieth-century writing endorses Shattuck's view of Renoir as the preserver of values, for better or for worse. Maurice Denis (1920) saw Renoir's late work as the provider of voluptuousness in the angular, dissonant and conceptual world of post-Cubist French art. It was precisely that esthetic which prompted Christian Zervos (1931) to write of Renoir's subservience to the physical. "That is why he has never been influential in painting. He has never put anything into his work other than the sensual element of art, which can do no more than create a series of minor impressions (unlike Cézanne)."

De Chirico's illuminating insights (1920) about the mood of Renoir's paintings tell at least as much about the writer as about his subject. In the writing of Fry (1920), Patrick Heron (1947) and Clement Greenberg (1950), Renoir is treated in terms of the increasingly formal values of modernist criticism. There are still traces of it in the personal and largely warm responses of Bridget Riley and Howard Hodgkin (1985). But in the 1980s writing of an art historian like Fred Orton, both the language and the first principles of this modernist criticism are called into question. And in this light, the assured and cultured writing of Kenneth Clark (1956), for instance, who places Renoir securely in a connoisseur's pantheon, may appear as the authoritative insensitivity of the privileged.

We may clearly understand the context of Gowing's observation that Renoir's pictures "have not attracted advanced support since they were painted. Serious critics do not take them seriously, unless to question their social enlightenment." Nevertheless, this anthology not only casts some doubt upon it as an accurate perspective, it also makes manifest how constant a focus of changing and conflicting critical concerns those paintings have remained.

NICHOLAS WADLEY

RENOIR

COLORPLATE 11. *Bather with a Griffon*. 1870. 72½ × 45¼″ (184 × 115 cm).
Museu de Arte, São Paulo (Assis Chateaubriand), Brazil (Photo Louis Hossaka).

COLORPLATE 12. *Bathing on the Seine, La Grenouillère*. c. 1869. 23¼ × 31½″ (59 × 80 cm).
The Pushkin Museum, Moscow.

GEORGES RIVIÈRE

RENOIR ET SES AMIS

"Renoir before Impressionism"

1921

*Georges Rivière (1855–1943), civil servant
who became a close friend of Renoir. He
published the broadsheets,
L'Impressioniste, in 1877.*

When I first got to know Renoir in 1874 he was barely more than thirty, being born on February 25, 1841; but with his solemn face furrowed with wrinkles he looked a little older than he really was. For a year he had been at 35 rue Saint-Georges, with a studio and small apartment and he stayed there until 1883.

Several biographical notes have been published which indicate that the painter was born at Limoges where his father was a "bespoke tailor" and that his parents came to Paris in 1844, as much to have their older son Henri taught a good trade as in the hope of finding themselves work which was better paid than in the provinces. They did not make their fortune in the capital but continued to live there modestly until the head of the family died, with the joy of having brought up their five children well!

Portrait of the Artist's Father. 1869.
24 × 18″ (61 × 48 cm). City Art
Museum, St. Louis.

It should not be assumed from this family background that Auguste Renoir's childhood was spent in uncultivated surroundings. Renoir's parents were artisans of the type who used to be plentiful in the old France. Sober, economical and appreciating beautiful things – there were some still to be found among the most modest utilitarian objects – many workers and peasants were able to recognize, even if they could not define it, the beauty of monuments and furniture as well as places all around them. They had respect, even a religious feeling for the past, and it is thanks to people's desire to preserve it that so many objects in everyday use have come down to us. These attitudes were not uncommon when Renoir was young. Two thousand years of civilization had refined the people of France, developed their taste and given them that remarkable aptitude for the arts that caused so many masterpieces of all kinds to blossom, even in the smallest villages of Ancient Gaul, to the extent that it places our country on a par with Ancient Greece. What is more, until the middle of the· last century, the different social classes did not live separately from each other as they do now. In old Paris, notably before it was completely changed by the prefect Haussmann, there were hardly any parts inhabited by either the rich or the poor exclusively. Most of the houses in the centre of Paris accommodated people from all walks of life at the same time. Everybody more or less knew everybody else through meeting daily. In many cases they took an interest in one another. This permanent contact between people belonging to different social milieux had a salutary influence on the attitudes of the underprivileged. It explains to a large degree the readily perceptible divergence that exists between the political ideas of workers in the first half of the nineteenth century, who mingled with the bourgeois of their time, and those of today's workers, who are set apart in particular areas, a long way from people of a different class. The latter, moreover, have ended up not knowing the poor, gradually losing all contact with them, and the nation has suffered from this separation which completed the process of disintegration begun by the revolution. Moral unity has been undermined. Yet the feeling that they had of belonging to the same French family as the bourgeois still persisted among the workers until mechanization embittered their minds, by generally reducing these intelligent collaborators of the past to the role of unskilled laborers.

Baron Georges-Eugène Haussmann (1809-91), who was responsible for redesigning central Paris.

These qualities were very much alive in the painter's family. Renoir has sometimes told me of his mother's exquisite sensitivity, her enthusiasm for the lovely skyscapes of the Parisian suburbs, which charmed her wonderfully when they walked together in the woods at Louveciennes.

The Renoir family were living in the rue d'Argenteuil at the time when the young Auguste was to make his first communion. He brought the same scrupulous conscientiousness to his preparation as to everything that he undertook. On that occasion his sensitivity also found one of its gratifications. It was then, in fact, that he learnt a little music under the direction of a talented composer: Charles Gounod. At that time the musician was the choir master of the Chapelle à Saint-Roch and the boy belonged to the parish choir school. Gounod noticed this intelligent child who had, what is more, a pleasant singing voice. He became fond of him, encouraged him in his study of music, even gave him private lessons and demonstrated the interest he took in him by coming to see him when Auguste was quite seriously ill.

Charles François Gounod (1818–93)

It must be acknowledged that in picking Renoir out from the other pupils, Gounod displayed a remarkable perspicacity, for the boy was, as he remained all his life, reserved and shy with an instinctive horror of everything that would make him stand out, seeking neither the front row nor rewards.

Perhaps under Gounod's guidance Renoir would have continued his musical studies further, had he not had to earn his living as soon as possible. It seemed that music would not fulfill this essential condition.

However, Renoir always retained grateful memories of Gounod for the lessons he had been given and which he did not forget.

So the time came to find Auguste a profession. The older son, ten years the senior of the future painter, had learnt the trade of a heraldic engraver and was getting on very well. That encouraged Auguste's parents to seek something similar for him, no doubt at his own request, in the workshop of a porcelain painter. The trade of a ceramic artist was then an excellent one and for the most talented workers it was also an art.

THÉODORE DURET

MANET AND THE IMPRESSIONISTS

"Renoir"

1910

Théodore Duret (1838–1927), critic, friend and champion of Manet, who published his first book on contemporary painting in 1867. He owned Summer *and* Lise *by Renoir.*

He was only three or four years old when his father, a tailor in a small way of business, came to live in Paris, thinking to make his fortune there. The tailor did not succeed in finding the fortune which he had anticipated; he had a great struggle to live in Paris, and, as he had five children to support, each of them was obliged to earn his own living as soon as he was able. Auguste took up the trade of painter on porcelain at the instigation of his father, who had seen it practised in Limoges. He continued at this occupation from thirteen to eighteen. To enter the manufactory at Sèvres as a porcelain painter was at this time the height of his ambition.

Limoges and Sèvres were the major centers for porcelain production in France.

His prospects, however, underwent a sudden change. The decoration of porcelain had hitherto been done by hand, but now a machine was invented which rendered hand labour unnecessary. Porcelain painters were suddenly deprived of their means of livelihood. Renoir after a certain period of unemployment, found another opening in the painting of window blinds. By this time he had acquired great dexterity of hand, and, as his own natural gifts were now fully developed, he was able to apply himself to his new trade with such superior skill, that after three or four years, he had saved enough to enable him to abandon it, in order to satisfy those artistic ambitions which were now making themselves manifest. Thus he entered the *atelier* of Gleyre, a painter of great repute at that time. It was there that in 1861-62, he first met Sisley and Bazille, and afterwards Claude Monet, and became friendly with them.

*The art historian John Rewald has questioned the accuracy of this reason for Renoir leaving the porcelain trade (*Studies in Impressionism, *1985, p. 25 n4); however Jean Renoir and Vollard both tell the same story, which suggests at least that Renoir himself circulated it.*

Alfred Sisley (1839–99); Frédéric Bazille (1841–70); Claude Monet (1840–1926)

JEAN RENOIR

RENOIR, MY FATHER

Renoir's Apprenticeship as a Porcelain Painter

1958

Jean Renoir (1894–1979), Renoir's second son, the film director, whose biography is a primary source.

Renoir began porcelain painting with the sober enthusiasm he put into everything he did. Deep down he doubted whether his employer's wares

Renoir's brother, Pierre-Henri

51

would ever represent the ideal of plastic beauty. They were copies of Sèvres and Limoges: vases adorned with delicate garlands, plates set off by fine arabesques, and always with a subject in the centre such as shepherdesses, Imperial Eagles, or historical portraits.

". . . It didn't set the world on fire, but it was good honest work. And there's a certain something about hand-decorated objects. Even the stupidest worker puts a little of himself into what he is doing. A clumsy brushstroke can reveal his inner artistic dreams. I prefer a dull-witted artisan any day to a machine. . . ."

Renoir began by painting the borders around the plates, which were fairly easy. He was so proficient that he was soon promoted to the historical portraits in the centre. Lisa, who had continued to interest herself in the welfare of others after her marriage, perceived that her brother was doing the work of a skilled decorator for an apprentice's pay. She went to see the owner of the porcelain works, called him an exploiter, and threatened to get a job for "Auguste" with a competitor across the street. The good man did not fancy losing his new recruit, who was, he said, "a quiet, polite boy." But he protested that he could not decently pay a youngster what he paid "a man with a wife and children." He constantly used the word "proper" and no doubt out of timidity punctuated his remarks with discreet little sniffs. My father described him vividly as being a small man, very near-sighted, and with a large beard like that worn by Napoleon III, which gave him a false air of vitality. He finally consented to pay Renoir by the piece.

"I'll start him on dessert-plates at two sous the plate; three sous for Marie Antoinette in profile."

"Marie Antoinette in profile!" Renoir's voice was scornful. "That nitwit who thought she was being so clever playing the shepherdess!"

My father painted her so many times that he could have done it with his eyes closed. And he worked so rapidly that his pocket was soon filled with sous. His employer sniffed and stroked his beard in disapproval.

"A mere boy . . . earning so much money!" he exclaimed. "It's not proper!"

He then proposed paying Renoir at the exorbitant salary of twenty francs a month. Believing that this would give him the financial security he might never otherwise attain, Renoir was ready to accept. But Lisa made him refuse the offer, so he continued working by the piece. He took advantage of his success with Marie Antoinette, however, to ask his employer to let him try other subjects. The good man was alarmed, but his wife, who sometimes liked to run her hand through the young artisan's light brown hair, persuaded him to agree.

Renoir tried his hand by copying nudes from a book his mother had given him, *The Gods of Olympus by the Great Masters*, illustrated with engravings of works by Italian artists of the Renaissance. I had at home for many years a vase decorated with a Venus against a background of clouds. Already it was a real "Renoir". Despite the banality of the object and the evident intention of doing a purely commercial piece, it revealed the hand of a great man. The vase unfortunately disappeared from my house during the second world war. . . .

Mme Lévy was a tall brunette. Renoir was terrified of her at first. He had never yet had his arms round a woman.

"As well as I can recall", Renoir told me, "she was quite attractive, but big-boned; and she had big legs, big arms and a shapely bosom. . . ."

As the Lévys' apartment was on the first floor, she would often come down to the workroom, watch my father as he worked, and sigh. "I am alone so much," she would say. "I am bored."

And Renoir added, by way of comment, "She must have read *Madame Bovary*, the sentimental hussy. I was a bit wary. Besides, I had other things to do. But I must admit she was a good sort, and all she really wanted was to help me."

Marie-Elise, Renoir's sister, who was seven years his senior.

The novel Madame Bovary *(1857) by Gustave Flaubert*

The manufacturing side of the work fascinated Renoir. But M. Lévy continued to oppose his desire to know more about it, for he was only interested in increasing the supply of Marie Antoinettes, which were selling better than ever.

"We owe that to the guillotine," said Renoir. "The bourgeoisie love martyrs – especially after a good meal, with plenty of wine and liqueurs!"

Even so, Renoir learned to mould vases and to shape them on the potter's wheel. The old workman who tended the kilns became his friend and taught him the secret of firing. In those days wood was still used for heating the ovens. Renoir soon became adept at regulating the degree of heat required and gauging the temperature inside by the colour of enamel in the process of fusion. There was a small opening in the side wall for keeping a watch on the progress of the operation. As he sipped his cheap red wine, the old man gave his pupil endless instructions.

"You must drink – but take wine with water in it. If you don't drink, the heat from the furnace will dry you up. I knew one fellow who got so dried up he had no flesh left on him. He was nothing but skin and bones. His heart and lungs wouldn't work any more . . . too cramped by the ribs . . . and he died. The colour of the vases mustn't go from dark red to cherry red too quickly. And, after that, you mustn't let the fire die down; if you do you'll have a lot of breakages."

Vase. 1857. Oil on porcelain. H. 11¾ (30 cm). Private Collection (Photo Sotheby's).

The firing usually lasted twelve hours. The owner's wife brought the kiln-tenders their meals. "Here, my boy," she would say to my father, "I've brought you some nice boiled beef." But Renoir was too occupied watching the pieces of china turning from red to orange and her attempts to lure him failed.

The old workman was amused. "You're too young and I'm too old," he remarked with a chuckle, after she had gone. "She's out of luck."

My father would describe these incidents in a haphazard way. But I believe I have succeeded in sorting the facts and assigning them to the correct period when he was at the porcelain works. I think he was there about five years, from the age of thirteen to eighteen. During those five years, Renoir was to learn the essentials of life: art and love. As regards the second item, I should perhaps have said more appropriately, "women." I must add that, with a few inevitable exceptions, for him women represented the materialisation of his art. Renoir rightly refused to be an intellectual.

"What goes on inside my head doesn't interest me. I want to touch . . . or at least to see," he would say. . . .

* * *

Boucher, *Diana at the Bath.* 1742.
22⅜ × 28¾″ (56.8 × 72.9 cm).
Louvre, Paris.

Renoir got into the habit of going to the Louvre at noon instead of lunching with his mates in a little café round the corner. "I had added Fragonard to my list of favourites, which included Watteau and Boucher, especially his portraits of women. Those bourgeois women of Fragonard's! They are distinguished and at the same time good-natured. You hear them speaking the French of our fathers, a racy language but dignified. Barbers were not yet 'hairdressers' and the word 'garçe' (hussy) was simply the feminine for 'garçon.' People knew how to let a fart in polite society as well as how to speak grammatically. Nowadays Frenchmen don't fart any more, but they talk like pretentious illiterates."

AMBROISE VOLLARD

RENOIR, AN INTIMATE RECORD

Renoir's Work as a Painter of Fans and Blinds

1925

Renoir: The first experiments in printing on faïences and porcelain had just been made; the infatuation of the public for this new process knew no bounds . . . invariably the case when hand-work is replaced by machinery! Our shops had to close, and I tried to compete with the machine-made product by working for the prices. But I was soon obliged to give it up. The dealers to whom I showed my cups and saucers all seemed to have conspired against me. "Oh that's hand-made," they would say. "Our clientèle prefers machine work. It's more regular." So I began decorating fans with copies of Watteau, Lancret and Boucher. I even used Watteau's *Embarkation for Cythera!* I was brought up, you see, on the eighteenth century masters.

To be more precise, Boucher's *Diana at her Bath* was the first picture that took my fancy, and I have clung to it all my life as one does to one's first love. I have been told many a time that I ought not to like Boucher, because "he is only a decorator." As if being a decorator made any difference! Why, Boucher is one of the painters who best understood the female body. What fresh, youthful buttocks he painted, with the most enchanting little dimples! It's odd that people are never willing to give a man credit for what he can do. They say: "I like Titian better than Boucher." Good Lord, so do I! But that has nothing to do with the fact that Boucher painted lovely women superbly. A painter who has the feel for breast and buttocks is saved!

Here is an anecdote that will amuse you. One day I was admiring a Fragonard – a shepherdess in a captivating little skirt which itself made the entire picture – when I heard someone remark that shepherd girls were probably just as slovenly then as they are now. What do you think of that! Wouldn't you admire an artist the more who can take a filthy model and give you a jewel?

Vollard: And what about Chardin?

Renoir: Chardin makes me sick. He has done some pretty still lifes, perhaps. . . .

But I was telling you about my fans. They were fortunately not my only source of income. My elder brother, who was an engraver, sometimes obtained coats of arms for me to copy. I remember doing a *Saint George with a Shield*. On the shield I drew another Saint George in the same position, and so on until the last shield and the last Saint George could only be seen with the aid of a magnifying glass. But the fans and the Saint George brought in very little, and I hardly knew which way to turn, when one day I saw at the back of a courtyard in the rue Dauphine a large café, enclosed in glass, with painters decorating the walls. As I came nearer, I heard a dispute going on: the employer was cursing and storming at his lazy workmen, because the paintings in his café were not going to be done in time. I immediately offered to do the decorations myself.

"Oh, I need at least three men, and I want regular workmen," said the proprietor contemptuously, for I was small and slightly built.

But without waiting for further objections, I took up a brush and showed him to his delight that I could paint as fast as any three workmen.

Ambroise Vollard (1868–1939), dealer and publisher, who met Renoir c.1895 and became an intimate of his house and circle, as well as his biographer.

The French painters, Antoine Watteau (1684–1721), Nicolas Lancret (1690–1743), François Boucher (1703–70)

Jean-Baptiste Chardin (1699-1779)

Pierre-Henri Renoir

When I finished the frescoes in the café, I went back to my fans without much enthusiasm, promising myself to get out of that kind of thing at the first opportunity. The opportunity soon came. As I was passing a shop I saw a little sign posted on the door: PAINTER WANTED FOR WINDOW SHADES. I went in.

"Where have you worked?" asked the proprietor. I was taken by surprise and said "Bordeaux" at a hazard. I had presence of mind enough to name a place far away, for I was afraid he would want to look up my references. But he evidently had some other idea in mind, for all he said was: "Bring me a sample of what you can do. Good-bye young man."

Before leaving, I had time to talk with one of the employees, who seemed a good sort, and I asked him for information about painting shades. "Come and see me at my house next Sunday," he answered. My first question was to find out if the boss was a good sort. "Oh, he's a fine man," came the reply. "He's my uncle."

After much hesitation I confessed that I had never painted window shades. "It's not very hard," he said. "Have you ever done the figure?" I commenced to breathe again. It was reassuring to find· that painting shades was not unlike other kinds of painting – about all you had to do was to add a certain quantity of turpentine to the colour.

This particular shade-maker worked for missionaries who carried with them rolls of calico painted with religious subjects in imitation of stained glass windows. When the missionaries reached their destination, they unrolled the calico around four poles, which gave the Negroes the illusion of being in a real church.

Before long I had dashed off a superb *Virgin with Magi and Cherubim*. My instructor could not conceal his admiration. "How would you like to try a *St Vincent de Paul?*" he asked. I must explain that in the Virgin pictures the background consisted of clouds which were done easily enough by rubbing the canvas with a cloth, but if you didn't know the trick, the colour ran down into your sleeves. Whereas the *St Vincent* required more skill. This personage was generally represented giving alms at the church door, which required painting a certain amount of architecture.

I emerged from the second test victoriously, and was engaged on the spot. I took the place of an old employee, the glory of the studio, who was sick and showed no signs of recovery. "If you follow in his footsteps," said my new boss, "you will some day be as fine an artist as he is."

Only one thing worried my new employer. He liked my work and even went so far as to confess that he had never found such a clever hand; but he knew the value of money and it disturbed him that I should be making it so easily, for we were paid by the piece. My predecessor, who was always held up to newcomers as the perfect example, never painted anything without long preparation and a careful preliminary sketch. When the boss saw me paint in my figures directly on the bare cloth, he was aghast: "What a pity it is you are so anxious to make money! You'll find that in the long run you lose your skill."

When he was finally forced to admit that the "squaring-up" process could be discarded, he wanted to cut down the prices. But his nephew advised me to stick to my guns. "He can't get along without you," he said.

When I had put by a tidy little sum, however, I decided to say goodbye to the shade-maker. You can imagine how upset he was. He even promised me a partnership if I would stay on. The offer was tempting, but I did not allow myself to be persuaded, and, having saved enough to live on for a while (if I were not extravagant), I went to learn "serious painting" at Gleyre's studio, where I could work from a living model.

ALBERT ANDRÉ

RENOIR
The Studio of Charles Gleyre

1919

Poor Gleyre, I made life impossible for him in the old days. He would pay
a weekly visit to the studio and he came to stand in front of my easel. . . .
It was my first week under him and I was applying myself as best I could
to copy the model.

Gleyre looked at my canvas and said to me coldly: "No doubt you
paint for your own amusement?"

"Oh, of course," I replied, "and please believe me that if it did not
amuse me I should not do it!"

I'm not sure that he completely understood.

* * *

I know that for my part I never wanted to play the martyr and if they
had not refused my canvases at the Salon there's no doubt I should have
carried on sending them in.

And, besides, it's fate that has driven me to make paintings. As a
young man I had no such ambition at all. My dream was to be admitted to
the Sèvres factory so as to have my livelihood assured, leaving me free to
pursue my passion for painting bits of canvas.

When I was a boy, I often went through the galleries of ancient
sculpture, without really knowing why; perhaps it was just that I went
through the courtyards of the Louvre every day, and that these rooms
were easy to get to and had no one in them. I used to spend hours there,
daydreaming. . . .

Painting didn't feel right for me . . . I must admit it struck me as very
difficult and even disagreeable. Even today I have to force myself, to fight
off my unwillingness, to make compositions instead of letting myself slip
into painting nothing but torsos and heads.

AMBROISE VOLLARD

RENOIR, AN INTIMATE RECORD
The Studio of Charles Gleyre

1925

Renoir: I chose the Gleyre studio because I wanted to be with my friend
Laporte, whom I had known as a child. I might have stayed on with the
shade-maker if Laporte hadn't begged me so often to join him. Our
comradeship did not last however; our interests were too dissimilar. But I
am more than grateful to Laporte for having influenced me to turn
seriously towards painting, which resulted in my meeting Monet, Sisley
and Bazille.

Gleyre was Swiss; he was a very estimable painter but of no help to his
pupils; he had the merit however of leaving them pretty much to their own
devices. Before long I met the three artists whom I just mentioned. Bazille,
after giving high promise, was shot down in the first battle of 1870, while
still a young man. The public has barely begun to do him justice. The first

*Albert André (1869–1954), painter, intimate
friend of Renoir from c.1895 until his death;
described by Jean Renoir as the only friend
who knew and understood Renoir. His
monograph (see also pp. 262 ff.) was written
in the last years of Renoir's life. Here he
quotes Renoir's words on his days as a
student.*

*Charles Gleyre (1808–74), was the respected
studio master at the Ecole des Beaux Arts,
Paris, under whom Renoir studied 1861–64.
His most celebrated painting was* Evening
(Lost Illusions), *shown at the Salon of
1843 (page 331).*

*The official Salon in Paris, at which all
French painters and sculptors were appraised
each spring by the establishment, the press and
their potential patrons.*

Photograph of Renoir. 1861.

*Emile-Henri Laporte (1841–1919),
childhood friend of Renoir, was later a
director of art schools and Mayor of Ville
d'Avray. A portrait by Renoir (1864) exists
(Daulte 9).*

*Frédéric Bazille was killed at the battle of
Beaune-la-Rolande, November 28, 1870.*

Bazille before his Easel. 1867.
41¾ × 29⅛″ (106 × 74 cm).
Musée d'Orsay, Paris.

buyers of "Impressionism" did not take Bazille's work very seriously, doubtless because he was very rich.

Vollard: What painters were your group mostly drawn to?

Renoir: Monet, being a native of Le Havre, had known Jongkind there and admired him a great deal; Sisley was influenced chiefly by Corot; my hero was Diaz. His pictures have become very black, but in those days they sparkled like precious stones.

Vollard: Did you ever work at the Beaux Arts?

Renoir: The Beaux Arts was far from being what it is today. There were only two courses then, one in drawing, from eight-o'-clock until ten in the evening; the other in anatomy. From time to time the School of Medicine near by would obligingly lend a corpse to the anatomy class. Sometimes I attended these two classes, but I really learned the elementary technique of painting at Gleyre's.

The only instructor I remember particularly was Signol. One day I was drawing a cast from the antique. When he came to me he exclaimed: "Don't you realise that the big toe of Germanicus ought to have more

Johann Barthold Jongkind (1818–91), Jean-Baptiste Camille Corot (1796–1875), Virgilio-Narcisse Diaz de la Pena (1808–76), all landscape painters who advised and influenced the young Impressionists.

Emile Signol (1804–92)

58

majesty than the big toe of the coal dealer round the corner?" He walked away muttering solemnly: "The big toe of Germanicus. . . ."

Just at that moment, somebody at the easel next to me, muttered an oath which Signol thought was intended for him. What is more, he imagined I was responsible for it. He had me expelled instantly. An oil study that I had brought to his class aroused his antagonism the very first day; he was fairly beside himself on account of an ugly red that I had used in my picture. "Look out you don't become another Delacroix!" he warned me sarcastically.

MARIE LE COEUR

Two Letters

March–April 1866

The painter Jules Le Coeur (1832–82) was a close friend of Renoir in his early years; Marie Le Coeur (1858–1937) was the daughter of his brother Charles, an architect.

MARCH 29, 1866

The poor boy is like a lost soul when he's not working on something. At the moment he doesn't know what to do next, having finished his paintings for the exhibition. The day before yesterday Jules had persuaded him that they should leave together, whereas he [Renoir] preferred to wait a little longer and finish mother's portrait, during which time his friend Sisley would find them both somewhere to stay over there. The friend Sisley, who had already left, was pulling him in one direction, Jules in the other. In the end, he turned up yesterday morning to start work, saying that he wasn't going to leave after all. This morning it was still all settled that he would stay, but he went to see Jules off at the station and, at the last moment, he left too. He has no luggage, so he'll have to come back to collect his things. I feel sure that at this moment he's regretting having given in.

i.e. for the 1866 Salon

* * *

APRIL 6, 1866

M. Renoir has been rejected, poor fellow. You see he had done two pictures: a landscape with two figures – which everyone says is good, that it has good points and bad – the other one was done in Marlotte in a fortnight, he considers it a sketch, and he only sent it to the exhibition because he had the other one that was a more serious matter, otherwise he would have felt that he shouldn't exhibit it.

On Friday, since no one could tell him if he had been accepted or rejected, he went to wait for members of the jury at the exit to the exhibition and when he saw MM. Corot and Daubigny (two well-known landscape painters) coming out, he asked them if they knew whether the paintings of a friend of his called Renoir were accepted. Then Daubigny remembered Renoir's painting and described it to him, saying: "We're very annoyed for your friend, but his painting was rejected. We did all that we could to prevent it, we asked for the painting to be reconsidered ten times, to no avail. But what could you expect, there were six of us supporting it against all the rest. Tell your friend not to be discouraged, there are great qualities in his paintings. . . ."

This means that in his misfortune, he has the consolation of receiving compliments from two artists whose talent he admires.

That evening he went into a café and heard some artists talking about the exhibition and one of them said: "There's a very good picture by someone called Renoir which was rejected."

Now what irritates him most is that he heard yesterday that his Marlotte painting had been accepted. With the other being rejected, he would have preferred this one to be rejected too.

*Barbara E. White (*Renoir, his Life, Art and Letters, *1984, p. 21) has identified this painting as* Landscape with Two Figures, *1865–86 (private collection, New York).*

Charles-François Daubigny (1817–78)

ÉMILE ZOLA

L'EVÉNEMENT

The Actualists

May 24, 1868

Émile Zola (1840–1902), boyhood friend of Cézanne, was a valued champion of new painting among the largely hostile critics of the 1860s such as De Lasteyrie and Chaurnelin, whose reviews of the same Salon exhibition of 1868 are quoted below.

. . . The other painting that I wish to speak of is that which Henri [sic] Renoir has called *Lise* and which represents a young woman in a white dress, sheltering beneath a parasol. This *Lise* appears to me as a sister of the *Camille* of Claude Monet. She is shown facing us, coming out of the trees, her supple body balanced, cooling herself from the burning afternoon heat. She is one of our women, or rather, one of our mistresses, painted with great frankness and a timely research into the modern world.

COLORPLATE 7

FERDINAND DE LASTÉYRIE

L'OPINION NATIONALE

A Review

June 20, 1868

I discovered in the furthest salon, the one known as the Room of the Outcasts, the figure of a fat woman daubed in white, labeled simply *Lise*, whose author, M R. (I trust he will allow me to designate him only by an initial) clearly was inspired no longer even by the great examples of Monsieur Courbet, but by the curious models of Monsieur Manet. And this is how the demise of the realist school, as it moves from imitation to imitation, becomes more and more inevitable. So be it!

Monet, *Camille (Woman in a Green Dress).* 1866. 91 × 59⅜"
(231 × 151 cm). Kunsthalle, Bremen.

MARIUS CHAUMELIN

LA PRESSE

A Review

June 23, 1868

M Manet is already a master apparently since he has some imitators; among their number is M Renoir, who has painted under the title of *Lise* a woman of natural grandeur walking in a park. This painting captures the attention of connoisseurs as much by the strangeness of its effect as by the justness of its tones. This is what, in the language of the realists, is called a fine touch of color.

ZACHARIE ASTRUC

L'ÉTENDART

"The Grand Style: Renoir"

June 27, 1868

Zacharie Astruc (1835–1907), amateur artist, musician and poet; friend of Manet, who had been reviewing the Salon since 1859.

The *Lise* of M. Renoir completes an odd trinity that started with the very strange, powerfully expressive and notorious *Olympia*. In the wake of Manet, Monet was soon to create his *Camille,* the beauty in the green dress, putting on her gloves. . . . Here now is *Lise,* the most demure of them all. Here we have the charming Parisian girl, in the Bois, alert, mocking and laughing, playing the "grande dame" somewhat gauchely, savoring the shade of the woods for all the agreeable diversions that may be had there: the dancing, the open-air café, the fashionable restaurant, the amusing dining room fashioned from a weird tree. . . .

Manet's Olympia, *1863, had been a scandal at the 1865 Salon; Monet's* Woman in the Green Dress *a relative success in 1866.*

Lise's hair is adorned with a dainty straw hat, she wears a white dress drawn in at the waist by a black sash. A parasol shields her face. She stops among the forest trees in a ray of sunlight, as if waiting for a friend. It is an original image. The painting has great charms: beautifully rendered effects, a delicate scale of tones, a general impression that is unified and clear and well conceived lighting. The art that has gone into this painting seems simple, but in fact it is very unusual and very interesting. Given a subject whose whole charm is its light, it could hardly have been executed with greater clarity. The sunlit whites are delicious. Wherever the eye wanders, it is enchanted by the finest of nuances and a very distinctive lightness of touch.

All praise to a joyful canvas made by a painter with a future, an observer who is as responsive to the picturesque as he is careful of reality. This canvas *Lise* deserves to be singled out. By an inconceivable error which I would rather think of as ignorance, she has suffered the fate of the rejected work. At the Salon with its array of marketable objects, such a work stands by virtue of its art, its taste and its exceptional character, which command our attention and our study. It was obvious to all the painters. But not to the jury? . . .

Drawing after Lise. *1878. Reproduced in Duret's* Les peintres Impressionistes *(1878).*

PAUL VALÉRY

LA REVUE HEBDOMADAIRE

"A Recollection of Renoir"

January 3, 1920

Paul Valéry (1871–1945), poet, probably met Renoir in the house of Berthe Morisot c.1892. In 1900, he married her niece, Jeannie Gobillard; it was a double wedding, the other couple being Julie Manet (Morisot's daughter) and Ernest Rouart.

Renoir would sometimes indulge in reminiscences. I forget what it was he would tell about Wagner, whose portrait he painted; but here is an incident from his own life which has an historic flavour to it. About the middle of the year 1869, he went to make some studies in the Forest of Fontainebleau. One day as he was painting, he was arrested by a sound, or by a feeling of being watched. He turned round in annoyance, to find an unknown gentleman, bearded, standing leaning on his cane. He bowed to Renoir, and with great politeness asked if he might watch Renoir paint. It is difficult to refuse such a request.

COLORPLATE 74

The session over, having shut up his paintbox and folded his easel, Renoir, carrying his kit, tried to get rid of his mysterious watcher, hoping to put him rapidly in the rear before leaving the woods. But the man became his shadow: and all the more mute because he seemed anxious to say something, he refused to be shaken off by any turning, put out of countenance by any expression, or outdistanced by any change of pace. . . . Renoir, after trying everything, after running, stopping, singing, whistling, after giving every sign of being at his wit's end with this nuisance, shouted out:

"But look, monsieur, which way are you going? Do you want me to show you the way?"

"Mon Dieu, monsieur," the man replied, "I was afraid to ask you. I am looking for the road that doesn't lead to Mazas."

"To Mazas?" asked Renoir, vaguely uneasy, thinking of his watch, of how deep in the forest they were.

"Yes," said the man, "I was given six months yesterday morning. I write for Rochefort's paper; they're after me, and I don't want to spend the fine weather in the Imperial cellars. I've made it this far, but I can't stay indefinitely under cover. It's hard to decide between staying with the squirrels and going to the police."

"That's the devil!" said Renoir.

The man went on: "I saw you coming just now, and choosing your spot. I thought, well, painters are good fellows, and you must know the district. . . . Anyhow, I didn't know what to do . . . so I passed the time watching you paint, waiting the chance to ask you for some advice."

Renoir had a resourceful mind. A classic age would have christened him the Ulysses of painting. He started smiling at an idea that had occurred to him.

"Ever dabbled with a brush?" he asked his journalist follower.

"A bit," said the other, "when I was twelve."

"Anyhow," Renoir went on, "it doesn't make any difference. If I were you I would get hold of a box of paints. I would rent a room in Barbizon, and I'd spend my days in the forest, sitting and smoking cigarettes over some everlasting sketch. There's not a policeman in the world who would dream of coming to look for me here!"

The man seemed to light up. Gripping Renoir by both hands and assuring him of his eternal gratitude, he made him promise that they would meet again, and before vanishing among the leaves, insisted on leaving his card. On the card was written: RAOUL RIGAULT. *Correspondent for La Marseillaise.*

"Never heard of him," thought Renoir. . . .

Came the war, and then the Commune. The latter coincided with the springtime. Renoir, who adored his work and contrived to make a living out of it, felt a wild longing for the country and the urgent need to paint a few landscapes which he could sell. But the gates were well guarded. Versailles without and Paris within put a ban on Nature. Where was there to set up an easel, and how could you contrive not to look dangerously like a spy, even if you did manage to slip past the outposts, the sentries, and the barricades, and set yourself down in some no man's land between the enemy camps?

Renoir had to make do with what the parks offered in the way of spring. One morning on his way to the Tuileries to see the growth of leaf, he was making for the chestnut trees by way of the Rue de Castiglione – his heart on the woods at Meudon, but his eye ever on the alert, ever engaged with the momentary dialectic between light and objects – when a photographer's window drew him to a halt.

How fine photographs were during the Second Empire, and even for some time after! As yet they made no pretence at the misty charms of a charcoal sketch, nor did they ape lithography, but they were simply themselves: remarkably delicate and clear, with handsome chocolate-

Henri Rochefort (1830–1913), founder of L'Intransigeant *was a leading figure of the Commune, for which he was later deported.*

Raoul Rigault (1846–71)

The Franco-Prussian war with its siege of Paris followed by the Commune, 1870–71, both seriously inhibited freedom of movement in and around the city.

coloured depths, and they were really fade-proof. . . .

On display were the upper officials of the Commune: Rossel, Dombrowski, Ferre. . . . And among them was the all-powerful *procureur*, Raoul Rigault. Renoir recognised his acquaintance of the woods. What an unlooked-for chance of getting a modest exit permit to the open country. So there he was, brooding on his newborn project and following it up with youthful energy. Turning left along the Rue de Rivoli, past the Châtelet, he made calmly for his objective.

Entering the Préfecture de Police, he went upstairs. A resplendent doorkeeper, whose function and whose majestic bearing might well have remained unchanged since Pietri's day, ushered him into the waiting room. There, many an anxious being sat in wait, widows of Communard fighters, in mourning, petitioners of every variety. The doorkeeper vanished, taking that same card of Raoul Rigault's, on which Renoir had scribbled his own name, to the master of the day. He reappeared. "Citizen Renoir!" he intoned, in a voice with a still rather Imperial ring to it. . . .

And when Renoir described his own entry, he would almost say that never in his life had he had such a reception. Rigault, sashed and booted, surrounded by numerous staff, welcomed him with open arms. He introduced "the citizen painter who saved my life" to all present. "The *Marseillaise!*" he commanded, "for Citizen Renoir!" After the *Marseillaise* came the champagne; and with the champagne came the toasts. To the Commune, to Painting, to Citizen Renoir. . . . But neither toasts, nor cheers, nor the *Marseillaise* were enough to make our citizen artist forget his vernal inspiration. Between one glass and another he gently gave the delegate to understand that a triumphal welcome was not exactly the thing he had come for. Rigault, doubtless expecting some request in proportion to his vast powers, and wanting nothing better than to make the visitor aware of their full extent, lavishly offered him his favours: "Anything you like, my dear citizen, you have only to ask!"

It was quite a surprise to him when Renoir explained how much he would enjoy having a sort of safe-conduct, which would allow him, without any untoward encounters, to go and paint a few studies on the slopes of the fortifications. . . . When Renoir left, he was the bearer of a wonderful missive, conceived in terms of the most flattering of his talent and his civic spirit. All the gates of Paris opened at its powerful agency, stamped as it was with all the seals of the Préfecture, and laden with all the requisite signatures and flourishes.

Different versions of this anecdote are told by, among others, Jean Renoir (1962, pp. 118–21) and Vollard (1925, pp. 57–60).

ARSÈNE HOUSSAYE

L'ARTISTE

A Letter to Karl Bertrand

June 1, 1870

Arsène Houssaye (1815–96), novelist, playwright, collector and editor of the relatively conservative journal L'Artiste.

The two real masters of this school, which is concerned less with art-for-art's-sake than nature-for-nature's-sake, are MM Monet (not to be confused with Manet) and Renoir, two true masters, like Courbet of Ornans, by virtue of the brutal candor of their brush. I am told that the [Salon] jury has rejected Monet, but had the good sense to admit Renoir. This painter, as we see, has a fiery temperament, which bursts upon the scene brilliantly in a *Woman of Algiers* which might have been signed by Delacroix.

COLORPLATE 54

His master, Gleyre, might well be surprised at having produced such a prodigal son, who mocks every rule of grammar by daring to do things in his own way. But Gleyre is too great an artist not to recognize art whatever its forms of expression.

So remember the names of M Renoir and M Monet. I have in my gallery the *Woman in the Green Dress* of Monet and an early bather of Renoir, which I shall present one day to the Luxembourg Museum, when the Luxembourg Museum opens its doors to all painting without prejudice.

The only Renoir now known to have belonged to Houssaye is a Seated Woman *of 1872 (Daulte 80).*

GEORGES RIVIÈRE

RENOIR ET SES AMIS

"Renoir before Impressionism"

1921

At that time Renoir lived in the rue Notre-Dame-des-Champs, one of those quiet old streets in the Luxembourg quarter, where the passer-by could hear cocks crowing behind garden walls. In 1873 he left it for the rue Saint-Georges, also a quiet street but in the middle of a more lively Paris than that of the left bank. So Renoir was closer to Manet and his other friends. I think anyway that this was the reason he decided to move, although the distance had not stopped him from frequently attending the meetings at the Cafe Guerbois, avenue de Clichy, before 1870.

In those days Renoir was hardly ever away from Paris. If before 1870 he had spent long periods in the villages adjoining the forest of Fontainebleau, after the war he hardly ever went further than the inner suburbs: Bougival, Saint-Cloud, Louveciennes where his mother lived. More often he stayed in Paris where he could find models more easily than anywhere else.

When he lived in the rue Saint-Georges he took nearly all his meals in a dairy opposite his lodgings which was patronized by just a few regulars. The small, cramped room, separated from the rest of the shop by a low partition, would not have had space for more than half a dozen to eat. Camille, the dairywoman, was an honest old girl who surrounded Renoir with discreet maternal attentions. In any case he was easy to serve, never complaining about anything and always finding a kind word of thanks for her services.

He always kept to this simple, frugal way of life, out of preference, his one pleasure all his life being to "daub canvases," as he himself would say.

Gradually some enthusiasts had emerged, the last survivor being Théodore Duret, who was also one of the first with Faure, the famous baritone at the Opéra. They were joined by an important ally, M Durand-Ruel, the art dealer of the rue Le Peletier, who had previously acquired several pictures by Edouard Manet and Claude Monet.

Jean-Baptiste Faure (1830–1914)

This early help, although slight, was precious, not to say indispensable to the development of the young group as a whole, who would perhaps have given up without this encouragement. Claude Monet was the most favored of the "Intransigents." The majority of the connoisseurs and Durand-Ruel preferred this handsome landscape painter, and that was fair. At the time Monet was the real soul of that little set. It was he who raised the sometimes flagging spirits of his friend when things were hard. With his fighting temperament he would bravely stand up to attacks like a magnificent bull that is excited by banderillas without being frightened.

COLORPLATE 17. *The Promenade*. 1870. 31½ × 25¼″ (80 × 64 cm).
On Loan to the National Gallery of Scotland, Edinburgh, from the British Rail Pension Fund Works of Art Collection.

COLORPLATE 18. *Lady Sewing*. 1879. 24¼ × 19⅞″ (61.7 × 50.7 cm).
Courtesy of the Art Institute of Chicago (Mr. and Mrs. Lewis L. Coburn Memorial Collection).

COLORPLATE 23. *Woman gathering Flowers*. c. 1872. 25¾ × 21⁷⁄₁₆″ (65.5 × 54.4 cm).
Sterling and Francine Clark Art Institute, Williamstown, Mass.

COLORPLATE 24. *The Pont Neuf, Paris.* 1872. 29⅝ × 36⅞″ (75.3 × 93.7 cm).
National Gallery of Art, Washington D.C. (Ailsa Mellon Bruce Collection).

Renoir often declared that at the time when everyone heaped sarcasm on the poor intransigents, Monet did them the greatest service with his liveliness, tenacity and unshakable confidence in their ultimate success. In 1873 the art critics' attacks had not yet reached the virulence that the modest exhibition of 1874 was to unleash, but the indifference of art lovers and the almost complete silence of the press were no less depressing for the young artists than were the insults that greeted their first collective event. Besides, at that time the cell formed by Claude Monet and his friends was resistant and nothing could break it.

It was in 1873 that Renoir painted *La Loge* which marked an evolution in his style. That attractive canvas with its harmonious tonality and delicate design figured in the 1874 exhibition at the Nadar Gallery and met with little success. No one bought it and for two years it lay in the studio in the rue Saint-Georges, that is until the painter's new technique was accepted.

We know how much Renoir's style has varied in the course of his long career, while remaining very personal and always recognizable in its evolution. That constant evolution, curtailed only by death, was the result of his perpetual search for progress in his craft which had haunted him. Shortly before his death, as he worked on his last canvases, Renoir was still saying: "I'm making progress." And he was right. Until the very end of his life he looked for and found some new secret, so to speak, of this difficult craft where you remain for ever an apprentice.

COLORPLATE 31

The first Impressionist exhibition of 1874 was held in the former studios of the photographer Nadar, 35 Boulevard des Capucines, Paris.

But the art lovers had some difficulty in following the painter through the incessant modifications of his technique. When he had painted *La Loge,* some of his friends were sorry that he had given up the tonality of *Lise,* or more recently of *The Little Dancer (La petite Danseuse).* Yet *Lise, The Dancer* and *La Loge,* although technically different, were certainly the work of the same mind, where the same sensitivity found expression, but the skill was modified in so far as the worker became more of a master, or the artist had a wider knowledge of the resources of his art. Those were only ever his reasons for changing his technique which was at first disconcerting for the public and marked stages in Renoir's work.

COLORPLATES 7, 27

Later, when the painter had won first the attention and then the admiration of everyone, the variety in his technique became one of the attractions of the exhibitions devoted to his work. It was possible to see twenty or thirty canvases by the same artist, side by side, without getting blasé because each one presented something special and new in its execution.

For this variety to be accepted, a collection of his pictures had to be shown – the result of twenty years' work – for the logical progression to be appreciated. But in 1873 this technical inconsistency disconcerted well-intentioned, conciliatory people who wanted to see Renoir become acceptable to the orthodoxy of the Beaux-Arts. It very often put an abrupt halt to the vague impulses to buy some of them. "Why do you change your style?" they kept saying to him after the *Dancer* and after *La Loge.* "You were beginning to be accepted and now you will have to start all over again." It was true, but of course Renoir paid no attention to these remarks which merely irritated him. "Why do they want me to re-do *La Loge,*" he said to me, "since I have found something else?"

The friendly criticism and sympathetic anxiety of men whose opinions had a certain influence in a wealthy social milieu did not prevent the earliest partisans from continuing their propaganda on Renoir's behalf, on the eve of the exhibition planned by the group of painters whom malevolent critics had designated "intransigents."

To understand the perfidy of this name, it has to be remembered that in those days, so soon after the Commune, it was meant to create in the public mind a sort of assimilation between the rebels of 1871 and the artists presumed to be in revolt against the order established by the Institut.

It was in these circumstances that Renoir and his companions went to brave the judgment of the masses.

JOHN REWALD

GAZETTE DES BEAUX ARTS

"Auguste Renoir and his Brother"

March 1945

The art historian, John Rewald, was born in Germany in 1912. His History of Impressionism *(1946) has been a foundation for all modern study of the subject. This passage was compiled from accounts of the early years given to Rewald by Edmond Renoir in conversations in Paris, 1939–40, and in writing c.1943.*

Despite the pessimism of his brother, Edmond Renoir was to launch himself upon a journalistic career, although the Franco-Prussian War interrupted its beginning. The two brothers served in the army and found each other again in Paris after the defeat and the Commune. It was then that Edmond Renoir became more intimately associated with his brother's work, either posing for him, or helping him, as he did in the execution of the view of the Pont Neuf painted by Auguste Renoir in 1872. Here is his account on the subject of this work:

"We established our quarters at the entresol of a little café at the corner of the quai du Louvre, but much nearer the Seine than are the present buildings. For our two coffees, at ten centimes each, we could stay at that café for hours. From here Auguste overlooked the bridge and took pleasure, after having outlined the ground, the parapets, the houses in the distance, the Place Dauphine, and the statue of Henri IV, in sketching the passers-by, vehicles and groups. Meanwhile I scribbled, except when he asked me to go to the bridge and speak with the passers-by to make them stop for a minute."

Edmond Renoir asked this gentleman the time and that lady where such and such a street was located. While he was given the unnecessary information, his brother had time to sketch the figure for his painting.

Among the numerous canvases for which Edmond Renoir posed, full face, profile, and often from the back, are *La Loge* and *The Henriot Family*. (Daulte 186) During the sittings he had the chance to observe his brother's methods. He says:

"He worked with such a prodigious virtuosity that a portrait required just one sitting. The model would leave his place and come to look at the canvas and find the painted image very like him, very good; but he expected to return. Auguste accepted this of necessity, but he had a bad time pretending to retouch the picture, occasionally satisfying himself with perfecting the background and certain details of the dress, without at all modifying the face. We argued about this and he said to me: 'Understand well: nothing is so mobile as a face. If the features remain constant, the physiognomy changes for a yes, for a no. The eyes will be more or less tired. The forehead may be wrinkled with preoccupation, the hair will not be in the same place and the amiable smile, natural today, may become affected tomorrow. Can I follow these evolutions? No!'"

GEORGES RIVIÈRE

RENOIR ET SES AMIS

"The Studio in the Rue Saint Georges"

1921

Renoir's studio in the rue Saint-Georges looked the same as all the others COLORPLATE 58 that the painter occupied in succession during his life.

The rectangular room had windows all along the long side that faced west. In summer the room was filled with sunlight despite the thick cloth curtains that were meant to filter it. The walls were papered in light gray and several unframed canvases hung there. Against the walls there lay piles of canvases, both used and unused, of which only the backs were visible. There was no other furniture except for two easels, a few cane chairs of the most common design, two squat armchairs covered in very faded floral rep, a worn-out divan covered in material of indeterminate color and a whitewood table on which lay jumbled up tubes of colors, brushes, bottles of oil or spirit and paint-stained rags.

* * *

A quick look at the painting that had just been begun, a more or less detailed inspection of the stretchers turned to the wall: this was how friends' visits to the studio in the rue Saint-Georges usually began, while Renoir, seated on a chair, knees raised to his chin – as Bazille has shown him – silently smoked a cigarette.

Bazille, *Portrait of Renoir*. 1867.
24⅜ × 20″ (62 × 51 cm). Musée
National des Beaux-Arts, Algiers.

We did not spend long discussing painting. We had convergent
opinions on art, as on almost everything, so that we had no need of
discussion in order to convince one another. Besides, Renoir had a horror
of discussion about anything. He also loathed all proselytizing, and never
tried to make anyone share his convictions.

Nonetheless, this communion of ideas sometimes made us rather
loquacious. In our rambling conversations, repeated daily, we always had
something to say to each other.

One remarkable feature of our talks was Renoir's marked penchant
(revealed on all possible occasions) for French art, quite irrespective of
any chauvinism. After the war of 1870, people sided passionately for and
against Wagner. It was the period when Pasdeloup, who was conducting
the Sunday concerts at the Cirque d'Hiver, would perform an excerpt
from a German composer at the end of the programme, the overture to the
Flying Dutchman or a passage from *Tristan and Isolde* or from *Lohengrin*. The
champions and adversaries of the composer thus had an opportunity for
magnificient altercations, in which the conductor played a large part. Both
camps applauded and booed with equal convictions. We applauded, but
Renoir never went with us to Pasdeloup's home. The Wagnerian spirit
was contrary to that of the painter.

Renoir knew all about Wagner's music. He had been saturated with
talk about Wagner before 1870 by Bazille, whose studio he shared.

*Richard Wagner (1818–83) (see also pp.
141–43); Jules-Etienne Pasdeloup (1819–
87), a conductor*

Through him and other friends, he knew all Wagner's scores, having heard them performed by incomparable virtuosi such as Judge Lascoux and Edmond Maître. They had not converted Renoir to their cult. It was not that he failed to recognize the value of Wagner and the beauty of certain parts of his work, but he undoubtedly regarded German music less highly than the music of the old French masters, whom he also knew well, and loved, as it were, instinctively. These old composers, who were despised at the time, like the painters who were their contemporaries, found favor once more with the public at the same time as Watteau and his successors, at the same time too as the spell of Renoir began to be understood. Cordey, Lamy and I, who had not been present at the musical sessions of Lascoux, Bazille and Maître, often used to go to Pasdeloup's, and we did not conceal our admiration for Wagner – an admiration which was by no means exclusive, since we also supported Berlioz equally energetically, and were already long acquainted with the *Damnation of Faust* when it was successfully performed at the concert Colonne.

As to Berlioz, Renoir would tell us of the failure of *The Trojans* at the old opera house. He and a few friends had been present at the performance, given to a virtually empty hall, but such audience as there was had been hostile. The music of one of the greatest modern masters then aroused anger or ridicule. Half a century would have to go by before the public accepted it. Berlioz's type of romanticism was still inaccessible when Victor Hugo's was beginning to seem outmoded.

It was not Berlioz' romanticism which appealed to Renoir, but the purely French and traditional aspect of his art. Renoir did not like displays of romanticism or realism, they were too alien to his temperament, his love of grace and measure.

Judge Lascoux was a Wagner aficionado and an amateur musician.
Edmond Maître (1840–98), amateur musician, close friend of Renoir in the early 1870s

Frédéric Cordey (1854–1911), Pierre-Franc Lamy (1855–1919), both painters and habitués of Renoir's studio in the 1870s

The Trojans (1855–58) was the major opera of Hector Berlioz (1803–69).

Victor Hugo (1802–85)

PHILIPPE BURTY

LA RÉPUBLIQUE FRANÇAISE

"The Exhibition of the Anonymous Society of Artists"

April 25, 1874

Philippe Burty (1830–1890), supporter of Manet and an important supportive critic of younger art at large in the 1860s and 70s.

This was the first of the eight Impressionist exhibitions.

The paintings are presented most advantageously, lit more or less as they would be in an average apartment, set in isolation, not too numerous, not detracting from one another by being too stridently or too dully juxtaposed. This was the main aim of this group of artists, who have already been seen briefly at the gallery of M Durand-Ruel. A wise and estimable aim, honorably achieved and well worthy of pursuit by other groups. These artists feel their mode of painting to be antipathetic to the majority which, with government support, is assured of a reception at the official Salon. . . . In a word, they believe – as we do – that the number and contrived arrangement of works at modern official exhibitions constitutes the very denial of judgment and pleasure; that it is impossible to come away from them with a clear idea of any one artist, any body of work, any endeavor which strays from the well-trodden and accepted ways. . . . Deliberately avoiding any invidious comparison with the masters of the past, who conceived their work according to their temperament, their training and the mood of their time. . . . We might say that this exhibition interests us primarily for the brightness of the color, the straightforwardness of the masses, the sheer quality of the impressions. Everyone – and here we are concerned only with those who are loyal and proud – everyone is taken by it and won over. A second viewing still offends received ideas on the degree of finish, on chiaroscuro, on the agreeableness of settings.

We shall not insist; but, even though there are discernible lacunae in these works, although the sensations transcribed are sometimes as fleeting as the very sensation of woodland coolness itself, or the burst of warmth of a stubble field, or the whiff of a seashore, or the glow of a young cheek or the brightness of a woman's dress, we must be grateful to these young artists for pursuing and capturing them. It is in this way that their work finds its links with that of the old masters. . . .

M Renoir has a great future. . . . *The Young Dancer* is strikingly harmonious. His *Parisienne* is less good, his *La Loge*, particularly in full light, achieves a total sense of illusion. The heavily-painted and impassive figures of the woman, one of her white-gloved hands holding a lorgnette and the other hidden in the muslin of her handkerchief, and the head and the bust of the man, who is leaning back, are fragments of painting as worthy of attention as they are of praise.

* * *

This is a young battalion which will make its mark. Already – and this is the important thing – it has won over those who love painting for its own sake.

COLORPLATE 27
COLORPLATES 30, 31

THE FIRST IMPRESSIONIST EXHIBITION

Other Reviews

April-May 1874

His *Jeune Danseuse* is a charming portrait. With her dark red hair, her too pale cheeks, and her too red lips she reminds us of the "thirteen year old woman" whose story was told so cruelly by Théodore de Banville in the *Parisiennes de Paris*. Already, as a result of work undertaken when too young, her legs have grown heavy, and her feet, in their pink satin slippers, are not dainty enough. But the long and spindly arms are surely those of a child, and below her boyish chest a blue sash, a ribbon from first communion, comes down and flutters over the winged skirt of the ballerina. Still a little girl? Doubtless. Already a woman? Perhaps. A young girl? Never.
(Jean Provaire, *Le Rappel*, April 20, 1874)

COLORPLATE 27

Renoir's *Danseuse* and the *Parisienne* are both sketches and nothing more. The figure should not be systematically treated in this loose way. Despite this reservation, the overall tone is attractive; the heads recall both English painting and Goya, and the fabrics are only thinly painted and have no depth or projection. It is an attractive approximation, but, at the most, it is a mere promise. Nature finds deeper expression than in such imperceptible appearances. There is something worse than taking reality for a shadow, and that is taking the shadow for reality. Despite these criticisms, one would search our official school in vain for a head whose distinction, quality, and reality of tone matched those of the *Danseuse*.
(Armand Silvestre, *L'Opinion Nationale*, April 22, 1874)

COLORPLATE 30

What a pity . . . that the painter, who has a certain understanding of colour, doesn't draw better: his dancer's legs are as cottony as the gauze of her skirts.
(Louis Leroy, *Le Charivari*, April 25, 1874)

Considered from a distance, for example from the back of the third room on the ground floor, the *Danseuse* is an original conception, a kind of fairy moulded in earthly forms. Nothing is more alive than her bright and tender, rosy skin. On this the heap of gauze that makes up her dress somehow delightfully blends with her luminous and tender tones. This is the Realism of the great school, the one that does not feel forced to trivialise nature to interpret it.
(Marc de Montifaud, *L'Artiste*, May 1, 1874)

The *Danseuse* is true to life and has a fine nervous elegance in its truth. However everything that is charming – the haziness of the gauze skirts, the notes of colour on the head, breast and legs – is unfortunately lost in a vague, entirely conventional background.
(Ernest Chesneau, *Paris-Journal*, May 7, 1874)

Photograph of Renoir. 1875.
Musée d'Orsay, Paris.

AMBROISE VOLLARD

RENOIR, AN INTIMATE RECORD

The Name for the First Impressionist Exhibition

1925

Vollard recalled Renoir giving him this account.

The title failed to indicate the tendencies of the exhibitors; but I was the one who objected to using a title with a more precise meaning. I was afraid that if it were called the "Somebodies," or the "So-and-So's," or even "The Thirty Nine," the critics would immediately start talking of a "new school," when all that we were really after, within the limits of our abilities, was to try to induce painters in general to get in line and follow the Masters, if they did not wish to see painting go by the board. . . . For in the last analysis, everything that was being painted was merely rule of thumb or cheap tinsel – it was considered frightfully daring to take figures from David and dress them up in modern clothes. Therefore it was inevitable that the younger generation should go back to simple things. How could it have been otherwise? It cannot be said too often that to practise an art, you must begin with the ABCs of that art.

AMBROISE VOLLARD

RECOLLECTIONS OF A PICTURE DEALER

An Anecdote

1936

Manet wanted one day to paint my wife and children. Renoir was there. He took a canvas too and began painting the same subject. After a while Manet drew me aside and whispered, "You're on good terms with Renoir and take an interest in his future – do advise him to give up painting! You can see for yourself that it's not at all his metier!"

Edouard Manet (1832–83). Despite the view expressed here, we know that Manet owned an early Renoir, Bazille before his Easel, *1867 (page 58). Monet told this anecdote to Vollard.*

GEORGES RIVIERE

RENOIR ET SES AMIS

"Montmartre – The Moulin de la Galette"

1921

At the top of the hill, facing the rue Lepic, a little taller than the Gothic-style red-brick house that Ziem had built for himself which had the dilapidated look of an old Provençal dwelling, the dance hall of the Moulin de la Galette spread out like a huge barn, behind a worm-eaten wooden fence, in the middle of steep ground covered in wild grasses. Beside the dance hall rose the blackened skeletons of the windmills and their useless arms.

In 1875 the Moulin dance hall looked very different from how it looked later, when Montmartre became fashionable and when elegant audiences came from all over Paris to the night clubs opened by cabaret singers. Then there was no *Chat Noir* or *Moulin Rouge* in the area round the old Moulin.

The Moulin de la Galette had no pretensions to luxury; it had retained its original rustic style, dating from the eighteenth century; it was contemporary with Ramponneau.

The Debrays, from father to son, had continued to run the establishment without really changing anything. One of the windmills which was situated in the garden, still sometimes turned to crush iris roots for a Parisian parfumier; the other, which did not work, offered curious visitors the chance, for a few sous, to look out over the panorama of Paris. On the land behind the windmills there was a roundabout with horses, operated manually, and some tables for the cabaret patrons, where they served the famous pancake which took its name from the windmill.

The dance hall was made out of wooden boards painted a horrible green, which happily time had partly worn away. At the end of the room a platform was reserved for the orchestra made up of a dozen unfortunates who were forced to blow their discordant instruments for eight hours every Sunday. A raised gallery ran round the area reserved for dancing. It was for the most part filled with tables with only a narrow gap between them and the balustrade where the pushing crowd moved around with difficulty.

Behind the orchestra platform there was a garden, or a courtyard more like, planted with stunted acacias and furnished with tables and benches. The ground which was made of rubble, was hard and fairly even, so that in summer there could be dancing there at the same time as in the dance hall which was then opened on all sides.

The entrance to the dance hall had nothing to commend it. It comprised a low, narrow door, opening into a fairly long corridor; a grill had been let into the wall to take the entrance money: five sous, which only the gentlemen paid.

On Sundays the dance hall opened at 3 o'clock in the afternoon and closed at midnight, with an hour's intermission to allow the musicians to eat.

The admission charge did not include dancing. Each quadrille cost the man four sous. For some dancing enthusiasts the total cost could be considerably more than the three franc charge at the Elysée-Montmartre, where dancing was free, but the Moulin patrons did not seem to think their entertainment was too expensive.

The Moulin was the normal meeting place for working-class families in Montmartre. Parents and small children would sit round tables eating pancakes and drinking wine or beer, while the girls threw themselves into dancing until it was time to eat. The female clientèle at the Moulin was not made up exclusively of these honest girls. There were quite a few young women there too who did not pretend to be virtuous, but like the others they came for the pleasure of dancing, with no other motive.

It was dancing too that attracted most of the young men to the Moulin de la Galette. There were few workers among them, since they preferred other establishments such as the *Reine Blanche* – replaced by the *Moulin Rouge* – the *Boule Noire*, on the boulevard Rochechouart, or the *Château Rouge,* in the rue de Clignancourt. The Moulin's usual customers were made up for the most part of non-manual workers who lived in the area, many of Montmartre's artists and some students. The young men and women who came to the dance hall were always the same, all of them more or less knowing one another and enjoying a certain camaraderie.

Young Girls. c. 1876. 17¼ × 14⅛″ (44 × 36 cm). Ny Carlsberg Glyptotek, Copenhagen.

The make up of this clientèle gave the Moulin dance hall a very different appearance from the others. You hardly ever saw those strange characters who had invaded the other dance halls in Montmartre. Besides, Debray was on the look out for them and would not tolerate their presence in the Moulin as they would have driven away his regular customers.

Among the most faithful regulars at the Moulin de la Galette were Renoir, Lamy, Goeneutte and myself, and other friends, Gervex, Louis Lefèvre and Cordey used to join us there. At the Moulin, Renoir found models who had, in his view, the advantage that they did not normally sit for painters. Nearly all the women in his paintings of 1875–1883 were dancers from the Moulin de la Galette: florists, dressmakers or milliners who used the enforced leisure of slack periods to pose for him.

It was not always easy to recruit these models. Most of the young workers did not generally agree straightaway to pose for a painter even when they knew him and it was only a question of appearing on a canvas in their normal clothes. They were afraid of being turned into professional models, who were also regulars at the Moulin, and could be recognized, depicted stark naked, in the canvases displayed by the art dealers in the rue Laffitte. To overcome the girls' reluctance, Renoir had to use a great deal of diplomacy. One of his most successful methods was to get their mothers on his side. He was able to win their confidence through being attentive in little ways which appealed to these good women. He listened with apparent interest to their chatter, bought pancakes for their children and drinks for the partners of the girl he had set his heart on, and when she was finally mollified she would agree to pose on condition she never took her bodice off.

Like Renoir, our group also gradually won general acceptance. We showed ourselves to be friendly: not aloof with the men, pleasant to the mothers and always ready to ask the girls to dance. Some of us, like Gervex and Lamy, were indefatigable dancers and full of spirit and good humor. They did not miss a single dance all evening. Handsome lads, who were known to all the women at the Moulin, they were, by their mere presence, of invaluable assistance to Renoir's diplomacy.

Degas used to sometimes come to the Moulin in those days, and was delighted by the sheer exuberance of Gervex and Lamy. Watching them he would forget his caustic comments and let himself be carried away by their youthful charm without ever dreaming of taking part in the spectacle before him. One might well ask how Degas, who used the Nouvelle-Athènes, the Cirque Fernando and the café-concerts of Montmartre, could not have been tempted by the Moulin de la Galette dance hall. It did not lack the coarser side which so appealed to Degas, yet it never became one of his special concerns.

The Moulin was an interesting little world. Strict virtue was not ready currency among the guests, but vice did not hold sway either. Love was generally unselfish, and most of those little working girls who gave their hearts so readily would not have agreed to sell them. Behavior there was neither wild nor dissolute. In addition there was a hierarchy of honor among the women of the Moulin which ranged from honest girl to kept woman, passing through a host of intermediary stages, which the uninitiated would have found hard to differentiate. The girls of Montmartre alone could judge why Zélia was more honest than Mathilde and give peremptory reasons for their judgment. Their mothers also had their reasoned ideas on the subject and those whose daughters admitted to a lover did not allow them to go with another girl who might be thought to be more fickle.

In this corner of Montmartre all the working-class families knew each other, like people living in the same village. They belonged to the same milieu, had similar habits and somehow formed an autonomous group within the whole Montmartre population. The families of the girls who danced at the Moulin professed a morality which was based on different

Norbert Goeneutte (1854–94), Henri Gervex (1852–1929), Louis-Valère Lefèvre (c.1840–1902), all painters

The Nouvelles-Athènes was a café-bar in Paris and the Fernando a famous circus, both of them subjects for Degas' paintings and drawings.

Self-Portrait. c. 1876. 29 × 22½″ (73.7 × 57.1 cm). Fogg Art Museum, Cambridge, Mass.

principles from those applied in other social groups. Moral freedom for a girl was not reprehensible so long as she stayed with her mother and helped her. The promiscuity which was a way of life for the poor crowded into old shacks on the hill meant, too, that downfall was almost inevitable, through the proximity of boys and girls who had played together in the street or courtyard since early childhood. Moreover the workshops where girls were sent at about the age of twelve were very often schools of corruption.

In their mothers' homes many of these poor girls had known only unstable "stepfathers," who changed with varying degrees of frequency. Most of the time the "stepfather" was a financial burden for the irregular household and the work of mother and daughter had to pay for the needs of them all.

ARMAND SILVESTRE

L'OPINION

"Exhibition in the Rue Le Peletier"

April 2, 1876

Paul-Armand Silvestre (1837–1901) wrote and published poetry, plays and short stories as well as criticism. Like Renoir's brother, he later reviewed exhibitions for La Vie Moderne.
The second Impressionist exhibition was held at 11 Rue Le Peletier.

This interesting school – interesting at least for the fervor of its convictions and the doggedness of its endeavors – thoroughly deserves a moment's pause to consider its tendencies. It proceeds from a truly novel principle of simplification, and one whose *raison-d'être* cannot really be impugned. Interested solely in aptness, it proceeds by elementary harmonies: little concerned with form, it is exclusively decorative and colorist. Certainly its ideal, in our humble opinion, is not all-embracing, but equally certainly its works will have a place in the legend of contemporary art.

This place has yet to be defined. Is it that of an art which is coming to an end or one which is beginning? In our view, its great merit is that it uses singularly skillful and subtle procedures, to seek renewal through a more direct impression of nature. Nothing is less ingenuous than its manner, nothing more simple than its aim. Beyond the longstanding convention of the modern landscape, it has discovered certain unexplored aspects of things, it has analysed them with infinite subtlety, it has extended the field of pictorial endeavor.

Even those who effect the most disdain for them are benefiting unconsciously from these works, which are easier to mock than to ignore.

It has made the "open air" effect more real than ever previously known; it has brought into fashion a singularly bright and delightful range of tones; it has sought out new relationships. It has replaced a vision of things spoiled by conventional abuse with a sort of analytic impression that is very succinct and clear. Personally, I find it has the sweetness of a perfect harmony after an avalanche of dissonance. It is not an orchestra, but a diapason. This is not a panegyric. . . . In all this I see merely a starting point. . . . I see this subtle and vibrant tonality as offering a completely new palette to anyone who wants to look beyond this initial statement. . . .

M Renoir paints flesh in a thoroughly agreeable range of pink. I was enchanted by his sketch of a naked woman. It gives a taste of a true colorist. . . .

COLORPLATE 44

I hope I shall not be accused of bias in favor of these examples of an art which is seeking its place. I know quite well that there is an element of incompleteness, but. . . . Once again, these endeavors will inevitably become part of the development of contemporary painting. . . .

ALBERT WOLFF

LE FIGARO

The Second Impressionist Exhibition

April 3, 1876

Albert Wolff (1835–1891), reactionary critic of the conservative Le Figaro

The rue Le Peletier has had bad luck. After the Opéra fire, here is a new disaster overwhelming the district. At Durand-Ruel's there has just opened an exhibition of so-called painting. The inoffensive passer-by, attracted by the flags that decorate the façade, goes in, and a ruthless spectacle is offered to his dismayed eyes: five or six lunatics – among them a woman – a group of unfortunate creatures stricken with the mania of ambition have got together there to exhibit their works. Some people burst out laughing in front of these things – my heart is oppressed by them. Those self-styled artists give themselves the title of non-compromisers, impressionists; they take up canvas, paint and brush, throw on a few colours haphazardly and sign the whole thing. . . . It is a frightening spectacle of human vanity gone astray to the point of madness.

Try to make M. Pissarro understand that trees are not violet, that the sky is not the colour of fresh butter, that in no country do we see the things he paints and that no intelligent being can accept such aberrations! Try indeed to make M. Degas see reason; tell him that in art there are certain qualities called drawing, colour, execution, control, and he will laugh in your face and treat you as a reactionary. Or try to explain to M. Renoir that a woman's torso is not a mass of flesh in the process of decomposition with green and violet spots, showing the state of complete putrefaction of a corpse! . . .

And it is this accumulation of crudities which are shown to the public, with no thought of the fatal consequences that may result! Yesterday a poor soul was arrested in the rue Le Peletier, who, after seeing the exhibition, was biting the passers-by. Seriously, these lunatics must be pitied; the benevolence of nature has endowed some of them with the superior abilities which might have produced artists. But in the mutual admiration of their common frenzy, the members of this group – vain and blustering mediocrity in the extreme – have raised the negation of all that constitutes art to the status of a principle: they have attached an old paint rag to a broomstick and made a banner of it. Since they know perfectly well that a complete lack of artistic training prevents them from ever crossing the void that separates mere effort from a work of art, they barricade themselves within their lack of ability (which is equal to their self-satisfaction), and every year they return, before the Salon opens, with their ignominious oils and watercolours to make a protest against the magnificent French school which has been so rich in great artists. . . . I know some of these troublesome impressionists; they are charming, deeply convinced young people, who seriously imagine that they have found their path. This spectacle is distressing. . . .

Self-Portrait. c. 1875. 15⅜ × 12½" (39.1 × 31.7 cm). Sterling and Francine Clark Art Institute, Williamstown, Mass.

THE SECOND IMPRESSIONIST EXHIBITION

Other Reviews

1876

NUDE IN SUNLIGHT (C. 1876)

If only Renoir were in less of a hurry to finish the subject he begins, he would certainly have the makings of a distinguished painter. He exhibits here a female nude and a portrait of a young girl that testify to his very real talents.
(Alfred de Lostalot, *Le Chronique des Arts et de la Curiosité*. April 1, 1876)

Let us throw a veil over Renoir's *Venus*, which he should have hidden behind a screen.
(Emile Porcheron, *Le Soleil*. April 4, 1876)

Study (Nude in Sunlight) *(Colorplate 44)*

It is not clear which painting this refers to; the catalog lists a portrait of a child belonging to Victor Choquet (possibly Daulte 220).

Looking at his *Etude de Femme Nue*, I struggle in vain to tell whether that thing wriggling in the background is a piece of fabric, a cloud, or a fantastic beast.
(Marius Chaumelin, *La Gazette*. April 8, 1876)

In his studies, as in his portraits, Renoir may be making a bet with nature that he stands a good chance to lose. . . . A large study of a female nude is depressing – its flesh has the purplish tones of meat gone rank. It certainly would have been kinder to let her put on a dress. Where did the artist manage to find such a pathetic model? But this is not systematic hostility toward Renoir – no artist will ever reproach me with that.
(Louis Enault, *Le Constitutionnel*. April 10, 1876)

PORTRAIT DE M. M. . . . (DATED 1875)   COLORPLATE 34

His portrait of Claude Monet is a strong piece that has been finished to perfection.
(Émile Blémont, *Le Rappel*. April 9, 1876)

Renoir is a painter who specialises in human faces. A range of light tones dominates his work, the transitions between them arranged with superb harmony. His work is like Rubens, illuminated by the brilliant sunlight of Velasquez. He exhibits a very successful portrait of Monet.
(Émile Zola, *Le Messager de l'Europe*. June 1876)

GEORGES RIVIÈRE

RENOIR ET SES AMIS
Renoir's Models in the 1870s

1921

Between 1874 and 1880 Renoir's usual model was a pretty blond girl called Nini. She was an ideal model: punctual, serious and discreet, she took up no more room than a cat in the studio where we would still find her when we arrived. She seemed to like it there and, when the sitting was over, she was in no hurry to get up from the armchair where she was bent over some sewing or reading a novel dug out of a corner; just as, in fact, we see her in many of Renoir's studies.

We know hardly anything about Nini's life. She had no father. The man living with her mother, her "stepfather," to use Montmartre's euphemism, was a provost in an arms room and it was said that he guarded the girl's virtue jealously. Her mother looked like a small theater usherette – and perhaps that was indeed her profession. From time to time she would come to Renoir's studio on the pretext of finding out about her daughter's behavior towards the painter, and each time she would tell him her worries, as if in confidence, about Nini's future. "Do you realize, monsieur Renoir," she would say, "the dangers for her? A pretty girl like that is so hard to look after! You understand that she will have to have a steady protector, a reliable man who will take care of her future. I do not dream of an English aristocrat or a Russian prince for her, I just want her to have a nice quiet little home. What she needs is someone who understands her – someone like you, monsieur Renoir," she would add as she left.

This good mother's dream did not come to pass. Nini fell in love with a third-rate actor at the Montmartre theater who was playing the part of

Renoir had two models named Nini in the 1870s. One, also known as "gueule de raie" ("fish-mouth" or "fish-face"), was the model for La Loge *(Colorplate 31). The Nini referred to here, however, was Nini Lopez, who posed for many paintings between 1875 and 1879, including* After the Concert *(page 87),* The Café *(Colorplate 47),* La Pensée *(Colorplate 60).*

Bussy in *La Dame de Montsoreau* – Montmartre's great success – and married him.

"My daughter has disgraced us!" she cried when this catastrophe happened.

At the same time a different model had a certain place in Renoir's work. She was called Margot and was a complete contrast to Nini. Nini had a marvelous head of shining, golden blond hair, long eyelashes beneath well-arched brows and a profile of classical purity. Margot's was rather thin dull chestnut hair, she had sparse eyebrows, and her reddened eyelids were without lashes. Her rather large nose seemed to sit between her plump cheeks as if between two pillows, and her sensual mouth with thick, bleeding lips would at times crease into a disdainful smile. Nini was

Margot was Marguerite Legrand who posed for several important paintings of the later 70s. (Colorplates 32, 47, 51 and page 105).

quiet and Margot was noisy. All in all she was typical of a coarse type of working-class girl.

Nevertheless, through the magic of Renoir's art, she was made to look pretty, almost dignified. It was she whom he depicted in a picture of 1880 which Paul Arène christened "Margot's chocolate." If I remember correctly, this canvas was shown at the Salon in 1881.

Few models tested Renoir's patience as much as Margot. She would deliberately miss a prearranged sitting, just when the painter needed her most. Then he would go down to Montmartre to chivvy her and most of the time ended up finding her sitting drinking wine by the liter with young tearaways. Giving in to the painter's pleas and insistence she would promise to come back to the studio the next day, but she did not always keep her word.

In 1881 an attack of typhoid killed her within a few days, and Renoir who was always full of pity, had her buried at his own expense. I really believe that he mourned that cruel woman although she used to drive him mad.

Several casual models also came to the studio at that time, including a tall, beautiful girl whom Renoir accosted one day in the Place Pigalle: she posed for the large figure of a woman which he painted for Georges Charpentier's smoking-room, where she was hung with the picture of a young man on the other panel in the room, which the painter's brother sat for.

This girl, who I think came from some seedy house on the Butte Montmartre, must have had connections in the shady world of the outer boulevards and Renoir, who was ill at ease when she was coming to him, wondered if she would have him robbed.

However Renoir turned her into a magnificent figure in the picture I have just mentioned.

When the canvas was in place, Henner saw it at one of Madame Charpentier's parties. Although Renoir's talent in no way resembled his own, he looked sympathetically on his young colleague.

After examining the two pictures at length, he took Renoir by the arm and led him into the smoking-room.

"What you haf done is very good," he said in his Alsatian accent, "but there is something that I must say."

"Say it."

"Well, men are always darker than women."

Now it happened that with the two models Renoir had used, the man was fair skinned while the woman had a bronzed, matt complexion.

Henner's remark amused Renoir without convincing him.

GEORGES RIVIÈRE

RENOIR ET SES AMIS

The Chabrier Nude

1921

It was in that same year, 1878, that Renoir painted the portraits of Madame Charpentier and her children in the drawing room at the rue de Grenelle. The two pictures were shown at the Salon in 1879.

Sometime before that Renoir had painted a very fine study of a nude modeled on Nana, the pretty girl from Montmartre. This work was certainly one of the most important that he did between 1875 and 1880

The Cup of Chocolate (Daulte 272) was shown in the 1878 Salon.

Woman on a Staircase. 1876. 65 × 24¾" (165 × 65 cm). Painted for Georges Charpentier's smoking-room. Present whereabouts unknown.

COLORPLATE 56

COLORPLATE 75 AND PAGE 239

The model was actually called Anna, although she had posed for Manet's celebrated Nana. *She was the model for Renoir's* Study (Nude in Sunlight) *(Colorplate 44).*

COLORPLATE 25. *Harvest Time*. 1873. 23⅝ × 28⅞″ (60 × 73.5 cm).
Private Collection, Switzerland (Photo Dräyer, Zurich).

COLORPLATE 26. *The Rose.* C. 1872. 11⅜ × 9¾″ (29 × 25 cm).
Musée d'Orsay, Paris.

COLORPLATE 37. *Young Girl Braiding her Hair*. 1876. 21⅞ × 18¼″ (55.6 × 46.4 cm).
National Gallery of Art, Washington D.C. (Ailsa Mellon Bruce Collection).

COLORPLATE 38. *Madame Henriot.* c. 1876. 26 × 19⅝" (65.9 × 49.8 cm).
National Gallery of Art, Washington D.C. (Gift of Adele R. Levy Fund).

and it marks a stage in the development of his talent. It was purchased by Emmanuel Chabrier shortly after his return from Spain, when he came back with *España*. Chabrier was not short of money and the success of his latest productions had given him additional resources. This encouraged him to acquire a work by Renoir, whose painting he admired more out of instinct than for any particular reason. So one Sunday he and Lestringuez came to the rue Saint-Georges.

He sat in one of the old armchairs and told us about his recent travels, while at the same time glancing at the canvases that Lestringuez put in front of him. I could see some confusion in his face. He was clearly perplexed. Would he choose a figure, a landscape or flowers? He kept coming back to the picture of Nana. That lovely girl with her elegant shape and enticing flesh tempted him. But she was outrageously naked and Chabrier intended hanging the picture he bought in his drawing room. After much hesitation, and an inner struggle between his artistic sense and his bourgeois concern for what people would say, he decided to admit his preference.

"I really want that lovely nude," he said, "but I can't afford the price. Oh, it's so beautiful; I'd take it if it weren't so expensive." It was as if he was hoping for a refusal.

After a moment's thought he offered three hundred francs for it, which Renoir accepted. It was barely enough to cover the cost of painting it.

Chabrier thanked the painter warmly. He had succeeded in conquering his scruples.

"You're giving it away, and I will treasure it: it's a magnificent piece. You can be sure that I will never sell it. I would have to be offered ten thousand francs to part with it," he added, laughing at the idea that a Renoir picture might ever fetch such a price.

But even so, I do not think that Chabrier waited for the picture to be worth ten thousand francs to get rid of it. This large naked woman was not well received at home. It was thought to be indecent and, if I remember correctly, the beautiful Nana with her lack of clothes had to leave the drawing room, where she was out of place amid the respectable family portraits, and hide in a dark corner to await her definitive departure.

GEORGES RIVIÈRE

RENOIR ET SES AMIS

"The Real Revolutionaries"

1921

Renoir, who was not keen on meeting politicians or influential people, had been presented to Gambetta by someone or other, Philippe Burty perhaps, and the *tribune* had immediately taken to the artist.

As the *Impressionists'* exhibition, which was to open in April 1877, drew nearer, Renoir violated his own principle of never asking anyone for anything and decided that in order to help his friends he would ask Gambetta to put a favorable notice of their exhibition in the *Republique Française*. One day, then, he went to the newspaper offices in the rue de la Chaussée-d'Antin, brooding over what he was going to say. Gambetta was not there and it was Challemel-Lacour who received him. He had scarcely heard the painter's request when he more or less flew into a rage. His normally sullen expression became even more stern. "What!" he cried, "you're asking me to talk about Impressionists in our paper! That's

The Conversation. c. 1878. 17¾ × 15" (45 × 38 cm). Statens Konstmuseer, Stockholm.

impossible, it would cause a scandal! Don't you know you're revolution-aries?"

Poor Renoir was completely thrown by this unexpected outburst and left without replying.

In the front porch he met Gambetta who asked him what he was doing there.

When Renoir repeated Challemel-Lacour's threatening remark, the people's advocate gave a loud laugh.

"You're Revolutionaries? Well what are the rest of us supposed to be?"

There would be nothing more disconcerting than this taunt of "revolu-tionary" directed at the Impressionists by a man of the fourth of September if one did not know, from many historical examples, that people who hold power, albeit since only yesterday, treat as insurgents those whose places they have just taken. That was indeed the case with the masters of Art, who had become official since the Revolution, and who counted as rebels those artists who had remained faithful to the old tradition of French art.

I do not want to get diverted by politics in connection with painting. This is not the place to take sides for or against the events which have so profoundly changed the life of our country and brought about the disappearance of what has been given the striking name of "the old regime." What I should like to make clear is that the movement called *Impressionism,* far from being an attempt to break with the classical past, marked, on the contrary, a return to that art in which technique and concern for the good use of materials was of first importance. "Be a good workman first and foremost," Renoir often used to say, "it will not stop you being a genius."

I should also like to show that among the Impressionists, Renoir was the most representative of that idea of a return to older French art, as it had developed over the centuries, and that was nearly wrecked by the invasion of a barbaric concept from outside. Challemel-Lacour's outburst was not the expression of his personal preference for a particular esthetic, it was a cry of indignation against men who, for him, constituted a threat to the great principles of '89.

GEORGES RIVIÈRE

L'IMPRESSIONISTE, JOURNAL D'ART

"The Impressionist Exhibition"

April 1877

The third group Exhibition of the Impressionists was held in a large second-floor apartment, 6 Rue Le Peletier.

Let us begin with the works of Renoir, and the most important of his works, *Dancing at the Moulin de la Galette*. In a garden inundated with sunlight, barely shaded by some spindly acacia plants whose thin foliage trembles with the least breeze, there are charming young girls in all the freshness of their fifteen years, proud of their light homemade dresses fashioned of inexpensive materials, and young men full of gaiety. These make up the joyous crowd whose brouhaha is louder than the band's music. Lost notes of a country dance are barely audible from time to time to remind the dancers of the beat. Noise, laughter, movement, sunshine, in an atmosphere of youth: such is the *Dancing at the Moulin de la Galette* by Renoir. It is an essentially Parisian work. These young girls are the same ones with whom we rub elbows every day, and whose prattling fills Paris

COLORPLATE 53

at certain hours. A smile and some shirt cuffs are enough to make them pretty. Renoir has proved it well. Look at the grace with which the girl leans on a bench! She is chatting, emphasizing her words with a subtle smile, and her curious glance tries to read the face of the young man talking to her. And that young philosopher, leaning back in his chair and smoking his pipe, what profound disdain he must have for the jigging of the gallant dancers who seem oblivious to the sun in the ardor of a polka!

Surely Renoir has a right to be proud of *Dancing at the Moulin de la Galette*. Never has he been more inspired. It is a page of history, a precious monument to Parisian life done with rigorous exactitude. No one before him had thought of portraying an event in ordinary life on a canvas of such big dimensions; it is an act of daring which will be rewarded by success, as is fitting. This painting has a very great significance for the future, which cannot be overemphasized. This is an historical painting. Renoir and his friends have understood that historical painting is not the more or less ludicrous illustration of tales of the past; they have blazed a trail that others will certainly follow. Let those who want to do historical painting do the history of their own era, instead of raising the dust of past centuries. What do those operetta kings, rigged out in yellow and blue robes, bearing a scepter in their hands and a crown on their heads, matter to us! When, for the hundredth time, we are shown Saint Louis dispensing justice under an oak, have we thereby made any progress? What documents will artists who indulge in such overlabored works bring to future centuries concerning the history of our own era?

Every conscientious artist tries to immortalize his work; by what right can such paintings, which bring nothing new in color or the choice of subject, hope for this immortality?

Treating a subject for the sake of tone and not for the sake of the subject itself, this is what distinguishes the Impressionists from other painters. For there are Italians, Belgians and others who paint miniatures of people in contemporary dress and who contribute also, it will be said, to the history of our period. We will not deny it, we will even add that the photographers and tailors who publish fashion illustrations contribute at least as much as they do; but are they artists for that reason? It is especially this pursuit, this new way of treating a subject, which is the very personal quality of Renoir; instead of seeking the secret of the great masters, of Velasquez or of Frans Hals . . . he sought and found a contemporary note and *Dancing at the Moulin de la Galette*, whose coloring has so many charms and so much that is new, will surely be the big success of this year's exhibitions.

If, as Boileau says, "One flawless sonnet's worth two lumbering odes," then I believe that a perfect painting like *The Swing* is every bit as good as *Dancing at the Moulin de la Galette*.

What calm and repose this painting has! These are undoubtedly people with time on their hands; here we no longer have the bustle, the all-pervading gaiety of the dance, whose protagonists are stealing a few hours' enjoyment which must last them the whole week. No, here the mood is of composure, tranquillity, in the midst of a large park, whose abundant vegetation blazes like a cluster of emeralds. Here one feels the absence of all passion; these young people are enjoying life, the marvelous weather, the morning sun filtering through the leaves; what do they care for the rest of the human race? They are happy, these are the words which come to the mind of anyone looking at this delightful painting. And none has given me greater pleasure. . . .

It is evident that the Renoir exhibition is very important, not only because of the number of canvases shown but also because of their worth. The show is even more complete than those of previous years.

We shall not say any more about it, it is up to the public to appreciate these works shown for its benefit; it is to the heart that the painting addresses itself; if the public is moved, the goal is met; nothing more can

Drawing after *Le Balançoire* for the front cover of *L'Impressioniste*. April 21, 1877. 4 × 3⅛" (10.1 × 8 cm). Bibliothèque Nationale, Paris. (See Colorplate 49.)

be asked of the artist, and the painter will be sufficiently rewarded for his labors we are sure.

Monet, whose works we are going to try to describe, seems to be the absolute opposite of Renoir. The strength, animation, in a word, the life that the painter of *Dancing at the Moulin de la Galette* puts into his people, Monet puts into things; he has found their soul. In his pictures, water splashes, locomotives work, the sails of boats swell in the wind, terrain, houses, everything in the work of this great artist has an intense and personal life that no one had discovered or even suspected before him.

ROGER BALLU

CHRONIQUE DES ARTS ET DE LA CURIOSITÉ

"Exhibition of Impressionists"

April 14, 1877

Roger Ballu was an inspector at the Ecole des Beaux Arts, Paris, and, as a critic, generally hostile to Impressionism.

. . . Despite the strangeness of his painting, M Renoir is not to be confused with the other exhibitors. His painting of the *Place St-Georges* has a ring of truth; but I confess I do not understand the *Portrait of Mlle S* . . . The well-known head of its charming model is virtually lost against its brutal pink background, which does not allow the flesh to bloom. The artist has been forced, on the lips and chin, to use blue shades in order to model this figure, drowned as it is in brightness. What an odd portrait! Nothing, it seems to me, is further removed from real nature! Whereas in *The Swing* and *Dancing at the Moulin de la Galette,* this same M Renoir has worked to render nature slavishly. At first glance it seems that his canvases have met with some mishap during their journey from his studio to their place of exhibition. They are dotted with round blobs, and apparently speckled in some parts. Looking at them closely, one understands what their author has tried to do: he has attempted to render the affect of full sunlight, falling through the foliage onto the people seated under the trees. The aim of these round blobs is to render the shadow cast by each leaf. This, I admit, is a truly Impressionist endeavor; but is not the undertaking of such a struggle with nature tantamount to exposing oneself to a defeat that is without excuses and without interest, because it will always be absurd?

This is the bust portrait of the actress, Jeanne Samary (1857–1890) (Colorplate 39).

Portrait of Madame Alphonse Daudet. c. 1876. 18½ × 14⅝″ (47 × 37 cm). Musée d'Orsay, Paris.

GEORGES RIVIERE

L'IMPRESSIONNISTE

"To the Ladies"

April 21, 1877

. . . You, Madame, have been to the Impressionist exhibition, you saw there paintings full of gaiety and sunlight, and as you are young and pretty, you found the paintings to your liking, you saw portraits of women.

I am too gallant to dream of implying that they are flattering, but anyway they are very pretty, this at least is your opinion and you personally would like to own a ravishing portrait which would capture the charm with which your dear person is blessed. But you have a husband. . . . Your husband, who may be a Republican, gets into a rage with a revolutionary who is sowing discord in the artistic camp. . . . He cries out against the political routine, against the government routine . . . but he looks at painting through old pictures. . . .

I saw some pretty women laughing in front of the paintings at the Impressionist exhibition. That saddened me. . . .

Renoir had sent more portraits than anything else to the 1877 exhibition, presumably in an effort to attract patrons.

PHILIPPE BURTY

LA RÉPUBLIQUE FRANÇAISE

"Exhibition of Impressionists"

April 25, 1877

Although generally greeted by jibes and outrage, this exhibition nonetheless continues to draw in the public. . . . The first impression almost certainly produces a reaction of great surprise. . . . The word "Impressionist" ill expresses the normal practice of a profession and characterizes them misleadingly. They are particularly impressionable people. Without entering into a systematic discussion which would certainly weary our reader, we may say that these artists try, on the whole, to capture the general aspect of things and beings, the character given off by conventional appearances; and that, in practice, they make use of bright color and proclaim the pointlessness of black or opaque tones. Is this to be laughed at, is this a matter for indignation? Certainly not. This is merely the eccentric development of what Corot had sought in giving up outlining forms, in constantly breaking up shadows by more or less accentuated shades of gray.

These works betray a bias too absolute for them to be accepted by the general public for a long time yet. But they have their buyers, and these buyers are by no means indiscriminate. As paintings, they shock. In position and as decoration, they have a brightness, a straightforwardness of effect that is undeniable. It will be a long time before they make their way into official exhibitions. But they will filter through to them as though by seepage.

* * *

M Renoir is certainly an Impressionist, but he would be more accurately characterized as a "romantic Impressionist." Highly sensitive in temperament, he is always afraid of being too assertive. By using the odd touch to emphasize all that is unmoving, in *Dancing at the Moulin de la Galette,* (chairs, benches, tables) he would leave the group of dancers and speakers a true sense of movement, the rays of sunlight their tremulous patches, and would imbue the whole scene with an air of reality which in fact is lacking. The drawing of the features in the portrait of our friend Spuller lacks solidity; but his expression is intense; the eyes think, the flesh is alive. The portraits of Mme Alphonse Daudet and Mme Georges Charpentier are true to life. The portrait of Mlle Samary renders the pretty face of a pert soubrette so well and so aptly evokes the particular stage atmosphere that one has to go back as far as the vivid sketches by

Jacques-Eugène Spuller (1835–96) was the senior editor of Gambetta's newspaper, La République Française. *(See p. 110.)*
Mme Alphonse Daudet (1847–1940)

Fragonard to find, not points of literal comparison, but similarities in the French temperament as applied to portrait painting.

We have found sustenance in these rooms that owe nothing to the government. . . . The Salon which is about to open does not include all endeavors, all convictions. . . . However little the various currents in art may be susceptible of direction, we must report on all of them. They are, in any case, less dangerous than a dead calm.

Jean-Honoré Fragonard (1732–1806)

Portrait of Jacques-Eugène Spuller. c. 1877. 18⅛ × 15″ (46 × 38 cm). Property of Mr. & Mrs. Charles Wohlstetter.

THE THIRD IMPRESSIONIST EXHIBITION

Other Reviews

April 1877

Unfortunately, placed next to those pretty canvases is *La Balançoire*. In it the effects of sunlight are combined in such a bizarre way that they exactly produce the effect of grease stains on the figures' clothing. (*L'Événement*. April 6, 1877)

COLORPLATE 49

Some of Renoir's portraits look alright – at a distance – so that you do not notice too much of his way of applying brushstrokes like pastel hatchings and the peculiar scratches that make his style seem so painful.
(Paul Sebillot, *Le Bien Public*. April 7, 1887)

. . . and because of our poor visual education we laugh blindly at the *Dindons* by Claude Monet, which resemble only puffs of smoke, and at the *Bal . . .* by Renoir, where the figures dance on a floor that looks like those purple clouds that darken a stormy sky.
(Georges Lafenestre, *Le Monitor Universel*. April 8, 1877)

Renoir is one of the prolific and daring ones in the place. I recommend his *Balancoire*, sublime in its grotesqueness and in its audacious impudence, and the *Bal du Moulin de la Galette*, which is in no way inferior to his other work in the incoherence of its draftsmanship, composition and color.
(Bertall, *Paris-Journal*. April 9, 1877)

COLORPLATE 53

Do you like vibrant landscapes? I admit that I am unable to figure out what a vibrant landscape is, but since the Impressionist painters who opened their exhibition on the rue Peletier the day before yesterday claim that they do vibrant work, so be it. It was necessary to find an adjective surprising enough to signify such an unheard of system. When you have done green hair, brick red flesh, turkeys like puffs of smoke and the dance floor at the Moulin de la Galette like a purple cloud, then you have done with vibrant painting. Even if you cannot argue with taste, you can at least laugh at it, and it really is amusing. . . .

We spoke of the *Bal au Moulin de la Galette* by Renoir, and of the impression produced by its floor, a minor detail. What must be added is that, except for the search for peculiar tonalities, this painting has real value because of the skilful composition of its many figures.
(*La Petite Presse*. April 9, 1877)

Cham, "But these are the colors of a cadaver?" "Yes, unfortunately I can't manage the smell!"
Caricature of the Third Impressionist exhibition. *Le Charivari*, 1877.

COLORPLATE 43

More blue! But this one is frighteningly intense. It has been applied to the picture of a young girl on a swing covered with azure pom-poms. I hope you like pom-poms, because the painter has scattered them everywhere, in the sky, the trees and on the ground. And everywhere the same ferocious blue. This dizzying work was signed by Renoir.
(Louis Leroy, *Le Charivari*. April 11, 1877)

The young girl of the *Balançoire* is eternally graceful in her springtime surroundings. . . .
I will be more reserved in my praise of the *Seine à Champrosay*, whose touch is quite brutal despite its impression of truthfulness. It is the high grass of the bank that ruins the river for me. . . .
The most important work, nevertheless, is the *Bal du Moulin de la Galette*. A dense crowd, some waltzing, the impetus of their whirling visible. Others watch, forming a line. Still others are drinking happily seated at tables. Some nonchalant young girls, sitting where their laughing faces seem to lean outside the frame, amuse themselves by talking of innocent trifles. In the shadow of a lightly sketched-in stage, the band plays and the luminous globes swing in the green leaves of the acacias. The clumps of leaves moving in the breeze break the horizon and set off the musicians. These are humble working girls, good people of the suburbs enjoying themselves decently. Nothing unwholesome here. They are treating themselves to a day off and accept the pleasure without a second thought. This, in an environment of lively, perfumed clear tones – nothing excessive, no heaviness. This is the face of a corner of nineteenth century Paris that will endure.
(Jacques, *L'Homme Libre*. April 12, 1877)

A catalogue of 1869 informs us that Auguste Renoir is a student of Gleyre. We would never have guessed as much. In his intelligent talks,

Gleyre used to tell his students that when Hercules was in love he spun wool at the feet of Omphale, and about the terrors of Pantheus when the maenads were after him. If he were still here, the master would be astonished that such teachings could have led Renoir to paint the *Bal du Moulin de la Galette*. But he would have been even more surprised by the techniques of execution that his student has adopted.
(Paul Mantz, *Le Temps*. April 22, 1877)

PIERRE-AUGUSTE RENOIR

L'IMPRESSIONNISTE

"Contemporary Decorative Art"

April 28, 1877

The decoration of buildings which, in our age of unbridled luxury, should occupy the foremost position in art, is in fact characterized by lack of balance.

Decorative paintings, in our public buildings, are stilted, breathless, out of all proportion and far from being in harmony with what they should be decorating. The paintings at the Opéra, for instance, do not accord with the building. Those by M Baudry, pale, wan, faded, and weak, disappear amidst the lights and gilding. The Pils ceiling is seen to better effect, but it draws a false strength from certain reminiscences of Delacroix interpreted by a sick man. In a word, it forms a broad swathe of tedium and indeed coarseness, in the midst of the luxury which surrounds it.

The other paintings at the Academy of Music all have similar faults. The painters were thinking of Venetians or Germans, of Delacroix or Ingres; none of them has managed to be a real decorator. Their works are easel paintings on a large scale, inspired by academic stereotypes, but they do not have the variety and power which enables a work to withstand the splendor of gold and to persist and take on life in the midst of the linear details of the surrounding arabesques.

In our time, only Delacroix has understood decoration, indeed he has actually changed its harmonic conditions. Thus his paintings in Saint-Sulpice are the most important thing; the Chapel itself is just a pretext to create art. In decoration, painted work has value only because it is polychrome; the more varied the tones are in their harmony, the more decorative the painting will be. Mosaic, for example, has no need to represent a subject, it works if it is harmoniously arranged, with no further concern. The stained glass windows of the Middle Ages are beautiful because they are in harmony with the monuments which house them and because they are beautiful in color.

Sculpture is in an even more irregular position than painting. From the main decorative themes down to the humblest accessories, modern sculpture is unsuited to, and in complete disharmony with, the architecture that surrounds it.

The statues which decorate Notre-Dame, for instance, are in complete unity with the building. The monsters, the gargoyles, the arabesques, the rose windows, all contribute to the life and variety of the work as a whole. Furthermore, all the decoration of past centuries has these same qualities, which is why we still warm to them today.

As to the intrinsic value of modern decorative sculpture, it is almost nil. The groups, statues, ornaments are coarse, if compared with the

This was Renoir's most considered theoretical statement, on the decorative arts or any other subject. Rather pompously self-conscious in the context of Impressionism at large, it provoked no more response than his 1880 Salon proposal (p. 136) or his Society of Irregularists of 1884 (pp. 164–65).

The painters Paul Baudry (1828–86), Isidore Pils (1813–75)
Eugène Delacroix (1798–1863)

Jean-Auguste-Dominique Ingres (1780–1867)

sculptures decorating the buildings of other periods. The Gorgons' heads at the War Office are horrible, while those on the Pont-Neuf are subtle, delicate, original. The ornaments of the old Louvre are a thousand times superior to those of the Palais de Justice, on the Place Dauphine. There, it is true, the finest decoration would not have saved the building, which is too grotesque by half, with its great wide shabby staircase, punctuated with public urinals, copied from something beautiful doubtless, but distorted as soon as it passed into the hands of the architect or modern craftsmen. On the façade there are large statues which the Assyrians would rightly have rejected from their bas-reliefs.

In Paris, the Halles Centrales are the only buildings with a truly original character and an aspect suited to their purpose. But there is not one modern building which can be compared to the Hôtel de Cluny or the old Louvre. Our buildings are more or less clumsy caricatures of these fine works, and that is all.

And yet there is a dependence on the past. The training given to architects, painters, and sculptors at the Ecole des Beaux-Arts is based entirely on the past. Architects are sent to Rome to reconstruct a Greek monument, painters are sent to Rome to copy Raphael. Sculptors too are sent to Rome to seek inspiration in Greek sculptures, more or less mutilated. When, after a few years' stay in the Eternal City, these young people, painters, sculptors, and architects, come back to Paris stuffed with antiquities, still dazzled by the masters of Greece and Italy, one might think that, freed of these obsessions by the modern trend, their works would gain some originality; no, the buildings contain all the lines, all the proportions which the architect has brought back from Rome. They have all the clumsiness, the hesitation of the half-obliterated memory. The painters have confused yearnings to resemble Raphael or some other Italian master ... the sculptors are content with a few movements provided by famous statues, and they go no further.

All these ineffective young artists, who are fervently patronized, end up believing themselves to be greatly gifted. They come to see their masters as plagiarists, and they live in eternal self-congratulation, which does not allow them to follow the modern movement. Who should bear the responsibility for this absence, or worthlessness, of decorative art? First and foremost the administrative organization of the Ecole des Beaux-Arts, then the training given to architects.

The architect with everything at his disposal, who is completely in charge of a building, should be an artist rather than a scholar. He should be not only a builder, but also a painter and sculptor, like the great architects of the Renaissance. Then, instead of leafing through some dusty old tome to seek out some forgotten column shaft, an unknown rose window or a facade dreamed of by Veronese or Michelangelo, he would go out into nature or withdraw into his own mind to search for a form and a color which would then have a value in a modern setting. If he wanted painters, he would look for them in a movement similar to that he himself followed; and he would do the same with sculptors. It is only in such conditions, that is to say if an architect has a modern education, that a building can be beautiful, and have a certain unity. The first revolution to be carried out is the suppression of the Ecole des Beaux-Arts. The Conservatoire des Arts et Métiers should be extended, so as to give the young people the scientific notions necessary for the practice of their art; their artistic attempts should be encouraged, but above all they should not be forced to copy the old masters, as is so crassly done today. So far no architect has left the path that his school had laid down for him. The Trinité, the Opéra, the Palais de Justice, the new Louvre, the Tribunal de Commerce, the Hôtel-Dieu are motley oddities, full of reminiscences of a long dead art. Strange alliances are formed from Gothic and Greek art. For some years, a fake Byzantine art has been prevalent in the building of churches. Tomorrow, something else will be dug up.

In a word, if the painters and sculptors who decorate modern buildings are, for the most part, without talent and without the least taste, the fact is that they are given their directions by a man who is absolutely ignorant of painting and sculpture. Despite the enormous learning accumulated in his brain over twenty years, the architect is as ignorant in matters of art as a vulgar astronomer. When he entrusts a painter or sculptor with the execution of any decoration, he is incapable of sensing whether the artist in whom he is putting his trust will not betray his hopes.

An architect must be in a position completely to execute his own building, he must be able to paint the pictures and create the sculptures, so as to avoid outlandish façades like that of the Opéra, where the group of the *Dance,* by Carpeaux, is so little at one with the building that it completely destroys its effect. In the Tuileries, this same Carpeaux refused to remain within the framework which the architect had assigned to him and took his group onto the roof, abandoning the pediment which was intended for him. All sculptors and painters have acted in the same way, because they sensed the powerlessness of the person who was directing their work.

In conclusion, I would add that until a new generation of architects emerges to overthrow the current *côterie* through a new training, it is to painters that the charge of a building should be entrusted.

I am convinced that they would give proof of an originality, and indeed a unity that one cannot ask of anyone except the person who can be at once the head and the arms.

The Dance, 1867–68, by the sculptor Jean-Baptiste Carpeaux (1827–75)

GEORGES RIVIERE

RENOIR ET SES AMIS

"Madame Charpentier's Soirées"

1921

Madame Charpentier's first receptions go back to the time when the publisher lived on the quai du Louvre, at the corner of the place Saint-Germain l'Auxerrois. They were already glittering occasions thanks to the quality of the guests, artists and men of letters, along with some Republican politicians.

When Georges Charpentier moved his bookshop to the building in the rue de Grenelle, Madame Charpentier's parties developed accordingly. The publishing house which had for a long time been on the old site of the Bibliothèque-Charpentier, was given new impetus by the success of a few writers who became leading figures in the contemporary novel. Charpentier's influence, and particularly that of his wife, a remarkably intelligent woman, was henceforth considerable in the world of letters, arts, and even politics.

At the time when Renoir regularly attended the publisher's parties, he already had several friends there, but Madame Charpentier's skills and persistence found him new ones, and the expressions of sympathy that he received in the drawing room at the rue de Grenelle after the 1877 exhibition were welcome comfort for the artist.

These cheerful gatherings where, without detriment to good manners, courtesy did not take the fixed form of ritual behavior, were animated without being noisy and infinitely rich in wit.

Mme Marguerite Charpentier (née Lemonnier, 1848–1904) was the wife of Georges Charpentier (1846–1905), publisher of La Vie Moderne, *etc., friend of Flaubert and the Goncourt brothers. The Charpentiers were Renoir's most important patrons of the 1870s, and through them Renoir met many more, not least at these soirées. (see also p. 137)*

Portrait of Théodore de Banville. Pastel. c. 1879. 20½ × 16⅛″ (52 × 41 cm). Cabinet des Dessins, Louvre, Paris.

With Alphonse Daudet and Zola, who were making the bookshop's fortune, came Gustave Flaubert, tall and well-set with a thick white mustache falling over his lips, "looking like a retired colonel selling wine," to use Daudet's words. To surprise his neighbors at the top table he would give loud voice to some crude traveling salesman's joke. Edmond de Goncourt, who sat in silence, his monocle in his eye, looking bored, acted out there as everywhere his role as "society inspector" turning his mournful gaze on the assembled company. Whenever I saw him like that I used to think of Barbey d'Aurévilly's joke about Jules de Goncourt's brother. When someone asked him if he had read *Les Frères Zemganno*, Barbey replied "No, not now the widow writes on her own."

Alphonse Daudet (1840–97);
Gustave Flaubert (1821–80)

The De Goncourt brothers, Edmond (1822–96) and Jules (1830–70), writers, best known for their essays on French 18th-century art and their Journal des Goncourt.
Jules Amédée Barbey D'Aurévilly (1808–89). A novel by Edmond de Goncourt.

General Billot, the hardworking host of this company, stood for a long time by the entrance as if he was afraid of missing the chance to clasp the hand of a future minister; he was the Republican Party's orderly.

Carolus-Duran, who always went in for some eccentricity of dress, would hold forth on art.

Charles-Emile Carolus-Duran (1838–1917), painter

"I don't like Raphael," he said one evening, "because he creates types."

If he was asked nicely, the good Carolus plucked his guitar, having always taken the precaution of bringing the instrument with him, first leaving it discreetly in the cloakroom. It seemed as though the guitar went together with his admiration for Velasquez.

Henner, with the slightly heavy walk of an Alsatian clog-maker, went from person to person, kindly and benevolent. He talked slowly with a rural accent which gave his words a certain goodnaturedness. One evening when I was complaining, in a group where he was, about the attacks directed against the painting of Renoir and other Impressionists, he talked about his own difficult beginnings.

Jean-Jacques Henner (1829–1905), painter

"How did you come to get the prix de Rome?" someone asked him, "since you were not in Paris?"

"It was like this. I had to leafe the studio because I could not pay my feess. So I went back to my own country and worked there. Later when I had safed some more I came back to Paris and got into the Ecole des Beaux-Arts. Sometime afterwards I got the prix de Rome. It's very simple."

* * *

Among so many famous or quite well-known men who came to the house, the man of the moment was the author of *L'Assommoir*, a book whose extraordinary popularity had been unexpected. Tall, upright, with a portly shape under his suit, his eye-glasses perched on an aggressive nose, his hair cut short and standing up on end, rather like a "Turk's head", and his quite closely cropped black beard, he looked both sad and forbidding.

Zola's novel, which Renoir illustrated in 1878 (page 116).

Zola, who was morose despite his success, bitter, even acid, always seemed to be arguing with the person talking to him. He made a striking contrast with Alphonse Daudet who was pleasant, fond of telling stories, charming, never having to make an effort to win over those who came up to him.

Near Zola there was often Huysmans, standing as solemnly as his companion. He was tall and thin, stiff and slightly sickly looking. With his square head crowned with short hair, his bony face, with its two shining foxy eyes, a spiky beard which was nearer yellow than red, he reminded me of those cardboard devils' heads which jump out on a spring when you open their box.

Joris-Karl Huysmans (see page 120.)

Théodore de Banville, of whom Renoir has done such a good likeness, belonged to a different age from the other two, as you realized when you saw them all side by side. Clean-shaven, with eyes which were both malicious and innocent and a sly mouth, he created in our mind the image of Pierrot, the charming Pierrot adored by the poet.

Théodore de Banville (1823–91)

* * *

Moving from one group to another through crowded rooms Manet, who was always very much "on the outside," summed up quite reasonable opinions in such incisive phrases that they were given a paradoxical appearance in the process. Less vocal than his colleague in Paris, de Nittis, the Neopolitan painter who had exhibited his work with the Impressionists in 1874 but without meeting with the success he hoped for, talked most frequently with Degas who seemed to take a mischievous delight in singing his praises in order to denigrate implicitly other exhibitors at the Nadar gallery; no one was deceived. . .

Among other regulars who were sympathetic to Renoir there were, notably, Emile Bergerat throwing out a multitude of witty remarks, amusing sallies that he delivered all over the place; Judith Gautier, his sister-in-law, an Athenian already taken with the grimacing fancies and devils on wallpaper of the country of Tin-Tun-Lin, her father's one-time servant; Jeanne Samary, the pretty actress whose small, enchanting portrait Renoir had shown at the exhibition in the rue Le Peletier, and finally Paul Arène, who was one of the most delicate poets of the second half of the nineteenth century.

I never met Gambetta at Madame Charpentier's, although I believe he went there a few times. But he did not much care for society parties and besides, from that time onwards, he was not able to devote much time to them.

Gambetta who, in working-class circles, had lost his earlier popularity, had become the idol of the liberal bourgeoisie. A few speeches, dotted with happy turns of phrase, had caused him to be dubbed a great statesman and his country's saviour. A legend grew up around his role during the war, portraying him as a hero defending his native land to the bitter end.

Illustration for Zola's
L'Assommoir. Pen and ink. 1878.
9⅝ × 14½″ (24.5 × 37 cm).
Private Collection.

Joseph de Nittis (1846–1884)

Emile Bergerat (1845–1923)
Judith Gautier (1850–1917), daughter of the
poet Théophile

COLORPLATE 39

This revolutionary whose mind was more than usually slovenly, was transformed by the recalcitrant bourgeois into a champion of order and craftsman of revenge. People were tired of the government of *moral order* whose *clericalism* offended the ideas of free-thinkers and whose reactionary attitudes disturbed the liberals, who were firm in their belief that the Republic would bring back the golden age on earth. All the hopes of the Government's opponents rested on the coming to power of the "great tribune."

Renoir, whose sympathies lay with Gambetta, whom he called "the only intelligent man in his party," told me the day after a party he had attended about the impression Gambetta had made on a society gathering.

It was just before the 1877 elections. Cernuschi, a rich banker of Jewish birth and Italian nationality, had given a party in honor of the *tribune* in his Parc Monceau hotel. Gambetta kept them waiting for a while and an impatient crowd was watching for his arrival in the large foyer. When he arrived perspiring, breathless and in a hurry, he had to pass between two rows of elegant women who were jostling each other to see him or be seen by him, greeting him with flattering comments and even with cheers. This heralded the great triumph that the Republican bourgeoisie had in store for him. Gambetta, who was not stupid, must have been highly amused by this enthusiastic reception, recalling how the same people had greeted him a couple of years before.

"The women," added Renoir, "were as always the most persistent in their acclamation of Gambetta. They were literally offering themselves to him, as if to a God."

In order to go to Charpentier's, Renoir and I would arrange to meet in a small café – no longer there today – at the corner of the rue des Saints-Pères and the rue de L'Université. It was hardly patronized at all except by old regulars who always sat at the same tables. Cats slept on the benches and a fat woman with her graying hair in a coil was behind the counter wearing a dapple-gray bodice of outmoded design.

One evening we were sitting with our goblets of dessert when two old people, husband and wife, came in, headed in our direction and suddenly stopped, looking uncomfortable and disoriented. They looked at the empty tables without managing to decide on one. Renoir who was watching them, guessed what was going on. He got up and spoke to the husband:

"We must have taken your table," he said to a smile. "Have it back, we'll be just as comfortable somewhere else."

The old couple beamed all over their faces. They thanked the painter warmly and once in their places silently began a game of dominoes.

When we left, the couple acknowledged us with a grateful smile and the waiter, who wore diplomat's sidewhiskers, showed us to the door. This little incident shows the care Renoir always took to avoid hurting anyone at all. How many times have I witnessed his thoughtfulness in equally trivial circumstances?

Although Renoir did not like society gatherings, he enjoyed going to Madame Charpentier's. There he was among intelligent people where, thanks to the tact and grace of the mistress of the house, there was no sign of aloofness or tedium. The painter felt supported and encouraged by the welcome of the friends he met there and that helped convince him that he was not as abandoned by God and men as the art critics made out in their reviews of the exhibition at the rue Le Peletier.

Henri Cernuschi (1821–96)

Portrait of Eugène Murer. c. 1877.
18½ × 15⅛″ (47 × 38.5 cm).
Private Collection of The
Honorable and Mrs. Walter H.
Annenberg, New York.

EUGÈNE MURER

An Anecdote from his Notebook

1877

Eugène Murer (Eugène-Hyacinthe Meunier) (1846–1906), was a pastry cook who painted and wrote novels and poetry. He ran a restaurant with his sister Marie. He was an important supporter and collector of the Impressionists and gave regular weekly dinners for the artists during the 1870s.

At that time I was living on the Boulevard Voltaire in a shop decorated by the Impressionists. Renoir had adorned the frieze with brilliant garlands of flowers. Pissarro, with a few strokes of the brush, had covered the walls with landscapes of Pontoise. Monet, who was always in search of a louis, had contented himself with coming in to see how it was all getting on. Every Wednesday for two years, we had met together, my friends and I, to partake of a little fraternal dinner presided over by my sister. That evening Pissarro had not come.

Over the dessert, Renoir told us that all day long he had been about from place to place with a picture under his arm trying to sell it. Everywhere he had been bowed out with the words: "You have come too late. Pissarro has just been here. I've taken a painting off his hands as a matter of humanity. You know. Poor chap. With all those youngsters." This "poor chap" – his name repeated at every door at which Renoir knocked – exasperated Renoir, who was very much put out at not having sold anything.

"What!" he cried, in that mock-ogre's voice of his, and, rubbing his nose nervously with his forefinger – a familiar gesture of his – 'because I am a bachelor and have no children, am I to die of starvation? I'm in just as tight a corner as Pissarro; yet when they talk of me, no one says 'that poor Renoir.'"

PHILIPPE BURTY

LA RÉPUBLIQUE FRANÇAISE

"Salon of 1879"

May 27, 1879

After long years of expectation, M Renoir is at last achieving success. In our view, he had delayed too long before making the concessions needed for firmness of rendering. His portrait of our friend Spuller, already exhibited with the Intransigents, was not the product of a palette as sober as this vast and harmonious portrait of Madame Charpentier. From the big Newfoundland dog, in the foreground, to the amusing walls of a boudoir decorated in Japanese style, everything is ruled by a general feeling of modern harmony. The poses are of a striking aptness, and the flesh which the children offer up innocently to the kiss of light, is firm as ripening cherries. It is more like looking at the bloom of an outsize pastel.

PAGE 110

COLORPLATE 75

CASTAGNARY

LE SIÈCLE

"Salon of 1879"

June 1879

Jules-Antoine Castagnary (1830–88), influential critic and administrator; he had been writing Salon reviews since 1857.

M Renoir is assuredly to be placed in the forefront of those who are driven by the new spirit, and who seek the material for an original art in the life that surrounds them, with neither imitation nor nostalgia. No one has fewer visible links. Where does he come from? No school, no system can claim him as their own. He is not a specialist, devoting himself to one exclusive genre, landscape or still life; he is a complete painter, painting history or everyday life (which will be history in a quarter of a century) and subordinating things to being, the scene to the actor. We have seen him several times associated with the Impressionists, and this has helped to create some uncertainty as to his style; but he does not linger there, and it is at the Salon, along with the main body of artists, that he is now demanding his share of publicity. The critics cannot fail to react favorably to him. His *Portrait of Madame Charpentier and her Children* is a most fascinating work. Possibly the figures are a little short, a little squat in their proportions; but his palette is one of extreme richness. A deft and witty hand has touched all the objects which make up this charming interior; they have been arranged and modeled by means of rapid brushstrokes, with the sprightly grace which creates the color's particular spell. Not the slightest trace of convention, either in the arrangement or in the technique. The observation is as sharp as the execution is free and spontaneous. We have here the elements of a lively art, whose further developments we await with confidence.

J. K. HUYSMANS

L'ART MODERNE

"The Salon of 1879"

1883

Joris-Karl Huysmans (1848–1907), writer, who after being a champion of Realism and Impressionism, became a leading figure of the Symbolist movement with his novel A Rebours *(Against the Grain) (1884). The long Salon review in which this extract appears was reprinted in Huysmans'* L'Art Moderne, *published by Georges Charpentier in 1883.*

COLORPLATE 69

The permanent, impossible laughter of this actress is perfectly captured; we find her (Jeanne Samary) again, still laughing, but dressed in pink this time, in a painting by M Renoir, so oddly placed high up in one of the Salon's dumping grounds, that it is absolutely impossible to gain any idea of the effect the painter intended. One might indeed range canvases along the ceiling while one is at it!

His other painting, on the other hand, is placed on the staircase. M Renoir decided that it would be better to represent *Madame Charpentier* in her own interior, with her children, at her usual tasks, rather than putting her stiffly, in a conventional pose, against some red or purple curtain. He was quite right, in my view. This is an interesting and praiseworthy exercise. This portrait has some exquisite flesh tones and an ingenious sense of grouping. The technique is rather shallow but showy, and somewhat fussy in planes in the accessories, but it is skillfully executed, and daring into the bargain! In short, it is the work of an artist of talent and one who, while figuring in the official Salon, is nonetheless an independent spirit; it is surprising, but pleasing, to come upon people who have long abandoned the old routines pickled so carefully by their colleagues in jars of brine.

COLORPLATE 75

THÉODORE DURET

RENOIR

The Impressionist Painters

1878

Renoir excels at portraits. Not only does he catch the external features, but through them he pinpoints the model's character and inner self. I doubt whether any painter has ever interpreted woman in a more seductive manner. The deft and lively touches of Renoir's brush are charming, supple and unrestrained, making flesh transparent and tinting the cheeks and lips with a perfect living hue. Renoir's women are enchantresses. . . . You will have a mistress. But what a mistress! Always gentle, gay, smiling, with no need of dresses or hats, able to do without jewels, the real ideal woman!

COLORPLATE 41. *Paris Boulevards*. 1875. 20½ × 25″ (52 × 63.5 cm).
Philadelphia Museum of Art (Collection Henry P. McIlhenny, in memory of Frances P.McIlhenny).

COLORPLATE 42. *Snowy Landscape*. c. 1875. 19⅝ × 25⅝″ (50 × 65 cm).
Musée de l'Orangerie, Paris (Collection Jean Walter and Paul Guillaume).

COLORPLATE 43. *The Seine at Champrosay*. 1876. 21⅝ × 26″ (55 × 66 cm).
Musée d'Orsay, Paris.

COLORPLATE 44. *Nude in Sunlight*. 1875. 31⅞ × 25½″ (81 × 64.8 cm.)
Musée d'Orsay, Paris.

COLORPLATE 47. *The Café*. 1876/7. 13¾ × 11″ (35 × 28 cm).
State-Museum Kröller-Müller, Otterlo.

COLORPLATE 48. *The Lovers*. c. 1875. 68⅞ × 51⅛″ (175 × 130 cm).
Narodni Gallerii, Prague.

EDMOND RENOIR

LA VIE MODERNE
"The Fifth Exhibition at *La Vie Moderne*"
June 19, 1879

By the late 1870s, Edmond Renoir (1849–1944), Renoir's younger brother, had established himself as a journalist, editor and man of letters, working chiefly for La Presse *and* La Vie Moderne. *This article is in the form of a letter to the editor, Emile Bergerat.*

My dear Bergerat,

When you decided to bring together some of my brother's works, I naturally suggested leaving it to you. But you asked me to overcome my rightful scruples and, upon my word, I believe you were right.

My brother, like myself, is a collaborator on *La Vie Moderne;* all of us there are his friends and, given the task of presenting him to the public, all could be accused of well-disposed partiality. If any of his friends is to be involved, it might as well be me, who has been living alongside him for fifteen years, not just as a brother, but as an associate. And what are we dealing with, after all? Not with art criticism in the strict sense, but with telling our visitors: "This is the man whose works you are looking at, this is where he started from, what he went through, where he is now." A twenty-line portrait – that is all: you will admit that I am well-placed to tackle my subject!

As you know us well, you will know that it was definitely not good fortune that hampered our beginnings: if one has to be poor in order to work courageously, let us admit, there too, we were well-placed!

At the age of fifteen, my brother was thus obliged to learn a trade which would ensure him a living later on. From his use of bits of charcoal on the walls, it was deduced that he might have a taste for an artistic profession. Our parents therefore placed him with a painter on porcelain. The choice was a lucky one, as chance would have it. The young apprentice took mightily to the trade; when his day was over, armed with a portfolio taller than himself, he would go off and attend free courses in drawing. This went on for two or three years.

He made rapid progress; after a few months of apprenticeship, he was asked to paint pieces usually reserved for the fully-trained workers, a fact which earned him a few jibes – they laughingly called him M Rubens – and reduced him to tears by their teasing. However, one of these workers was a nice old man whose hobby was oil-painting: possibly pleased to have a pupil, he offered the young man a share in his stock of canvases and paints. After some time, he asked him to paint a work on his own.

The apprentice set to work and, one Sunday, the visit of the first master of the future painter of *Lise* and *Dancing at the Moulin de la Galette* was announced. I remember it as though it were yesterday. I was still a boy, but I was quite aware that serious things were afoot: the easel bearing the precious painting was put in the middle of the largest room in our modest lodgings in the rue d'Argenteuil; everyone was feverish with impatience, I had been tidied up and told to behave myself. The atmosphere was positively awesome. The "master" arrived; I assure you, the Renoir family felt very small indeed. At an agreed signal, I brought a chair up for him in front of the easel and he sat down and began to look at the "work." I can see it still, it was an "Eve": behind her, the serpent was coiling around the branches of an oak tree, coming towards her with bared fangs, as if to hypnotize her.

COLORPLATES 7, 53

The inspection lasted a good quarter of an hour; after which, with no further comment, this poor nice old man went up to our parents and uttered these simple words: "You should allow your son to become a real painter; in our trade, at most, he will finally earn twelve or fifteen francs a day. I foresee a brilliant future for him in the arts: see what you can do."

That evening, dinner at the rue d'Argenteuil was a somber affair; the

Edmond Renoir at Menton. Crayon and ink. 1881. 15 × 11⅜″ (65 × 81 cm). Private Collection, New York.

joy produced by this success vanished before the terrible prospect of having him abandon the trade which would give him a secure living, for the arts, which might lead him straight to destitution. At last, everyone resigned themselves, and the Ecole des Beaux-Arts had one more pupil. Auguste entered Gleyre's studio, studied anatomy, entered competitions in sketching and perspective, like everyone else.

How, as a pupil of Gleyre's did he become what he is? This is how: at that time, even more so than now, groups of art students swept down on the forest of Fontainebleau; they did not have their own studios, as they do today – that was an unknown luxury; they would stay at inns in Chailly, Barbizon or Marlotte, and they would go off to work in the open air, with their bags on their backs. It was there that my brother met Courbet, who was the idol of the young painters, and Diaz, whom they admired even more. It was Diaz who gave him the best lesson he may ever have had in his life: it was Diaz who told him that "no self-respecting painter ever touches a brush unless he has his model before his eyes."

This axiom remained deeply engraved in the memory of the young painter. He told himself that living models were too expensive and that he could find such models much more cheaply, since the forest was there, ready and eager to allow itself to be studied at leisure. He spent the summer there, and the winter, and whole years on end. It is by living in the open air that he became an open-air painter. The four cold walls of the studio did not weigh him down; the uniformly gray or brown tone of walls did not dull his eye; thus the environment has an enormous influence on him; having no memory of the constraints to which artists subject themselves, he lets himself be carried away by his subject and above all by the setting in which he finds himself.

This is the hallmark of his work; it is to be found everywhere, always, from *Lise*, which was painted in the forest, to the *Portrait of Madame Charpentier and her Children*, painted in her home, without the furniture having been moved from its usual place, without anything having been specially arranged to bring out any particular part of the picture.

Now he is painting the *Moulin de la Galette:* so he sets himself up there for six months, gets to know the locals with their idiosyncrasies (which models imitating their poses could not express) and by mingling with the popular tumult, he renders the rumbustious scene with marvelous verve.

Now he is painting a portrait; he will ask his models to keep their usual bearing, everyday clothing, sit as they normally sit, so that there should be no sense of preparedness or artificiality.

Thus quite apart from its artistic value, his work has all the *sui generis* charm of a faithful painting of modern life. We see the matter of his paintings every day; it is our own existence that he has recorded, in works which will surely remain among the liveliest and most harmonious of our time.

Thus for the *Acrobats* (Two Little Circus Girls), there is really no sense of arrangement. It is as though a process of inconceivable subtlety and immediacy had enabled him to capture the movements of the two children in the act. It was precisely thus that they walked, waved, smiled, on the circus floor. I shall not use the grandiose words "realism" or "impression-ism" to say that what we have here is real life with all its poetry and all its savor. This absence of the "conventional" which I am so stressing, gives me extreme pleasure; it gives the impression of nature with all its unexpectedness and its intense harmony: it is nature which is speaking to me, without my having to reckon with the artist's "talent," this talent which pursues you, itself, and destroys all sensation.

It is by considering my brother's work as a whole that one comes to realize that it is innocent of "technique." One may possibly not encounter the same fashion of proceeding in any two of his works, and yet the work has a unity, it was thoroughly felt from the very beginning, and pursued with the sole concern of attaining, not perfection of rendering, but the most complete perception of the harmonies of nature.

You have mostly pastels; do they not give you the same impression as oils? I might mention the portrait of Alphonse Daudet's little "baby," the *Boy in the Blue Hat*, the *Portrait of Banville;* carried away by their profound feeling for nature, did you pause to consider their technique?

I promised you a twenty-line portrait: rapt, absorbed, somber, remote, you have seen him rushing across the boulevard dozens of times; forgetful, disorderly, he will come back ten times for the same thing and still forget to do it; always running in the street, always motionless indoors, he will spend hours without moving, without speaking; what is he thinking of? Of the painting he is doing or about to do; he speaks about painting only as little as possible. But if you want to see his face light up, if you want to hear him – oh the wonder of it – humming some gay tune, don't look for him at table, or in places where one normally seeks amusement, but try to catch him unawares while he is working.

And now, my dear Bergerat, if some morose spirits find my apprecia-tion too flattering, I would answer that my conscience is my own affair; I think I have spoken sincerely.

If, in short, people have been given an inkling of the emotion, mingled with a touch of respect, with which I speak of my elder brother, they will have been given the right impression.

So who could dream of reproaching me for it?

Affectionately yours, Ed. Renoir

Study of Two Circus Girls (Francisca and Angelina Wartenberg) of the Cirque Fernando. Black chalk. 1879. 12½ × 8⅞" (31.8 × 22.5 cm). Saltwood Castle Collection. (See Colorplate 63).

These were drawings that Renoir made specially for La Vie Moderne.

PIERRE-AUGUSTE RENOIR

Letter to Théodore Duret

February 13, 1880

I shall be quite restored within a week. I owe this speedy recovery to Dr. Terrier, who has been marvelous. I amused myself working left-handed, it's great fun and the result is even better than I did with the right. I think I did well to have broken my arm, it has caused me to make some progress. . . . I can't feel pleased at the emotion my accident has caused you, but am very flattered by it and I greatly appreciate all of the sympathy I have received from everyone. I have been spoiled with all sorts of dainty morsels. Even so, I don't feel like doing it again.

JEAN RENOIR

RENOIR, MY FATHER

The Luncheon of the Boating Party

COLORPLATE 76

1958

Just as Montmartre had served as an artistic inspiration for Renoir, the banks of the Seine between Chatou and Bougival stimulated him to the same degree, especially in the years before his marriage. The large "Boatmen's Lunch," now in the Phillips Memorial Gallery in Washington, was the crowning achievement of a long series of pictures, studies and sketches at the Grenouillère Restaurant at Chatou. It was the railway line to Saint-Germain which made the success of the place possible. The station at the Chatou bridge was only twenty minutes from Paris by train, and the restaurant, out on the island of Chatou, could be reached in a few minutes' walk from the station. . . . The spot had been discovered by young lovers who liked to wander under the great poplar trees. As outdoor sports were then becoming popular, a far-sighted Bougival hotel-keeper called Fournaise decided to enlarge a small house on the island where he sold lemonade to Sunday visitors. He built a landing-place at the river's edge. He himself was something of an oarsman and had bought some excellent boats, which he rented to his Parisian customers. He even had several skiffs, as slender as knitting needles and very speedy: but these he would hire only to experts. It was not long before the Fournaise restaurant had developed into a sort of boating club. Both upstream and downstream from the restaurant, the river bends in a well-proportioned curve. Renoir had painted there as early as 1868.

COLORPLATES 12, 13

The name *Grenouillère* derived not from the numerous batrachians which swarmed in the surrounding fields, but from quite a different species of frog. It was a term applied to ladies of easy virtue: not exactly prostitutes, but rather a class of unattached young women, characteristic of the Parisian scene before and after the Empire, changing lovers easily, satisfying any whim, going nonchalantly from a mansion in the Champs-Elysées to a garret in the Batignolles. To them we owe the memory of a Paris which was brilliant, witty and amusing. Among that group, moreover, Renoir got a great many of his volunteer models. According to him, the *grenouilles* or "frogs" were often "very good sorts." Because French

people love a medley of various classes, actresses, society-women, respectable middle-class people also patronized the Fournaise restaurant. The tone of it was set by young sportsmen in striped jerseys, who vied with each other in rowing, beating records and becoming accomplished boatmen. When Bibesco first took Renoir to the Grenouillère, he brought along a captain in his regiment, the Baron Barbier. The Baron was a most congenial fellow, totally ignorant of painting, and interested only in horses, women and boats. He and my father struck up a great friendship.

Apart from the beauty of the place and the ample supply of models, one advantage especially attracted Renoir: its proximity to Louveciennes. Despite his busy life, he did not forget his mother. He loved and admired her more than ever. . . .

* * *

From Louveciennes to the Grenouillère it was only an hour's walk. Renoir made friends with the Fournaise family. Madame and Mlle Fournaise figure in several of his pictures. He also did a portrait of M. Fournaise. The Fournaises would rarely give Renoir a bill. "You've let us have this landscape of yours," they would say. My father would insist that his painting had no value: "I'm giving you fair warning; nobody wants it." "What difference does that make? It's pretty, isn't it? We have to put something on the wall to hide those patches of damp." My father smiled as he thought of those kind people again. "If all art-lovers were like that!"

La Grenouillère. 1869. 25½ × 36½" (65 × 93 cm). Oskar Reinhart Collection, Winterthur.

Prince George Bibesco, wealthy Parisian, for whose house Renoir had made decorations, now lost, in 1868.

133

He was to give them a number of pictures, which later became immensely valuable. And the Fournaises were not the only examples of this kind. I could cite any number of families, and important ones, who, thanks to the pictures Renoir had left with them, saved themselves from financial difficulties and even complete ruin.

"I am certainly a lucky man. I am able to help my friends, and it costs me nothing."

My father sometimes came across Maupassant at the Fournaises'. The two men were friendly enough but frankly admitted they had nothing in common. Renoir said of the writer, "He always looks on the dark side" – while Maupassant said of the painter, "He always looks on the bright side." There was however one point on which they did agree: "Maupassant is mad," asserted Renoir. "Renoir is mad," declared Maupassant.

One day as he was painting a young woman sitting in a boat, someone came up behind my father on tiptoe and put his hands over his eyes for a joke. It was the Baron Barbier, who had just returned from Indo-China, "cleaned out to the last sou," as he expressed it. . . .

My father was enormously pleased to see him again, and told him that he was planning a large picture of boatmen lunching with friends on the terrace of the Fournaise restaurant. Barbier offered to serve as stage-manager, getting boats for the background and rounding up models. "I know nothing about painting, and still less about yours; but I'll be glad to do you a favour."

Guy de Maupassant (1850–93)

Boating Couple. Pastel. 1880/81. 17¾ × 23″ (45 × 58.5 cm). Museum of Fine Arts, Boston (Given in memory of Governor Alvan T. Fuller by the Fuller Foundation).

Alphonsine Fournaise. 1879.
28 × 36¼″ (71 × 92 cm). Musée
d'Orsay, Paris.

It took Renoir several years to make his project "mature." He had a
number of pictures underway; then, too, his sketches for the subject did
not please him. He finally made up his mind in the summer of 1881. "I am
going to start the 'Luncheon,'" he told Barbier and his friend immediately
got in touch with the faithful. I am not certain of the identity of all the
people in the picture. Lhote is there, in the background, wearing a top hat;
Lestringuez is to be seen leaning over a friend who is perhaps Rivière. The
young woman with her elbows on the railing is Alphonsine Fournaise,
"the lovely Alphonsine," as the habitués of her parents' restaurant called
her. She died penniless in 1935, at the age of 92, having invested all her
money in Russian bonds. The young person drinking is "little Henriot;"
and the woman looking at Lestringuez must be Ellen André. The figure in
the foreground, patting a little dog, is my mother.

I paid a visit to the place last year [c. 1957]. How depressing it was!
Nothing but factories, mounds of coal, blackened walls and dirty water.
The leprosy of modern industry had eaten away the little woods and
luxuriant grass. North African labourers, weighed down by their wretched
fate, were forlornly unloading large metal drums from a barge smeared
with grease. Baron Barbier, the boatmen, the carefree young girls, have all
disappeared from this part of the river. They live now, for eternity, in the
imagination of those who love painting and dream of days gone by as they
gaze at "The Boatmen's Luncheon."

PIERRE-AUGUSTE RENOIR

LA CHRONIQUE DES TRIBUNAUX

"Plan for an Art Exhibition"

May 23, 1880

This proposal was quoted in an article by Eugène Murer.

PLAN FOR ART EXHIBITION
For the year 1880.

Article 1. The Salon is divided into four groups, which will run from the Salon of Honor to the end rooms, where each group will be divided into two [?].
1st group. Members of the *Institut* and previous award winners.
2nd group. Foreign artists judged by their delegates in Paris.
3rd group. Idealists. History, genre, etc., etc....
4th group. Naturalists, Impressionists, still Lifes, etc....

Article 2. Each group will be constituted in advance. It will comprise 400 members. This number shall not be exceeded.

Article 3. Each group will nominate its jury, who, working together, will separately and freely judge those canvases that they consider to belong to their section.

Article 4. No jury will be allowed to accept more than 4,000 canvases.

Article 5. After a final reconsideration by all four juries together, the remaining canvases submitted but not accepted shall be hung in separate rooms as *unclassified*. They will not appear in the catalogue.

Article 6. Awards of any category will no longer entitle artists to automatic acceptance, *hors concours*.

ÉMILE ZOLA

LE VOLTAIRE

"Naturalism at the Salon"

June 19, 1880

Émile Zola increasingly subscribed to his friend Manet's view that, for a young painter, "the Salon is the real field of battle;" hence his warmth towards Renoir here.

... M Renoir was the first [of the Impressionists] to understand that commissions would not come his way by those means [independent exhibitions]. Since he needed to earn a livelihood, he started again to send paintings to the official Salon, which led to him being treated as a renegade. I am a defender of independence in all things: however, I confess that the conduct of M Renoir appears to me to be perfectly reasonable. One must recognize the admirable means of publicity that the official Salon affords young painters; in the current climate, it is uniquely there that they may achieve serious recognition. Certainly one must keep one's independence in the work itself, one must waste nothing of his temperament and then one must go into battle in full sunlight. ...

JEAN RENOIR

RENOIR, MY FATHER

A Dinner at the Charpentiers'

1958

An incident recounted to Jean Renoir by his mother, Aline.

Once when my father was out painting in the Forest of Marly, he suddenly remembered an invitation for that evening to a large dinner party at the Charpentiers'. He was to be introduced to Gambetta, then at the height of his power. Charpentier wanted the Premier to commission Renoir to decorate a large panel in the new Hôtel de Ville.

Renoir gathered his equipment, hurried to his grandparents' house in Louveciennes, and dashed over to the town of Marly just in time to see the train for Paris pull out of the station. Luckily the station-master knew him and allowed him to jump on a goods train. It took him to the shunting yard in the Batignolles district, which in those days was still a suburb. He climbed down from the train and ran like mad through the empty streets. Finally he found a horse cab which took him into Paris.

Formal evening clothes always annoyed him, and once he reached home, instead of changing his shirt, he saved time by putting on a strange combination of starched collar and false shirt front, quite a popular device at the time.

At the Charpentiers' house, he solemnly handed his top hat, scarf, gloves and overcoat to the footman, and walked into the drawing-room before the astonished footman could stop him. He was welcomed by a burst of laughter; and with good reason. For in his haste he had forgotten to put on his dinner-jacket and was only in his shirt-sleeves. Charpentier was highly amused and, to make him feel at ease, took his coat off. All the other men did the same. Gambetta declared that it was very "democratic." And the dinner went with an extra note of gaiety.

Charpentier discussed the proposed decoration frankly with Gambetta. "This young artist is capable of reviving the art of fresco painting. He would bring glory on your Republic."

Gambetta then took Renoir aside. "We can't give you any commissions, or any of your friends, either. If we did, the government might fall."

"Don't you like our kind of painting?"

"Yes, indeed. It is the only painting that counts. And those others we are giving commissions to are no good at all. But you see. . . ."

"See what?"

"You are revolutionaries; that's the trouble."

My father was dumbfounded. But he could not keep from retorting: "Well what about you?"

Compare this with George Rivière's anecdote, "the real revolutionaries" (pp. 105–6) to witness a story that Renoir probably repeated to everyone being put into a different context.

"That's just it," answered Gambetta, "That point has to be overlooked: and our opinions as well. We have to get our democratic laws passed, and throw inessentials overboard. It is better for the Republic to live with bad painting than to die for the sake of great art."

MADAME AND JACQUES-ÉMILE BLANCHE

Two Letters to Dr Émile Blanche

July 1881

Dr Emile Blanche was a famous psychiatrist; his son Jacques-Emile (1861–1942), taught painting by Renoir, became a well-known painter. These are two letters from Mme Blanche and Jacques-Emile respectively, to the doctor, about a visit by Renoir to the Blanche house in Dieppe.

[M. Renoir] gets so carried away, in his painting, in his conversation, completely uneducated, very good-natured but with no time for healthy conventions; and I think (by having him leave) I have done absolutely the right thing for Jacques, who is so clean, so caring about his studio; he needs paint in pots, he makes his own canvases. He [Renoir] doesn't mind rain or mud. He wants to make a big picture of naked children bathing in sunlight; for this he needs it to be sunny, but not too hot; the children will want no wind or cold if they are going to pose in the water for two or three hours; it promises to be quite an undertaking.

If I had thought he was going to be a permanent fixture here and not just staying for five or six days, I might have lost my self-control, since all his twitches at table and his conversation during dinner have had just as bad an effect on Nanny as on me. You must remember that we have no manservant, and that, even if our house were ready, Dinah would not be at all pleased at having to serve men, wash their dirty trousers and clean their filthy shoes. He is not one to be daunted by our local mud, but that is no reason to allow the fabrics and mats in our lovely new rooms to get spoiled.

* * *

Renoir came to see us yesterday. As you know, Mother had invited him here to work with me. Since there was no room ready, we were not able to put him up, and this was very lucky as you'll see. Mother invited him to stay for dinner. We stayed at the table for nearly three-quarters of an hour (usually we take fifteen or twenty minutes). Mother became so impatient that she said it would be impossible for her to dine with him. After having invited him, she said the most damning things about him to me, finding him humorless, a poor painter, a slow eater who is prone to infuriating nervous twitches. Finally, Mother is going to do all she can to uninvite him. . . .

Renoir painted an effect of sunset in ten minutes. That exasperated Mother, who told him he was only "wasting paint." It's lucky this was said to him, who notices nothing. As for me, I said nothing to Mother, out of displeasure.

PIERRE-AUGUSTE RENOIR

Four Letters from Italy

1881-82

Between October 1881 and January 1882, Renoir traveled in Italy, visiting Venice, Rome, Naples, Calabria, Sorrento, Capri.

LETTER TO MADAME CHARPENTIER, FALL 1881, VENICE.

Dear Madame,

I was to have lunched with you one morning, a prospect which pleased me enormously, for it had been a long time. But suddenly I found myself on my travels, seized by the feverish desire to see the Raphaels. I am therefore in the process of "swallowing" my dose of Italy. Now I shall be able to say firmly, yes sir, I have seen the Raphaels. I have seen Venise la belle, etc, etc. I've started with the north, and am going down the whole boot while I'm at it, and when I've finished I shall allow myself the delight of lunching with you.

So, despite my ingratitude, I hope that you will receive me all the same. A man who has seen the Raphaels. . . . Would you like me to tell you what I saw in Venice. Here goes. Take a boat and go to the Quai des Orfèvres, or opposite the Tuileries, and you will see Venice. For the Museums, go to the Louvre. For Veronese go to the Louvre, with the exception of Tiepolo, whom I did not know. But it's rather a high price to pay.

No . . . it's not true, the lagoon is very beautiful, very beautiful, when it's fine. St Mark's, the Doge's palace, all the rest is wonderful. Give me St Germain L'Auxerrois. . . .

Goodbye Venice, I'm off to Rome, my promised land, my paradise, my lovely home.

I'm doing a study of the doge's palace – never before attempted.

Would you be very kind and remember me to grandma Charpentier and tell Paum that he shall pose on my return, for which he will have to wait a bit despite his impatience and greeting to Georges.

Kindest regards, R

* * *

LETTER TO DURAND-RUEL, NOVEMBER 21, 1881, NAPLES

Dear Monsieur Durand-Ruel,

I've been wanting to write you for some time, but I also wanted to send you a mass of canvases and I'm still plagued by my researches. I am not satisfied, and I scrape off, again and again. I hope I'm nearing the end of this mania, which is why I'm sending my news. I shan't bring much back

Alfred Bérard and his Dog. 1881. 25¾ × 20¼″ (65 × 51 cm). Philadelphia Museum of Art (The Mr. & Mrs. Carroll S. Tyson Collection). Bérard was also the recipient of letters from Renoir in Italy.

from this trip, but I have made some progress, the kind that comes after a long period of study. One always comes back to one's old loves, but with something added. Finally, I hope that you will forgive me for not bringing you back very much. You'll see what I shall do for you when I get back to Paris.

I'm just like a schoolchild. The white page should always be neatly written and *splat!* – a blot. Here I am, 40 years old and I'm still making blots. I went to see the Raphaels in Rome. They are very beautiful and I should have seen them earlier. They are so knowing and full of wisdom. Unlike me, he wasn't looking for the impossible. But they are beautiful. I prefer Ingres for oil painting. But the frescoes are admirable in their simplicity and grandeur.

. . . But, I shall see you very soon, because Italy may be very beautiful, but Paris. . . . Ah! Paris. . . .

I'm making a start on something. I shan't tell you what, because it might not come off. I'm superstitious about some things.

* * *

LETTER TO CHARLES DEUDON, DECEMBER 1881, NAPLES

My dear friend,

I am not quite sure of my correspondence because I changed my mind en route after having been given addresses which I never went to. So please forgive me if by any chance I have failed to answer one of your letters. I haven't heard anything from you for a long time and I'm now demanding news clamorously. A brief word.

I am in Naples with wonderful weather and I am going to spend some time on Capri. So far I have spent my time searching. I do not dare tell you that I have found anything because for about twenty years now I've thought I had found art.

Still, in a few days I am going to send off one or two still lives, one of them is good. I don't know if you saw what I brought back from Venice. It's nothing, I hope to do better, but there's one which isn't bad.

I get a bit restive away from Montmartre and I am carrying on with my journeys only so as not to have to start off again later. I dream of the church tower and conclude that even the ugliest Parisienne is better than the most beautiful Italian. I've tried figure drawing, which has caused me to waste a lot of time. I have a host of models, but all of them, once seated, offer a three-quarter view, their hands on their knees, it's sickening.

I remember Venice. Following a girl who was carrying water, lovely as a madonna. My gondolier tells me he knows her, I hug him with delight. Once seated, three-quarter view, she was frightful. To get someone to pose you have to be a close friend, and above all to know their language.

I've just been on a trip right down to Calabria. I saw marvels; but the person who was traveling with me couldn't stay longer, and everyone was talking a jargon incomprehensible even to the Italians. Otherwise, I'd have stayed a month. If I ever travel again, I'll go back there. It is certainly the loveliest place I've seen. I hope to be back about Jan. 15 and to find you in good health. Send me a line, won't you?

Your friend, Renoir.

* * *

Charles Deudon (1832–1914), lawyer and collector, was probably introduced to Renoir by Théodore Duret. The Dancer (1874) was the first of several Renoirs that he acquired.

January 14, 1882

My dear friend,

I am very worried about my letter, since once it was sealed, I weighed it, wondering whether to put two stamps on it. But as I've sent several letters at the same time, I could easily have put it inside another. Where the devil has it ended up? Luckily I still have a torn-up draft, so I shall try to recopy it just as it is without any apology. You know quite well that I can't write. Enough said!

After holding out against my brother for a long time, he sends me a letter of introduction to Naples from M. de Brayer. I don't read the letter, above all I don't look at the signature and there I am on the boat with at least fifteen hours of sea-sickness ahead of me. It crosses my mind to look in my pockets, no letter, I must have left it at the hotel. I turn the boat upside down, not a sign of it, so you can imagine my situation once I arrive at Palermo. The town strikes me as gloomy and I wonder whether to catch the boat back the same evening. In the end I walk dolefully towards a bus bearing the words: Hôtel de France. I go to the post office to find out where Wagner lives; no one speaks French and no one knows Wagner, but at my hotel where there are some Germans, I eventually learn that he is at the Hôtel de Palmes. I take a cab and visit Monreale where there are some beautiful mosaics and, on the way, I let my mind wander over a number of gloomy topics. Before leaving I telegraph Naples, without any hope incidentally, and I wait. Seeing nothing arrive, I decide to introduce myself, so here I am composing a letter asking leave to pay my respects to the master. My letter ended more or less like this: I shall be pleased to take news of you back to Paris, to M. Lascoux and to Mme. Mendès among others. I can't say to M. de Brayer, of course, because I hadn't looked at the signature of my letter of introduction. Now I am at the Hôtel des Palmes; a servant takes my letter, comes down again after a few moments, tells me in Italian *Non salue il maestro (sic)* and turns his back on me. The following day my letter arrives from Naples, I present myself again to the same servant who this time takes my letter from me with marked disdain. I wait at the *porte-cochère*, concealing myself as much as possible, not wishing to be received, since I had made up my mind to this second attempt only to make clear to this family that I hadn't come to beg 40 sous.

At last, along comes a young blond man whom I take to be English, but who turns out to be Russian and is called Joukoski. He eventually finds me in my corner and shows me into a small room. He says that he knows [my work] well, that Mme. Wagner is most unhappy not to be able to receive me at the moment and he asks me if I would like to stay another day in Palermo, as Wagner is putting the final touch to *Parsifal* and he is unwell and suffering from his nerves, can no longer eat, and so on. . . .

I beg him to send my apologies to Mme. Wagner, but I want one thing only and that is to leave. We remain together for some time and I tell him the purpose of my visit. I sense from his smile that it's hopeless, then he confesses to me that he is a painter and that he too wanted to do the master's portrait and that for two years he has been following him everywhere to realize this dream, but he persuades me to stay by saying: What he has refused me, he might grant to you and anyway you can't leave without seeing Wagner. This Russian is charming and in the end he quite consoles me and we arrange to meet the next day at two. The following day I meet him again at the telegraph office. He tells me that Wagner completed his opera yesterday, February *(sic)* 13, that he is exhausted and that I mustn't arrive before five, and that he will be there to put me at my ease. I accept enthusiastically and leave well satisfied. On the stroke of five there I am and I bump into my servant who greets me respectfully, invites me to follow him and leads me through a small conservatory into a little adjoining room, sits me down in an immense armchair and, with a gracious smile, asks me to wait a moment. I see Mlle. Wagner with a lithe fellow who must be a young Wagner, but no sign of the Russian. Mlle. Wagner tells me that her mother is not there, but that her father is coming and then she pushes off. I hear the sound of steps muffled by the thick carpets. It is the master, wearing his velvet garment with wide sleeves lined in black satin. He is very handsome and most friendly and he holds out his hand, invites me to sit down again and there begins one of the most hare-brained conversations ever, interspersed with *hi*'s and *ho*'s; half French, half German with gutteral endings. I am delighted, Ach! Oh! and a gutteral sound, you have come from Paris. No, I have come from Naples and I tell him of the loss of my letter which amuses him greatly. Our conversation covers just about everything. When I say we, my part was only to repeat: Yes Maestro, No Maestro, and I stood up to leave, at which he took my hands and thrust me back in my armchair. Vait a little, my vife vill come, and the good Lascoux, how is he? I tell him that I haven't seen him, that I have been in Italy for some time and that he doesn't even know that I'm here, Ach! Oh! and a gutteral sound in German. We speak of Tannhäuser at the Opéra, and all this goes on for three-quarters of an hour, during which time I am constantly looking round to see if the Russian has arrived. At last he comes in with Mme. Wagner who asks me if I know M. de Brayer well. I look up. M. de Brayer, goodness no, Madame, not at all, is he a musician? But was it not he who gave you this letter?

Oh de Brayé, yes of course, forgive me, we pronounce it differently and I apologize, blushing. But I retrieve my ground with Lascoux, I imitated his voice to put it beyond doubt that I knew him, then she tells me that when I go back to Paris, I should send regards to all their friends and especially to Lascoux; she even repeated this as I left. We spoke of the impressionists of music. What a lot of nonsense I must have talked! I ended up boiling hot, babbling incoherently and scarlet with embarrassment. It was a case of the timid man throwing himself into it and going much too far, and yet, even so I know he was pleased, though I no longer know why. He hates the German Jews, and among others, Wolff. He asked me if people in France still liked *Les Diamants de la Couronne*. I blasted Meyerbeer. In short, I found time to voice every stupidity imaginable. Then suddenly he said to M. Joukovski, If I am up to it at midday, I could give you a sitting until my lunchtime, you know you'll have to bear with me, but I shall do what I can and if it turns out not to last very long, it won't be my fault. M. Renoir, please ask M. Joukovski if he's agreeable to you [painting me] as well, that is, if that doesn't put him out. Joukovski says: But Maestro, I was going to ask you just that, etc., etc. . . . How would you like it done? I suggest full face. He says to me that will be fine, I'd like to do you from the back, because I have a composition all prepared. Then Wagner tells him, you will do me turning my back on France and M. Renoir will do me from the other side. Ach! Ach! Oh!. . .

The following day I was there at noon and the rest you know. It was very cheerful, but [I was] very nervous and regretting that I'm not Ingres. In a word, I think I used my time well, 35 minutes, which isn't much, and it would have been very good had I stopped sooner. But then my model lost some of his gaiety and became stiff. I paid too much attention to those changes, anyway you'll see for yourself.

Afterwards Wagner asked to see it and he said Ach! Ach! I look like a Protestant minister, which is true. I was pleased anyway not to have made a complete fiasco; and I have a little souvenir of that admirable head.

Greetings   RENOIR

I'm not re-reading this, or I would tear it up again, for the fifteenth time. If I left anything out, I'll tell you.

He repeated several times that the French read the art critics too much. Ach! Ach! and a great laugh. The German Jews! but, M. Renoir, I know that there are some good fellows in France and I'm not confusing them with the German Jews. Sadly, I can't put across the frank and good-humored spirit of this whole conversation on the master's part.

PIERRE-AUGUSTE RENOIR

Letters to his Dealer

March 1881-February 1882

ALGIERS, MARCH 1881

My dear Monsieur Durand-Ruel,

I shall now try to explain why I am sending to the Salon. There are in Paris barely fifteen collectors capable of appreciating a painter unless he has exhibited at the Salon. There are eighty thousand who will not buy even a nose if a painter is not in the Salon. That is why I send two portraits each year, little though that is. Furthermore, I am not going to fall into the obsessive belief that something is bad just because of where it is. In a word, I don't want to waste my time resenting the Salon. I don't even want to seem to do so. I believe a painter should produce the best painting possible. . . . That is all. Now if people accused me of neglecting my art, or making sacrifices which go against my own ideas of an idiotic sense of ambition, then I would understand the criticism. But since this is not the case, I cannot be criticized in this way, quite the contrary. All I am concerned with at this moment, as always, is making good things. I want to make you splendid paintings which you will be able to sell for very high prices. I shall soon manage to do this, I hope. I have stayed in the sun, away from all painters, to reflect at length. I think I have reached my aim, and have found what I am looking for. I may be wrong, but it would greatly surprise me. A little more patience and soon I hope to give you the proof that one can send work to the Salon *and* do good paintings.

I therefore beg you to plead my case with my friends. The fact that I am sending work to the Salon is purely a matter of business. In any case, it's like certain medicines. If it does no good, at least it does no harm.

I think I have recovered my health. I shall be able to work solidly and make up for lost time.

Which reminds me, I wish you good health. And a lot of rich collectors. But keep them for my return. I shall be here for another month. I don't want to leave Algiers without bringing back something of this marvelous country. Fondest wishes to our friends and yourself,

Renoir.

* * *

Paul Durand-Ruel (1831–1922), came to prominence as a dealer through handling the Barbizon painters and then through the 1870s and 80s established himself as the Impressionists' dealer. He became a close friend to Renoir and to Monet.

Renoir's (and Monet's) decision to send paintings to the Salon had been criticized by other Impressionists as a betrayal of their collective cause. Renoir here puts his case.

Portrait of Paul Durand-Ruel. 1910.
25½ × 21″ (65 × 54 cm).
Collection Durand-Ruel, Paris.

L'ESTAQUE, FEBRUARY 24 1882

Dear Monsieur Durand-Ruel,

If you were organizing an exhibition of which you were in absolute charge, and if this exhibition were to be held even at La Bastille or indeed somewhere even less salubrious, I would eagerly say: take all my pictures, quite aware that it might mean complete disaster. That is not the problem. I would like to think that you are not personally committed to the strange alliance they are hoping to involve you in, and into which no one shall tempt me. It is no exaggeration to say that the exhibition planned by these gentlemen has been conceived and devised quite without me, that I was consulted only late in the day, when gaps had occurred, that after the previous Independents exhibition I had not been required . . . I was going to say, pursued!

At present I am racking my brains to imagine the reason which made them think of me at all. . . .

But I shall not go on in this vein . . . I might seem to be regretting something that is not regrettable. That would be most distressing and I am too delighted that I have been left in peace in the past, not to beg for that state of affairs to continue.

With Monet, Sisley, Mlle Morisot, Pissarro I would accept, but only with them.

The five or six of us, including the elusive Degas, might make an exhibition which would be an interesting event.

Berthe Morisot (1841–95)

Edgar Degas (1834–1917)

144

COLORPLATE 49. *The Swing*. 1876. 36¼ × 28¾″ (92 × 73 cm).
Musée d'Orsay, Paris.

COLORPLATE 50. *In the Garden: Under the Trees of the Moulin de la Galette.* c. 1875/6. 31⅞ × 25⅝″ (81 × 65 cm).
The Pushkin Museum, Moscow.

COLORPLATE 51. *At the Moulin de la Galette*. Pastel. c. 1875. 18½ × 24″ (47 × 61 cm).
National Museum of Belgrade.

COLORPLATE 52. Study for *Dancing at the Moulin de la Galette*. 1875. 25⅝ × 33½″ (65 × 85 cm).
Ordrupgaard Museum, Copenhagen.

COLORPLATE 54. *Woman of Algiers ("Odalisque")*. 1870. 27¼ × 48¼" (69.2 × 122.6 cm).
National Gallery of Art, Washington D.C. (Chester Dale Collection).

COLORPLATE 53. *Dancing at the Moulin de la Galette*. 1876.
51½ × 68⅞″ (131 × 175 cm). Musée d'Orsay, Paris.

But I bet you that Monet for one would not go along with these gentlemen.

To sum up, then, I absolutely refuse to have any dealings with this group, whom I do not even know.

However, if you personally need canvases, I repeat, I shall make them available to you.

I conclude convinced that one day you will share my view and that it is out of pure goodness of heart that you have passed on to me a message which you would blame me for having taken seriously.

Warmest greetings, Renoir.

* * *

L'ESTAQUE, FEBRUARY 26 1882

My dear Monsieur Durand-Ruel,

. . . This morning I sent you a telegram as follows: "The paintings of mine that you have are your property. I cannot prevent you from disposing of them, but it will not be me who is exhibiting."

These few words express my thought completely.

It is therefore quite clear that I am not having any part of the Pissarro – Gauguin group and that I do not agree to be included in the so-called group of Independents for a single moment.

The first reason is that I am exhibiting at the Salon, which does not fit in with the rest.

Therefore I refuse, and refuse again.

Now you may put in the canvases that you have, without my permission. They are yours, and I do not claim the right to prevent you from disposing of them as you see fit, if it is in your own name. Only let it be clearly agreed and accepted that it is you who, as the owner of canvases signed with my name, are exhibiting them, and not me.

In these conditions the catalog, posters, brochures and other information to the public shall state that my canvases are the property of . . . and exhibited by M Durand-Ruel.

In this way, I shall not be an "independent" despite myself, if I am not allowed not to be an "independent" at all.

Please do not resent this decision which should scarcely affect you personally, since it is not you who is organizing this exhibition, but M Gauguin, and believe me your ever devoted and faithful artist. Only, I am protecting our common interest, for I believe that to exhibit there would be to devalue my canvases by 50%. I repeat once more, nothing in my refusal should wound you, for nothing is addressed to you and everything to the gentlemen alongside whom I do not wish to find myself, for my own good, because of my own taste, and in your own interest.

I send you my sincere wishes for your good health and a warm-hearted assurance of my friendship, Renoir.

Paul Gauguin (1848–1903)

* * *

My dear Monsieur Durand-Ruel,

In order to prove to you that my brother is not exhibiting for serious, genuine and artistic reasons. I am sending you the rough copy he wrote from his bed. Style apart, it expresses his thought: it is up to you to judge whether you should override it.

Kind regards, Edmond Renoir.

* * *

DRAFT OF THE LETTER OF FEBRUARY 26, 1882 (ADDED BY EDMOND RENOIR)

. . . Unfortunately I have one aim in my life, which is to raise the value of my paintings. The means I employ are perhaps not very good, but it suits me. To exhibit with Pissarro, Gauguin and Guillaumin is like exhibiting with any old rabble. For two pins Pissarro would invite the Russian Lavrof (the anarchist), or some other revolutionary to join in. The public does not like anything that smacks of politics and at my age I do not want to be a revolutionary. To associate with the Israelite Pissarro is tantamount to revolution.

Furthermore, these gentlemen know that I have taken a great step forward because of the Salon. They are in a hurry to make me lose what I have gained. They will overlook nothing with that aim, only to leave me once I've fallen. I will not have it. Get rid of these people and present me with artists like Monet, Sisley, Morisot etc, and I am all yours, for that is no longer politics, it is pure art.

Renoir.

* * *

Jean-Baptiste Armand Guillaumin (1841–1947)

UNDATED (EARLY 1882)

I hope indeed that Caillebotte will exhibit, and I also hope that these gentlemen will drop this ridiculous title *"Indépendents."* I would like you to tell these gentlemen that I am not going to give up exhibiting at the Salon. This is not for pleasure, as I told you, but so as to dispel the revolutionary taint which frightens me. . . . It is a small weakness for which I hope to be pardonned. . . . Delacroix was right to say that a painter ought to obtain all honours possible at any cost.

Gustave Caillebotte (1848–94)

J. K. HUYSMANS

L'ART MODERNE

"The Independents' Exhibition of 1882"

1883

The seventh Impressionist exhibition was held in March-April 1882. Durand-Ruel sent 25 Renoir paintings from his holding.

James Abbott McNeill Whistler (1834–1903)

A gallant and adventurous magician. Like the American Whistler who gave his paintings titles of the kind: *Harmony in green and gold, amber and black; Nocturnes in silver and blue,* M Renoir could give several of his canvases the titles of harmonies, adding the names of the freshest shades.

This artist has been very productive: I remember, in 1876, a large canvas representing a mother and her two daughters, an odd picture whose colors look as though they had been rubbed over with a piece of cloth, where the oil vaguely imitated the pale tones of pastel. In 1877, I found M Renoir again with more solid works, firmer in color, more confident in their feeling of modernity. Undoubtedly, and despite the visitors sniggering inanely before them, these canvases revealed a precious talent; since then, M Renoir seems to me definitively to have found his footing. Fascinated, like Turner, by mirages of light, by the golden haze which shimmers, tremulous, in a ray of sun, he has managed to capture all this despite the poverty of our chemical ingredients. He is the true painter of young women, he renders, in this sparkling sunshine, the sheen of their tender skin, the velvet of their flesh, the luster of their eyes, the elegance of their toilettes. His *Woman with a Fan,* painted this year, is delectable, with the exquisite sparkle of her great black eyes; I am less fond, for instance, of his *Luncheon of the Boating Party;* some of his oarsmen are good; some of his oarswomen are charming, but the picture does not have a strong enough smell to it; the girls are spruce and cheery, but they do not give out the scent of the Paris girl; they are fresh-faced wenches newly arrived from London.

Girl with a Fan. 1881. 25½ × 21¼"
(65 × 54 cm). Sterling and
Francine Clark Art Institute,
Williamstown, Mass.

Draner, *A Visit to the Impressionists.*
Caricature of *Young Girl Sleeping.*
Le Charivari, March 9, 1882.

Young Girl Sleeping. 1880.
19¼ × 23⅝″ (49 × 60 cm). Private
Collection, Courtesy Ellen Melas
Kyriazi.

THE SEVENTH IMPRESSIONIST EXHIBITION
Other Reviews
1882

The *Dejeuner à Bougival* is full of movement and is one of the most successful pieces of this Independent Salon. The eye of the painter found new colours for the flora around Paris in the bouquet of wine. And one can scarcely say that it is grey.
(Jean de Nivelle, *Le Soleil.* March 4, 1882)

Un Dejeuner à Bougival is a charming work, full of gaiety and spirit, its wild youth caught in the act, radiant and lively, frolicking at high noon in the sun, laughing at everything, seeing only today and mocking tomorrow. For them eternity is in their glass, in their boat and in their songs. It is fresh and free without being too bawdy. This work and the *Partie de Besigue* by Caillebotte share the honours of the exhibition.
(Paul de Charry, *Le Pays.* March 10, 1882)

Renoir is unique among this essentially liberal group. His *Dejeuner à Bougival* seems to me one of the best things he has painted; shaded by an arbour, bare-armed boatmen are laughing with some girls. There are bits of drawing that are quite remarkable, drawing – true drawing – that is a result of the juxtaposition of hues and not of line. It is one of the most beautiful pieces that this insurrectionist art by Independent artists has produced. I found it absolutely superb.
(Armand Silvestre, *La Vie Moderne.* March 11, 1882)

It is as if the artists have different pairs of glasses that they anchor on their noses when they want, with lenses made to give the tones they seek. That is the only way to explain categorically the orgy of tones that can be found in a single painting. For example, in Renoir's *Vue de Venise*, the artist, through a marvel of imagination, has given the impression of a tempest in the Grand Canal.
(Jean de Nivelkle, *Le Soleil.* March 4, 1882)

COLORPLATE 76

COLORPLATE 72

Renoir's Venetian views made me stop for a long time. One of them has reflections that overlap like a roof of polished tiles. Transparency is not an issue here. The painter has posed the problem of how to make the water . . . solid. On this water the gondolas could roll on wheels, yet its surface – choppy, splashed, zebra-striped – could never be taken for land. He has admirably overcome this difficulty, and the result is like nothing ever known.
(Louis Leroy, *Le Charivari*. March 17, 1882)

Renoir is also showing two poor little *Saltimbanques* who were born with legs too short. To console them the artist has given them hands that are too long, full of great oranges.
(Gaston Vassy, *Le Reveil*. March 2, 1882)

COLORPLATE 63

LIONELLO VENTURI

ARCHIVES DE L'IMPRESSIONNISME

Renoir's One-man Exhibition, 1883

1939

This was Renoir's first major one-man exhibition, comprising seventy works.

In April (1883), Renoir's one man show was undoubtedly more carefully prepared than that of Monet. The catalog contained a preface by Théodore Duret who gave this account of Renoir's "progress": "We see him developing a touch that is increasingly broad and personal, giving more and more suppleness to the figures, surrounding them with more and more air, bathing them in more and more light; we see him constantly accentuating his coloring and ultimately achieving the boldest color combinations, apparently quite effortlessly."

Armand Silvestre in *La Vie Moderne* (April 14, 1883), Gustave Geffroy in *La Justice* (April 16, 1883) praised Renoir's figures and especially the portraits. In contrast, Geffroy showed less enthusiasm for the landscapes and G Dargenty (*Courrier de l'Art* March 29, 1883) spoke of Renoir with great reservations, although on the whole he preferred him to Pissarro and to Monet.

Not one of these four critics identified the new tendency that had surfaced in Renoir's painting. In 1883 he had painted the two *Dancing in the Country* and the *Dancing in the Town;* in 1876 he had painted *Dancing at the Moulin de la Galette.* Can one speak, in 1883, of progress with regard to light and air? Quite the reverse! It may be true that the colors are increasingly intense, but this does not work in favor of the overall coloring. In *Dancing in the Town* we can see the danger that Renoir exposes himself to in struggling to become more *"distingué"* in the social sense of the word. It is also true that, even in his mistakes, the genius of Renoir always shines through. And the 1883 landscapes that did not appeal to Geffroy rank among his masterpieces.

COLORPLATES 82, 83
COLORPLATE 53

A letter from John-Lewis Brown of September 5 speaks of Renoir's discouragement. Possibly he had submitted several canvases to the Salon: only one portrait was accepted. His adversaries on the jury had described one of Renoir's works as a "blonde Delacroix," which might be taken as something of a compliment.

John-Lewis Brown (1829–90)

Portrait of Mme Clapisson, *1883. Art Institute, Chicago (page 162)*

To indulge himself, Renoir went off to Guernsey in September. He was enchanted: as much by the landscape as by the "ravishing" bathing costumes and the emancipation of the women. Perhaps it was in Guernsey that he first conceived the idea of the *Bathers.*

COLORPLATE 97

PIERRE-AUGUSTE RENOIR

A Letter to Durand-Ruel from Guernsey

September 27, 1883

Renoir visited Jersey and Guernsey in September and October 1883.

I've found myself a charming beach here which is quite unlike our Normandy beaches, sadly a bit late but not so late that I haven't been able to take advantage of it. They bathe here among the rocks, which serve as cabins since there is nothing else. This mixture of men and women clustered on the rocks is charming. It feels more like being in a Watteau landscape than in the real world.

So I have a source of motifs that are real, graceful and which may be of use to me. The bathing costumes are ravishing; and, as in Athens, the women are quite unabashed about the proximity of men on the neighboring rocks. There's nothing more diverting, moving among the rocks, than to surprise young girls changing to swim and who – despite being English – are not at all put out. I hope to give you an idea of these charming landscapes, despite the slightness of what I shall be able to bring back.

Landscape with Bathing Boys. 1882. 21¼ × 25½″ (54 × 65 cm). Ny Carlsberg Glyptotek, Copenhagen.

PIERRE-AUGUSTE RENOIR

A Trip to the Riviera with Monet

December 1883

In December 1883, Renoir and Monet traveled along the Riviera to North Italy in search of new motifs. Each artist refers to it in these letters to Paul Durand-Ruel.

GENOA (?), DECEMBER 1883

Dear M Durand-Ruel,

We are delighted with our trip. We have seen wonders, we probably won't be bringing much back because we really only wandered around, but what wanderings! You have to stay in a place much longer actually to do anything. This year the weather is very changeable and you can always be sure of getting the effect you want if you stay long enough. But we decided it was preferable to look at the landscape carefully so as to go back there and know immediately where to stop. We saw everything, or almost, from Marseilles to Genoa. It is all superb, Skylines you have no idea of. This evening the mountains were pink.

Hyères is superb. St Raphael, Monte Carlo and Bordighera are wonderful places, all pines, but too changeable at the moment.

We shall write to you tomorrow or Thursday if we are to bring you anything back. So far we have just made a mess on a few canvases and used some lovely colors.

Warmest greetings, Renoir.

* * *

GIVERNY, JANUARY 12, 1884

Dear M Durand-Ruel,

. . . I should also like you to put aside for me a 500 franc note, which I shall come to Paris to collect on Wednesday, as I have decided to leave for Italy immediately. I want to spend a month in Bordighera, which is one of the loveliest places we saw during our trip. I hope to bring you back a whole series of new works.

I'd also like to ask you not to mention this trip to *anyone*, not that I want to make a mystery out of it, but because I want to make it alone. Much as I enjoyed traveling with Renoir as a tourist, I would find it awkward to travel with him if I were working; I've always worked better on my own, according to my own impressions. So please keep it to yourself until you hear to the contrary. With Renoir knowing that I am about to leave, he would probably want to come with me, which would be disastrous for both of us. I'm sure you agree.

Ever your devoted, Claude Monet.

Photograph of Renoir 1880/5.

GEORGES RIVIERE

RENOIR ET SES AMIS

The "Crisis" of the 1880s

1921

Renoir's pictures during the five or six years that followed his travels in Italy differed considerably from everything he had painted previously. The design of the figures, the color and even the technique appeared different from the canvases painted between 1875 and 1881. These pictures, to anyone looking at the whole of the artist's work, indicate the extent of Renoir's inner disturbances at that time. He underwent both an intellectual and a moral crisis. The intellectual crisis was brought about by the lesson of the masters that the painter had examined on his travels; the moral crisis was the result of a change in the artist's life: he had got married and felt his new responsibilities weighing heavily upon him.

All the time he lived alone Renoir had accepted poverty and its privations without any anxiety or difficulty; he did not suffer from it, so to speak, being totally absorbed in his art. But he did not want his wife and child to suffer these privations. He was haunted by a preoccupation with providing for their existence and making life as comfortable for them as he could. From then on, he strove to find a formula that would satisfy both his artist's conscience and his public's taste. This moral crisis did not last very long but it was long enough to be reflected in a certain number of important pictures which I can never look at without a feeling of sorrow.

These are certainly not negligible works, there are even some attractive ones among them, but they lack that freedom of expression, that expensive sincerity which is one of Renoir's noblest qualities.

To overcome material preoccupations and to resolve his intellectual crisis, the painter had his will to work which saved him from the danger of inertia, and a levelheadedness which enabled him to guard against discouragement and anger.

With time the circle of his admirers gradually increased and if sales prices did not noticeably go up the number of paintings sold was greater each year. This result restored all Renoir's mental freedom; henceforth he was concerned only with making his painting even more supple, perfecting his technique and expressing his sensitivity as clearly and as simply as he had done in the past, but having in addition the experience acquired on his travels, since we have to add to his stay in Italy, his journey to Spain and the impression made on him by the works of Velasquez.

The serious attack of bronchitis which nearly killed Renoir in 1882 left the painter's respiratory system much weakened. From then on he had to be on his guard against the rigors of the Parisian winter and each year he left to spend the winter in some part of Provence: at Cannet, Magagnose, Beaulieu etc, before finally coming to a halt at Cagnes. His stays in Paris were shortened which, no doubt, deprived us of a certain number of canvases which would have followed the *Moulin de la Galette* and *The Luncheon of the Boating Party*.

COLORPLATES 53, 76

What is more, from 1885 onwards he spent some time each summer at Essoyes, where his wife was born. Paris was by then no longer his main place of residence.

In Paris between 1883 and 1890 Renoir did a series of portraits, some of which are sheer masterpieces, like that, for example, of Madame Clapisson, and those of Madame Manet (Berthe Morisot) and her daughter, a dark canvas expressing a rare emotion in that it reveals so much of the soul of the characters. It was also at Paris that he worked out the many pictures of bathers, where Monsieur Meier-Graefe thinks he can see the influence of Ingres, but in which there is simply the teaching of the Italian masters, which Ingres also received. That common source exploited by both painters also explains the comparison made by the German critic; Renoir and Ingres are linked through the primitives.

PAGE 162

Julius Meier-Graefe, whose biography of Renoir was published in 1912. (see pp. 247–56.)

By "primitives," he means classical and/or Renaissance art.

These bathers who are so different from those painted before the Italian journey are of particular interest. The design has been modified and the outlines of the figures have been lightly defined in a way they were not prior to 1882. The tones are simplified. In some figures they become almost flat with shadowy tints, in the style of ancient frescoes. There can be seen an attempt at color synthesis, in contrast to the diffusion of tones previously adopted by the painter. The attitude of the figures is also different from the bathers of the earlier period. We can no longer see, as in the beautiful bodies of 1875-1880, modern woman splashing about in the water or drying off on the river bank. She has been replaced by Venus in her bath. The gestures are nobler and closer to the movements adopted by Greek esthetics, the principles of which were renewed by the Italian painters. In these modifications we can observe the effects of the intellectual crisis that followed Renoir's Italian journey.

Ingres, *Portrait of Madame Senonnes.* 41¾ × 33" (106 × 84 cm). Undated. Musée des Beaux Arts, Nantes.

Portrait of Madame Clapisson. 1883. 32⅛ × 25⅝" (81.8 × 65.2 cm). Courtesy of the Art Institute of Chicago (Mr. and Mrs. Martin A. Ryerson Collection).

Jean Racine (1639–99)

Yet his originality was so lively that the masters the painter most admired have left only a faint – and fleeting – trace on his work. Venus as painted by him brings out the model's Parisian origins. She is one of us, just as the beautiful princesses in Racine's tragedies come from the château at Versailles and not the palace of Theseus.

In Renoir's constantly evolving technique, in his work's extraordinary variety, there is no more eventful period than the one we are considering here. Alongside the broadly treated figures there are a few landscapes where the concern for detail is taken a very long way, almost to the point of meticulousness. In memory of his erstwhile preoccupations Renoir had kept a small landscape where all the leaves are, so to speak, drawn and separate from one another. On a panel he had painted the portrait of a woman in a garden, the size of the lid of a tobacco tin; everything in it was finished with the minute care of a porcelain painter. These were obviously experiments, but they are typical of the painter's state of mind at that time.

AMBROISE VOLLARD

RENOIR, AN INTIMATE RECORD

"Renoir's Dry Manner"

1925

I was going to tell you last time . . . about a sort of break that came in my
work about 1883. I had wrung Impressionism dry and I finally came to
the conclusion that I knew neither how to paint nor how to draw. In a
word, Impressionism was a blind alley as far as I was concerned.

I finally realised that it was too complicated an affair, a kind of
painting that made you constantly compromise with yourself. Out of
doors, there is a greater variety of light than in the studio, where to all
intents and purposes it is constant. But for just reason, light plays too
great a part outdoors; you have no time to work out the composition; you
can't see what you are doing. I remember a white wall which reflected on
my canvas one day while I was painting; I keyed down the color to no
avail – everything that I put on was too light. But when I took it back to
the studio, the picture looked black.

Another time I was painting in Brittany, in a grove of chestnut trees. It
was autumn. Everything I put on the canvas, even the blacks and the
blues, was magnificent. But it was the golden luminosity of the trees that
was making the picture; once in the studio, with normal light, it was a
mess.

If the painter works directly from Nature, he ultimately looks for
nothing but momentary effects; he does not try to compose, and soon he
gets monotonous. . . .

I'm sick and tired of the so-called "discoveries" of Impressionism. It
isn't likely that the Old Masters were ignorant of them; and, if they did not
use them, it was because all great artists have despised mere effects. By
making Nature simpler, they made it more impressive. For instance, if the
magnificence of a sunset were permanent, it would wear you out, whereas
the same landscape, without those special light conditions, is not at all
wearing. With the ancient sculptors, action is reduced to a minimum. Yet
you instinctively feel that their statues could move if they wanted to. . . .

I have told you how I discovered, about 1883, that the only thing
worth while for a painter is to study the museums. I made this discovery
on reading a little book that Franc-Lamy picked up along the quays; it was
a treatise on painting by Cennino Cennini, and gave some precious
information on the methods of the fifteenth century painters.

The public is always convinced you are a fool if you abandon one style
to which it is accustomed and adopt another; even my best friends
complained of these new leaden colours of mine "after such pretty tones!"

I had undertaken a large picture of *Bathers* and slaved away at it for
three years. (The portrait of Mlle Manet with a cat in her arms is also of
the period.) The best that people could find to say about it was that it was
a muddle of colour!

On the other hand, I must admit that some of my paintings of this
period are not very soundly painted, because, after having studied fresco, I
had fancied I could eliminate the oil from the colour. The surface then
became too dry, and the successive layers of paint did not adhere well. I
did not know at that time the elementary truth that oil-painting must be
done with oil. Of course none of those people who established the rules of
the "new" painting ever thought of giving us this precious hint! Another
reason that induced me to dry the oil out of my colour was my search for a
means of preventing the paint from blackening; but I later discovered that

*This is Renoir's own account of the "crisis"
that occurred in his work in the mid-1880s, as
retold by Vollard.*

*Julie Manet, Three-Quarter View,
with Cat.* Charcoal and pencil.
1887. 24 × 18⅞″ (61 × 48 cm).
Private Collection.

On Cennino Cennini, see pp. 241–42.

COLORPLATE 97

oil is the very thing which keeps colour from becoming black; only, one must know how to handle the oil.

At this time I also did some paintings on cement, but I was never able to learn from the ancients the secret of their inimitable frescoes. I remember also certain canvases in which I had drawn all the smallest details with a pen before painting. I was trying to be so precise, on account of my distaste for Impressionism that these pictures were extraordinarily dry.

After three years of experimentation, the *Bathers,* which I considered as my master work, was finished. I sent it to an exhibition at the Georges Petit Galleries [1886]. I got roundly trounced for it, I can tell you. This time everybody, Huysmans in the lead, agreed that I was a lost soul; some even said I was lazy. And God knows how I laboured over it!

PIERRE-AUGUSTE RENOIR

"The Society of the Irregularists"
May 1884

In all the controversies matters of art stir up daily, the chief point to which we are going to call attention is generally forgotten. We mean irregularity.

Nature abhors a vacuum, say the physicists; they might complete their axiom by adding that she abhors regularity no less.

Observers actually know that despite the apparent simplicity of the laws governing their formation, the works of nature are infinitely varied, from the most important to the least, no matter what their species or family. The two eyes of the most beautiful face in the world will always be slightly unlike; no nose is placed exactly above the centre of the mouth; the quarters of an orange, the leaves of a tree, the petals of a flower are never identical; thus it seems that every kind of beauty draws its charm from this diversity.

If we look at the most famous plastic or architectural works from this point of view, we can easily see that the great artists who created them – careful to proceed in the same way as that nature whose respectful pupils they have always remained – took great care not to transgress her fundamental law of irregularity. Even works based on geometric principles, like St Mark's (Venice), the little house of Francis I in the Cours la Reine . . . as well as all the so-called Gothic churches . . . have not a single perfectly straight line, and the round, square or oval forms which are found there and which it would have been extremely easy to make exact, are never exact. So we can conclude, without fear of being wrong, that every truly artistic production has been conceived and executed according to the principle of irregularity; in short, to use a neologism which expresses our thought more completely, it is always the work of an irregularist.

At a time when our French art, which until the beginning of this century was still so full of penetrating charm and exquisite imagination, is about to perish of regularity and dryness, when the mania for false perfection makes engineers diagram the ideal, we think that it is useful to react against the fatal doctrines which threaten to annihilate it, and that it is the duty of all men of sensitivity and taste to gather together without delay, no matter how repugnant they may otherwise find combat and protest.

An association is therefore necessary.

Although I do not want to formulate a final platform here, a few projected ideas are briefly submitted:

The association will be called the Society of Irregularists, which explains the general ideas of the founders.

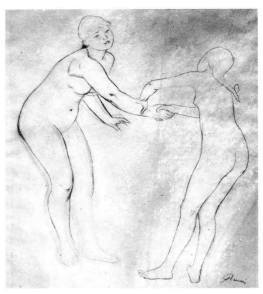

Bathers. Sanguine and pencil, heightened with chalk. c. 1884. 26 × 14¾″ (66 × 37.5 cm). National Museum, Belgrade

This proposal, expressing Renoir's lament for the passing of the individual craftsman, remained a dream. Neither the grammar of art, nor the archive of photographs was realized.

Its aim will be to organise as quickly as possible exhibitions of all artists, painters, decorators, architects, goldsmiths, embroiderers, etc, who have irregularity as their aesthetic principle.

Among other conditions for admission, the rules stipulate precisely, as far as architecture is concerned: All ornaments must be derived from nature, with no motif – flower leaf, figure, etc, etc – being exactly repeated; even the least important outlines must be executed by hand without the aid of precision instruments; as far as the plastic arts are concerned, the goldsmiths and others . . . will have to exhibit alongside their finished works the drawings or paintings from nature used to create them.

No work containing copies of details or of a whole taken from other works will be accepted.

A complete grammar of art, dealing with aesthetic principles of the organisation, setting forth its tendencies, and demonstrating its usefulness, will be published by the founding committee with the collaboration of the members who offer their services.

Photographs of celebrated monuments or decorative works which bring forth evidence of the principle of irregularism will be acquired at the expense of the society and placed in a special room for the public.

OCTAVE MIRBEAU

LA FRANCE

"Notes on Art: Renoir"

December 8, 1884

Octave Mirbeau (1848–1917), poet, critic and amateur painter, was one of Renoir's prominent champions at a time when other critics and some patrons were turning away.

He is truly the painter of women, alternatively gracious and moved, knowing and simple, and always elegant, with an exquisite visual sensibility, a touch as light as a kiss, a vision as penetrating as that of Stendhal. Not only does he give a marvelous sense of the physique, the delicate relief and dazzling tones of young complexions, he also gives a sense of the *form of the soul*, all woman's inward musicality and bewitching mystery. Contrary to the majority of modern painters, his figures are not frozen over by layers of paint; animated and vivacious, they sing out the whole range of bright tones, all the melodies of color, all the vibrations of light . . . I do not understand why all women do not have their portraits painted by this exquisite artist, who is also an exquisite poet, and who is to M Jacquet, the fashionable portrait-painter, what Victor Hugo is to a churner-out of love songs.

Stendhal (Marie-Henri Beyle) (1783–1842)

JEAN RENOIR

RENOIR, MY FATHER

The Birth of Renoir's First Child, Pierre

1958

Jean Renoir here recalls the birth of his elder brother, Renoir's first child, March 21, 1885. It appears that Jean may not have known that his parents were married only five years later.

More important than theories to my father was, in my opinion, his change from being a bachelor to being a married man. Always restless, unable to remain long in one place, jumping into a train with the vague notion of enjoying the misty light of Guernsey, or else immersing himself in the rose-coloured atmosphere of Algeria, he had, since leaving the rue des Gravilliers, lost the meaning of the word home. And here he was, installed in an apartment with his wife, taking meals at regular hours, his bed carefully made every day and his socks mended for him. To all these benefits another was soon to be added in the form of his first-born child. The birth of my brother Pierre was to cause a definitive revolution in Renoir's life. The theories aired at the Nouvelles Athènes were now made to seem unimportant by the dimples in a baby's bottom. As he eagerly sketched his son, in order to remain true to himself he concentrated on rendering the velvety flesh of the child; and through this very submission, Renoir began to rebuild his inner world.

ÉMILE VERHAEREN

SENSATIONS

"Impressionism"

June 15, 1885

The painter who is attracting the most vehement notice after Monet is a figure painter: Renoir. All the refinements and unflagging enthusiasm that the former applies to capturing the subtlest tones of nature in broad daylight. . . . Renoir employs in the rendering of flesh tints. Here too, is an

Emile Verhaeren (1855–1916), Belgian poet and critic, reviewing an exhibition at the Hôtel du Grand-Miroir, Brussels, which included 32 Renoirs.

After the Bath. 1885/7. 23⅝ × 21¼″ (60 × 54 cm). Nasjonalgalleriet, Oslo.

utterly new vision, a quite unexpected interpretation of reality to solicit our imagination. Nothing is fresher, more alive and pulsating with blood and sexuality, than these bodies and faces as he portrays them. Where have they come from, those light and vibrating tones that caress arms, necks and shoulders, and give a sensation of soft flesh and porousness? The backgrounds are suffusions of air and light; they are vague because they must not distract us.

Renoir's preferred subjects are women, and especially young girls. His brush is superb at capturing their blushing ingenuousness and chastity – the blossom becoming a flower. His art is most certainly of French lineage. He is descended from the magnificent eighteenth century, when Watteau, Fragonard, Greuze, Madame Vigée-Lebrun, [Angelica] Kauffmann, and Drouais were producing works of marvelous inventiveness. The resonant and high-pitched quality of his color, however, is more reminiscent of that great genius, Eugène Delacroix. . . .

PIERRE-AUGUSTE RENOIR

Letter to Durand-Ruel

September/October 1885

Dear Monsieur Durand-Ruel,

I think you will be pleased this time. I have gone back to the old painting, the gentle light sort and I don't intend ever to abandon it again. I want to come back only when I have a series of canvases, because, now that I'm satisfied, I make progress with each one. My work is quite different from the last landscapes and that dull portrait of your daughter. More like the woman fishing or the woman with a fan, but with a subtle difference given by a tone that I was looking for and which I've found at last. It's not so much new as a continuation of eighteenth-century painting. I don't mean the very best, of course, but I am trying to give you a rough idea of this new (and final) style of mine. (A sort of inferior Fragonard).

I've just finished a young girl sitting on a bank which I think you'll like.

Please understand that I'm not comparing myself to an eighteenth-century master, but it's important to try and explain to you the direction I'm moving in. These painters, who didn't seem to be working from nature, knew more about it than we do.

BERTHE MORISOT

JOURNAL

Early 1886

Visit to Renoir. On a stand, a red pencil and chalk drawing of a young mother nursing her child; charming in subtlety and gracefulness. As I admired it he showed me a whole series done from the same model and with about the same movement. He is a first class draughtsman; it would be interesting to show all these preparatory sketches for a painting to the public, which generally imagines that the Impressionists work in a very casual way. I do not think it possible to go further in the rendering of form; two drawings of women going into the water I find as charming as the drawings of Ingres. He said that nudes seemed to him to be one of the essential forms of art.

The Toilette ("Young Girl Sitting on a Bank"). 1885. 20¼ × 14⅝″ (51.5 × 37 cm). Private Collection (Photo The Lefevre Gallery, London).

Durand-Ruel was not alone in having reservations about Renoir's change of manner in the 1880s. The regular patrons of his early work were not the collectors of his later painting.
(Daulte 409)

Berthe Morisot (1841-95), a close friend of Renoir in the 1880s. Here she seems quite oblivious to the fact that the young mother in the drawing is Aline Charigot and the child Renoir's son. Renoir did not introduce them to Morisot until July 1891, a year after his marriage.

CAMILLE PISSARRO

Letters to his Son Lucien

1887

Camille Pissarro (1839–1903). His (sometimes grudging) respect for Renoir was not altogether reciprocated. Renoir mistrusted his left-wing political sympathies and was, anyway, unapologetically anti-semitic.

MAY 14, 1887

As for Renoir, again the same hiatus. I do not understand what he is trying to do, it is proper not to want to stand still, but he chose to concentrate on the line, his figures are all separate entities, detached from one another without regard for colour; the result is something unintelligible. Renoir, without the gift for drawing and without his former instinctive feeling for beautiful colours, becomes incoherent.

This is Pissarro's reaction to Renoir's large Bathers *(Colorplate 97), which had just gone on view at Petit's gallery, Paris.*

SEPTEMBER 20, 1887

Then I went to the Murers; I had lunch and then we had a talk. As if by plan, though we did not meet, Renoir and his family came by the same train to the Murers. A tremendous discussion of the dot! At one point Murer said to me: "but you know perfectly well that the dot is impossible!" Renoir added: "You have abandoned the dot, but you won't admit you were wrong!"

Renoir had no time for the pointillist technique of neo-Impressionist painting, with which Pissarro had until recently been experimenting.

Nettled, I replied to Murer that he no doubt took me for a cheat, and to Renoir I said, "My dear fellow, I am not that senile. Besides, you Murer know nothing about it; and as for you Renoir, you follow your caprice, but I know where I am going!" Then there was much abuse of our young friends: Seurat discovered nothing; he takes himself for a genius, etc. You may be sure that I did not let these remarks pass unchallenged. I had imagined that they knew something – if ever so little of our movement but no, they knew nothing about it.

VINCENT VAN GOGH

THE COMPLETE LETTERS

1958

Vincent Van Gogh (1853–90)

ARLES, MAY 4 AND 5, 1888

I very often think of Renoir and that pure clean line of his. That's just how things and people look in this clean air. . . . There are women like a Fragonard and like a Renoir.

* * *

ARLES, MAY/JUNE 1888

You will remember that we saw a magnificent garden of roses by Renoir. I was expecting to find subjects like that here, and indeed, it was that way while the orchards were in bloom. Now the appearance of things has changed and become much harsher. . . . You would probably have to go to Nice to find Renoir's gardens again.

The Rose Garden at Wargemont.
1879. 25 × 31 ½″ (63.5 × 80 cm).
Private Collection. © CNMHS
(Arch. Photo. Paris/SPADEM).

PIERRE-AUGUSTE RENOIR

Letter to Philippe Burty

April 8, 1888

The novelist George Sand (1804–76), and the feminist writer, Juliette Adam (1836–1936)

I think of women who are writers, lawyers or politicians – George Sand, Mme. Adam and other bores – as monsters, mere freaks. The woman artist is just ridiculous, although I am all in favor of women as singers or dancers. In Antiquity and among simple peoples, the woman who sings or dances is no less a woman for that. Gracefulness is her natural domain, even her duty. I realize that today all this has been compromised, but what can one do? In olden times, women sang and danced for nothing, simply for the pleasure of being agreeable and gracious. Today, they are overpaid, which takes all the charm out of it.

Washerwomen. c. 1888.
22¼ × 18½″ (56 × 47 cm).
Baltimore Museum of Art (The
Cone Collection, formed by Dr.
Claribel Cone and Miss Etta
Cone of Baltimore, Md.).

PIERRE-AUGUSTE RENOIR

Letters to Berthe Morisot and Eugène Manet

December 1888 – January 1889

Berthe Morisot and her husband, Eugène Manet, had invited Renoir to join them at a villa they had rented at Cimiez, above Nice.

DECEMBER (?), 1888, ESSOYES

My dear friends – I am of course using the plural – my answer will be a little late because I am painting peasant women in Champagne so as to escape the expense of Paris models. I am doing laundresses, or rather washerwomen, on the banks of the river; moreover I am taking advantage of the springlike weather that I hope will continue for some time, since I promised to bring back something. All this will explain my delay, now I have only to answer your letter. The white house and the orange blossoms both tempt me, and above all the sun, yet despite that I cannot answer yes. It is not that I should not like to come, but I have to paint my washerwomen and then to move. If all these complicated matters go as well as I wish, I shall try by the beginning of January to visit the white house and my friends who live in it.

Ah, if I only could get on well with my washerwomen, how glad I should be to paint a few people sitting under the orange trees! I shall write

COLORPLATE 59. *At the Milliner's*. c.1878. 12¾ × 9⅝″ (32.4 × 24.4 cm).
Fogg Art Museum, Cambridge, Mass. (Annie S. Coburn Bequest).

COLORPLATE 60. *Young Woman Seated ("La Pensée")*. 1876/7. 26 × 21⅝″ (66 × 55 cm).
The Barber Institute of Fine Arts, The University of Birmingham.

to you and if it is not too late I hope to visit you in January. I hope that the beautiful sun agrees with all of you and that I shall find you glowing like gold (horrible idea!)

It is very sweet of you to have thought of your friend who thanks you and wishes you continued good weather and good health. Many, many regards.

* * *

DECEMBER 29, 1888, ESSOYES

My dear Manet, I am still hoping that my displacements can be carried out without difficulty: this will enable me to visit you and to see whether the climate of orange trees agrees with you. We have had a fairly sunny winter for the north; it is true that I am in a country where one takes advantage of the slightest ray of the sun that passes unnoticed in Paris because there one is too busy and the houses are too high.

I am becoming more and more rustic, and I realise a little late that winter is the really good time: the fire in the large fireplaces never gives you a headache, the blaze is cheerful and the wooden sabots keep you from the fear of cold feet, not to mention the chestnuts and potatoes cooked under the ashes, and the light wine of the Côte d'Or. It is with regret that I shall return to Paris where the starched collars forgotten for months will again get on my nerves, but I hope not to stay there long enough to have to endure these tortures. The blue sea and the mountains constantly lure me; only if I cannot afford to go shall I linger beside the studio stove, unless I get many orders for portraits, which would surprise me a great deal.

* * *

JANUARY (?), 1889, ESSOYES

My dear Manet, I must say farewell to the oranges and to the pleasure of seeing my friends. I am held captive: I have caught cold in the country, and I have a facial, local, rheumatic etc, paralysis. . . . In short, I can no longer move a whole side of my face, and for diversion I have two months of electrical treatments. I am forbidden to go out for fear of catching another cold. It is not serious I think, but up until now nothing has improved. I need not tell you that I am bored with being kept here in this dark foggy weather; I shall let you know when I am better, this will be my solace. Otherwise I am all right; I have no pain. I have waited a little to tell you this news, as I hoped to find a medical man who would cure me. My hopes were frustrated, and so I am forced to tell you about my illness; this is the least I can do.

GEORGES RIVIÈRE

RENOIR ET SES AMIS
Renoir's Declining Health

1921

At the end of 1888 or the beginning of 1889, Renoir's health, which was already very doubtful, suffered another setback. One day he woke up with one side of his face paralyzed. This misfortune caused him great embarrassment for a long time. He would not go out without a big woolen scarf tied round his head. Yet he did not complain: physical disorders never affected his spirit. He could paint and that was enough to protect him against all forms of suffering. He was even able to laugh at any misunderstanding that arose from his getup, as when, one Sunday, he was coming to see me with his head wrapped up in his scarf and his coat collar

Draner, *A Visit to the Impressionists,* Caricature of *Sleeping Girl with a Cat. Le Charivari,* March 9, 1882.

Photograph of Renoir. 1896.

turned up, and was not allowed in by the deaf old caretaker who did not recognize him.

"No, Monsieur, the owner doesn't like it," she said, to Renoir's astonishment, as he repeated his question.

"Monsieur, I'm telling you that the owner doesn't like people singing in the courtyard," the good woman finished.

She had mistaken the painter for a wandering singer!

Despairing of making the deaf old woman understand, Renoir waited for the moment when she turned her back in order to come up to me; the caretaker's mistake had greatly amused him.

He had already been the object of similar misunderstandings; servants' failure to discern the quality of their masters' visitors always delighted him rather like a good farce.

GUSTAVE GEFFROY
MONET, SA VIE, SON OEUVRE
"The Impressionist Dinner"

1924

Gustave Geffroy (1855–1926), critic and novelist, friend of Clemenceau and of the Impressionist painters. His two-volume monograph on Monet is a major document in the writing of Impressionism's history.

It was between 1890 and 1894, through Monet, that I got to know the Impressionist painters. I had the honor of being present at the monthly dinner which took place at the Café Riche. These dinners were attended, with Claude Monet, by Camille Pissarro, Auguste Renoir, Alfred Sisley, Gustave Caillebotte, Dr de Bellio, Théodore Duret, Octave Mirbeau, sometimes Stéphane Mallarmé.

Georges de Bellio (1828–94), Rumanian-born doctor, friend and patron of the Impressionists; Stéphane Mallarmé (1842–98)

They were evenings of conversation where the events of the day were mulled over with the open-mindedness brought to bear by artists who stood outside all official organizations. It must be admitted that the company was somewhat boisterous, and that these men, at rest from work and worry, had the high spirits of schoolboys at play. Discussion was sometimes heated in tone, particularly between Renoir and Caillebotte. The former, edgy and sarcastic, his tone mocking, his face, already ravaged by illness, marked by a kind of Mephistophelian irony and bizarre laughter, found malicious pleasure in taunting the latter, red-faced and irascible; Caillebotte's countenance would turn from red to purple, and even to black, when his opinions met the bantering verve Renoir liked to counter them with. He would then exhibit a heatedness which verged on anger, though quite inoffensive. Debate touched not only on opinions on art and painting, but on any subject of literature, politics and philosophy with which Caillebotte, in all good faith, happened to engage, and he was a great reader of books, reviews and newspapers. Renoir had brought himself up-to-date with everything by buying an encylopedic dictionary where he found topics to "stump" Caillebotte. Naturally, Mirbeau too launched headlong into these witty scuffles, and naturally Mallarmé was heeded when he handed out his balanced judgments. Pissarro and Monet were also keen appreciators of literature, both having sure and sophisticated taste. I remember a positive battle for and against Victor Hugo, where the whole gamut of enthusiasm and restraint was engaged, and from which everyone emerged reconciled to go to sit at some café terrace, before the ever-magical spectacle of night-time Paris. On other occasions too, discussion would continue as they left, out on the boulevard, and indeed I think some of them have not ended yet.

I feel that it is necessary, during the course of the study devoted to Monet, more particularly to mention the painters who were his companions. These men, inseparable in life and so strongly united in their love of art, will always form an indissoluble group.

TÉODOR DE WYZEWA

PEINTRES DE JADIS ET D'AUJOURD'HUI

"Pierre-Auguste Renoir (1891)"

1903

Téodor de Wyzewa, Polish-born writer, critic of art and literature, wrote regularly for Revue des Deux Mondes. A friend of Renoir from c. 1886 until his death, in poverty, in 1917.

Last summer, as chance would have it, I was present at the opening of the Salon du Champ-de-Mars. This, it may be remembered, was a joyful baptism: I was entirely surrounded by bright dresses, beaming faces, arms raised heavenwards in enthusiasm. And as I was proceeding through the grandiose rooms, by a strange contrast I felt welling within me the distressing sense of being at a funeral. The admiring passions of my adolescence were dying by the dozen.

All the painters whom I was seeing there once again were the ones who, when they started out, had seemed to me so personal and so bold! I saw them again through the same works, or at least the same qualities applied in the same way. Some continued to capture the sense of outdoors, others to emphasize chiaroscuro, others yet to conceive forms of a paradoxical clarity . . .

Indeed the unfortunate thing is that these bold innovators had not changed enough. Each one, having found a note, was sticking to it unchanged . . .

This is a disappointment which no one will feel with the paintings of M Renoir. He discovered twenty notes which were both original and charming; and no sooner had he discovered one, than he started off again in search of another, having the severest critical sense and the highest conception of art that any creative artist has possessed for a long time.

I know nothing of M Renoir's first style. I can only guess at the works he once painted, in Gleyre's studio, when the practice of painting on porcelain had already formed his eye and loosened his hand. But, just like everyone else, I am acquainted with his second style, the one he practiced during the heroic age of Impressionism, together with MM Monet and Sisley, his fellow students in Gleyre's studio. Surely no one who has seen these enchanting paintings can fail to remember them, paintings wherein the Impressionist method was a mere pretext to set bright colors humming with a freer, more varied sense of harmony.

And within this same second style, one might easily distinguish two or three successive styles, a sort of continuous process of lightening and cleansing, concluding with the boating scenes, the rustic dances, the views of Asnières and Venice, where forms of an exceptional indolence and ingenuity appear enveloped in a mysterious violet atmosphere.

M Renoir had become famous: of all the Impressionists, he was the most delicate, the most feminine, the one in whom we recognized the most perfect expression of our less wholesome feelings. And it was this weaker, feminine character of his work which he took against at that moment in his career. For several years he experienced unease, and sometimes despair, as he studied the old masters, whose fervent and fearful admirer he remained. He was looking for a more solid, more classical art, self-sufficient, beyond the sensual charm he was so adept at adding to it. *The Bathers*, which he exhibited at the rue de Sèze in 1887, will continue to bear witness to these years of quest and hesitation. I cannot forget the quite unearthly emotion aroused in me by this gentle but strong painting, this delicious mingling of looking and of dreaming.

The effort of so many years ended in triumph, M Renoir finally took possession of this pure and knowing beauty of form and never lost it; so

COLORPLATE 97
(Galerie Petit)

far, he is alone amongst us in holding its secret. Some of the portraits, nude studies and heads of children which he painted after his *Bathers* are works that have all the life-like sense of relief, the soberness and trenchancy of execution of the great works of the old masters. All he had to do now was to add the external grace of his earlier works; but that too was ennobled, raised to the level of an art which had by now become completely classical. And it is upon this reconciling of life-giving power and grace of expression that M Renoir has been working since. Today, each of the pictures he paints represents a distinct manner: for he has not spent ten years on these patient and varied studies, studies to which none of our fashionable young painters has either the time or the inclination to devote themselves. He has not stopped being a master for ten years to become a pupil once more, without gaining an abundance and suppleness of vision capable of bringing, to the different subjects, the different forms appropriate to each of them.

But perpetual change, in art, has no more importance than constant immobility. Alongside the painters who have produced only a single note, at the Salon du Champ-de-Mars, I have seen painters who produced a new note every year; and I have not been able to bring myself to admire them, either. The fact is that they have broken new ground without retaining anything of the old. They themselves being nothing but clever machines for making paintings, they had not been able to use their various styles to develop an originality the seed of which has always escaped them.

What constitutes the artistic merit of the work of Renoir is that, beneath his twenty successive styles, he has always remained the same, absolutely the same, so that it is enough to have seen one of his early pictures to recognize him in his current works. No painter has brought more personal, innate and singular qualities to the service of art. . . .

The innate qualities of the art of M Renoir are, unfortunately, easier to appreciate than to define in words. I believe that they may be summed up as an extraordinary feeling for those aspects of nature which are elusive, capricious, feminine. Unbeknown to himself, M Renoir brings life to everything that he sees with a particular characteristic which is at once naive and sophisticated, agitated and serene. His type of young girl has tried in vain to alter herself: everywhere, in all her attitudes and under all her guises, we find the same delicious little being, like a cat in a fairy tale, peering sleepily out at the world through strange little eyes, tender and malicious. And this expression is not just the result of the form of the body and the facial features; it is to be found in the half-imaginary settings which serve the figures as décor; it may be found even in those simple and powerful real landscapes which M Renoir loves to paint from time to time, knowing, along with the old masters, that nothing contributes more to imbuing the eye with the feeling of life. One may recognize M Renoir's very soul in his paintings of flowers, the loveliest flower-paintings ever created, marvelously alive, bursting with color and ever-alluring by virtue of a very feminine intermingling of gentle langor and a perturbing capriciousness.

Thus M Renoir is a painter of our time: for if there is any remotely artistic feeling among the feelings of our time, it is indeed that restless and elusive sensual melancholy which he manages to capture in everything he paints. And yet in another way M Renoir is a classical painter; and that is what makes him so very dear to us. He is concerned with formal perfection, he abhors exaggeration, he is increasingly tending towards an art of discreet and simple harmony. Thus he goes back to the old French masters, whose spirit is preserved for us today by him alone. And so, going beyond Impressionism, going beyond all the restless and unhealthy painting of his time, he links up with the admirable master in whose company he will not fail to appear to posterity: the poet of the *Lesson in Love* and the *Embarkation for Cythera*.

(both by Watteau)

ARSÈNE ALEXANDRE

"Renoir"

May-June 1892

He has been exquisitely attentive and sensitive in his rendering of the clear, happy eyes of a child, the red mouths of women, the dazzling harmony of flowers (which, whatever they may be, always go well together). Renoir himself never thought he could find a line that was supple and fluid enough, a color that was soft enough, or matter that had the qualities of enamel, but was more alive.

He wanted the contours of these fragile things, of these beings which will always be subjects of wonder to discerning spirits, to be as rare and iridescent as fine plumage. Furthermore, he placed them in lovingly conceived settings, under tender greenery, where rays of sunlight play and shatter in reflections, or else among personal finery and rare ornaments which he has embelished with his color – or lastly, intoxicated and almost hesitant, in a setting richer still, though indeterminate: in hazy atmospheres all shimmering with gold, emeralds and rubies.

His draftsmanship, which Renoir's most dogged adversaries never dared attack head-on, even in the old heroic days, has a childlike grace. Indeed, his felicity, on occasions, is that of a witty child. His is the draftsmanship of a master who has retained, through the bitterness of life and all the anguish of art, all the candor and responsiveness of his youth.

Young Girl. Pencil. c. 1886/7.
11 × 9¼" (28 × 23.5 cm).
National Museum, Belgrade.

MAURICE DENIS

LA REVUE BLANCHE

"The Renoir Exhibition"

June 25, 1892

Maurice Denis (1870–1943), young painter and theorist, member of the Nabis group and a great admirer of Renoir's late work. (see also pp. 282–84.)

... There are some other painters of whom we might have wished to speak, but our spirit is drawn irresistibly towards another exhibition, infinitely more suggestive of esthetic emotions and thus infinitely more moral. It is that of the master Renoir – (and we advise you to read the catalog preface by M. Arsène Alexandre which is a masterpiece of precision and discretion in its praise). Renoir's exhibition offers us the pure satisfaction of a group of his works from the Durand-Ruel gallery: a whole lifetime's silent, unaffected work, the fine honest life of a true painter. Idealist? Naturalist? Whatever you please. He has succeeded in confining himself to the translation of his own emotions: the whole of nature and the world of dreams, always using his own particular methods. He has composed marvelous bouquets of women and of flowers, which so delighted his gaze. And since his heart is generous and his will firm, he has made only beautiful things. While awaiting a better occasion to speak our whole mind on this oeuvre, we remain content to ponder on this example and the lesson it contains.

see above

ALBERT AURIER

"Renoir"

1892

G.-Albert Aurier (1865–92), critic whose essays in Le Moderniste, Le Décadent, La Pléiade, Mercure de France, *etc., made a brief but important contribution to the early writing on post-Impressionist painting.*

In Renoir, the original and perhaps very wise conception of the famous "eternal feminine" does not seem to be in the least the outcome, intentionally deduced, of a scepticism acquired through bitter experience. It strikes me as more spontaneous, more naive, more instinctive, and if one insists that it must proceed from some sort of scepticism, then it must be one which is not at all bitter, not at all experimental or closely reasoned, or indeed conscious, but from a merry scepticism which is natural and innate. . . .

With such ideas, with such a vision of the world and of femininity, one might have feared that Renoir would create a work which was merely *pretty* and merely *superficial*. Superficial it was not; in fact it was profound, for if, indeed, the artist has almost completely done away with the intellectuality of his models in his paintings, he has, in compensation, been prodigal with his own. As to the *pretty*, it is undeniable in his work, but how different from the intolerable *prettiness* of fashionable painters.

PIERRE-AUGUSTE RENOIR

A Letter to Berthe Morisot

1892

PORNIC. AUGUST/SEPTEMBER 1892

Renoir was on a family visit to Brittany.

Every day I want to write to you and I do not because I am in a very bad humor. I have ended up by being stranded at Pornic where I am teaching my son to swim; so far so good, But I should be painting landscapes. The country here is quite pretty, and that is why I am so cross. To paint landscapes is becoming for me an ever greater torture, all the more so because it is a duty: obviously this is the only way to learn one's craft a little, but to station oneself out of doors like a mountebank, this is something I can no longer do.

In my moments of enthusiasm I wanted to tell you, "Do come," but then I am seized by the boredom of the seashore, and I do not want to play a bad trick on you by telling you to come to a place where I am so bored, a place I should quickly leave were I alone. Nevertheless I went to Noirmoutiers; it is superb and quite like the south, far superior to Jersey and Guernsey, but too far away, much too far. If I were bolder, there would be lovely things to do there, as everywhere else for that matter.

. . . Are you still worried about where to live? This is something I want to put out of my mind, I find it so troublesome. To relieve myself of the studio problem I toyed for a while with the idea of going to Algeria with some friends, but I think it is bad to be always travelling. I shall write to you when I have painted an interesting landscape.

ALINE RENOIR
A Letter to Renoir
June 1893

Aline Charigot (1859–1915), a young seamstress whom Renoir first met and used as a model c. 1879. They married on April 14, 1890. This letter, full of domestic concerns, is one of few that survive between them.

Wednesday night

My dear:

The leak in the roof of your studio has not been repaired yet. The men were to come and mend it on Monday, but there was a wedding. Tuesday was a holiday. Today it rained all day, and they say they must wait until it clears up. However, I hope it will be done by the time you come back. I showed Monsieur Charles the drawing for your bed. He will make it as soon as you return. He wants to talk to you about it. You know how stubborn he is. I don't know what he thinks is too high about it. You can discuss the matter together.

I don't know if I will have enough money to last to the end of the month, because we must buy some more material. We haven't enough for the big curtains to hang at the side of the large window where most of the sun comes in. It is on the west side, I think. Monsieur Charles did not understand that we wanted some hung there. Isn't that what you explained to him? The calico curtains next to the beam and the linen ones on the other side.

I shall be able to buy just the number of yards needed. I found a shop where they sell by the piece. But as I have already spent forty francs for you, I am afraid I won't have enough to buy the material. If you are not planning to return before the end of the month, please send me some.

Tell me, my poor dear: Are you cold up there in Dieppe? We are freezing here in Paris.

Are you working hard? Will your portraits be finished soon? A month seems so long. Our trip this winter seemed much shorter than the past two weeks without you.

Write to me often, and tell me if you are well.

All my love,
ALINE

Aline Renoir (Detail). 1885. 25¾ × 21¼″ (65 × 54 cm). Philadelphia Museum of Art (W.P. Wilstach Collection).

Photograph of Renoir on the Steps of the Château des Brouillards. c. 1890.

JEAN RENOIR

RENOIR, MY FATHER

The Caillebotte Bequest

1958

Gustave Caillebotte (1848–94), a painter who exhibited in five of the Impressionist exhibitions and was an important collector of his peers' work. Renoir was named in his will as executor of the bequest.

The godfather Renoir had chosen for my brother Pierre was one of the most devoted of Renoir's many friends. Gustave Caillebotte belonged to a family of bankers. His brother Martial had followed his father's profession, but Gustave wanted to be a painter. And he painted with as much passion as any member of the Impressionist group. He and my father had first become acquainted in 1874. He had exhibited his pictures along with Renoir, and had had his share of the criticisms and insults. The canvas he had shown in the Durand-Ruel exhibition of 1876 depicted a group of house-painters, executed in very realistic style. Renoir praised it, and Caillebotte, being an exceedingly modest man, had blushed. He was only too well aware of his limitations. "I try to paint honestly, hoping that some day my work will be good enough to hang in the ante-chamber of the living-room where the Renoirs and Cézannes are hung."

* * *

Caillebotte had gathered the most important collection of his friend's works. His enthusiastic purchases were often made just in the nick of time for those who benefited by them. How many artists in financial straits at the end of the month were saved by his generosity and far-sightedness! "He had his own little plan. . . . He was a sort of Joan of Arc of painting."

Caillebotte died in 1894, after making Renoir the executor of his will. The resulting negotiations proved very complicated, for he had left his collection to the Louvre in the hope that the Government would not dare to refuse it and that in this way the official ostracism from which the modern French School still suffered would be finally overcome. That was the "little plan" Renoir referred to.

In carrying out his legal duties, my father had first of all to deal with a certain Monsieur R., who was a high official of the Beaux-Arts. "A good sort, but very annoyed at having to make a decision." The gentlemen paced up and down in his office in the Louvre, while Renoir examined the sculptured doors and took the liberty of running his hand over the moulding, remarking aloud, "A beautiful door!" But Monsieur R., in a plaintive voice, asked him point-blank:

"Why the devil did your friend decide to send us his white elephant? Try and put yourself in our place. If we accept it we shall have the entire Institute after us. If we refuse we shall have all the people in the new movement down on us. Please do not misunderstand me, Monsieur Renoir. I am not against modern painting. I believe in progress. I am even a Socialist, and you know what that means. . . ."

Renoir asked him politely to drop theories and to get down to facts by taking a look at the pictures. With the exception of two or three, Monsieur R. had to acknowledge that the Manets and Degas seemed acceptable. And he consented to take the "Moulin de la Galette" because it represented the working class. "I like the working class," he said. But as soon as he came to the Cézannes he began to wring his hands. "Don't try to tell me that Cézanne is a painter!" he protested. "He has money, his father was a banker: and he took up painting as a pastime. I should not be surprised if he did his painting just to make game of us."

Everyone knows the sequel. At least two-thirds of this unique collection, one of the greatest in the world, was turned down. The remaining third did not get past the doors of the Louvre but was stored away in the Luxembourg Museum. On the death of Charlotte Caillebotte, those works which had been rejected went to various heirs, who got rid of them as quickly as possible. Scorned by France, they were well received in foreign countries. A good many were brought in the United States. I tell this story to any French friend who accuses Americans of having emptied France of its masterpieces by means of the almighty dollar.

GUSTAVE GEFFROY

LA VIE ARTISTIQUE

"Auguste Renoir"

1894

I   THE SAFE PLACES

The work of Renoir is a source of enchantment for the eye. It is also a consolation, a balm for the spirit.

On two occasions, the walls have been graced by the delectable feast his paintings offer: in April 1883, in boulevard de la Madeleine, and in May 1892, in the gallery of Durand-Ruel. The reception, on the first occasion, was one of mockery or indifference; the second time it was one of astonished welcome for the same works – the very same, I assure you – and the beginnings of a triumph.

Those who knew of the artist's labor and struggle, of the obscurity in which he had been too long held by those who dispense publicity – dealers, collectors, critics, Salon juries, inspectors, directors and ministers of the Fine Arts – such people felt the harshness of so prolonged an injustice, of this cold-shouldering of one of the most original and passionate talents of this century, of this virtual silence which, for Renoir, was to follow the insults formerly meted out so generously to the Impressionist group.

But now the truth has been established, a balance has been achieved and no more proof is needed. And for myself, one of life's bystanders, an observer of this artistic spectacle, I refuse, once and for all, to feel sorry for Renoir.

It is those who failed to appreciate him who are to be pitied, those who refuse him not only fame, a place on the Salon wall, a space in the museum, but who denied him his very livelihood. His upright spirit, untouched by compromise and disdainful of intrigue, had enabled him, and some others, to choose the best course from the very first. Of course he experienced the harshness of fate, the sadness of life; but oh the safe places he also found, which gave him incomparable joy, a joy which no one could take from him.

The safe places are these:

He discloses them to us, through them he tells us of the charm of his disquiet and the secret of his happiness. He found them simply through his ability to see, destined as it was to revel in the appearance of things, all that enchanted blossoming where light-beleaguered forms are celebrated and reconciled.

These safe places are everywhere, in nature, and in man. It is man's part to know how to discover them and to take possession of them, and he does this when he has discovered himself, when he has divined the melancholy and beauty of his fugitive passing, and when he realizes that he must hurry if he is to see the eternal whole that he will never see again.

Renoir has observed the spectacle of this world with the most artless and also the most clear-sighted and devoted gaze. It is with a lover's

The bequest was made to the Luxembourg Museum, not to the Louvre, on condition that it was accepted as an undivided collection. There was violent reaction from the Ecole des Beaux Arts and elsewhere, with threats of resignation. The celebrated academic painter Gérôme said the government could not accept such filth. Renoir was obliged to compromise and only half of the 65 or so paintings were accepted, including 6 of the 8 Renoirs. They are now in the Musée d'Orsay, Paris.

One of the most important supportive essays on Renoir's work in the 1890s.

The one-man show of 1883 and the retrospective of 1892.

Bathers in the Forest. c. 1897.
29 × 39⅜″ (73.5 × 100 cm). © The
Barnes Foundation, Merion, Pa.

fervor, an eager desire to contemplate and to possess, that his eyes and
mind have gone towards these safe places which were offered him, and
which present themselves in the delectable guises of leaves, water,
flowerbeds, landscapes – the living, breathing flesh of women and children
– faces lit up with looks and smiles – scenes of civilized life enacted in town
or country settings, in color-filled gardens, in light-filled theaters, in
crowd-thronged pleasure gardens. These are the scenes and lively beings
that are imbued by Renoir's poetry, a happy, impetuous, painter's poetry,
which throbs and quivers and feeds on warmth and light.

The desire for and achievement of harmony, the pursuit of young and
supple bodies, the contemplation of beings in motion, seeking oblivion in
the frenzy of the dance and the sensuality of love, bouquets inhaled, flesh
caressed, reveries first indulged in at the stream's edge, spreading to the
ebb of dazzling seas, fading with the fleeting clouds – this is Renoir's
philosophy of melancholy joy as expressed in his work.

II · LANDSCAPES AND WOMEN

He is a landscape painter, although this is perhaps the quality most
doggedly denied him. How could it be otherwise? How could he have
failed to sense running through all of nature that frisson he surprised in
eyes and faces? How could he not have seen it in the play of light? How
could he have failed to see, in the world at large, the lovely undulations
and the fervent desire for life he pursued in the breathing surfaces of
bodies? Thus his observations as a landscape painter, in Guernsey, in
Toulon, in Algeria, wear their harmony of blue and gold, an extraordinary
appearance of flamelike glimmering, they are conflagrations of brightness,
mirages of light. Renoir set fire to these landscapes with the tip of his
brush, forced them to reflect a portion of the dazzling star which lights up
the worlds, forced them to express and eternalize the memory of what was
to be his own particular radiant dream.

He is so continuously a landscape painter, he is so haunted by the
glory of nature unfolding under the summer light which shines forth and
will die, that he has regarded women's flesh as an emanation of these
astral splendors, and that he has delighted in installing living creatures,
unveiled, in a foreground of vague and lush expanses where bluish water,

woods of purple and gold, hills like precious stones, are resplendent in the powdery atmospheric haze of the most sumptuous fall. From these exalted surroundings, from this shimmering heat he has conjured the creation of marvelous sun-hued women, sharing in the life of the elements, within whom a univeral sap truly rises.

One, flecked with light and shade, her stomach of gold, her flesh a rich and subtle substance, her breasts unhindered, her shoulders round, is truly porous and breathing. Another, in front of a green and blue sea and purple-blue sky, is as white and cold as though a chilly breath were passing over her soft young flesh. Her lips, her cheeks, her hands and breasts just barely tinged with pink, her head of hair touched with the pale blond of the North, has all the dazzle of the living snow. *The Bathers* has this same clear, cold grace, with movements of the most marked but delicate draftsmanship, a flesh that is more intensely present, breasts which have their own true weight, broad backs, rounded legs. *The Bathers* bears witness to bitter effort and admirable application. Here Renoir has doggedly worked towards an intellectual and pictorial ideal, he has tried to crystallize his analysis into a summary, a firm and skilful synthesis. At the root of this life's work, with its compelling charm, lie both the luminous purity of the primitives and the serene draftsmanship of Ingres.

COLORPLATE 97

Bather arranging her Hair. 1885. 36¼ × 28¾" (91.9 × 73 cm). Sterling and Francine Clark Art Institute, Williamstown. Mass.

But nature, once summoned, came to dominate the original conception, and it is she who has provided the rightness of the structures, the youthful grace of the faces, the perfectly-rendered joints, the heaviness of the breasts, the fold of the hips, the softness of the hair, the brightness of cheeks and eyes, the harmony of the flesh tones, from the dusky brown of the stomachs to the faint veined blue of the throats and the complexions of the faces modeled in light.

Yet other women, more recent, complete the revelation of Renoir's art of sensual delight. Compare them with those naked women he painted in the past, and who are so lovely, one, arms raised, another, surrounded by clothes, with their fresh torsos and pink cheeks. These new ones too have the bodies of women, but their faces are almost those of children. They have the soft grace of bodies entirely of flesh, so slightly built, with so little sense of bone, and their round heads with their diminutive profiles, their shy and blushing faces, have both the self-possession of extreme youth and the awkwardness of puberty at the first awakening of the senses, the innocence of the little girl glimpsed through the developing body of the young woman in love.

III EXPRESSION

This face and this expression must have been so intensely conceived of and favored by Renoir that he found himself unable to disengage from them; they are recognizable everywhere. "A Renoir woman!" people will always exclaim before those figures he has immortalized in art. Their eyes and lips are all touched with something strange and unconscious, as are all eyes which see existence anew, all smiling mouths eager to kiss and sing. Their characteristic expressions, both tender and sharp, steal from under bruised eyelids, mouths half-open for heedless kisses and cruel bites, they have the untamed grace of sinuous animals and the falsely innocent air of schemers, they are close to nature and yet acquainted with the veneers of civilization.

With all of them, the characteristics Renoir chose were the low forehead, with its implications of niceness and obstinacy, and the slightly heavy jaw implying animal appetite and sensuality. In his portraits, even in those which stray furthest from his ideal as observer, he goes straight to those favorite details, he emphasizes those features, which he no doubt sees as being some of the decisive proofs of femininity. All the great painters of women show this same instinctive selectiveness, this same creation of a type of beauty, whether haughty, passionate, melancholy or charming, through which they have expressed their desire and rendered their thought visible.

Nonetheless, differences and nuances do persist, as perceived by a keen intelligence: one from among the abundant proofs of this diversity should suffice, namely, those portraits of little girls in violet dresses, sewing in the garden – the little seamstress with the white, frail hands, her fingers moving so charmingly and her attentive profile softly outlined in an atmosphere pervaded by a sort of vermeil gilding – a woman's head, the lower part of her face lit up, her eyes in shadow – and the little girl in a muslin dress threaded with satin, trimmed with green, in a greenish room, who has all the grace of the dainty well-dressed child, the germ of the woman-to-be indicated in the little girl with an exquisite gentleness and poignancy by the rose-soft face, the velvety eyes, the tiny hands.

There are many other expressive portraits in the work of Renoir: the *Reader* who in this case is Claude Monet, alert, shrewd and full of energy – Richard Wagner, lips tightly closed, pink and childlike, the long narrow blue eyes gleaming in a broad placid face, enigmatic, ageless, like a placid and unforgettable Scandinavian god – the portrait, both veiled and exact, of Mme Charpentier – heads of children, some absorbed in play, others, very little ones, sleeping, milky-faced and swollen-cheeked. But one always returns to the women who gaze out, their eyes moist with light,

COLORPLATE 16
COLORPLATE 74

COLORPLATE 75

proffering the fruit of their mouths – the *Woman with a Fan*, with her luscious flesh – the figure of *Coquetry*, a small finger on her smiling lips – the figure of *Sleep* with her low neckline, her throat veiled in greenish shadow, her face damp with heat, closed eyes softly ringed, sensuous lips pouting – and the *Woman Leaning on her Elbow* dressed in blue, the most pensive and disquieting of all, her gaze elusive, her mouth showing both a flicker of a smile and a hint of dawning bitterness, the possible rêverie of a woman of pleasure, the Mona Lisa of the rowing-boat.

PAGE 156

PAGE 157

It is not clear to which painting this refers.

IV THE POETRY OF THE CITIES

Renoir's vision remained equally keen, concentrated and expressive when he portrayed people in action, when, indeed, he mobilized whole crowds. A rare charm emanates from the woman in *The Swing* in her white peignoir with blue ribbons, as she stands and sways in the avenue of shadow riddled with sunlight; an intelligent woman's rêverie emanates from the society woman in her black and white dress in the magnificent picture *La Loge*, where everything is in harmony: the wonderful painting of the pink in her hair, of her icy white gloves, of all the delicious frothy flounces of blue-white and soft black which fill the box, of the outline of a man in evening dress and the calm of the woman's face, camelia-hued, with her clear eyes.

COLORPLATE 49

COLORPLATE 31

Another *Loge*, some *Young girls at the Piano, Dancing in the City, Dancing in the Country* are astoundingly varied versions of this same vision of civilized humanity. The Bougival couple whirls gaily in the drunkenness of a summer night, to the sound of music heard through the trees. The elegant couple waltzes slowly over the parquet of a drawing-room floor. The open-air festivities shine in every glass, every fruit, every face in the *Luncheon of the Boating Party;* we have here the very essence of the lull in conversation which follows a meal, the uninhibited attitudes, the gay and enthusiastic phrases spoken to women from near to. There is not one of these faces, so perfectly within their plane, so lapped by the warm summer air, which does not express a state of body and soul, a rapport with the general conversation, with the muddle on the table with its glow of fruits and liqueurs. The whole canvas seems filled as if with a warm breath.

COLORPLATES 100, 82, 83

COLORPLATE 76

The poem ends with one of the loveliest pages ever inspired by the girls of Paris, always so touching: the delicious *Moulin de la Galette*. No one can now claim that the Impressionist painter, who is so adept at capturing the fleeting appearance of landscapes, comes up against the human being as against an insurmountable obstacle. Renoir proclaims the power of the disparaged art. Through his depiction of a single moment, he fixes the truth of the movements, the subtlety of expressions on the faces, for all time, he is a great observer of eyes and souls. It is the variety of shades and effects that make his evocations a triumph, he is a masterly portrayer of life in full light, and at the same time one of the most sincere and personal chroniclers of our time. Wonderfully gifted, the painter reproduces complexions, materials, the play of light, with a rare truthfulness and a well-schooled ease. Necks grow perfectly from shoulders, eyes swim, hair is heavy or light, skin is transparent and pale pink, or mat, or sunburnt. And this painter is a portraitist: his Impressionist palette has yielded the secret of disposition and character, physiological and social life.

COLORPLATE 53

The *Moulin de la Galette* is one of these rounded summaries, made up of lively observation and luminous atmosphere: the intoxication of the dance, the noise, the sun, the dust of outdoor merry-making – the excited faces, the casual postures – the pattern of dresses, pink, light blue, dark blue and black, which whirl and stand stock-still – a sudden passionate movement, an encroaching shadow, a leaping fire, pleasure and exhaustion – all the poor lovesong heroines with their finely cast faces and expressive hands, moving lightly, or suddenly, or wearily, expressing hope, abandon, drunkenness, grim tedium.

Photograph of Gabrielle in
Renoir's Studio, Cagnes. c. 1910.
(Photo Durand-Ruel.)

JEAN RENOIR

RENOIR, MY FATHER

The Arrival of Gabrielle (1894)

1958

*Gabrielle Renard (1879–1959), cousin of
Renoir's wife Aline. One of Renoir's favorite
models until 1913, when she left to marry.*

He was born September 15, 1894.

Let us go back now to the period when my mother was pregnant, shortly
before I was born. She suddenly got the idea of having a cousin from
Essoyes come to Paris and help her with the housework. Gabrielle Renard
was fifteen at the time. She had never been out of her native village. The
nuns had given her a good education. She knew how to sew and iron. She
owed her religious education to her father, because he wanted to annoy the
local lay school-teacher, who in his opinion was too pretentious.

The instruction the nuns had given her was amply supplemented by
the lessons the young Gabrielle learned at home. At ten she could tell the
year of any wine, catch trout with her hand without getting caught by the
game warden, tend the cows, help to bleed the pig, gather greens for the
rabbits, and collect the manure dropped by the horses as they came in
from the fields. The manure was a treasure which everyone coveted.
Hardly had it fallen on the white road in steaming lumps than a horde of
competitors rushed out, shovel and pail in hand, to gather it up. Every
youngster in Essoyes was proud of the family's manure-heap which
dominated the courtyard, and was eager to bring in a fresh supply. Their
rivalry resulted in epic battles, from which Gabrielle generally emerged
victorious but with her clothes in rags. Her mother, being insensitive to
the aesthetic qualities of the booty, would end the incident by boxing her
ears. Parents' hands were always ready for action in Essoyes. The young
fry were often sent away howling, but they were none the less healthy for
it. Gabrielle never wore shoes except in the morning, when she went to the
nuns' school, and she took them off as soon as she left in the afternoon.
When the nuns met her on the street they would tell her that little girls

who went barefoot would never grow up to be like Mlle Lemercier, the pride of the village, who wore a veil over her face, had received her diploma and was going to marry a Colonial official. Gabrielle would retort that she hadn't the slightest desire to be like Mlle Lemercier. As a rule the nuns were fairly successful in giving their pupils a veneer of gentility; with Gabrielle, they failed completely. . . .

On Sunday, Gabrielle went with her mother to Mass, where, ill at ease in her starched dress, she was called upon to distribute the pieces of blessed bread. But that did not keep her from joining the other youngsters when they followed the priest down the street and mocked him by imitating the cawing of a crow. Essoyes was proud of its tradition of anti-clericalism. The women went to church, but the men rarely set foot in it. In fact Essoyes was one of the few villages left in which the men still performed the ritual of gathering on the square in front of the church on Good Friday and eating slices of sausage to show that they had got beyond the superstitions of the Middle Ages.

Gabrielle arrived in Paris one summer evening in 1894. My mother met her at the Gare de l'Est. Gabrielle already knew my father, whom she had often seen in Essoyes. For the moment he was away visiting Gallimard in Normandy. When she saw the Château des Brouillards she exclaimed, "A fine garden you have! There's no manure heap!" The next morning, as she did not appear for breakfast, my mother knocked at her door. There was no response. Gabrielle was already out in the street, playing with the children she found there. My mother decided it was a good omen, for all she intended asking her young cousin to do was to play with me after I came into the world. She would trust no one but herself to look after her children and prepare their meals.

Several months later, at the beginning of 1895, I was taken ill with pneumonia. It was freezing hard and the walls of the Château des Brouillards gave little protection against the winter's blast. For an entire week Gabrielle and my mother did not sleep at all. While one was busy bringing up wood, the other was making swaddling clothes to keep me warm. I had to be carried about constantly in their arms, for if I was laid flat on the bed I began to suffocate. They finally decided to telegraph my father. He was painting down at La Couronne, near Marseilles, along with my godmother Jeanne Baudot and her parents. He left his canvas and brushes, hurried to the station without even taking his suitcase, and jumped on the first train for Paris. He arrived home just in time to relieve the two exhausted women. Thanks to love of these three devoted people, I was pulled through a crisis which might otherwise have been fatal. Yet once the danger was passed, no one made further mention of it. If it had not been for Gabrielle, I should never have known anything about it.

JEAN RENOIR

RENOIR, MY FATHER

The Family of Berthe Morisot

1958

When Renoir received my mother's telegram about Berthe Morisot's death, he and Cézanne were out in the country working on the same motif. He folded up his easel at once and hurried to the station without even stopping at the Jas de Bouffan. "I had a feeling of being all alone in a desert. Once I had got on the train, I recovered my composure by thinking of your mother and Pierre and you. On such occasions you realize what a good thing it is to have a wife and children." Before she died, Berthe Morisot had asked my father to look after her daughter Julie, then aged seventeen, and her nieces Jeanie and Paule Gobillard. Being a trifle older than the other two girls, Paule took charge of "the Manet house" as my parents called the mansion at number 41, rue de Villejust. Jeanie was to marry the poet Paul Valéry, after whom the street was later to be renamed. Paule became so wrapped up in playing the part of a big sister that she never married. Julie, a painter herself was to marry the artist Rouart. In Berthe Morisot's day the Manet circle had been one of the most authentic centres of civilized Parisian life. Although my father, as he grew older, avoided artistic and literary sets like the plague, he loved spending an hour or two at the house in the rue de Villejust. It was not intellectuals that one met at Berthe Morisot's, but simple good company. Mallarmé was a frequent visitor. Berthe Morisot acted like a special kind of magnet on people, attracting only the genuine. She had a gift for smoothing rough edges. "Even Degas became more civil with her." "The Manet girls" as they were called, carried on the family tradition. And when Rouart and Valéry married into the family, it was further enriched. Whenever I have the opportunity to go and see my old friends, I feel as if I am breathing a more subtle air than elsewhere, a remnant of the breeze which stirred gently through the Manet drawing-room. . . .

My mother had the idea of bringing together the little Manet girls and Jeanne Baudot. So began an eternal friendship. In view of their belief in the hereafter, the word is surely not misplaced. Paule Gobillard is no more; and my godmother, Jeanne Baudot, died not long ago in the house in Louveciennes that my father had persuaded her parents to buy. Right up to the last, she had her eyes fixed on the pictures that my father had painted of me when I was six years old. Every one of the paintings that she did herself is a tender tribute to Renoir, who was to remain the only love of her life. My father's relations with my godmother were on a purely spiritual basis, as they had been, equally, with Berthe Morisot. As he grew older this gift for friendship with women developed more and more. He would set out on a trip with Jeanne Baudot; they would stay in village inns, take refuge in some farmhouse when it rained, laugh and paint, eat plain country food. Whenever my mother could spare the time – for I was a fretful, demanding baby – she would join them. . . .

Julie Rouart and Jeanie Valéry often talk to me about my father. They always tell me of his gaiety, and how infectious it was. They speak of the absolute passion he had for painting, and how free it was of any complexes. . . . It had been the same with Bazille, Monet, Berthe Morisot, Pissarro, Sisley and his first companions. One of them would get excited over a motif and set up his easel, and the others would instantly follow his example. Passers-by would stop in astonishment to see these bearded young men, their eyes concentrated on their work, their minds miles away from material preoccupations, carefully applying little patches of colour to their canvases. And to make the sight more unusual, a woman in a light summer dress, Berthe Morisot, was often to be seen with the group. My godmother Jeanne de Baudot took me not so very long ago to see a clearing in the Forest of Marly, where she and Renoir had painted. "He would stop as if by chance, then, if he began humming to himself, I knew he was pleased with the motif in front of him. He would unfold his easel and I would do the same, and in a few minutes we would both be painting away furiously."

(see pp. 213–14.)

COLORPLATE 67. *Path Through the Long Grass*. 1876/7. 23¼ × 29⅛″ (59 × 74 cm).
Musée d'Orsay, Paris.

COLORPLATE 68. *Girl with a Falcon (Mlle Fleury in Algerian Costume)*. 1880. 49¾ × 30¾″ (126.5 × 78.2 cm).
Sterling and Francine Clark Art Institute, Williamstown, Mass.

COLORPLATE 71. *Place Clichy*. c. 1880. 25½ × 21¼″ (65 × 54 cm).
On Loan to the Fitzwilliam Museum, Cambridge.

COLORPLATE 72. *View of Venice*. 1881. 17⅞ × 23¾″ (45.5 × 60.5 cm).
Collection Mr. & Mrs. David Lloyd Kreeger, Washington D.C.

COLORPLATE 76. *Luncheon of the Boating Party.* 1881.
51 × 68″ (129.5 × 172.7cm). Phillips Collection, Washington D.C.

COLORPLATE 75. *Portrait of Madame Charpentier and her Children.*
1878. 60½ × 74⅛″ (153.7 × 190.2 cm). Metropolitan Museum of Art, New York
(Catherine Lorillard Wolfe Collection).

JULIE MANET

JOURNAL *August 1895 – August 1899*

Julie Manet (b. 1878). Extracts from the journal she kept in the years between the death of her mother, Berthe Morisot, and her marriage in 1900 to Ernest Rouart, son of the artist Henri Rouart (1833–1912).

AUGUST 23, 1895

[A visitor had spoken of a painting that was a fine portrait, despite being covered in craquelure.]

Renoir comments: "That only proves that it's a bad painting; painting is a craft that must be learned. A good painting is well painted. . . ." M Renoir said that he was always learning more of his trade and wasn't satisfied with what he was doing. "I would rather not paint at all than be a mediocre painter."

SEPTEMBER 19, 1895

Mme Renoir spoke of her trip to Italy after their marriage. It amused us to hear her recounting this because we had so often heard Renoir describe it as if he had traveled there alone, and we knew nothing of his wife then. She was 22 and very thin, she said, which is hard to believe. She also told us that the first time she saw Renoir he was with Monet and Sisley: all three of them wore their hair long and their appearance was something of an event in the rue St Georges where she lived.

M Renoir, when he was a lot younger, spent his summers working in the Forest of Fontainebleau, where he could stay for 50 sous a day and Diaz, who was there too, sold his paintings for him as Rousseau's. He used to paint about eight a day. So that many Renoirs now pass for Rousseaus.

Photograph of Julie Manet. 1894.

OCTOBER 4, 1895

M Renoir has been so good and charming the whole summer. The more one sees him, the more one recognizes the artist in him; he is subtle and extraordinarily intelligent, but so sincere and uncomplicated as well.

MARCH 4, 1896

[Renoir, Monet and Degas are assisting Julie Manet with the hanging of the Berthe Morisot memorial exhibition, March 1896. Degas says it's not for the public, it's only for us, writes Julie Manet. Monet and Renoir disagree.]

Early the next day, Monet and Renoir were there first thing. "Degas won't be here," Renoir said. "He'll turn up in the course of the day to bang a nail in from the top of a ladder, then he'll say – Couldn't we put a rope across the door to stop people coming in? I know him."

DECEMBER 31, 1896

M Renoir came to see us at the same time as Mallarmé. . . . These two – animated painter and beguiling poet – chatted together as they had so often on those Thursday evenings at home in the high-ceilinged pink room. . . . I thought of the phrase of Renoir's that so touched Mother when it was repeated to her. The same painter and poet were returning home after one of Mother's dinner parties and, in talking of the charming manner in which she entertained and her talents (as a painter), etc, M Renoir said: "any other woman with all of those qualities would manage to be quite insufferable."

SEPTEMBER 28, 1897

M Renoir attacks all mechanical inventions, saying that we live in decadent times, where people think of nothing but traveling at so many kilometers per hour; that this serves no purpose; that the automobile is idiotic; that one has no need of such speed. . . . "The government is more monarchical than ever with all-powerful machines at its command. The worker can no longer think or improve his conditions: without the means to change, he will remain forever where he is. What point is there in going so fast? The Gentleman who has a factory which makes 100,000 pairs of shoes a week doesn't always find a market for them. At a certain point the factory can't go on and it's for this reason that we have to go and sell shoes to the savages, persuading them that it is necessary for them to wear shoes in order to sustain the working life of a Gentleman's factory. We have built an empire in order to dispose of our products. Slavery has been abolished but this is worse than slavery: the worker who knows that he cannot get anywhere has no hope of change and is more unhappy than the slave."

OCTOBER 11, 1897

We also spoke of the Natansons: M Renoir said that it was very dangerous to support anarchists like Fénéon, who work in the literary field before launching themselves into politics and who will end badly. Is he not right? Writers give too much support to doubtful characters; painters are much saner. Pissarro, however, is an anarchist.

Félix Fénéon (1861–1944), critic, champion of post-Impressionist art

DECEMBER 5, 1897

He spoke with enthusiasm of Alexandre Dumas who will be read, he said, long after Zola, who despises him. M Renoir's principle is that art must be both entertaining and comprehensible.

Alexandre Dumas the Elder (1802–80)

JANUARY 15, 1898

In Renoir's studio there was talk of the Dreyfus affair, and against the Jews.

"They (the Jews) come to France to make money and then, if there is any trouble, they run to hide behind a tree," said M Renoir. "There's a lot of them in the army because the Jews love to strut around in fancy uniforms. They have been hounded from all other countries and there must be a reason for it. They shouldn't be allowed to occupy a prominent position in France. People say that the Dreyfus case must be brought out into the open, but there are some things which can't be said and people refuse to understand that."

M Renoir started off on the subject of Pissarro, a "Jew" whose children have no country of their own and who do no military service whatever. "It's tenacious, this Jewish race. Pissarro's wife isn't Jewish and yet all the children are more Jewish than their father."

The "Dreyfus Affair" centered upon a debate about the guilt or inocence of an army captain, Alfred Dreyfus, a Jew, who was convicted on suspect evidence of selling military secrets to Germany and court-martialed. The bitter political crisis around the case lasted from 1874 to 1906, promoting ministerial resignations and arousing a hostile wave of extreme anti-semitism, to which Renoir – along with most of the French nation – subscribed. Emile Zola, who wrote an heroic pro-Dreyfus pamphlet, J'Accuse (1898), was among its most vocal opponents. After several retrials, Dreyfus was eventually pardoned by the President of the Republic.

JANUARY 20, 1898

M Renoir spoke of Zola, of his habit of only seeing one side of things and describing the ordinary people. Renoir said, "It's rather like a person who half opens the door of a cottage and says that it smells bad in here and leaves without ever going right in." Then he said that in the past, when he used to go to the Moulin de la Galette where all the Montmartre families got together, he'd always noticed how sensitive these people were, while Zola spoke of them as barbaric creatures.

JANUARY 30, 1898

He spoke of the appeal that is currently being signed by Jews, anarchists and writers for a review of the Dreyfus case and which Natanson called to ask him to sign. He refused, of course, just as he refused to attend a dinner among such people, where on a previous occasion, he had this exchange:

"Where does the bourgeoisie begin and end? Am I a bourgeois?" – "No," came the answer, "We are intellectuals."

FEBRUARY 5, 1898

We went to Renoir's studio to say goodbye, since tomorrow he leaves for the Midi; that is, this is what he tells us from time to time, whereas at other times he no longer knows what he is doing, he's so changeable. He was so funny today. "What I really need," he tells us, "is a woman to lead me by the nose." "But isn't this just how things are?" we ventured, Paule, Jeanne Baudot and I. M Renoir appeared astonished and afterwards he said several times that we had just taught him something about himself that he had never suspected.

APRIL 21, 1899

M Renoir's philosophical attitude and his acceptances are remarkable. We spoke of the suffering that one sees in the hospitals. "It's a crime to complain," he said, "when you see others suffering like that. We should all count our blessings." How good it is to find someone who is so ill, but not feeling sorry for himself.

APRIL 22, 1899

We spoke afterwards of Sisley and of the withdrawn manner in which he lived his last years at Moret, believing that everyone had it in for him. When he re-met M Renoir – with whom he had lived – he would cross the street in order not to speak to him. He made himself very unhappy. M Renoir told me that when I went to Valvins with Mother we had met him one day on a visit to Moret. Mother invited him to visit her at Valvins, he accepted. Then, after saying goodbye, he ran after her saying "After all, no. I shan't come to see you."

JULY 28, 1899

Then he spoke about socialism and all the harm it does. "It has taken working people away from their religion – which was always a source of consolation to them – and replaced it by an extra 25 cents a day. Happiness isn't achieved by working fewer hours. . . . The worker who, in the past, took great pleasure in making a chair in his own way, now has no interest in it. One man makes the legs, another makes the backs and another puts it all together. The work is finished as quickly as possible in order to get paid. In the old days, a painter would devote loving care to the painting of a Virgin who would lead him to heaven; now he goes pell mell at his Virgin to get her finished as soon as possible."

AUGUST 4, 1899

What intelligence! [M Renoir] sees everything with the same clarity and judgment that are in his painting. "Knowledge is mankind's great loss," he says. "Just consider all those people who no longer believe in God and who are just left with science." This is the same idea as Edgar Poe puts forward when he says that science represents a great loss to mankind.

AUGUST 7, 1899

Pissarro persuaded Georges Lecomte to write in his book on Impressionism [1892] that it was necessary to banish black as being quite useless. This is something I know a lot about and there's a certain buoyancy that one can only get from using black. Titian said that a great painter is one who knows how to use black. It seems to me more important to listen to Titian than to Pissarro. There is nothing so difficult in painting as the use of black. Manet's blacks are marvelous – always painted at a stroke.

Portrait of Alfred Sisley. 1875.
25⅛ × 20⅞" (64 × 53 cm).
Courtesy of the Art Institute of Chicago (Mrs. Lewis Larned Memorial Collection).

Edgar Allen Poe (1809–49)

JULIE MANET

JOURNAL

The Tuition of Julie Manet

1895-99

These are the most expansive of many references in her journal to the help and advice that Renoir gave Julie Manet with her painting during the later 1890s.

. . . I went to work with M Renoir and after searching for a sheltered spot for an hour, we ended up back at the river. M Renoir advised me not to place the horizon line too high in a painting, but rather in the middle, this being the point that attracts the attention. Also not to start the foreground too close to one. He showed me how the river appeared to flow and to vanish among the trees at the back more convincingly, when they were placed in the middle of the canvas rather than high up, as I had placed them. Then he said that I should paint very lightly to start with.

* * *

M Renoir said that one should paint still lifes in order to learn to paint quickly.

* * *

He gave me an excellent lesson. He said that when one starts a still-life or anything else, it is most important to look at the tones in their relation to each other, and to sketch very lightly, observing the blacks, greys, whites. "There is only black and white in painting," said M Renoir. Then he added that one gives intensity to the whites by the value of what surrounds them, not by putting on more white. "In the works of a great painter, the whites are so beautiful because he knows where they belong – look at the whites of Titian, the whites of Manet, the whites of Corot." . . .

He said it was very good to paint houses precisely, to learn how to render white walls under brilliant sunlight.

* * *

M Renoir says that the only real painting is with oil; the only reason to paint with turpentine is if you have to do something in a hurry.

* * *

M Renoir said that you can learn more about painting by looking at painting, than by looking at nature.

* * *

"I think that an art with secrets is inferior. In the painting of Rubens or Velasquez, there's nothing hidden, nothing underneath, it's painted straight off. Those who speak of glazing don't know what's involved: colors floated in a transparent medium over something else can only have a dulling effect. One makes light tones with impasto, mixed with white. One can look for things underneath which have never existed. . . .

"Degas is worrying as a teacher. I heard him say to an amateur: when you start a landscape, look first of all to see if the dominant color is green or violet etc, and make a study, an underpainting in one of those colors. Personally, I think one should start a canvas brushing in lightly, trying to reproduce the colors immediately. Then you have to paint each bit straight off as old Ingres used to do, being prepared to start over again until it seems right."

JEANNE BAUDOT

RENOIR

The Tuition of Jeanne Baudot

1949

He advised me to go to the Académie Julian, where there would be models, but instead of showing my work to the professor, I was to bring it back to the house where he would come to look at it . . . he suggested that "sometimes" I should work with him in his studio. . . .

Thus I was allowed to make a study of the *boulangère*, the model, alongside Renoir and to order my palette like his: flake white, Naples yellow, yellow ocher, burnt sienna, Venetian red, vermilion, madder lake No. 1, cobalt blue, terra verte, emerald green, ivory black. Later he introduced me to cobalt green and Chinese vermilion.

Renoir was not taken in by brilliant colors like chrome or cadmium which, when mixed, were liable to darken with age; he preferred to rise to the challenge of producing the desired effect, rather than watch his works changing with age as a result of chemical combinations. In his concern with this question, he made me carry out a study of the colors used by the old masters and of their technique.

. . . it was by personal effort and by analyzing the works of the masters that Renoir found his way as a painter. How many times did I hear him regret that he had not been guided by an artist, like the Italian Renaissance master who passed on all that he had learnt to his students and so saved them from floundering and wasting their time. . . .

* * *

Jeanne Baudot (b. 1877), a doctor's daughter; she was a student of painting when Renoir met her in 1893 and he gave her some private tuition and they shared painting trips together. She became godmother to Jean Renoir in 1894. These are extracts from her memoirs.

"La boulangère" *was Marie Dupuis (d. 1948), who – after Gabrielle – was Renoir's most used model of the later years; he first met her in 1899. She was named* la boulangère *(the baker's wife) because she lived with a man who worked at the bakery where Renoir bought rye bread. She posed for* The Judgement of Paris *(Colorplate 111).*

In winter, when all colors were suppressed by the somberness of the sky, Renoir, frustrated at not being able to make luminous paintings, would come and fetch me to look at exhibitions in the rue Lafitte. He would say: "This weather is made for Carrière, but not for me."

* * *

[After an account of the 1894 Caillebotte bequest to the nation, of which Renoir was executor] Renoir, to whom Caillebotte had given the choice of a major work [from the collection] as a souvenir, opted for a Degas and Degas wrote to him expressing his pleasure. Several years later, Renoir suffered an extreme attack of rheumatism which obliged him to stop working. He was in dread of not being able to work again and was plagued by fears for the future security of his family. Durand-Ruel learned of his worries and suggested to Renoir that he might buy the Degas for 45,000 francs, a considerable sum in those days and one which was particularly high in comparison with the price commanded by other, less highly regarded Impressionist paintings. Renoir, after much hesitation, decided to accept the offer. When Degas learnt of this, he felt hurt and, not appreciating the family considerations involved, he returned one of the Renoir paintings that he owned. Renoir responded by sending back a small Degas from his collection together with a note. On the first page, he said that his reply would take just five letters, and turning the page, one found the word: *"Enfin. . . ."*

(see pp. 186–87.)

The number of times I went to the Louvre with Renoir! That was my greatest pleasure. When his work wasn't going well, or when his model hadn't turned up, he would come down to eat at our house in the rue Taitbout. Having fortified himself at our table, he would take me to the Louvre. We used to go in at the porte Denon. Renoir was in ecstasy before the mosaics which met his eyes just inside the door. "Ah," he would say to me, "look at that fish, sparkling like a diamond, and yet the whole effect is achieved simply by surrounding a white stone by others of Venetian red, ochre and grey."

We went up to the Poussin room. Most especially he admired the *Apollo and Daphne*, pointing out the disposition of the groups and the whole composition. . . . He couldn't pass Delacroix's *Women of Algiers* without exclaiming: "You can smell the sherbet. . . ."

PAGE 334

* * *

In the Louvre, Renoir made me copy the right hand group from the *Rape of the Sabines* by Poussin . . . Renoir also advised me to copy the first four dancers on the right from Mantegna's *Parnassus*. This was in order to give me some discipline and to make me appreciate different techniques.

* * *

Renoir would often receive various friends at the end of a day's painting. The wife of one of them had misgivings about her husband's constancy and used to think that he was more attracted by the models than by the artistic concerns. She confided her anxiety to Renoir who replied, smiling, "Just look at them, these are good girls not seducers; I paint them just as I would paint carrots."

* * *

Techniques and method cannot be taught; you have to find them for yourself. No two things should be painted in the same manner. Certain things in a painting gain from being simply roughed in, left to be improvized with. It's a matter of sensibility. Oil accelerates the cracking of a painting. I've managed for a long time without it. That's a matter of temperament. Cézanne worked very well towards the end of his life with turpentine. At the start he painted with oil, and I prefer the canvases he painted with oil. It is obvious that Velasquez used oil.

THADÉE NATANSON

LA REVUE BLANCHE

"Renoir"

May 1896

Thadée Natanson (1868–1951), writer, a founder in 1890 of La Revue Blanche, *principal journal of the Symbolist movement.*

A constant agitation hastens Renoir's stride, bows, then straightens his back, sets his twisted fingers moving, ceaselessly propels the frail, restive, irritable frame, lost in loose folds of clothes too large for it. It puckers his skin and makes every facial feature twitch, makes his eyelids flicker, focuses and quickens the nervous gesticulation of the body on the narrow mask: a ravaged face, shrunken, desiccated and drawn, and bristling with gray hairs, where the eyes sparkle, but kindly, above protruding cheekbones.

The nimble fingers constantly pluck and smoothe the gray mustache and beard: sparse, rebellious hairs which put the finishing touches to an appearance which is forbidding at first sight, but promptly redeemed by the vivacity of the features and the goodness they express.

He comes and goes, sits down, stands up, has hardly stood up than he decides to sit down again, gets up and goes in search of the latest cigarette forgotten on the stool, no, not on the stool, or on the easel, no, on the table, not there either, and at last he decides to roll another which he may well lose before he has had the time to light it, but which is replaced by a third whose ash may have been cold for a day at least. The fact is that between whiles he has disparaged a hundred other practices of his time, and voiced all his other well-known complaints into the bargain and, equally often, regretted the lingering mist of times gone by; once again proclaimed his passion for Delacroix, his devotion to Watteau, the respect he has for Monet. Laughing and shouting, more often standing than seated, he touches on a whole range of topics. And yet he allows you to look at – without actually showing you – what he has just done. His working practice tolerates no audience, even of one, and his volubility is some measure of compensation for the silence his work demands. Once he has finished working, he always finds another means to talk passionately again about painting. He will laugh at some joke in passing, relish some anecdote, become indignant or protest, come back once more to the eighteenth century masters of whom (as far as his modesty permits) he regards himself as but a very distant, or indeed aspiring, descendant.

Or he will admit that he and those around him were slow in coming to feel a sense of reverence for the old masters, and particularly in understanding Chardin, for instance, or Poussin, whom he confesses he has only recently comprehended. And the prejudice which kept him and his contemporaries clear of museums as young men, obsessed as they were with the open air, in the grip of an enthusiasm which he now mocks at but which they then felt could teach them more. And when he is feeling at his most mellow, he talks at greater length of the journey he made to Italy, fifteen odd years ago when, already over forty, he realized how much he did not know. This frequently leads him to attack the faults of his early works, which he sees more clearly than anyone, to give lengthy and almost naive explanations of the difficulties he is having with his current ones, and to expatiate on the plans that so absorb his quinquagenarian youth.

He has a particularly nice and sprightly gift for mime, which enables him to highlight his already vivacious conversation, and he uses a range of apt, expressive gestures, tracing the shape of a hat, the pleats of fulness of a skirt, a panel, a flower or the corner of a famous painting. He is at his best when mimicking the attitudes of his models. Even those who seemed at first to have the most natural grace, to his despair rigidly adopt poses they have learned from a sitting or two in some studio, and so mulishly, that one has to abandon all hope of doing anything with them. On another occasion he will do a complete mime of a young woman in a wood: her skirt snared on a twig, she tugs, leaves the fraying ribbon caught, turns back; her fingers, at the hem of her dress, tweaks a silky thread which unwinds, snags, then droops like a rag, unraveling endlessly until suddenly the stroller, maddened, turns back, pulls at it and promptly rewinds it, all smiles. Then we are back with Monet or Corot, "Corot whose palette is the most admirable France has known since Watteau!" And then after Fragonard and the marvels of Watteau, we have Velasquez and the frescoes he is going to look at in the Louvre; his admiration for Pompeii, the source of his most intense enjoyment, but then, fearful of wronging them, he returns to the decorations over which Raphael reveled on the walls of certain Roman villas. The topics flow, jostling each other until night drives him from the studio or an attendant finally moves us towards the door . . .

FRANTZ JOURDAIN

LA PATRIE

June 23, 1896

Frantz Jourdain (1847–1935), influential critic and later President of the Salon d'Automne; normally a champion of the Impressionist cause.

. . . I find myself incapable of speaking equitably of the painters who have, this week, invited the critics to inspect their wares at the various *petits salons*, whose interest is most definitely waning.

Nonetheless, I would make an exception in the case of Renoir, whose place is – or was – too pre-eminent for an exhibition of his work to pass unnoticed. My zealous and long-standing admiration for this artist, who has long occupied a leading role in modern art, counsels extreme reserve. But I am unable to extend blindness and fetishism to a point where I do not deplore the misguided zeal of M Durand-Ruel, who, in order to promote their sale, has brought together in his gallery thirty or so distressingly feeble canvases.

It would have been respectful, it would have been proper not to reveal the failings of a man of high standing whose irreparable errors we have followed, with sadness, for some time. These plastery women, these clumsily modeled bodies, these feet and hands that resemble chunks of raw meat, these invariably squashed profiles, these leaden seas, these cliffs of mauve tow, these mindlessly puerile arrangements, between them make an affirmative appreciation quite out of the question – or even a sincere or convincing defence. One may still find some canvases, the portrait of Mme Monet, for instance, which conjure up a memory of the luminous and exquisite painting of times gone by, but, alas! such canvases are rare in the exhibition at the rue Lafitte. The most genuine proof of concern that one can now show to M Renoir will be – as far as I am concerned – to prevent his current works from painful and untimely exhibition.

* * *

Jeanne Baudot records Renoir's reaction to this criticism as follows:
Renoir was sent this article by Durand-Ruel. He read it and ranted against "these word-merchants who understand nothing about painting." In order to get the whole thing out of his mind, he suggested to me that I should take my paint-box and go with him to paint in the woods. We traveled some kilometers without finding a landscape to Renoir's taste – Renoir who would normally have settled for any tree or stream! We arrived back at our lodgings without stopping once! In this way, Frantz Jourdain deprived us all of another work by Renoir.

JEAN RENOIR

RENOIR, MY FATHER

The Beginning of Renoir's Illness

1958

The accident which was to turn my father's life into a martyrdom was a fall from a bicycle in 1897, at Essoyes. . . .

Our cousin, Paul Parisot, had his shop near the Porte des Ternes in Paris, where he sold, repaired and even manufactured bicycles. Whenever he came to see us, we were lost in admiration of his beautiful bicycle, a shiny model and absolutely noiseless. . . .

Almost all the young painters who came to see Renoir when he was at Essoyes rode bicycles. Among the Paris friends were Albert André, and his wife Maleck, d'Espargnat, Matisse and Roussel. Abel Faivre was a keen cyclist. Monsieur and Madame Valtat rode a tandem. . . .

My father finally decided to do as everyone else did, and he had cousin Parisot send him a bicycle. Abel Faivre taught him how to ride it. He never used it when he went out to paint, as his equipment was too cumbersome, but he found it convenient when he was searching for subjects, which he noted down with a few quick pencil strokes on his sketch pad. . . .

On that particular day Renoir, to the surprise of the entire household, was doing nothing. The rain had stopped. The heavy carts were coming back from the fields. My father took it into his head to go out on his bicycle as far as Servigny to see "what the tops of the poplars look like under a stormy sky." Servigny was one of the places which enchanted him. I use the word "enchant" in its literal sense of casting a spell. At Servigny he muttered the name of Watteau to himself, and hummed one of Mozart's airs. The place had once been the property of some nobleman. The château had been razed during the Revolution. The few bits of wall which had survived were buried in a mass of vegetation. Renoir meditated with some emotion on the spectacle of a human achievement reverting to Nature. He saw in it a subtle marriage, a blending of Nature and art somewhat akin to what he was so passionately seeking in his painting. . . .

As Renoir was riding along on his bicycle on that rainy day in 1897 he skidded in a puddle of water and fell on a heap of stones. When he got up he realised that he had broken his right arm. He left his bicycle in the ditch and returned home on foot, only thankful that he was ambidextrous. . . .

Dr Bordes . . . put Renoir's arm in a plaster cast and advised him not to do any more bicycling. My father had therefore to paint with his left hand, and he was obliged to ask my mother to prepare his palette and to wipe off with a piece of cloth dipped in turpentine those parts of the picture that did not satisfy him. It was the first time he had ever asked anyone to help him with his work. He went back to Paris at the end of the summer with his arm still in plaster. At the end of the customary six weeks Dr Journiac, our Montmartre doctor, came to the house and removed the cast. He announced that the bones were completely knitted. Renoir then began painting with either hand as it suited him, believing the incident to be closed.

On Christmas Eve that year he felt a slight pain in his right shoulder. However, he went with us to the "Manets" in the rue de Villejuste, as Paule Gobillard was giving a Christmas party. Degas was present, and he told Renoir quite cheerfully of all sorts of cases of frightful muscular rheumatism resulting from fractures. Everyone seemed to think it exceedingly funny, Renoir above all. Even so, he consulted Journiac, and

Henri Matisse (1869–1954) (see pp. 260–61), Albert André (see pp. 262 ff), Ker-Xavier Roussel (1867–1944), Louis Valtat (1869–1952), Jules-Abel Faivre (1867–1945)

was informed to his dismay that medical science had not been able to solve the mystery of arthritis. All that was known was that it could become extremely serious. He prescribed antipyrin. Dr Baudot was even less reassuring and recommended frequent purges. Renoir followed the orders of the two men, and on his own initiative started taking physical exercise. He had no great faith in the benefit of walking, which brings into play only certain muscles. He believed in ball games. He had always liked juggling as an amusement, so he began practising every morning for ten minutes before going off to his studio. . . . Whenever he had the chance he would play battledore and shuttlecock. Tennis seemed too complicated for him. . . . He liked billiards, because it makes you adopt all sorts of awkward postures. With the addition to our house at Essoyes, my mother had a billiard table installed, and she herself became quite expert at the game. In spite of her corpulence she beat my father at it regularly. . . .

Towards the end of May my father took us to visit the Bérards at Berneval. We rented the house which Oscar Wilde occupied in the winter. . . . We returned to the rue la Rochefoucauld (Paris) in time for Pierre's autumn term at Sainte-Croix. In December Renoir suffered a new

Jeanne Baudot's father

Oscar Wilde (1854–1900)

Photograph of Renoir painting at the Villa de la Poste, Cagnes. 1903. (Photo Archives Durand-Ruel.)

attack, really terrible this time. He could not move his right arm and he was unable to touch a brush for several days.

His story from then on is the story of his fight against illness. For him the important thing was not to find a cure – he was not a bit interested in his own health – but to continue painting. . . . There was also the practical side of the dilemma. He confided to my mother his fear of not being able to assure the material needs of the family. His output by now was enormous, but he sold immediately almost everything he produced. The money he made sufficed amply for our carefree life, but no more. . . .

Renoir's malady grew worse at irregular intervals. I should say that his condition changed radically after my brother Claude [Coco] was born in 1902. The partial atrophy of a nerve in his left eye became more apparent. It had been caused by a bad cold caught some years before while he was out painting a landscape. His rheumatism made this semi-paralysis worse. Within a few months his face took on this fixed expression which so startled people who met him for the first time. All of us in the family, however, soon got used to his changed appearance, and except for the attacks of pain, which grew steadily worse, we completely forgot that he was so ill.

Each year his face became more emaciated, his hands more twisted. One morning, he decided to give up juggling the three balls, at which he had become so expert. He was no longer able to pick them up. He threw them as far away as he could, saying in an irritated tone, "The devil take it, I'm going gaga!" He had to fall back on the game of bilboquet, played with a ball and peg, "just like the one Henri III used in Alexandre Dumas!" He also tried juggling with a small log. He asked our coal and wood dealer to cut one for him very evenly, about eight inches long and two inches thick. He scraped it with a knife himself and sandpapered it till it was perfectly smooth. He would toss in in the air, making it turn round and round, and catch it adroitly, being careful to change hands from time to time. "One paints with one's hands," he would say. And in this way the fight to save his hands went on.

He now began to have difficulty in walking. I was still young when he decided to try using a cane. As he had to lean on it more and more, the cane would sometimes slip, and he had to have a rubber tip put on it, "just like an invalid." He became more sensitive to temperatures, and would catch cold easily when working out of doors.

We returned to Essoyes every summer. Our house there had been finished by then. My mother would invite friends in continually so as to provide Renoir with the social life he was so fond of and could no longer seek away from home.

PIERRE-AUGUSTE RENOIR

Two Letters to Claude Monet

August 1900

AUGUST 20

Dear Friend,
I have allowed myself to be decorated. Believe me that I'm not telling you about it in order to say that I'm right or wrong, but rather that this little ribbon should not get in the way of our long friendship. So feel free to insult me with whatever disagreeable words you choose – that's O.K. by me – but no joking about whether or not I've done something stupid. I value your friendship; for the rest, I couldn't care less.
Your friend, Renoir.

In July 1900 it was announced that Renoir had been appointed a Chevalier de la Légion d'Honneur. *While Renoir saw fit to accept the honor, his ambivalence vis-à-vis his contemporaries' attitude is clear from these two letters. Monet's reaction to the news was "How sad!"*

Dear Friend,
I realize today, and even before, that the letter I wrote to you was silly. I felt unwell, nervous and harried. One shouldn't write at all under those conditions. I am wondering a little what it matters to you whether I'm decorated or not. You have an admirable code of conduct for yourself, whereas I can never know on one day what I shall do on the next. You ought to know me well by now, better probably than I know myself, just as I very probably know you better than you do. So please tear up that letter and don't let's talk of it again, and *vive l'amour!*
Regards to Madame Monet and all at home, *A toi*, Renoir.

Renoir had apparently refused an offer of official decoration as early as 1890. He was later to accept further appointments in the Légion d'Honneur: Officier *in 1911,* Commandeur *in 1919.*

PIERRE-AUGUSTE RENOIR
Letters to Durand-Ruel
March 1902 – March 1910

During the last two decades of his life, Renoir's paintings were widely exhibited and increasingly in demand. These excerpts from letters to his dealer give some idea of his mixed feelings.

MARCH 9, 1902. LE CANNET
On the subject of exhibitions, it seems to me that you should already have all you need at the gallery, but I would prefer on my return to give you some canvases that are not new – or that are at least a year old – because they never speak clearly to you when they're too fresh.

However, I would prefer you to settle for the works you have: there are some that aren't bad, and that haven't been shown, or only very little. In addition I think that limited exhibitions with a few canvases carry much more weight. I find that over-large exhibitions of figure-subjects make it look as if the paintings were made too easily, which strips them of any rarity value. This was a criticism made of the Impressionists who showed too often. It used to be said that they laid pictures like eggs. This gives – or will later give – a very bad impression.

* * *

SEPTEMBER 18, 1904. ESSOYES
Do whatever you want for the autumn exhibition; I can't say anything else to you. Personally I neither want nor feel able to get involved in it. I can hardly move and I really feel that this is the end, as far as painting goes. I shan't be able to do anything else. You will understand that in these circumstances, nothing interests me.

* * *

SEPTEMBER 20, 1904. ESSOYES
I would ask you not to put too many things into this exhibition; it is rarity that pushes up the price not abundance. . . .

* * *

OCTOBER 19, 1904. PARIS, TO GEORGES DURAND-RUEL
People ask me why, if I never normally exhibit, I have decided to exhibit at the Salon d'Automne. My reply is that I never exhibit when people don't want me to, but that it's not my intention to hide my work, that I was asked very courteously if I wanted to exhibit. I accepted because I had confidence in the organizers of this Salon. And I asked your father to look after the exhibition since I was very ill and at Bourbonne. I'm delighted with what I had done, everyone was happy. The people I've managed to speak to thought this the most interesting exhibition, and organized with taste, which is rare. It is a success. What more could one want? I was afraid, in view of the vast number of exhibitions, that it would be a failure. I was mistaken, so much the better.

A Renoir room at the Salon d'Automne, Grand Palais, which in the event, in October/November 1904, contained 35 of his works.

OCTOBER 29, 1906. PARIS

I have received an enquiry from a M Gustave Cohen, a solicitor of 61 rue
des Petits-Champs, about the price of a nude No. 1469 at the Salon
d'Automne; could you look into this.

P.S. I've told you that I wasn't thinking of selling these paintings yet.
Make them very expensive. I leave tomorrow evening.

MARCH 24, 1908. CAGNES

I don't know if I should accept this new honor of taking part in the Société
Royale de Bruxelles. I should do so with pleasure if I believed that it
would help you sell even one painting more, but – rightly or wrongly – I
don't. The last thing I want is to dishearten you, but soon there will
inevitably be a major and a lasting collapse in public interest, caused by
the excessive number of exhibitions. This collapse may come tomorrow, it
may come in ten years, I don't know, but come it will. Too much utterly
worthless stuff is produced. You can do no more about it than I can. But
the only wise thing is to expect the worst and guard against it. All the
same, I am sending you my acceptance for this *société nationale,* and you can
do what you wish.

JANUARY 6, (TO GEORGES DURAND-RUEL); FEBRUARY 11, 1909. CAGNES

Please tell your father to send nothing to *La Libre Aesthétique,* the Belgians
are really far too advanced for me. . . .

*   *   *

At the *Libre Aesthétique,* they only like artists like Van Gogh and
Gauguin. Since I am neither one nor the other, I don't see what good will
come from being involved in it, unless it is to be roundly abused and sell
nothing, which is what generally happens.

MARCH 1, 1910. CAGNES

Please choose three good paintings for the Brussels exhibition. The
reclining female nude included. Everyone is pressing me to send to this
exhibition. . . . To avoid sending bad paintings, I am asking you to make
the choice. . . .

P.S. For all that, if you consider it pointless or inadvisable to submit, then
don't. The Belgians don't buy, but since it's an international exhibition it
will attract foreigners.

TÉODOR DE WYZEWA

PEINTRES DE JADIS ET D'AUJOURD'HUI

"Post-script"

1903

Téodor de Wyzewa's most substantial essay on Renoir, seeing him in the historical context of Dutch 17th-century painting and, more conventionally, of Watteau and the French tradition.

It is not without a touch of embarrassment that I have decided to reprint this old article, an unworthy testimony to my admiration for a man whom I regard as the greatest of today's painters – the last of the great painters, probably, for I do not see whence we may now hope for another. On twenty occasions, over as many years, I have tried to define M Renoir's work more exactly, and in greater detail, or rather to define the ever deeper impression it has made upon me; but there is certainly nothing more difficult than writing well about things one loves, especially when these things happen – as is the case with impressions made by art – to be of a kind which no word can ever translate. Twenty times, after feasting my eyes on the paintings of M Renoir, I have planned long studies on the master to whom I owed this unparalleled delight; but each time I ultimately realized that the intended study could quite well be reduced to one or two lines: "What marvelous painting! Don't fail to go and see it, and may it give you the pleasure it has always given me!" Because art criticism, which may hold the future in its hands, has not progressed beyond the stage of futile babble; and Fromentin himself, when he learnedly explained why the *Nightwatch* is not a good painting, may be read with profit only by those who have not yet been affected by the genius of Rembrandt. "Criticism has one right," said Victor Hugo, "the right to keep silent." But the situation of the art critic is particularly awkward; because if a work leaves him unmoved, one cannot hope that he will write well about it; and if he likes a work, if he really feels a deep-seated joy in beholding it, then from that moment onwards he is irresistibly drawn to complete silence on the subject.

Eugène Fromentin (1820–76), painter and writer on Flemish and Dutch art

Alongside art criticism there is, of course, art history, whose seriousness and usefulness I would be one of the first to appreciate. While Fromentin, with all his talent, succeeds only in spoiling my pleasure in the *Nightwatch*, I would be very happy if a historian took the trouble to investigate the various influences – family, training, background, temperament, affinities, literary sources etc – which have gone into making Rembrandt the man he was. The biographies of artists would not be as useless a literary genre as they are, if their authors were less insistent on telling us only things that we could get on quite well without knowing. Every artist has two lives, one consisting of eating and drinking, paying his rent, loving his or his neighbor's wife, and the other being the one which gives rise to his work. It is that life which biographers omit to tell us about; yet it is almost always more interesting than the other: more varied, more eventful, richer in romantic or tragic vicissitudes. Does not the work of a painter such as Rembrandt, for example, when considered in chronological order, immediately suggest a whole drama, the drama of a poet of genius in a state of constant, unconscious struggle against the artistic conditions of his time and race? What did his teachers teach him? What works did he see subsequently which encouraged him to modify his style? And when, and how, and why did he progress from the *Anatomy Lesson* to the *Nightwatch*, from the latter to the *Syndics*, and then to the *St Matthew* in the Louvre and the *Jewish Bride?* A biography which would enlighten us on all this would help us to understand and relish the art of Rembrandt in quite another way than one which might succeed in determining whether or not the old master ended by marrying his housekeeper. But unfortunately such historical studies can be undertaken only when a certain period of time has elapsed. In a hundred years – always supposing of course that the world still has the leisure to concern itself with beauty – a historian will inevitably be found to attempt to reconstitute the admirable life of M Renoir the artist. He will show the stages M Renoir too went through from one of his successive "styles" to another, and the variety of reasons which caused him to do so. M Renoir's work will appear to him as a whole, having become detached from the background of our contemporary painting, as the work of Rembrandt or Watteau appears to us today; and I would gladly believe that what he says about this work will help his readers to know it better. Today, those to whom it appeals must be satisfied with enjoying it in silence.

And yet here is an observation, purely historical in kind, that may be made even today, on the position occupied by M Renoir in what has come to be known as the "Impressionist movement:" a completely negative observation, furthermore, and one which consists simply in protesting against a mistake too long widely circulated. Today, any man of good faith can see clearly that it is a mistake constantly to associate the name of M Renoir with those painters who, with him, were formerly the first representatives of *Impressionism*. For impressionism, at the already distant period when it was invented, was not a school, nor even a doctrine, but a new language, with its advantages and disadvantages, like all other artistic languages. Perhaps, when all is said and done, it actually had more disadvantages than advantages, at least for current practice; and I cannot help thinking, for example, that the artistic dreams of M Besnard would not distress us so insistently if this skilful man had allowed them to find expression in the language of Paul Delaroche, rather than in that of M Renoir. But a language, of whatever kind, may serve to express different things; and the truth is that M Renoir, using the same artistic language as his companions, nonetheless used it to quite another end than did most of them. There is a profound difference between their art and his own, a difference which, furthermore, could and should have remained unobserved in the past, when we did not yet understand the language which these painters had just invented in common; but today the methods of impressionism are sufficiently known to us for this difference to appear to us with conclusive clarity. We now perceive, with no possibility of error, that the painting of M Renoir does not lend itself to being classed as it was at first, with that of M Monet, Sisley and the rest of the Impressionist masters. These admirable artists were, in some sense, the "prose writers" of Impressionism; M Renoir is its "poet."

Albert Besnard (1849–1934), popular sub-Impressionist painter
Paul Delaroche (1797–1856), successful Salon painter

* * *

And there are, in all the arts, men of a different kind, who not only see and feel things differently from ourselves, but who, by instinct, feel and see them as more "beautiful," with more light, or color, or purity and harmony. Involuntarily, inevitably, they transfigure the objects they perceive; and their works do not give us the impression of "reality" at all, but ravish us with a mysterious and delightful "beauty." They are the poets: I really cannot think of any name that better befits them. And sometimes, in order to delight us, these poets do not even need to possess a very high mastery of their craft. Ruysdael, for instance, certainly does not draw or paint better than Van Goyen, Van den Hagen or Hobbema or a dozen other landscape painters of his circle; but none of them has his gift of *beautifying* a bush, a sand-dune or a field of wheat, of lending them a soul or a voice, of hearing and making us hear the music of the earth. I would add that the real poets are those who *beautify* things without meaning to, while trying to reproduce them just as they see them. The slightest drawing by Ruysdael, faithfully copied from nature, contains as much

The Dutch landscape painters, Jacob van Ruysdael (c.1628–82), Jan van Goyen (1596–1656), Joris Van den Hagen (1615–69), Meindert Hobbema (1638–c.1709)

poetry as his biggest paintings, and more. And yet I know of nothing more pitiable than the efforts of painters such as Théodore Rousseau, Daubigny, Millet and all the painters of the "school of Fontainebleau," to give their works a poetry which these decent burghers simply did not have in their hearts. And in the same way the clumsiest of the masters of Siena, from Duccio down to Beccafumi, bring to their vision of the world a sweetness, a rhythm, a poetry which the most skillful of their Florentine confrères lacked. And what would remain of Corot's painting if we were to judge it, like that of a Rousseau or a Troyon, purely from the point of view of its "reality?" All these painters move us only because external things appear more "beautiful" to them than to the rest of mankind, that is, more bedecked with an indefinable grace to whose allure, sooner or later, we shall succumb. And M Renoir is one of them. In vain, with his admirable craftsman's conscience, he has been trying for forty years to reproduce things exactly as they are to his eyes; they are not the same to his eyes as to ours and, despite himself, he transfigures them, thinking he is reproducing them. This marvelous flower painter seems from birth to have had the art of changing everything into flowers. His portraits and his landscapes, his "bathers," his "oarsmen," his groups of children, are always flowers, and so fresh, so alive, so charming are they that their colors dissolve within us and inebriate us like sweet scents.

Unlike his companions in Impressionism, M Renoir is a poet. Beneath the outward resemblance of his language and their own, the meaning of his art is quite different: it is an art whose main effect is not to arouse in us the illusion of a perfectly reproduced reality, but to release, for us, an

Théodore Rousseau (1812–67), Charles-François Daubigny (1817–78), Jean-François Millet (1814–75)

Constant Troyon (1810–65)

After the Meal. 1879. 39⅜ × 31⅞" (100 × 81 cm). Städelsches Kunstinstitut, Frankfurt.

224

COLORPLATE 77. *Blonde Bather*. 1881. 32¼ × 25⅞″ (81.8 × 65.7 cm).
Sterling and Francine Clark Institute, Williamstown, Mass.

COLORPLATE 78. *The Seine at Chatou.* c. 1881. 28⅞ × 36⅜″ (73.5 × 92.5 cm).
Museum of Fine Arts, Boston (Gift of Arthur Brewster Emmons).

COLORPLATE 79. *Rocky Crags at l'Estaque*. 1882. 26⅛ × 31⅞" (66.5 × 81.9 cm)
Museum of Fine Arts, Boston (Juliana Cheney Edwards Collection)

COLORPLATE 80. *Landscape near Menton*. 1883. 25⅞ × 32″ (65.8 × 81.3 cm).
Museum of Fine Arts, Boston (Bequest of John T. Spaulding).

image of this reality whose lines have greater sweetness, whose shades are at once lighter and more vivid, where the siren song of an eternal spring floats on the air. And thus it is that, even more than that of his companions, M Renoir's art originally surprised and shocked public taste. He had ranged against him not only the novelty of his style, but more importantly still that deeper originality which the works of poets always have, and which always makes them difficult for their contemporaries to understand. In Holland, in the past, when the good "prose writers" of painting, from Frans Hals to Gerard Dou, could get all the money they wanted from their works, the "poet" Ruysdael was so utterly despised that the dealers sold his paintings for five or six florins each. . . . Rembrandt, that other poet of Dutch painting, was less and less appreciated, as he gave himself over increasingly to his poetic genius. At each of his new "styles," dealers and public suddenly discovered the beauty of the previous one which, till then, they had derided: in precisely the same way as we are aiming to contrast Renoir's more recent paintings with those of thirty years ago, *La Loge*, the *Luncheon of the Boating Party* which, thirty years ago, met almost solely with witty mockery and howls of indignation. And let it not be thought that Watteau – with whom I am always particularly tempted to associate Renoir's name – was, for his contemporaries, the marvelous poet he is for all of us today! He had a few friends who enjoyed his painting. . . The painter of the *fêtes galantes* was criticized for the poor quality of his draftsmanship, excessive use of color contrasts, and for lowering the dignity of his art both by his choice of subject and by what we today would call his "lack of an ideal;" of all the faults that have been observed in the painting of M Renoir, there is not one that authoritative judges did not find and deplore, formerly, in the work of Watteau.

And then, gradually, eyes became accustomed to those "faults in draftsmanship," to these "orgies of color," as they had become accustomed to the chiaroscuro and impasto of Rembrandt. People realized that the *Embarkation for Cythera* was not to be regarded as a reproduction of that moderate and middle-of-the-road vision which is conventionally known as "reality," but as the evocation of a different reality, just as, through a fortunate privilege, it had been revealed to the soul of a poet. People realized that Watteau's draftsmanship and color were precisely as they had to be to make the *Embarkation for Cythera* the most charming of dreams, the living reflection of a marvelous land of enchantment, utterly imbued with tenderness and sensual pleasure. And who would then think of objecting to a "lack of an ideal" in a master who diverts us and consoles us for the ugliness of life just as much as Watteau?

The same thing will happen, the same thing is happening, with M Renoir. Already the art of this delectable poet has stopped surprising us, and all eyes have begun to feel its beauty. As false geniuses and artificially created reputations crumble – alas! how many "great painters" have we seen passing that way over the last thirty years, how many schools which, we were assured, had at last discovered the infallible formula of the beautiful – the charm of the innocent and pervasive art of M Renoir is entering us more deeply; soon, I am sure, there will be no one who does not succumb. But it will be on condition that they are willing to do so. It will be on condition that M Renoir's painting is no longer required, any more than that of Rembrandt, or Watteau, to offer an "accurate" image of reality. Because our so-called "reality" itself is only an illusion, imposed on most of us by by the mediocrity of our souls; and there is no doubt that, in all the arts, we like "prose writers" (who know this reality better than we do) to devote themselves to revealing its thousand delicate nuances to us; but, despite all their genius, constant contact with so commonplace a "reality" would finally sicken us if the genius of the "poets," by associating us with their particular vision of the world, did not afford us a glimpse of a higher reality from time to time.

Frans Hals (c. 1581/5–1666), Gerard Dou (1613–75)

COLORPLATES 31, 76

Antoine Watteau (1684–1721)

233

TÉODOR DE WYZEWA

Reflections from a Journal

1903

JANUARY 29, 1903

"You and me," our good Renoir said to me just now, "we are the two last suckers." It's true, and there's no other man whose thoughts are so close to mine nor whom I love and understand so well down to the smallest nuance. He did not speak to me today of manual labor, for the sake of the body and the spirit. He told me about the genius of Rubens, of the tremors of delight that one experiences in front of his painting.

FEBRUARY 19, 1903

I went to the home of my dear Renoir, whom I found preoccupied with the start of a large figure. I often think that is a solemn and mysterious thing for me, the fact that I am endlessly in contact with the only man of genius of my time. Each touch of the brush from this man creates for us the impression of a miracle. And it truly is a miracle to witness how with his poor deformed hands, he can transform into color, light and beauty the miserable objects he has chosen as models.

MARCH 28, 1903

Renoir has in his blood an uneasy need for change, which is aggravated by his illness. He can't stay in the same place for more than two years: his nerves become impatient and he needs to try to get better somewhere else. In this sense he has always been like Watteau, and he's very like him in many other ways.

MARCH 29, 1903

Renoir almost finished today a marvelous little portrait of Mimi reading and he has another underway of Mimi sitting in the garden which will also be mine if it's ever finished. All this is to recompense me for those few pages I wrote . . . and, really they weren't written with any thought of reward. And, in all of this, he is always so modest, with such a strange reserve, that he has not said a word to me about those pages and that I am left to divine whether they give him a little or a lot of pleasure. No matter, I praise the heaven that has blessed me with knowing and loving such a man. This is a man whose friendship people will envy me for, later, more than all the other favors that this life may bestow upon me. . . .

PIERRE-AUGUSTE RENOIR

Two Letters

August-September 1904

BOURBONNE-LES-BAINS, AUGUST 21, 1904

My dear Durand-Ruel,

. . . It seems that I have come to the right place; a lot of people here seem well-satisfied with the waters. As soon as I get even a mediocre result, I shall let you know.

Renoir attended various spas for water treatment from the 1890s onwards.

As far as the autumn exhibition goes, I think there is already too much, which won't encourage them. However, as I can do nothing about it, I shall just have to see. Please tell me in your next letter when it is going to be and I'll let you know my views.

Yours affectionately,   Renoir

BOURBONNE-LES-EAUX, SEPTEMBER 4, 1904

My dear Durand-Ruel,

. . . I am just starting my last week of treatment and find it suits me. If this continues, in a short time I hope to be able to start work again. The most awkward thing at the moment is that I can't stay seated because I am so thin: 97 pounds. That can't be called fat. My bones are sticking through my skin and so after a short time I have to stand up. I've got a good appetite, though. Let's hope I'm bound to put on a bit of weight.

At the end of the week I go back to Essoyes.

Yours affectionately,   Renoir

I'll talk to you later about the exhibition.

C.L. DE MONCADE

LA LIBERTÉ

"Renoir and the Salon d'Automne"

October 15, 1904

De Moncade: One of the big attractions, if not the biggest, of the Salon d'Automne is certainly the exhibition of the works of the painter Renoir, the Impressionist master. According to certain of our colleagues, the person who is generally portrayed as a fierce independent had always refused to have any of his paintings appear in any Salon.

Let's see how this version of the story is commented upon by the artist.

I have been to see the painter Renoir, and I confess that my first impression was one of complete stupefaction. I thought I was going to meet an ardent, impetuous man, pacing feverishly the width and length of his studio, delivering indictments, demolishing established reputations, vindictive, if not to say full of hatred, in short, an intransigent revolutionary; and he is a sweet old man, with a long white beard, a thin face, very calm, very tranquil, with a husky voice, a good-hearted manner, who welcomes me with the most amiable cordiality.

Renoir: It's a very big mistake . . . to think that I am an adversary of exhibitions. On the contrary, no one is more a proponent of them than I am, for painting, in my opinion, is meant to be shown. Now if you are astonished not to have seen my canvases in the Salons and if you want to find out why, the reason is much simpler. My paintings were rejected. The jury welcomed them – welcomed in a manner of speaking – with a burst of laughter. And when by chance these gentlemen found themselves one day in a less hilarious mood and decided to accept one, my poor canvas was placed under the moulding or under the awning so that it would go as unnoticed as possible. I estimate that I sent in canvases for about twenty years; about ten times I was mercilessly rejected; the other ten times about one out of three was taken, and placed just as I told you.

Photograph of Renoir. c. 1900. (Photo Archives Durand-Ruel.)

You see . . . my existence has been exactly the opposite of what it should have been, and it's certainly the most comical thing in the world that I am depicted as a revolutionary, because I am the worst old fogey there is among the painters.

Moreover the misunderstanding began when I was at the Ecole des Beaux Arts. I was an extremely hard-working student; I ground away at academic painting; I studied the old masters, but I did not obtain the least honourable mention, and the professors were unanimous in finding my painting execrable. I began sending canvases to the exhibitions in 63, when I was rejected, 64 rejected, 65 rejected, and so on. Let's not be unjust! I did have one canvas, just one to be exact, but indeed a canvas that was very well placed. It was, it's true, the portrait of Madame Charpentier. Madame Charpentier wanted to be in a very good position, and Madame Charpentier knew the members of the jury, whom she lobbied vigorously. This did not prevent what happened the day when I sent in the little Mendès, they were put under the awning where nobody saw them.

All these rejections and bad placements were not helping my paintings to sell, however, and it was necessary to earn enough money to buy food, which was difficult.

In 1874, we (Pissarro, Monet, Degas and I) founded the Salon of the Impressionists. We had accepted the participation of any painters who wanted to join us. There were twenty five in all, for it was surely necessary

One Renoir was accepted at the 1864 Salon and two in 1865.

COLORPLATE 75

The Daughters of Catulle Mendès *(1888) in the 1890 Salon*

The Daughters of Catulle Mendès. 1888. 63¾ × 51⅛″ (162 × 130 cm). Private Collection of the Honorable and Mrs. Walter H. Annenberg, New York.

to fill the walls. Oh! It was a great success! The public came alright, but after having made a tour of all the rooms, screeching like peacocks, they would demand their twenty sous back.

I don't know what would have become of us if Durand-Ruel, who was convinced that we would be appreciated one day, hadn't kept us from dying of hunger.

He wasn't very rich himself at that time, but he did all that he could and we owe him a great deal of gratitude. I was painting canvases then that I was selling at from twenty five to a hundred francs. One of them, *The Dancer,* was on sale at the Hotel Drouot. I myself pushed the price up to 120 francs, but since I didn't have the six louis needed to take it, one of my friends loaned them to me, and I let him have the canvas. Today it is the property of Durand-Ruel, who has refused a hundred thousand francs for it. It's strange isn't it?

COLORPLATE 27

* * *

[. . . later in the interview, De Moncade asked Renoir if he will exhibit regularly in future.]

I really don't know. To tell you the truth, I'm not the one who's exhibiting, it's Durand-Ruel who asked me to permit him to send several of my old 'canvases [to the *Salon d'Automne*]. Personally I would have preferred to exhibit some new canvases, although, fundamentally, I'm a little tired of sending things. And then, what do you want me to say? This *Salon d'Automne* seems to me fairly useless. Certainly I'm in favour of Salons, they're an excellent lesson in painting. One thinks one has a marvel which is going to bowl everyone over. In the studio it's enormously effective, and your friends come and pronounce it a masterpiece. Once in the Salon among the other canvases, it's not at all the same thing any more, and it doesn't bowl anyone over. So it's also a lesson in modesty. But there are really too many exhibitions and it seems to me quite sufficient to bother the public once a year.

De Moncade: There is my conversation with the painter Renoir. What I am unfortunately unable to reproduce here is the charming good-heartedness with which things were told to me.

LÉONCE BÉNÉDITE

THE BURLINGTON MAGAZINE

"Madame Charpentier and her Children by Auguste Renoir"

December 1907

The art historian Léonce Bénédite (1859–1925), author of a study of 19th-century painting (Paris c. 1902), discusses the past and present history of Renoir's great portrait (Colorplate 75), recently purchased by Roger Fry for the Metropolitan Museum of Art, New York.

The Metropolitan Museum of New York made last spring an acquisition which may be termed sensational: it purchased the *Portrait of Madame Charpentier* by Auguste Renoir for the sum of 92,000 francs. Whatever may have been the recent rise in the prices of the productions of the so-called "Impressionist" school, this is an enormous figure for a modern work by a living artist. Until then Degas alone had reached or passed it. It has occasionally been possible to contest the sincerity of certain valuations at public sales, reserves being based on prices artificially obtained by skillfully arranged bidding; but this case is different. The acquisition was made under conditions of incontestable good faith: 92,000 francs were really paid for this portrait.

Oddly enough, this price caused less astonishment than might have been expected. It did not make a scandal. Even those who formerly accepted the commanding position in the American market of masters officially consecrated, such as Meissonier or Jules Breton, and of them alone, raised no clamour about speculation and aberration. Can things possibly have changed in France? Alas! We dare not hope so. Artistic battles have doubtless lost some of their bitterness. The excesses in audacity or in imagination which went as far as mystification have resulted in making even the most hostile minds indifferent to the most formidable liberties of the Impressionists. Conflicts about principle have degenerated into economical quarrels, leaving only the grudges of those who do not sell or who no longer sell against those who alone are still supposed to sell.

Jean Louis-Ernest Meissonier (1815–91), Jules Breton (1827–1906)

Possibly then, it is because the raising of prices brought about in the Parisian art market by American intervention has become so general that people have resigned themselves to these unaccustomed prices. Possibly it is merely owing to a mood of weariness or indifference; or else, what is equally possible because the canvas in question had acquired an exceptional notriety.

The *Portrait of Madame Charpentier and her children* is indeed the classical work *par excellence* of Auguste Renoir. And, as such, when many another of his works was violently discussed and rejected, it was so favorably received even by his detractors that it served them as a weapon for attacking its author. The picture is very well known, for it has been exhibited several times . . . and it is one of the artist's most popular works. With the *Loge* and the little *Danseuse* in the Durand-Ruel collection, it is considered one of the principal triumphs of the Impressionist master. It belongs to the same period, being dated 1878, and it is certain that this lapse of about thirty years has aided its recognition and contributed to its charm, for the patina of time has added its warm and amber-hued harmony to a painting the technique of which, slightly rough and disconcerting at first, but fresh and healthy, becomes only richer with time.

COLORPLATES 31, 27

The *Portrait of Mme Charpentier* was exhibited at the Salon in 1879. It was accompanied by that of Jeanne Samary; and M. Duret, in "Histoire de l'Impressionisme," gives us to understand that Renoir owed his admission to the Salon less to the merit of these two works than to the names of the well-known publisher and the celebrated actress. . . .

COLORPLATE 69
Théodore Duret, Histoire des Peintres Impressionistes *(Floury, Paris, 1906)*

Nevertheless this group of works found critics indifferent. They appear not even to have shown hostility. The two fairly serious passages which are devoted to Renoir are favourable. One of the two writers, indeed, Arthur Baignières of the *Gazette des Beaux Arts,* was capable of believing that Renoir had now made an *amende honorable* for his uncompromising principles. He was doubtless given credit for special merit in not holding aloof like the others (other Impressionists) and in continuing to exhibit at the salon. We know, in fact, that Renoir, like Manet and Sisley, did not persist in defiant solitude. For a long time he took part, though irregularly, in official exhibitions, perhaps expecting medals which never came, and accepted without protest the cross offered him in 1900.

see p. 219.

In any case, it appears that these two works alarmed the public less than might have been feared. . . . Here is the passage by Baignières. . . .

". . . Monsieur Renoir, that converted rebel who is right in thinking that he has talent enough to compare with anyone else. The general effect of the *Portrait of Madame Charpentier* is very agreeable. It is gay and full of life. Ought one to take it seriously and study it a long time? Perhaps that would hardly be wise. One would discover legs that are a little. . . . But we must not quarrel with Monsieur Renoir. He has returned to the fold of the Church. Let us greet him in welcome. Let us forget the form and talk only of the colour."

"Let us forget the form!" That was always the great reproach which was brought and is still brought against the Impressionists. We are accustomed to the precise drawing of school formulas, and make no effort to understand that drawing must not be considered as the proportion of a body against a background, a kind of architectural plan which merely fixes the outlines, but as the means to succeed in giving the illusion of the appearance of the body, as seen through the play of light, in the fluid and coloured masses of air.

Castagnary's tone is bolder; the praise is less circumspect, because in this case the critic is open, in all sympathy, to the new ideas. Castagnary was, indeed, with Champfleury, Duranty and Burty – all those critics who rhymed in Y, as had been playfully observed – one of the supporters of realism. Impressionism, which is a direct derivative of realism, did not appear so distinct as it seems today from the past which gave it birth. Claude Monet, Renoir, Pissarro, like Manet, had at first followed the furrow of Courbet; and Zola, their first champion, could confuse them, in his "Salon" of 1866 with the recognised realists of this group. . . .

(see p. 119–20.)

* * *

For Renoir, his [Castagnary's] pen is animated by a truly sympathetic current. We shall not find it difficult to agree with this just and sagacious appreciation, and, what is more, extraordinary, even today very little of it need be retracted. The remark about the dumpy appearance of the figures is the only one which seems to us open to discussion, but the critic's impression is explained by the position of the figures, which are placed on the canvas in ascending perspective. Otherwise, there could hardly be a better description of this fresh, gracious and living painting, to which we are not afraid of applying the term masterpiece, a word which in these days is so much abused but which has rarely been better deserved.

M. Theodore Duret . . . tells us the state of mind of Renoir at the moment he executed this painting. His position was precarious; ill luck pursued all his pictures. The little group of the galleries of the rue Le Peletier and of the Hôtel Drouot was pursued with pitiless ridicule. A few portraits of his friends had gained him a modest success among them. Thus he hoped to find in this path a humble but assured income. The portrait of M. Choquet was the first which he accomplished. The publisher Charpentier, who, we must not forget, was Zola's publisher and had probably been drawn by him into this artistic circle, was seized in his turn by the idea of commissioning Renoir to paint a portrait of his wife. Need we say that Renoir accepted with pleasure? He had an admirable model in Madame Charpentier, a beautiful young brunette, at the zenith of her prime, with eyes shaded by long black lashes, distinguished features, a pretty well-shaped mouth, fresh and smiling. He painted an exquisite little portrait of her, a bust with the head turned three-quarters to the right against a background of tapestry, the throat veiled by a transparent black lace, a knot of white satin poised like a butterfly near the low-cut black bodice, her expression mysterious and dreamy, a smile of ardent life on the flower-like flesh of the lips, the throbbing pulses animating the face where the blood seems actually to circulate beneath the silken tissue of the skin. This charming likeness, exhibited at the rue Le Peletier in 1877, obtained a well-merited success with the limited public interested in the new movement. As to the Charpentier family, they were extremely pleased, and in the mind of the publisher, as in that of his wife, was conceived the plan which their children have today carried out, the plan of bequeathing this canvas to the Luxembourg in order that later it may take its place in the Louvre. We may be sure that it will occupy this position worthily.

Touched by his success, Renoir had the idea of using this seductive original as the motif of his picture to be exhibited at the next Salon. M. Th. Duret tells us that it was Charpentier who asked the painter for this second portrait. The youngest daughter of Charpentier, Mme Dubar, tells us on the other hand that she learned from her father that it was Renoir

The Portrait of Victor Choquet *(Colorplate 35) was not, of course, Renoir's first, not by ten years or so.*

Portrait of Madame Georges Charpentier. c. 1877. 17⅞ × 15″ (45.5 × 38 cm). Musée d'Orsay, Paris.

239

who begged for the honour of making a larger composition from the model who inspired him with confidence in a further success. Charpentier and his wife assented enthusiastically. Renoir began to work slowly and patiently, for it appears that he required a great many sittings from the amiable and gracious mother and her dainty little people.

He places her with her children in the familiar room of her home. She is seated in the middle distance, wearing a black dress trimmed with lace, the bodice fastened at the neck by a knot of ribbon but opening immediately to show the upper part of her throat. She is seated full face, her hair curling over her forehead, her right arm extended upon a bronzed leather cushion, her left hand folded on her knee, and she is watching with a pensive smile the tranquilly animated little group formed by her children. They are both dressed in pale blue, the little boy sitting on the sofa in front of his mother, the little girl on the back of a large black and white dog which is good-naturedly on the matting by which the whole floor is covered. Quite at the back, on the right, there is an armchair of Japanese style in coloured cane, and a bamboo table bearing a plate of grapes, a Dutch glass bottle and a vase of Italian earthenware full of roses. A background of tapestry serves as a warm vibrating decoration to this intimate little glimpse of happy peaceful contemplative life.

. . . Renoir is really the painter of women, and never did he paint a woman more successfully than in this famous portrait. To quote once more the realist critic [Castagnary] – with what master, with what school can this work be connected? It has often been said, yet without thereby determining his character, that he resembles Watteau in his charm, his naturalness and his persuasive warmth, and Fragonard in his imagination, his passionate love of light, his delicate sensuality and the richness of his harmonies. He is said, also, to recall the English school by the fluidity of his materials, his transparency and his brilliance. Doubtless; but is that enough . . . to connect him with the past?

There is no more disturbing figure. He has tried to paint the mobility of existing things and the elusive play of solar and atmospheric phenomena, and no one has been more mobile, more unstable and more capricious; I would add as a mark of special distinction, more deliciously unequal. No one makes such candid mistakes. But there is nothing indifferent or banal in his works; they are in themselves interesting and instructive.

Sometimes he has tried to envelop things in the fluid masses of the atmosphere, sometimes he prefers to define the form decisively in the full light of the sun. Now his brush delights to glide in the thinnest transparency of glazes; then again it lingers to spread gravely a dense impasto of colour. He is continually modifying the theme of his harmonies. Sometimes he seeks paradoxical chords among the sharpest dissonances.

* * *

He is really undefinable and that is why he is so personal. Assuredly he will remain one of the most original masters of the French school in the second half of the nineteenth century, one of those who may be most truly called "painters." He is the most ingenuous, the most spontaneous, the most attractive, the least artificial, the least inhibited by conventions and school formulas.

It is certainly to be regretted that the canvas which may be considered one of his finest works should have left France, where its place awaited it by the side of the masterpieces of our national artists. But it will carry this message of light, youth, life and joy to the gallery of a great city where French art has already found a particularly hospitable and generous refuge. And we must congratulate the curators who have added to the *Femme au Perroquet* and the *Enfant a l'Epee* by Manet the *Portrait of Madame Charpentier and her children* by Renoir, wondering at the same time whether there may not be a moral in all this to be learnt by the French museums.

PIERRE-AUGUSTE RENOIR

Preface to Cennino Cennini's
Libro dell'Arte

1910

Dear Monsieur Mottez:

Your intention to publish a new edition of your father's translation of the book by Cennino Cennini is naturally inspired by your filial piety, by your desire to give a highly deserved tribute to one of the most upright and talented artists of the last century. That in itself would be enough to make us grateful to you. But the republication of this treatise on painting has a wider significance, and it comes at the right time, which is an essential condition of its success.

So many wonderful discoveries have been made in the last hundred years that the men of today are dazzled, and seem to have forgotten that others have lived before them. It is a good thing, I believe, to remind them sometimes that they had ancestors whom they should not disdain. The publication of the present work contributes to that end.

. . . Certainly there will always be Ingres and Corots, just as there have been Raphaels and Titians, but they are exceptions, for whom it would be presumptuous to write a treatise on painting.

Those young artists who take the trouble to read Cennini's book, in which the author has described the way his contemporaries lived, will note that the latter were not all men of genius, but they were always marvellous craftsmen.

Now, to make good artisans was Cennini's only aim. Your father understood that fully.

. . . I imagine that the artist, who dreamed of restoring the art of fresco-painting to its former place, felt a great joy in translating Cennini's book.

He found in it, indeed, the encouragement to persevere in his efforts to renew the art, regardless of the difficulties it entailed.

Your father, who could have said with the poet that he had come too late into too old a world, was the victim of a splendid illusion. He believed that it was possible to do again what others had achieved several centuries before us.

He was not ignorant of the fact that the great decorative compositions of the Italian masters are the work not of just one man, but of a group of men: of a workshop where the master was the animating spirit. And it was this collaboration that he hoped to see repeated so as to give birth to new masterpieces.

The milieu in which your father worked kept his dream alive. In effect, he belonged to that phalanx of young artists who worked in the shadow of Ingres, and this fraternal group was like the workshops of the Renaissance in appearance only. For one can live only in one's own time, and ours does not lend itself to reconstituting such coteries.

. . . We can never know this métier entirely, because we are emancipated from its traditions and hence no one can teach it to us. . . .

Now, this métier of the painters of the Italian Renaissance was the same as that of their predecessors in all past ages.

If the Greeks had left a treatise on painting, you can be sure it would be identical with Cennini's.

All painting, from that of Pompeii, done by Greek artists (the boastful and pillaging Romans would probably not have left anything if it had been for the Greeks, whom they conquered but were unable to imitate), down to

The Libro dell'Arte *by the Renaissance sculpture Cennino Cennini (c.1370–c.1440), an artist's handbook, exemplified for Renoir all of the professional craftsmanship that he thought lost to the modern artist. This is part of Renoir's draft preface written in 1908/9 as a letter to Henri Mottez, who published it in Paris, 1910, in a new edition of the translation by his father, the painter Victor Mottez (1809–97).*

that of Corot, by way of Poussin, seems to have come from the same palette. Formerly all pupils learned this way of painting, under their master. Their genius, if they had any, did the rest.

... The stern apprenticeship imposed on young painters never prevented them from having originality. Raphael was the pupil of Perugino, but he became the divine Raphael nevertheless.

But to explain the general value of the older art, one must remember that over and above the master's teachings so docilely accepted there was something else, which has also disappeared, filling the soul of Cennini's contemporaries, namely the religious feeling, the most fecund source of their inspiration. And that is what gives to all their works a double character of nobility and innocence, and saves them from the ridiculous and from excess.

Among civilized people it is the conception of the Divine which has always implied the idea of order, hierarchy and tradition. If we recognize the fact that men have conceived a heavenly society in the image of an earthly one, it is still more true that this divine organization has in turn had a considerable influence on people's minds, and conditioned their ideas.

... If Christianity had triumphed in its primitive form, we would have had no cathedrals, or sculpture, or painting.

Fortunately, the Egyptian and Greek gods were not all dead; it is they who saved beauty by insinuating themselves into the new religion.

... It must be noted, however, that, along with the religious feeling, other factors helped to confer on the artisan of former times qualities which make him incomparable.

Such for example, is the rule laying down that an article shall be made, from its inception to its completion, by the same workman.

The workman could then put a great deal of himself into his work, and take an interest in it because he was doing it all himself. The difficulties he had to overcome, the taste he wanted to display, kept his brain alert: and success filled him with joy.

These elements of interest, this mental stimulation which the artisan found in his work, no longer exist.

The machine and the division of labour have transformed the work-man simply into a mechanical hack, and have killed the joy of work.

... Whatever the secondary causes of the decadence of our métiers, the principal cause, in my opinion, is the absence of an ideal. The most skilled hand is never anything but the servant of the mind. Moreover, the efforts being made to give us artisans like those of the past will, I fear, be fruitless. Even if the professional schools should succeed in producing skilled workers trained in the technique of their craft, nothing could be done with them if they had no ideal.

So we are very far, it seems, from Cennino Cennini and from painting. And yet – no. Painting is a métier like carpentry or ironmongery; it is subject to the same rules.

Those who carefully read the book so well translated by your father will be convinced of it. Furthermore, they will find in it the reason for his admiration for the old masters, and also an explanation of why they have no successors today.

Believe me, dear Monsieur Mottez,

I am yours, etc.

WALTER PACH

QUEER THING, PAINTING

"Pierre-Auguste Renoir"

1938

Walter Pach (1883–1958), American painter and writer about art, who had earlier interviewed and written about Monet (Scribner's Magazine, June 1908).

[A slightly expanded version of an article that was first published in *Scribner's Magazine* in May 1912. It is based on a series of conversations that Pach had with Renoir in Cagnes between 1908 and 1911. Pach submitted a draft for Renoir's approval. Renoir's reply included the following editorial comment in a letter of March 1911: "For instance, I mention Saint-Saëns in connection with Wagner. Saint-Saëns is an extremely talented man, and very *lively* into the bargain; I would be most unwilling to appear to criticize him, since I know little about music. I probably plucked his name out of the air, since I couldn't think of anyone to contrast with Wagner. . . . Above all, steer clear of personalities (Gauguin, for example). . . . To sum up, an interview is not literature, it's journalism. Furthermore, I can see no interest whatever in knowing whether a man ate lentils or beans, whether he was rich or poor. What's interesting is to assess the significance of the art. So: I don't know whether Homer ate lentils or beans, but he's still Homer." It is clear from what follows that Pach was sensitive to Renoir's feelings.]

* * *

If any modern painter seems a demigod to the world of today, it is Pierre-Auguste Renoir. I am sure that the beauty of his work – something to place beside that of the supreme colorists of all time – must make him appear more remote and mysterious than Monet or Rodin, his exact contemporaries. In genius he was impressive enough, but in person he was the simplest, most accessible of men. As I had written for the old *Scribner's Magazine* the account of that visit to Claude Monet . . . people encouraged me to try calling on Renoir. It appeared that no one had got him to speak for publication since 1878. . . . Vollard and Meier-Graefe were preparing books founded on intimate conversations with the great artist, but their writings were not given to the public till some years after the time I speak of – 1908.

(see pages 55, 247.)

It would have been enough for me just to have caught a glimpse of the man whose beautiful "Liseuse" I had copied in the Luxembourg, but when I presented myself at his apartment, in a quiet street of the Montmartre that he had always loved, he made me welcome, bade me stay, and expressed an almost boyish interest in the idea of speaking for an American audience. . . .

COLORPLATE 36

There were other visitors, his son Pierre, . . . M. Gangnat, the collector, who was devoted to him, and then Vollard, who was none too favorable to the idea of my writing. Once he suggested that, for my article, I simply interview Gabrielle, the model for so many of Renoir's pictures and, at that time, general caretaker of the household. She was a dear, as good to the old man as she was inspiring to paint; if we stayed too long, she would rattle the dishes or otherwise disturb him until we took the hint and left. Once she followed me to the stairs and asked if I could not do something to dissuade Renoir from working at the sculpture which he had begun on and which she feared would be too much for his strength. . . .

(see pages 308–11.)

Within a year or so afterwards, his work in clay was ended by an increase in his infirmities. When I first knew him he could still walk with the aid of two canes. Then the terrible rheumatism from which he suffered – often in the cruellest way – made all locomotion impossible, though he could still use his hands freely. Later on again, these were too crippled for him to model, though by attaching his brushes to a little clasp he continued to manipulate them, and with a mastery that increased until his last days, in December, 1919.

I do not know whether anyone has told in print of the production of the later sculptures, so I relate the wonderful tale here as his son Pierre gave it to me. Renoir had for so long had the ambition to work in the round, he was so enchanted with his progress in sculpture, that even when he became the "Raphael without hands" as Meier-Graefe called him in the last years, he refused to give up. Providentially, a young assistant was discovered, a Mexican, who was so sensitive to Renoir's thought that he could execute it in modelling under the master's guidance but without a word being said, neither artist speaking the other's tongue.

A sketch on paper by Renoir would furnish the general set-up of the mass of clay. With a light wand the old man would indicate how the work was to continue, at one place making a mark on the maquette where the ready modeling tool of the young sculptor was to cut away an excessive volume, at another place showing by a pass through the air how the contour was to swell out by the addition of more material – which the nimble fingers of the assistant molded on until the desired form was achieved. Then the figure would be turned on its pedestal and would need trimming down to compensate for an excess visible from another angle. The wand would again travel lightly down the surface of the clay, the tool in the firm hand of the young man following and scraping to the desired depth.

"They communicated by grunts when the thing got so close to the definitive result that it grew exciting," as Pierre Renoir described the scene. "My father would say, 'Eh, eh, eh – aaah! *ça y est,*' and the sculptor would be making little jabs with his tool, so much like my father's brush-strokes that you'd think the work came from his hand, as indeed it almost did; and they would be working together so closely that the young chap would say 'Eh? eh? eh?' – only with a note of interrogation that made you feel he was responding to those other grunts and did not propose to go too far by the thickness of a cigarette paper."

* * *

. . . I now give the salient features of those hours with Renoir, as I wrote them down each time at the nearest cafe, where I would go so as to let no new impression come into my mind and perhaps cause me to forget something. Try as I would, later on, I was never able to make an addition to the notes, which I merely joined together, as if all the talk had taken place on a single day.

Pach: "When you have laid in the first tones, do you know, for example, which others must follow? Do you know to what extent a red or green must be introduced to secure your effect?"

Renoir: "No I don't; that is the procedure of an apothecary, not of an artist. I arrange my subject as I want it, then I go ahead and paint it, just like a child. I want a red to be sonorous, to sound like a bell; if it doesn't turn out that way, I put more reds or other colours till I get it. I am no cleverer than that. I have no rules or methods; anyone can look over my materials or watch how I paint – he will see I have no secrets. I look at a nude; there are myriads of tiny tints. I must find the ones that will make the flesh on my canvas live and quiver.

"Nowadays they want to explain everything. But if they could explain a picture it wouldn't be art. Shall I tell you what I think are the two qualities of art? It must be indescribable and it must be inimitable. . . . The work of art must seize upon you, wrap you up in itself, carry you away. It is the means by which the artist conveys his passion; it is the current which he puts forth which sweeps you along in his passion. Wagner does this and so he is a great artist; another composer – one who

Richard Guino (1890–1973)

Venus Victorious. Bronze. c. 1914 16. H.71⅝″ (182 cm). Les Collettes, Cagnes. (Photo Jasia Reichardt.)

knows all the rules – does not do this, and we are left cold and do not call him a great artist.

"Cézanne was a great artist, a great man, a great searcher. We are in a period of searchers rather than of creators. We love Cézanne for the purity of his ideal. There never once entered his mind any thought but that of producing art. He took no heed of money or of honors. With Cézanne it was always the picture ahead of him that he cared for – so much so that he thought little of what he had done already. I have some sketches of his that I found among the rocks at l'Estaque, where he worked. They are beautiful, but he was intent on others – better ones that he meant to paint – that he forgot these, or threw them away as soon as he had finished them.

"I like so much a thing that Cézanne once said: 'It took me forty years to find out that painting is not sculpture.' That means that at first he thought he must force his effects of modelling with black and white and load his canvases with paint, in order to equal, if he could, the effects of sculpture. Later, his study brought him to see that the work of the painter is so to use colour that, even when it is laid on very thinly, it gives the full result. See the pictures by Rubens in Munich; there is the most glorious fullness and the most beautiful colour, and the layer of paint is very thin.

Renoir had visited Munich in 1910.

Here is the Velasquez . . . it is a perfect picture. See that dress with all the heavy silver embroidery that they used in Spain at the time. If you stand away from the painting, it gives you the impression of the weight of that dress. When you come close, you find that he has used only a very little pigment – a tone, and some touches for the metal. But he knew what the painter must do. Cézanne was a man of big qualities and big defects. Only qualities and defects make no difference. What counts is always that passion of the artist, that sweeping of men with him. The person who goes hunting for the defects is the professor. . . ."

[*Pach:* "Have you found, M. Renoir, that your opinions of the Old Masters change much in the course of time?"]

"No – only for some pictures it takes very long until one reaches the judgment one finally holds. With some pictures I do not think that I realised their true beauty till I had known them for thirty years – the Poussins, for example. The greatest works reveal a new beauty each year I come back to them. There is the *Marriage at Cana* [by Veronese]. I admired

Veronese, *The Marriage at Cana.*
1562. 262¼ × 354¼″
(666.1 × 899.8 cm). Louvre,
Paris.

it when I was young; one can scarcely avoid doing so; one knows that it is a great thing. But it was only at a much later time that I could feel I had something of an intimate understanding of it – of the way he has controlled the architecture of that enormous picture, and the way all those brilliant, even violent colours work together without a break.

"Titian is a man who always stays great for me. His painting is a mystery. Raphael's you can understand, and you can see how he worked (that doesn't mean that you can paint Raphaels). But you can't tell how Titian worked. No one ever painted flesh as he did. And then that *Virgin with the Rabbit* seems to have light coming out from it, like a lantern. It seems to rise above painting.

"There is nothing outside of the classics. To please a student, even the most princely, a musician could not add another note to the seven of the scale. He must always come back to the first one again. Well, in art it is the same thing. But one must see that the classic may appear at any period. Poussin was a classic; Père Corot was a classic. When I was a student, Corot was unknown, Delacroix and Ingres were laughed at. . . . That seems strange today, but it was really so. And the thing that corrupts taste is government patronage of art. Here is a case within my immediate knowledge. A rich banker had chosen among the most illustrious painters of his time to have the portraits of his family painted. These portraits are criticised, and he replies very sagely: 'I know about finance; I don't know about painting. If those portraits are bad, it is through no fault of mine, for I looked through the catalogue of the Salon, and chose the painter with the most medals, just as I would do in buying my chocolate. If I had gone to the painter you recommended, people would say I was trying to economise.'

"The bad system begins in the schools. I was in all of them and they were all bad. The professors were ignorant men; they did not teach us our trade. Even today I do not know whether my pictures will last. When I have noticed them yellowing, I have tried to find out the cause. I have changed the colours on my palette ten times and yet I cannot be certain yet that I have arrived at a choice that will yield a permanent result.

"Now this was not always so; it is only since the Revolution that the principles of the old masters have been swept away. Look at Nattier's pictures – how well they are preserved; then look at what follows and you will see what I mean. The Old Masters were taught each step of their trade, from the making of a brush and the grinding of a colour. They stayed with their teachers until they had learned well the ancient traditions of the craft. And the tradition has never been an obstacle to originality. Raphael was a pupil of Perugino; but did not prevent his becoming the divine Raphael. . . ."

Jean-Marc Nattier (1685–1766), portrait painter to Louis XV

PAUL DURAND-RUEL

A Letter Written during a Visit to Renoir

1912

Renoir is in the same wretched state, but his force of character is always astonishing. He can neither walk nor even lift himself from his armchair. Two people carry him everywhere. What torment! Yet there is the same good humor and the same joy when he is able to paint. He has done several things already and yesterday, in a single day a complete torso that he only started in the morning. It's lightly done, but superb.

JULIUS MEIER-GRAEFE

AUGUSTE RENOIR

1912

Julius Meier-Graefe (1867–1935), German art historian; his perceptive and original monograph based on first-hand knowledge of the artist was the first substantial, serious study of Renoir.

Renoir – the very name, the sound of those two syllables, conjures up melodious rhythms in the mind. The same is true of Fragonard, and this common trait probably partly explains the tendency that has arisen to speak of the two artists in the same breath. Renoir is considered as the Fragonard of our time. It is intended as an honor that he is awarded this title which, among art lovers, passes for one of the surest guarantees of glory. We shall have to examine to what extent he is worthy of this title, and to what extent this title is worthy of him. What is beyond doubt is that the harmonious epithet underlines a relationship which actually exists. Renoir is a living synthesis of our age and of the eighteenth century, a synthesis so manifest and clear that one is almost tempted to believe in a quite conscious intention on the part of its author. But it is far from being the only synthesis of this kind.

Who will ever discover everything that the great anarchists of our age owe to the curlicued style of a past so remote, apparently so hostile? Who will write the history of the Baroque in the nineteenth century, of that particularly elusive Baroque which sways the entire work of Delacroix like a great wave, which holds out against the naturalism of Courbet, with which Manet wrestled in vain; which lifted Rodin to the highest peaks and sent him plummeting into the abyss; which twirled Monet's brushstrokes in his best paintings, and provided Cézanne with the extravagant framework for his mysticism; which inspired the rapturous visions of Van Gogh and is still at work in the discreet and restrained impressionism of today's young painters, a Bonnard, or a Roussel, like the light wind which ruffles those shallow pools that are left by the sea in sand-dunes.

Alongside the forces which tend to free the spirit of modern art, alongside the new which commands our attention at once, the new which is both war-cry and rallying-cry and which took upon itself, as it were the responsibility of representation, this Baroque, which worked covertly and which is even today barely noticed, seems to us to have been the conserving element which brings unity and order to everything the revolutionary powers have shattered. These two powers combine and work together in every great French artist. Where they cannot unite and counterbalance one another, where one of them succeeds in definitively supplanting the other, where the new element excludes all participation of the Baroque, the lasting value of the result is more than merely jeopardized; and no innovation, however favorable to the organism of art as a whole, whatever beauty, in certain conditions, it may bring to the works of other, luckier artists, can save the daring innovator who has cut himself off from his past entirely. Only the old, traditional element, everything we understand by the very broad term Baroque, gives novelty strength and meaning; just as no new piece of knowledge has value except in the context of the sum total of the knowledge that man has already accumulated. The greatest beauties, and the rarest and freshest too, are to be found precisely where the synthesis is deepest, where the new is utterly pervaded with tradition while not losing anything of its creative power.

In the scarcity of its external events, the life of Renoir as we see it unfolding before us up to his seventieth year, is just such a synthesis. But the reader need not fear that this book, which is much too short for the scale of the task it sets itself, will contain many theories or hypotheses more or less problematical. By its very nature, the synthesis Renoir brings us has no room for the meditations of a pale dreamer. It would give a very

Gustave Courbet (1819–77), Auguste Rodin (1840–1917)

misleading idea of the artist's happy disposition if the things which concerned him were not treated with a touch as light as his own. Renoir's earliest works give no hint that he might become the Fragonard of our time. He aims at expressing what he sees with the greatest possible vivacity. The first paintings of his that we know represent man in nature, and reflect the astonishment he himself felt in seeing human forms in the midst of nature. The fine painting in these works cannot conceal the very primitive character of the impression. Their strength enters us so deeply only because it avoids circuitous routes. This is the period of Courbet's influence. No other Impressionist reveals this influence as patently as Renoir at the beginning of his career. It is like a meeting of two kindred spirits, and indeed certain common traits persisted. It seems that Renoir was born with something of Courbet's animal instinct. He has that same productive energy, for which no canvas is too large, and the same speed of execution. It seems likely that Manet, Cézanne and Degas together have not produced as much as Renoir alone. He himself estimates the number of his canvases at two or three thousand. This is the fecundity which we like to associate with the enthusiasm of genius. But it is also something he shares with the master from Ornans. Renoir's maturest and richest pictures do not have the bravura that distinguishes those of his predecessor. It is reasonable to wonder whether one may truly attribute him with that deftness of touch before which all difficulties melt away, the virtuosity

There is no complete oeuvre catalog, but the total of extant works is believed to be around 6000.

Bathers. 1916. 28¾ × 35½" (73 × 90 cm). © The Barnes Foundation, Merion, Pa.

which enabled Courbet to juggle with all the secrets of the old masters. Renoir has one advantage over him. This advantage is not a painter's gift; it is not a sensory gift, it lies beyond the fingertips, beyond the eye. It is more a matter of placing man above man than artist above artist, and it helps us to determine Renoir's position among the other great artists of his time. He is the most natural among them. More natural than Courbet, despite, or rather actually because of, Courbet's naturalist doctrine, more natural than Manet, Cézanne or Degas, despite all the revelations that they brought us about Nature, which is all the artist has to look for. And this is because the physical and mental tension of the man confronting nature does not occur in Renoir with such violence, because he is the most innocent among them, because in his works, alongside a great magnificence, alongside a natural talent, cultivated to the last nicety, alongside the greatest daring and most sober wisdom of a great master, there is a childlike laughter, a voice of Nature, primitive and irresistible. All the others carry the hallmark of our time, the sign of the struggle. They wrestle with nature, tug it violently towards them, and their daemon contorts their movement. He alone seems born with it, like a Greek, a Poussin, a Mozart. He paints as the bird sings, as the sun shines, as buds blossom. Never has anyone created with less artifice. His is the movement of the infant towards its mother's breast: an instinct which becomes a life's work.

* * *

Fragonard, *Bathers*. c. 1765. 25½ × 31½″ (64.7 × 80 cm). Louvre, Paris.

The Folkwang Museum at Hagen in Westphalia owns Renoir's first masterpiece, the *Lise* of 1867. There is a story behind this painting. It originally belonged to Théodore Duret, who had met Renoir in 1872 at the home of Degas. According to his account, the painter then had the air of a total Bohemian and appeared literally penniless. Degas praised Renoir's talent and, thereupon, Duret went off to look at some of his paintings, scattered among various small dealers in Montmartre. For four or five hundred francs he bought the portrait of a young girl (the second *Lise*) mentioned above, which is now in the National Gallery in Berlin. When he met Renoir again, the latter naturally expressed his delight at having sold his canvas, but added that there were still better ones available. Duret was extremely eager to see more. Renoir finally admitted that he had a large number of canvases in a studio which were not bad at all but that, not having been able to pay the rent, he had been forced to leave the studio and leave the paintings with the concierge as security; that the latter had permission to sell them all and that Duret might perhaps buy some of the canvases and thus pay his debts which amounted to 700 francs; and that indeed there might be a little money over for Renoir himself. Duret went to see the studio, found a large number of paintings, including the *Lise* which he particularly liked. The canvas was rolled up in a corner on the floor because the concierge had sold the frame. No one had wanted the painting. Duret offered 1200 francs for it, an exorbitant sum for the time, and Renoir accepted with delight. A small drawing after this canvas is on the cover of Duret's booklet entitled "The Impressionist Painters" (Heymann and Perois, Paris 1878). Duret later exchanged this painting with Durand-Ruel for the Puvis which is now with Moreau-Nélaton. Durand-Ruel did not think much of the canvas and sold it some six years ago to Osthaus for ten times the price Duret had paid. A tenfold multiplication of this figure would scarcely be more than the current commercial value of the canvas.

* * *

Now let us look at some figures. On March 24, 1875, Durand-Ruel organized a sale of paintings by Monet, Sisley, Renoir and Berthe Morisot at the Hôtel Drouot. On the day of the viewing, there were wild scenes of scandal which degenerated into scuffles, and the sale could take place only with police intervention. The twenty paintings by Renoir together fetched 2251 francs. And again, according to Durand-Ruel, some prices were "pushed" by friends and had to be reimbursed after the sale. There were several masterpieces among these paintings: *The Spring* was withdrawn at a bid of 110 francs (30 years later Durand-Ruel sold it for 70,000 francs to the Prince de Wagram). *Before Bathing* was sold for 140 francs to the collector Hecht (he later sold the painting to Duret. At the Duret sale, on March 19, 1894, Durand-Ruel bought the canvas for 4900 francs). *Fisherman with Rod and Line* was knocked down to the publisher Charpentier for 180 francs (at the Charpentier sale, in 1907, the painting made 14,050 francs). The highest price, of 300 francs, was paid for one of the artist's finest early landscapes, *View of the Pont Neuf*. On May 28, 1877, 45 paintings by Caillebotte, Pissarro, Renoir and Sisley were sold at the Hôtel Drouot. Durand-Ruel, who organized the sale, did not attend it because the second Impressionist exhibition, which he had organized a short time before in his own premises, had once again unleashed a storm of indignation and he hoped to soothe tempers in this way. The outcome was the same. Renoir's sixteen paintings brought in 2005 francs. Prices changed little during the next ten years. The portrait of Madame Charpentier and her children was purchased from Renoir by his friend the publisher Charpentier, for 300 francs (it made 84,000 francs in 1907 at the Charpentier sale.) The portrait of the actress Samary which figured with the *Charpentier* family at the Salon of 1879, one of the artist's loveliest works, was brought by Durand-Ruel from the artist for 1500 francs. (He

COLORPLATE 7

Summer (COLORPLATE 6)

The Spring. c. 1895. 25¾ × 61¼" (65.5 × 155.5 cm). © The Barnes Foundation, Merion, Pa.

(Daulte 144)

COLORPLATE 33

COLORPLATE 24

COLORPLATE 75

COLORPLATE 69

sold it to the Prince de Polignac and bought it back from him about 1890 for 8000 francs. The painting then passed through different collections and was finally bought, some years ago, by the collector Morosoff, of Moscow, for a large sum.) At the Hoschede sale, in June 1878, three paintings by Renoir together fetched 156 francs. They were the *Bridge at Chatou* (42 francs), *Young Girl on a Bench* (30 francs, currently in Durand-Ruel's private collection) and the *Girl with a Cat* which was exhibited in Paris in 1900 at the Centennial (84 francs), also in Durand-Ruel's gallery. After 1880 prices rose slowly. The *Mussel Fishers at Berneval* was bought from Renoir by Durand-Ruel for 2500 francs. The first Renoir exhibition which was organized by Durand-Ruel in an apartment in his house, 9 Boulevard de la Madeleine, from April 1-25, 1883, and for which Duret wrote a short introduction, had a certain success in a limited circle. But in 1900 one could still buy a number of paintings for almost nothing. The portrait of *Mme Henriot as a Page*, today one of the jewels of the Prince de Wagram's collection, hung for a long time in the window of a junk-shop in rue de Rennes. The dealer had chalked the asking price, 80 francs, on the canvas. Another painting from the same collection, *The children of Catulle Mendès* (Salon of 1890) made 100 francs for the gallant painter, whose situation was still very precarious, by his friend (!) Catulle Mendès. But even the going price for works not belonging to the particularly highly-valued period of 1870-80 was very modest in the big sales of recent years. Renoir's major work, *Children's afternoon at Wargemont* (National Gallery in Berlin), with an estimate of 20,000 francs at the Bérard sale in May 1903, was sold for 14,000 francs. In his "Impressionist painters" Duret gives a detailed account of the difficulties Renoir had as Caillebotte's executor, at his death in 1894, to get even a portion of the bequest accepted by the Luxembourg Museum. I still remember the horror originally inspired by the salle Caillebotte.

(Daulte 148)
COLORPLATE 64

(Daulte 292)

(Daulte 123)

PAGE 236

COLORPLATE 91

* * *

Fragonard has painted the indolent abandon of the dreaming woman, and often with great mastery. And yet, when looking at a Renoir [Sleeping Girl with a Cat] we cannot help feeling a certain disdain for Fragonard's somewhat superficial eroticism. Under Renoir's spell, one might almost feel that the famous painter of eighteenth century women held an artificial being before his gaze.

COLORPLATE 64

Renoir painted several hundred similar paintings. Always young girls, sleeping, seated, lying down, naked, dressed, absorbed purely by their dreams, women in the first flower of youth with their children. Their very quantity has been criticized. One might reproach Rubens for the same thing with equal justice. He who blames quantity has no sense of nuance where nuance is all. There are thousands of individuals in this great family, which is bounded by beauty alone. What makes them alike – the painter's sense of color and form – seems to get to the very essence of woman which no individual difference can efface, and indeed their very resemblance guarantees for us the vital energy of these creatures. The common mark of the species is no obstacle to extreme variety. There are working girls, good bourgeois girls, aristocratic girls. We do not distinguish them at first glance, the painter does not make use of tired, superficial distinctions; it is in his nudes that Renoir reveals their class. There we see the solid country girl who, in the midst of all the wretchedness of the big city, retains the delicious simplicity we so often admire in the little Parisiennes. Here we have the born city-dweller, slender and graceful. She looks more natural than connoisseurs of the Frenchwoman are disposed to admit. But does the connoisseur look deeply enough into this contradictory being, who preserves within her an indestructible fund of joie-de-vivre? Many of these young Renoir women may be seen on the streets of Paris even today, by those with sharp eyes. The type is at least as genuine as that of Lautrec's *cocottes*. Here we have the spoilt pampered beauty, strutting in her opulent train, with a greedy brashness just perceptible in her expression and bearing, leading her gentleman while allowing herself to be led by him. Here she is, dancing at Bougival in a cheap summer dress, all given over to Sunday revelry. One finds relatively few such scenes which resemble genre paintings, but which a powerful hand, able to garner and to concentrate, raises infinitely higher than the "genre." Renoir has no need of man to paint a woman as he sees her. He gives her only what she gives to men. Her instinct rises above sexual relations, which debase and falsify her image. He prefers to show us a woman alone, thereby reaching out towards the enchanted aloofness of the divine feminine principle in our world. Or he may show her with a woman friend, a confidante, he shows the completeness of tender relations to which the male world, today coarser than ever, can never aspire.

Anyone who criticizes these works in terms of quantity does not love womankind, does not know her range, is himself poor in spirit. One might just as well criticize those ever-burgeoning rose-trees one sees in the gardens of ruined mansions, and which outlive all of man's labor, because they are putting forth new blooms. Life flows in great waves from the hundreds and hundreds of women's eyes, women's lips, women's breasts. Renoir puts before us a divine celebration of flesh, still innocent of desire, not yet tainted by passion; still idyllic and yet brimming with powerful sensuality. The love of these superb creatures is not unsettling. We have the evidence in Renoir's children. Who ever painted such babies? The "putti" of the old Italian masters look like stage props in comparison. Besides, how could an age that did not risk everything in the name of color ever have rendered that colored and yet formless thing that is young flesh?

But anyone who sees Renoir purely as a colorist has never really seen him. Of course color – his particular color and no other – the blue and pink swimming in white which, even when it is completely exposed, seems to be merely the outer skin of richer colors which burn in the depths – this color is his alone, it envelops him as the body envelops the soul. Only he can speak in this way. His language sounds like the voice of a close friend whose every new word is a repetition of all the other words he has ever spoken. We shall probably never be able to disengage ourselves from this mark of his art, we would never want to have to do without it, we can never exhaust its mystery, nor admire it enough. It is the key which has let us into an enchanted castle. But once one has entered it completely, once one feels as at home in his world as with a close friend, then the key is no longer just the key, the mark no longer just the mark, and the means which guided us seems to us a small thing in comparison with the bounty which is revealed to us. We would then like to command words to fall silent. We no longer see with our usual sense organs, we have no more need of signs. Where is the man who, touched to the depths of his being by the power of a thought, would pause to meditate on the mere sound of the words which transmitted it to him?

The role of colorist is too narrow for a Renoir, just as it seems to us too finite for a Rubens or a Delacroix. The work flows before our eyes like a broad river. Its waves, in which magical images shimmer and reflect one another, transport us upwards into the sphere of a lofty vision. This vision is Renoir, it is more than his palette, it has a higher value, it is more rare, unique. Our epoch has its intellects. We make astonishing analyses and reduce the world to a couple of numbers. Here, we find a man who, from the mists of the great city, conjures up a garden flowing with milk and honey, peopled with beings who have never known decay. He creates them of flesh and blood, without phantasmagoria, with a light which skims the surface of living models; he kneads them from our earth, abandoned as it is by the gods, with our materialism, as naive as a Giotto, as frothy as a Rubens. None of the great men of France in the last century has given such a convincing testimony to the lasting health of this people, tales of whose

Portrait of a Young Girl. Sanguine heightened with white. Drawing. c. 1906. 23¼ × 18⅛″ (59 × 46 cm). Louvre, Paris.

corruption and decline are on everybody's lips. Nothing is less surprisng than that this Parisian art, bursting with color as it is, should have produced yet another colorist. As this painter is a great artist, he must inevitably contribute in some way to a positive development, a sense of progress. One is the consequence of the other. But that in our day such positivism could have been so clearly formulated, that the country of the great sceptics and petty cynics should have produced so obvious a statement of a joyous affirmation of life – that might pass for incredible, but miraculously so.

* * *

It was in this great bathing scene of 1885, in the Blanche collection, that Renoir first used a type of bather he had just created in the composition of a painting with several figures. . . . In this painting we see a lakeside spot in a wood with five young girls on the bank or in the water. Two are seated or lying on their bathing towels; a third is standing in the water and threatening to splash another, who has already dried herself and who is lifting her hand and legs to protect herself; in the background, in the water, are two other young girls, one in the pose we already know, with her hands in her hair.

COLORPLATE 97

This picture has an important part to play in the master's work. He worked on it for a long time, did a large number of drawings in preparation for it, and went back to this subject on several occasions. It represents one of Renoir's culminating points, not the only one, not the highest one, just as the development of which it is the climax is not the only one in his fertile existence. It is a rallying point; it offers the most precious information to the critic. It is from here that, looking forwards and backwards, one may best survey Renoir's work as a whole and – those many supporters of Renoir who deny this work their approval must grant me this at least – it is alone of its kind; there is no other in nineteenth century French painting which offers such great insights of this sort.

Of the five girls in the picture, only the three in the foreground really matter; the two others, of whom only fragments are visible, are part of the movement of the water and have been added by the landscape-painter, as the drawings prove. The decrease in the number of figures, which we already observed in the stage which separates the two major works which precede it, the *Moulin de la Galette* and the *Luncheon of the Boating Party*, is thus already carried a little further here. Multiplicity, which the Impressionist had needed to give life to his picture, disappears to the advantage of the type. And with the type, the linear element is emphasized. Composition, in the sense it had with the old masters, emerges more strongly here than in any other painting. And in no other painting does Impressionism so recede into the background. The bodies are not formed by means of a loose play of patches of color which leaves to the eye the task of composing the image. They rise up before us, hard and firm as calligraphic signs, formed of a dense substance that one could take for enamel obtained by dissolving mother of pearl. One cannot imagine anything more foreign to the spirit of Manet, Cézanne and Monet than these bodies.

COLORPLATES 53, 76

But if the means themselves do not seem to be modern in appearance, the spirit of the author of this picture remains nonetheless very close to our own. We feel Renoir in as positive a way as we see these bodies; he has simply taken on a firmer outline than before, a more definitive form. The new style comes from the old, but rises above many of his earlier creations, and we enjoy his independence from the fashion of the day in the same way as we do the proud stance of a monument, scornful of all that is small.

The sources of this work are to be found far back in time. The artist's immediate sources of inspiration remain in the wings, even Ingres, whom one might think of first of all. Ingres would have been beside himself if anyone had thought him capable of showing four legs thrashing in a single corner of the canvas. Of the twenty or thirty women in the *Turkish Bath*,

Le Bain Turc *(1862) by Ingres*

253

barely four feet are visible. There is a new spirit implicit in this break with
the traditional decorum which conceals everything that might jeopardize
the solemnity of the pose. Renoir's form is extracted from an infinitely
more abundant raw material, and it thus has a far richer range of
variations. No doubt something of the feminine world of the *Turkish Bath*
has gone into the *Bathers,* but everything additional in Renoir is not in the
Turkish Bath. Ingres' naked slaves are seated in the cramped space like
dolls which marvelously reflect some aspects of the woman. Their
existence is as limited as that of women in a harem and they look like rare
hothouse plants. Renoir's young girls are in the open air and one senses
that they are free agents. Their harem is nature. Here again, despite the
severity of the forms, it is as if no restraint inhibits their being. The vision
of Ingres never penetrated so deeply, never did he give so powerful a sense
of depth as that of Renoir's figure in the middle ground, which embraces
space in all dimensions. And, in just the same way, this whole picture,
which speaks to us so profoundly, also seems to encompass a vast expanse
of time and of artistic culture. One would have to go back well before
Ingres, and deep into earlier centuries, to find remotely similar forms.
Elsewhere I have compared the *Bathers* and the painting by Fragonard
which bears the same title, but without reaching any conclusion. We know
how much of the eighteenth century there is in Renoir. It provided him
with everything that could be called decorative in his work. The panels
made for Blanche, and more particularly the decoration executed for
Charpentier, works which were done shortly before the *Bathers,* are
inspired by the eighteenth century. They are light, flimsy improvizations

Girardon, *Nymphs Bathing.* Iron
bas-relief (detail). 1668/70. Allée
des Marmouseïs, Versailles.
(Photo Bulloz.)

254

that could have decorated the salon of Mme Du Barry, for instance. There is nothing of all this in the present painting. M Blanche, its owner, put me on the scent. At his suggestion, I found the model for our work in the park at Versailles, among the lead reliefs of the beautiful ornamental pool on the Allée des Marmousets. The reliefs are by Girardon, who made so many lovely things for the gardens at Versailles, and they represent Diana bathing. Naked women play in the water; some are lying at the water's edge. Among them is a figure whose pose resembles that of the main figure in our painting. The little one who is in the water and about to splash the other, is there too, the whole scene is similar. Renoir copied it. So far I have not managed to find this drawing. Blanche saw it; it was in the possession of the painter and collector Maître, Renoir's friend. The resemblances are even more pronounced in one of the first sketches where the composition still included seven figures (Collections of Vollard and the Prince de Wagram).

Jacques-Emile Blanche

These are essentially just common elements of subject matter. . . . The forms have scarcely anything in common. One feels the presence of the relief in Renoir's painting, but the way it is expressed far surpasses the sprightly play of Girardon's delicate figures, which give the surface of the work a picturesque movement similar to that of the lapping of waves. In Renoir's work, we find quite other rhythms of French art, older, flowing more powerfully. Harsher representations of women come to mind, a prouder physique, a Diane de Poitiers, the soaring lines of a haughtier painting, that bright, fresh, youthful painting by an unknown seventeenth century painter, the jewel of a now completely vanished school which graces one of the rooms in the Louvre: the *Diana the Huntress*. There are pictures whose power brings up a whole series of forgotten connections, like a young prince entering a room long abandoned by his forebears and sending long-gathered dust flying from the walls at the sound of his voice. The trees in Fontainebleau, where the young Renoir painted his *Lise*, part to reveal the turreted castle of the lavish Francis I, who summoned artists to his court from Italy. Behind Primaticcio, the leaders of the old school of Fontainebleau, we see the great masters of the sister-nation. They seem reborn in a new guise, quickened by a breath of the freedom which pervades the work of their descendant. All the grandeur of Latin art, allied to the pure joie-de-vivre – and what would not emerge happily with it in this exultant art – seems to come to life again.

Prince de Wagram (1883–1918), a prodigious collector in the 1900s

Francesco Primaticcio (1504–70)

* * *

It is not so much as a painting among so many masterly paintings that Renoir's *Bathers* (and the other works linked to it) are important – arguably, at least – but because it is one of those pointers, infinitely rare in our time, which show the way towards a simple monumental form, obtained without compromise and without abandoning essentials. I say a pointer, and I do not claim that the aim has already been reached. The artist's will alone is not enough for such a task, as we know. We still have nothing more than one easel painting before us. But the same is true of this work as of so many paintings by Márees, in whose presence we feel that mere mechanical enlargement would suffice to turn them into a monument. The only thing lacking now is our inability to feel the need of worthy monuments of our style and our way of thinking.

Hans von Marées (1837–87), German painter

And it is on this reef, clearly, that this period of our master was to founder. There was no State to commission a monument from this artist. . . .

Renoir did not pursue this line any further, but he tried to transfer the results he had achieved to other areas of his activity. Many paintings of this period have a touch of the severity of the *Bathers*. Form, which had always seemed to gain by opening itself to colors, now tightens again and seeks at the same time to augment this intensity of color. A scheme governing both color and line gives the freest subjects a power which the painter had never before achieved. Yet this scheme does not hamper the artist's creative power. The works Renoir painted around 1885 leave the rich harvest of the years 1870-80 far behind. The inner richness of these works is maintained too, but on a far higher level. We are struck by a more coherent, more powerful vision, one which in some way redoubles the multiplicity of motifs.

* * *

Not all Renoir's champions will implicitly accept my judgment on the works of the last period, to say nothing of those uncommitted people who do not know Renoir at all. . . . The paintings of this last period are like young wine: they need to be left to mature. In the past Renoir had never worried about the material quality of his colors and of their rational use from a technical point of view, and to this he attributes this or that inadequacy of his earlier work. Today, he is also concerned about the effect of the passing of time on colors and color contrasts, and he heightens all the tones which, subsequently, tend to lose their intensity, in particular the lakes. Hence the exaggerated red of certain flesh tones. The colors "ferment" for several years until they blend perfectly into a beautiful enameled surface.

Many find his range of colors cloying. But these delicate folk have no sense of delicacy for those things which truly warrant it. They cheerfully devour paintings by the dozen at exhibitions, mentally convert the Renoir they see into a coarse-grained image, similar to those hideous three-color prints where any remotely delicate shading is done away with and where all that remains is the mauve, the candy-floss pink and blue white, accredited symbols of conventional taste. They do not see the tones that lie between these overworked extremes of a rich and original range, and reason just like those literacy wiseacres who think that the rhyme "fire" and "desire" must inevitably belong to the poetry of love-lorn school girls. Perhaps the vision of the former painter on porcelain does indeed reflect a color symbolism typical of his time, and somewhat vulgar. But in my view it is a rare advantage still to be able to find this popular scheme in the artist's most opulent variants.

Probably, opinion on Renoir's most recent works would change if they were more readily accessible. The public collections, which in any case are only beginning to take an interest in Renoir, contain nothing of this period (the few paintings of his last period given to the Louvre in the bequest of Count Camondo have not greatly changed the situation). Exhibitions, as a general rule, neglect the old Renoir for the young. The review of Renoir's works, organized in 1904 by the Salon d'Automne, took place a little too early for this period. Dealers have only isolated paintings, and in fact no period of Renoir lends itself less to being surveyed piecemeal. A few works suffice to acquaint us with the previous ones. The latest one, whether this is to its advantage or not, rests precisely on the wealth of the variations. The great dance panels may be his most remarkable work of all, and may rightly pass for the culmination of Renoir's decorative art; and yet even had they never existed, its richness would not have been diminished thereby. This richness, this superabundance, is a characteristic trait of a son of Delacroix and a grandson of Rubens. We cannot and would not wish to imagine his old age any other way. The three previous periods are great rivers on whose majestic banks no one can pause without pleasure. They have come together and now flow along a hundred branches towards the river mouth. None of these branches has banks as powerful as the three rivers. But the territory watered by them is Renoir's happiest domain. It is an empire on which the sun never sets.

The collection of Count Isaac de Camondo (1851–1911) was bequeathed in 1908 and entered the Louvre in 1911.

OCTAVE MIRBEAU

RENOIR

1913

Mirbeau's book was published on the occasion of a large Renoir exhibition, of 52 works, at Bernheim-Jeune, Paris.

In this exhibition and this book containing his complete works year by year we see Renoir as the equal even of those whose glory is firmly rooted in universal acclaim. And yet it is among us that he lives and paints, paints and lives. His painting is inseparable from the man himself. Other painters have set themselves problems, the great problems. They have given us sonorous meditations on the purpose and limits of life, the relation between art and life and the place of art in life and life in art. Esthetes, critics, philosophers, apostles and pedants all offer us an explanation of the world when they condescend not to save it. They have solved all the problems, as if life were a problem, as if there were some solution to life other than life itself, and as if a picture were something other than the happiness that it wrests from nature and gives to men. Renoir has been painting. And I can imagine the astonishment of the beautiful women and young poets. He has been painting, yes painting, in the true sense. Since when has a painter needed to paint?

Renoir paints as you or I breathe. For him, painting has become the corollary of vision. Other people's eyes cannot resist the temptation to wander. But with Renoir his hand has to set down in space the happiness he has seen with his eyes. That is why, even outside his working hours, he is often to be seen on a walk or a journey, covering minute pieces of cardboard cartons, painting what is in front of him: sunflowers growing in a level crossing keeper's garden, a wall, bench or flowerbed, anything.

Not only has he refrained from saving the world: he has even refrained from saving France. Ever since a young student resolved to conquer Morocco to save Poussin's pictures from the Muslims, painters have thought of their mission as being patriotic, social and traditionalist. They unearth Poussin's Italian formulae as an architect would reconstruct a seventeenth-century façade for a world exhibition, just as one day – or so we might hope – Brittany and the Massif Central will be transformed into a Trianon garden. It is not a question of painting but of defending tradition, which is an indivisible whole whether we are talking about painting, literature or politics. First you have to learn the tradition. If you know that, then according to your own inclination you will be able to paint pictures, write books, sculpt statues, or govern and colonize as necessary. Painting, painting nature, being moved by it and summoning up all your strength to come close to it – what madness! I will go so far as to say: how shameful! When you have a tradition which is sufficient for everything and self-sufficient, a closed system like that of the universe where nothing is either lost or created, a tradition which is like an animal who, on the pretence of biting its tail, thinks it is a perfect, unbreakable circle. Why not paint this tradition, this archetype, this canon?

As a young man, Renoir is reported as saying: "I never believe I am saving the Republic when I paint."

Against the unending succession of artistic themes, doctrines, esthetics, metaphysics and physiologies, Renoir's work has developed by the year, by the month and by the day, as simply as a flower opens out its petals or a fruit ripens. Renoir has not given a thought of fulfilling his destiny. He has lived and painted. He has done his job. It is perhaps there that his genius lies. Furthermore, his whole life and work are a lesson in happiness. He has painted joyfully, with joy enough not to shout from the rooftops that joy in painting that sad painters proclaim lyrically. He has painted women and children, trees and flowers with the admirable sincerity of a man who believes that nature is at the disposal of his palette as simply as if it had been created from all eternity to be painted.

He is no prophet. He does not have a self-appointed mission to pronounce the last judgment on the soul of things. Their appearance is enough for him. He paints neither the soul nor the mystery nor the meaning of things because you can reach a little of their meaning, mystery and soul only if you pay attention to their appearance. Therein is the secret of his youthfulness and joy. Nature is amenable and indulgent only towards those who trust in nature and do not demand its great secrets all at once. He shares the optimism of all those who surrender to the twin forces of nature and instinct. Like a scholar who does not pretend to know his subject but tests it in its manifestations with a meticulous, ingenuous optimism, so Renoir has followed the most subtle movements from one color and one nuance to another. The world lies before him like a rainbow, whose colors are shaded and distributed differently with each new picture.

Renoir is perhaps the only great painter who has never painted a sad picture. Joy with him is no more willed than it is chance. It summons him to his craft as naturally as light bathes objects and reveals them. When the eyes of a Renoir contemplate objects he witnesses their constantly renewed immersion in light, a light which is itself visible. A double serenity is born in him out of the joy he feels in looking at them and the certainty he has of equating the image he reconstructs of them with the image which he receives. He knows that the world is there and that he is there to depict it.

He is ill. His hands are painful. His misshapen fingers find it difficult to hold a brush. Anybody else might be said to be infirm, but not him, since he can still paint and makes no distinction between work and happiness. What sorrow could he know? Even the thought of death holds no bitterness for him who believes in external beauty and loves it more than himself. A great artist thinks of death with the peacefulness of a faithful witness who will leave the court with a clear conscience having delivered his testimony.

As in company with Monet and Pissarro he opposed the academics of 1875, so he offers the same healthy opposition to the academics of 1913. Today he appears younger and even more necessary than in 1875. For the painters of anecdotal, naughty or sentimental canvases are not only in the official Salons. In their hypocritical imitations of Poussin and Cézanne they have tried to corrupt the very tradition which gave life to Renoir.

Nature herself seems grateful for the faith he has placed in her. The effects of oxydation and patina were never completely favorable to any painter. His canvases have aged magnificently. And now he looks ahead: his skills seems to prejudge the future as it delights in the present. In his recent works the color seems intemperately youthful. It has that acidity which is retained only by fruit that has ripened too soon. The years will add a still fuller harmony, brought about by nature and foreseen by Renoir, as if nature, through the humblest effects of the physical world, sought to bring her mysterious contribution to the man who could enhance and expand the visible world.

Photograph of Renoir in His Studio. 1912. (Photo Archives Durand-Ruel.)

MARY CASSATT

Letters

January 1913 – February 1914

Mary Cassatt (1844–1926), American painter who exhibited in four of the Impressionist exhibitions.

I must take some of your nuts to Renoir, who suffers at times greatly, senile gangrene of the foot. His wife I dislike and now that she has got rid of his nurse and model, she is always there. He is doing the most awful pictures or rather studies of enormously fat red women with very small

This must refer to Gabrielle Renard, who left Renoir's house after nearly 20 years, apparently to marry.

heads. Vollard persuades himself they are fine. J. Durand-Ruel knows better.

Joseph Durand-Ruel (1826–1928), eldest son of Renoir's dealer

* * *

I have only to look around me ... to see Degas a mere wreck, and Renoir and Monet too.

* * *

I saw Renoir this afternoon, very well and painting and with pretty color, no more red. Madame was not there, she had gone to Nice. He told me she was also very well. But their cook told Mathilde that that wasn't true, that she was not herself and that she (the cook) thought that her diabetes was going to her head. The woman has been in her service a very long time. Now he won't follow a diet, but they say if you go to Vichy regularly it isn't necessary.

Renoir's wife, Aline

Renoir was taking water treatment at various spas.

AMBROISE VOLLARD

RENOIR, AN INTIMATE RECORD

"The Family"

1925

... Then war broke out.

The two eldest sons, Pierre and Jean, enlisted immediately.

I had gone to the Renoirs' to ask for news of them. There were other callers. Everybody was optimistic.

Dorival, the actor, a friend of the family, had just brought an "extra" which announced a thunderous advance in Lorraine.

Everyone was discussing the event, when Monsieur Z., a deputy, arrived with further tidings.

"I have just left the War Ministry," he said, still a little out of breath from having run up the stairs four at a time. "The ministers have just had a conference, and the government thinks that the Russian steam-roller will reach Berlin by the first days of October [1914] at the latest. ..."

Renoir had taken up his brushes, but he was so tormented by the thought of his sons that he was unable to finish the little still-life – a cup and two lemons – that he was working on. "I can't paint any more!" he said of a sudden, letting his arms fall. Madame Renoir, who was knitting a soldier's muffler, took off her glasses, looked at her husband, and without saying a word, stifled a sigh and lowered her hand again over her work. Renoir, in an effort to hide his apprehension, started to work again, but mechanically – it was the first time I had seen him paint without passion. He began to hum one of his favorite airs, a tune from *La Belle Hélène*. But there was no life in it.

La Belle Hélène, *the opera by Offenbach*

Nevertheless, news from the "children" arrived regularly. The graphic letters they wrote to their parents confirmed what the papers said about the joyous life of the *poilus*. Renoir and his wife were beginning to breathe freely again, when out of the clear sky came the news that Pierre, the eldest, was in a hospital at Carcassonne; "I hope that Jean –".

poilus = *"tommies," First World War soldiers*

But Jean, unable to bear the inactivity which was the fate of the cavalry, secured a transfer to the Chasseurs Alpins.

"Just think, mamma, I have a *béret.* . . ." The *béret* was the cap the Blue Devils were so proud of.

And then word came that Jean was in the hospital at Gérardmer.

"At least he isn't fatally wounded," said Madame Renoir, reading the letter to her husband.

"I suppose not," said Renoir, forcing himself to be calm. Jean took it as a joke. His thigh had been punctured by a bullet.

"The doctor," he wrote, "tells me my leg will be stiff for some time. What luck! They'll be taking me for an officer now!" Madame Renoir left for Gérardmer the same day.

"You'll see," said Renoir. "I know perfectly well that if I receive a telegram with too many details, it will be because they want to hide something from me."

A short and optimistic despatch arrived; but Renoir was not in the least reassured.

"I'm sure they are going to cut off his leg. I think I'll write to Clémentel. You laugh because I'm thinking of asking the Minister of Commerce to keep them from cutting off a leg? You know very well that nobody is in his right place in this war. Think of the director of a theatre as chief surgeon of a hospital! Doctor Abel Desjardins was reprimanded by the Undersecretary of State for Hygiene because his report, in proportion to the number of beds in his ward, did not show as many amputated arms and legs as the ward next door."

My bedroom was next to Renoir's; I could hear him moaning, all night. The least distraction kept him from sleeping, and in his restless condition, his infirmities gave him particular trouble, but did not lessen his energy. When he was seventy-eight, he was carried groaning to the studio, after a sleepless night, and his strength came back under the stimulus of his work.

The telephone rang. It was the Cagnes Post Office, which was rather far from *Les Collettes,* calling to give the contents of a telegram that had just arrived for Renoir. Jean was to keep his leg. He had fallen into the hands of a major who preferred to let the leg get well rather than cut it off – an ambitionless major, who got nothing for his forebearance but reprimands.

After all the excitement Jean and Pierre had caused, peace settled again at *Les Collettes.* Madame Renoir could go back to her chickens and her rabbits with a tranquil heart.

It was the season for gathering orange-blossoms. I recollected that Renoir had told me when he bought *Les Collettes* that one could make a good living from the fruit alone. I asked Madame Renoir if the property was making a good return. "Well, if Renoir were younger," she replied, "and we could work the garden together. . . . But I suppose we have done best to count on his painting!"

ALFRED BARR

MATISSE, HIS ART AND HIS PUBLIC
"The Visits with Renoir"

1951

It was on the last day of 1917 . . . that Matisse first called on Renoir in the villa at Cagnes. It was a troubled moment for the aged artist: he had just dismissed the young craftsman who at Vollard's insistence had been

Richard Guino

260

serving as Renoir's "hands" in modelling his sculpture. Renoir and Matisse became good friends. The older painter, crippled by arthritis, welcomed the visits of the younger, who often came at the end of the day, the time when Renoir began to dread his nightly bout of pain.

Early in 1918 Matisse for the first time took some of his paintings to show Renoir. . . . Renoir in the past had not been prejudiced in favor of the art of the *roi des fauves* but he now studied Matisse's paintings with interest, especially *The Open Window*. He was amazed at Matisse's control of strong mixed colour areas which to an impressionist were non-existent in nature and therefore almost sinful. He was astonished that the solid blue of the sea seen through the window held its place instead of jumping forward, and went into a half-genuine rage over the intense black curtain rod or valance at the top of the picture which against all good practice and common sense stayed in its proper place. Renoir's influence may have contributed to the softening and relaxation of Matisse's art during his early Nice period.

After Renoir's death Matisse continued to visit the villa at Cagnes occasionally. In 1925 he made a number of drawings and sketches of the garden dominated by Renoir's sculptured Venus. Once Purrmann went with Matisse and was astonished at the cheap furniture, gaudy pillows and general bad taste of the interior of the villa. Matisse explained that the impressionists cared little for the quality of their furnishings and "even put tawdry frames on their own pictures."

Matisse had been recognized as the leader of the fauves *in 1905.*

Hans Purrmann (1880–1966), German painter

FRANÇOISE GILOT/CARLETON LAKE

LIFE WITH PICASSO

Henri Matisse Recalls Visits to Renoir

1964

During a conversation with Picasso, around 1951, Matisse was asked what he thought of the recent work of Jackson Pollock and other younger painters. It made him think of Renoir.

I have the impression I'm incapable of judging painting like that. . . . It's completely over my head.

When I was young, I was very fond of Renoir's painting. Towards the end of the First World War, I found myself in the Midi. Renoir was still living, but very old. I still admired him and I decided to call on him at Les Collettes, his place at Cagnes. He received me in very friendly fashion and so, after a few more visits, I brought him a few of my paintings, to find out what he thought of them. He looked them over with a somewhat disapproving air. Finally he said, "Well, I must speak the truth. I must say I don't like what you do, for various reasons. I should almost like to say that you're not really a good painter or even that you're a very bad painter. But there's one thing that prevents me from telling you that. When you put on some black, it stays right there on the canvas. All my life I have been saying that one can't any longer use black without making a hole in the canvas. It's not a colour. Now, you speak the language of colour. Yet you put on a black and you make it stick. So even though I don't like at all what you do, and my inclination would be to tell you you're a bad painter, I suppose you are a painter, after all."

Matisse, *The Open Window.* c. 1917. Private Collection, Switzerland, © DACS 1987.

ALBERT ANDRÉ

RENOIR

1919

This account was written during the last years of Renoir's life and only slightly modified in later editions.

He remained as simple a man as when he started out, unsusceptible to vanity or flattery, unconcerned about honors.

At one point, late in life, when illness threatened to interrupt his work and when his name carried very little weight in the art market, He gave in to friends and allowed himself to be decorated. Certain friends knew how to break down the last defences of his modesty.

Describing the typical celebratory banquet given for a well-known artist at 50 sous a head, a friend asked him "When will yours be?" "Whenever you like . . . this summer would be fine, a picnic on the Seine . . . a dozen or so good friends, people I know who won't start making speeches about me. . . ."

There were no celebrations in his honor. There never was a Renoir banquet. This master was not deemed worthy!

There was an occasion, however, when he was visibly moved by a tribute. It was in July 1917. One of his paintings was exhibited at the National Gallery on its way to an Irish museum. He was sent a letter signed by one hundred or so English artists and collectors, which said: "From the moment your painting was hung amid the masterpieces of the past, we had the pleasure of observing that one of our contemporaries had immediately taken his rightful place among the great masters of the European tradition." On that day, recognition seemed to him a good thing! . . .

The Umbrellas (1881/85) (Colorplate 90), part of the Hugh Lane Bequest, arrived in London from Ireland in 1917.

. . . He has only one real passion; to hear concerts or to attend literary discussions only prevents him from getting into his studio first thing in the morning. So he has cut them out of his life.

"I have had to drop, if not actually quarrel with quite delightful friends who would never arrive on time, who never go to bed, and who talk endlessly about art. I have always hated that sort of chatter."

He is passionately involved in all types of discussion, but his better judgment carries the day. He is a painter, and wishes to be nothing else!

"What am I getting mixed up in? I barely know my *own* business, . . . this mania for getting involved in things we weren't meant for is fatal."

While he has some pet aversions, which he makes no secret of, he is never guilty of jealousy. "With artists," he would say, "jealousy is often just fear for their own immortality." He lives in no ivory tower; he is always curious about what was going on in the world of painting. When he could still walk, you might be sure to bump into him at all the exhibitions where his younger colleagues were showing. He was always one of the first visitors, the most attentive, the most benevolent. If someone's talent had caught his eye, he would want to meet them. He would go and visit them, invite them to his studio, even exchange works with them. He never pontificated. He was simply a fellow-painter who was a bit older.

Now that infirmity confines him to his armchair, he keeps himself informed on all topics that interest him. He never mocks, even at things that are quite antipathetic to him, if he feels that they are sincerely held. This compulsive worker respects the labors of others.

"You mustn't think too much of yourself," he says, "anymore than you should think yourself inferior to everyone else. You must know yourself and what you are worth."

"When I look at the old masters, I feel very small, but nevertheless, I believe that enough of my work will remain to ensure me a place in the French school that I love so much: it is so kindly, so simple, so congenial . . . and so restrained."

* * *

It is astonishing, when you visit him, to see how little luxury there is around him. He loves fine things, certainly, but to find them takes time. His luxury is in his eyes.

His studios, whether in Paris or in the country, are empty of any furniture that might encourage visitors to stay for long. A broken down divan, covered in clothes and old flowered hats for his models; a few chairs that are always cluttered with canvases. But for the eyes there is a riot of color, an Aladdin's cave: finished paintings, waiting to dry, and canvases that are still being worked on. They are all tacked on the wall or lying about the floor, with no thought of presentation. If by chance there is a painting that is framed and hung in a presentable way, it will have been done for, and by, someone else in the Renoir circle.

He wears no special painter's garb. He sits in his armchair, his spindly legs crossed; his poor feet clad in woolen slippers; his body wrapped in shawls; his pale, fine head muffled to the ears in a cap, or a white linen hat according to the season; and in his fingers the ever-present cigarette, which he constantly relights.

He welcomes friends joyfully. But if he suspects that anyone has come to see him out of curiosity, he withdraws into himself, says nothing and becomes totally disagreeable. As soon as he has rid himself of such unwelcome visitors, and is back in front of his easels, he is a man transformed. He whistles, hums the tunes which his models so often sing to him and goes into ecstasies over the beauties which only his eye can find in them.

It is only really in such moments that he may be persuaded to divulge his theory of art in all its simplicity.

This man, who has put painting above all else in his life, speaks very little of the painting he has done.

"Just look at the light on the olive trees . . . it glitters like a diamond. It's pink, it's blue. . . . And the sky coming through them. It's enough to drive you crazy. And those mountains over there which change with the clouds. . . . They're like the background in a Watteau."

"Ah! this breast! How very soft and heavy it is! That pretty fold underneath with its golden color. . . . It's enough to bring you to your knees. If there had never been any breasts, I don't think I should ever have painted figures."

He loves things filled with light. A gray landscape never tempts him to put brush to canvas. The sun must be part of it. Even so his prodigious eye can invent sumptuous harmonies for the most lifeless motif.

His studio accessories more often than not are of a shabbiness and simplicity that is disconcerting, when you see what he can make of them.

His painting offers a constant contrast to his external life. He lives almost like a petit bourgeois, but he creates nothing that isn't bold and generous. It is as though his creative abilities felt the need of this tame and uneventful existence in order to burgeon.

"Painting is intended to decorate walls, isn't it? So we must make it as rich as possible. For me a painting – since we are obliged to make easel paintings – must be agreeable, joyful and pretty – yes, pretty!"

"There are enough depressing things in life without our creating still more. I know that it's difficult to accept that a painting can be a great painting if it is joyful. Because Fragonard put laughter into his work, it quickly became the accepted thing to call him a minor painter. People who laugh aren't taken seriously. It's the solemn, full dress art – whether it's painting, music or writing – that will always impress.

"The most simple subjects are timeless. A naked woman emerging from the sea or getting out of bed, whether her name is Venus or Nini – you could never invent anything better than that."

"All one needs is an excuse for grouping several figures together. There musn't be too much literature, not too many figures who express thought. Old Man Corot used to say: 'When I paint I want to be an animal.' I feel

Model's hat on a table in
Renoir's studio.
Musée Renoir, Cagnes. (Photo
Nicholas Wadley.)

rather the same. Besides, all these self-consciously expressive elements are almost always at odds with good sane art."

"Look at the Greeks of the classical age or later at Rubens, Titian, Veronese . . . and Corot himself!"

"I really took against one of my paintings when they named it *Thought*. . . ."

This is the Young Woman Seated *of 1876/77 (Colorplate 60), which was retitled "La Pensée" ("Thought") on the occasion of an auction at Sotheby's.*

For several years now, pain has prevented him from holding his palette. He balances it on his knees and on the edge of his easel.

This palette is surprisingly clean and bright, even after a long painting session. It only serves as a measure of flexibility of color that he was going to put on his canvas. Its composition had changed several times since the days when Diaz, who took a great liking to Renoir, had made him open an account with his own color merchant. It is very simple. He doesn't hide it, since he makes no mystery of his working methods, but he avoids offering them as an example to others for fear of being accused of acting the teacher.

"A painter's palette doesn't mean anything," he says, "it's his eye that does it all. There are some colors that you like more than others and you end up using them."

"I used to use chrome which is a superb color, but which can play some nasty tricks, apparently. I tried cadmium; I had great problems with it; it used to make me paint heavily. Then I wanted to act the little Rubens. I started to paint with Naples yellow, a rather dull color. It gave me all the brilliance I needed. Still, it's always the same story. . . . It all depends on what colors I surround it by."

Given the appearance of his pictures, it comes as something of a

COLORPLATE 87. *Girls in Black*. 1880/2. 32 × 25⅝″ (81.3 × 65.2 cm).
The Pushkin Museum, Moscow.

COLORPLATE 88. *Nude in a Landscape*. 1883. 25½ × 21⅝″ (65 × 55 cm).
Musée de l'Orangerie, Paris (Collection Jean Walter and Paul Guillaume).

surprise to realize that he uses black and ochers so constantly, if carefully. His first trade as a painter of porcelain has left him with a taste for clear and transparent tones. The white ground of his canvas today plays the same role as the kaolin plates of his apprenticeship.

When his subject is simple, he sets to work on his canvas by drawing a few summary brushstrokes, usually in a red brown, to give him an idea of the proportions of the component parts. "The volumes . . ." he says with a slightly sardonic air. Then straightaway using pure colors diluted with turpentine, as if he were working in water-color, he rapidly covers the canvas and you can see something vague and iridescent appearing, colors running into each other, something that enchants you, even before a sense of the image is intelligible.

At the second session, when the turps has dried out a little, he reworks this preparation, proceeding in almost the same way, but with a mixture of oil and turps and slightly denser color.

He lightens those areas which are to be luminous by applying pure white directly to the canvas. He reinforces the shadows and the half-tones in the same way, directly on to the canvas. There is no mixing of colors – or almost none – on his palette, which is covered only in little commas of almost pure colors. Little by little, he defines the forms, but always allowing them to merge into each other. "They must kiss . . ." he says.

A few more touches still . . . and out of the colored mist of the first state, soft rounded forms emerge, glittering like precious stones, enveloped by transparent, golden shadows.

* * *

When starting on a complicated composition, he doesn't make what you would really call a study. Once his motif is decided on, he does some little paintings in the spirit of the subject. Sometimes it is a single figure, sometimes several. This process is a sort of practice for the definitive work.

When it is fixed in his mind, he next draws his composition in sanguine, and traces it on to his canvas.

Drawing with a hard pencil doesn't suit him, even though he has done some admirable studies in that medium. He needs something that is softer than the pencil, and more colorful, in order to realize large masses. His preference is for charcoal or for a brown-red pastel.

He can no longer change brushes while he's working. Once the brush is selected, and strapped between his paralyzed fingers, it travels from the canvas to his pot of turps to be cleaned, back to the palette to be recharged, and then returns to the canvas.

When his hand becomes numb with exhaustion, someone has to retrieve the brush from his fingers, since they cannot open by themselves. He asks for a cigarette, rolls back his wheelchair, screws up an eye, gives a dissatisfied grunt or a modest expression of praise before getting back to work.

"How difficult it is in a picture to find the exact point at which to stop copying nature. The painting must not smell too strongly of the model, but at the same time, you must get the feeling of nature. A painting is not a verbatim record. For myself, I like the sort of painting which makes me want to stroll into it if it's a landscape, or if it's a female figure, to run my hand over a breast or back. Corot had some very coarse ways of describing what I mean."

"Don't ask me whether painting should be objective or subjective, because I can assure you I couldn't care less. It always fills me with trepidation when young painters come here and ask me about the purpose of painting. Some of them tell me why I put a red or a blue in such and such a spot. Of course our trade is a difficult and complicated one and I understand why people read so much into it. But just the same one needs a little simplicity and innocence."

"I struggle with my fingers until they are truly at one with the landscape that acts as their background; I don't want them to feel flat, any more than I'd want my trees to feel flat. The main thing is, it has to remain painting and nothing else. But then you can go on saying 'it has to . . .' till the cows come home."

"I love painting that is mellow and rich, as smooth as possible. That's why I love oil paint so much."

"I have tried all possible ways of getting the results I was looking for – and still look for. No one could criticize me for staying locked within one system."

"I painted two or three canvases with the palette knife, following the technique so dear to Courbet; then I painted with the brush in full-bodied paint. Perhaps one or two of these pieces came off, but I found it very awkward to come back to (and rework) these paintings. I had to lift off the mistakes with a knife. After the first session, I couldn't make necessary changes to the position of a figure without scraping my canvas. I tried painting with small brushstrokes which made it easier for me to break colors into each other, but this manner produced a rough sort of painting and I don't like that very much: I have my little quirks and I like to be able to stroke a painting, to run my hand over it; and with pictures that are painted like that, it would be no exaggeration to say that I've been tempted to strike matches on them. And besides, dust gets into the crevices and interferes with the tones."

"A painting must be able to withstand all the varnishes, the dirt and the tricks it might suffer at the hands of time and the restorers."

* * *

"The model is only there to set me going," he says. "She enables me to dare things that I couldn't invent without her, also to help me back on course if I go too far." So he always likes to have a model in the house, on a permanent basis.

Woman Tying her Shoe. c. 1918.
19⅞ × 22¼″ (50.5 × 56.5 cm).
Courtauld Institute Galleries
(Courtauld Collection).

He has a taste for heavy hands and feet. The beautiful, robust girls who have served, almost exclusively, as his models during his last twenty years, have been his youngest children's nurse-maids.

Almost all of his figures reveal this single type of feminine beauty that he favored most. The mouth coming forward as if for a kiss; the bright, joyful eyes; the long torsos with exaggerated hips; the slightly short legs, rounded but not particularly muscular; the feeling of bonelessness. This type becomes more emphatic around 1880; he finds it all around him and imparts it, despite himself, to all of his figures.

A new model disturbs him, holds him back a little. He doesn't feel relaxed enough to work, but often he dares not send her away. Without a word, he gets on with painting a rose in the corner of his canvas, or some clothes draped over a chair, while the girl – quite unaware of her irrelevance – continues to pose.

* * *

"If I hadn't been obliged to make paintings for a dealer, and in order to live, I could very well have spent my life painting nothing but sketches, but my old friend Durand-Ruel took care of that and would remind me that he was waiting for my pictures. Dealers have their good points, whatever people say, ever since the Medicis. . . ."

"If the unfortunate painter had been obliged to run after the collectors until they ran after him, he would have died of hunger. . . ."

"And then sometimes, they force you to do things that you would never have thought of yourself and you have to be grateful to them. For instance, if I have tried to make sculpture, it isn't to take issue with Michelangelo, nor because painting was no longer enough for me, but because M Vollard has very gently forced me into it."

"I had modeled a medallion and a bust of my youngest son. Vollard then very shrewdly asked me to give some advice to a talented young sculptor who might do some work based on one of my paintings. I went along with it, we made a small statuette, and then, as one piece of advice led to another, a large statue came into being. But this art is a Herculean task . . . and you can see my condition . . . so I didn't carry on."

* * *

"One's art must be of one's own time. But it's there, in the museums, that one gets a taste for painting which nature, by herself, cannot give you. It's not in front of a beautiful landscape that you declare: 'I shall be a painter,' it's in front of a painting."

"Theories cannot make a good painting. As often as not, they are just a disguise for what's wrong with the means of expression. Besides, they're cobbled together only after the event. A beautiful painting doesn't need commentaries. . . .

"I have always put myself at the mercy of fate. I have never had a fighter's temperament and would have given up on many occasions if my old friend Monet – one who *does* have a fighter's temperament – had not been there to put me on my feet again. Today, when I look back at my life, I compare it to one of those corks thrown into a river. It bobs along, then gets caught in a whirlpool, spins back, goes down again, surfaces, gets tangled in a weed, makes desperate efforts to free itself and then vanishes from sight altogether. . . ."

* * *

The last great joy he had as a painter, three months before his death, was when M Paul Léon (director of the Beaux-Arts) arranged for him to visit the Louvre, which was then in the course of rearrangement. "I saw the *Marriage at Cana* on the line," he would say when he described this tour, during which he was carried through the rooms of the Louvre like the pope of painting.

"On the line" means at the optimum viewing level. Paintings hung at spectators' eye-level in the Royal Academy (or the Salon) were hung "on the line" ("en cimaise"). Renoir, carried high in his sedan, had a rare vantage point for viewing the enormous Veronese painting.

275

ABBE BAUME
Funeral Oration to Renoir

1919

"My dear friends and brothers,

It is not for me, neither is it the time nor the place, to attempt to retrace the eventful, hard-working and fruitful life, the glorious life of Auguste-Pierre Renoir.

This distinguished artist, to whom we are paying our last respects, will be the subject for all writers whom the Fine Arts number among their experts on painting, as he is already in France and throughout the world.

They will discuss the magnificent line of masters of the brush from which Renoir descended, the burden of that heritage that he bore so lightly, and the school to which he might best belong; similarly they will tell how, as a disciple of Watteau or Fragonard, he in turn became a master and assumed immortality in his lifetime through his boundless skill with light and color.

There will no doubt be many anecdotes told and retold which reveal his remarkable mind, upright nature and his limitless warm-heartedness.

At all times in his life he was ever the same, in adversity as in success, in full youth and vigor as well as in the midst of the infirmities which had made his life one long martyrdom; in him people will acclaim the perfect craftsman of beauty, the mystic whose firm faith in his art always held him above the epic struggles waged by the schools, and also the aged master whose suffering no more got the better of the freshness of his brush than of his sympathetic and welcoming disposition.

Yes, they will say all that and the many other things that Arts writers say so well, along with those experts who are adept at presenting their judgment in a form that is appealing to the public.

For some it will be a professional duty, for others the opportunity to repay a debt of gratitude, and for all of them there will be the need to pay a tribute, as affectionate as it is glowing, to the man who has just passed on in triumph, advanced in years and laden with honors.

For me, his priest and something of a friend to him and his family, the task is easier, but no less noble – perhaps nobler than others – since it falls to me to pay homage to Auguste-Pierre Renoir as deeply spiritual and a Christian idealist.

Those who were close to him know all this. . . .

But perhaps none of them has attributed to that side of the great man the importance that I have been led to attach to it through my temperament and calling. And you will understand straightaway if I say that not only in hours of leisure or musing, but even in the midst of the most absorbing work, certain words – God, Soul, Justice, Duty, Providence, Eternity . . . were enough to bring him back to himself, whether his eyes were gazing into space or fixed on some color.

That gaze, with its famed acuteness, would then become more alive, full of an extraordinary light whose brightness would spread across his face, driving out his usual impassiveness and preceding by several seconds the words his lips were about to utter.

And there would follow true expressions of faith in God's greatness, adoration of his majesty, confidence in his justice and hope in his goodness . . . as if he were worshiping the unfathomable mystery of creation, nature's magnificence and the infinite sweetness of the light – the light that he loved so much and would contemplate for hours at a time, motionless as if he were drinking it down in a long, unending draught!

He did indeed drink it in with his eyes, which were created to see what ours cannot. And I remember one evening when the light at sunset seemed

The Abbé Baume was the Curé-Doyen of Cagnes; the text of this oration was first published in La Vie, *Paris, in January 1920.*

Renoir's Obituary. *The Times,*
London, December 14, 1919.

Photograph of Renoir's Wheelchair in Front of his Easel. Musée Renoir, Cagnes. (Photo Nicholas Wadley).

Photograph of Renoir. 1915.
(Bibliothèque Nationale, Paris).

more fascinating than usual – I will give you just this one illustration:
Renoir was sitting riveted in his invalid chair, his face turned towards the
watery horizon with its fading light, where the landscape of the cap
d'Antibes seemed to be sinking down to sleep. Suddenly, emerging from
his silent meditation, the master said to me in an undertone: "Imagine the
beauty of the God who made that!"

After a moment of prayerful contemplation, I replied: "You remind me
of Ampère after some famous discovery suddenly exclaiming in his
laboratory: 'How great God is!' and repeating for more than an hour,
'How great God is! How great God is!'"

A moment later, still speaking under his breath as if confidentially,
Renoir replied: "What a noble mission you have, my dear curé! Teaching
the existence of God, preaching his beauty. . . ."

It was as if this illustrious old man envied me.

And in his own way Renoir was also a priest, a faithful priest of the art
which is immortal because it is the earthly reflection of eternal, divine
beauty. That is how he came to God; and it is with the reputation of an
artist of integrity that he will remain among men . . . and that is why I
loved him as you yourselves have loved him.

I wanted to say this here in front of everyone, his friends, and
especially in front of you, his three sons, at the time when we are about to
lay his remains alongside those of your mother and reunite in the peace of
that final sleep those whose greatest and purest joy lay in the pleasure of
cradling you and the pride of watching you grow up.

May that thought, my friends, be always with you on the different
paths where your destiny may lead you. To you who have been given a
Christian upbringing, may this memory of a father and mother filled with
faith in God be to you a private source of peace and tranquillity and in
public a reason for pride among men who will never shake your hand
without thinking of the heritage of that famous name whose weight you
bear.

And now, dear and revered Master, we say the magnificent prayers
that befit the indefatigable worker for whom the hour of rest has tolled –
requiem aeternam – and the hour of light, that unending light on whose
divine radiance we pray that your eyes will gaze eternally – *et lux perpetua
luceat eis . . . Amen.*

CLIVE BELL

THE ATHENAEUM

"Renoir"

July 27, 1919

Clive Bell (1881–1964), British writer and critic, important champion of modern French painting in Britain. This article is a review of the monograph by Albert André (see pp. 262 ff).

Renoir is the greatest painter alive. . . .

He is over forty: to be exact, he is seventy-seven years old. Yet, in the teeth of modern theories that have at least the air of physiological certainties, one must admit that he is alive still. A comparison between the five-and-thirty photographs reproduced by M. Besson and those at the end of Herr Meier-Graefe's monograph suggests that even since 1910 his art has developed. But what is certain is that, during his last period, since 1900 that is to say, though so crippled by rheumatism that it is with agonizing difficulty he handles a brush, he has produced works that surpass even the masterpieces of his middle age.

Renoir observed one day to an astonished disciple, "Avec la Nature on ne fait rien;" and on being asked where, then, the student should learn his art added, without any apparent sign of shame or sense of sin – "Au musée, parbleu!"

"One makes nothing from Nature"

"In the museum, by God!"

* * *

Renoir thus affirmed what every artist knows, that art is the creation and not the imitation of form. In his eyes the most valuable part of an artist's education is the intelligent study of what other artists have done. For his own part he studied Courbet and then Delacroix, and, assuredly, from these picked up useful hints for converting sensibility into significant form. Sensibility he never lacked. Renoir's painting gift may, without unpardonable silliness, be compared with the singing gift of Mozart. His conspicuous characteristics are loveliness and ease. No painter, I suppose, gives more delight, or gives it more frankly. That is why his name provokes an odd, personal enthusiasm in thousands of people who have never seen him. That is why Frenchmen, who have sometimes a terribly intimate way of explaining themselves, have been known to assert that they feel for Renoir the sort of grateful affection that every sensitive man feels for a woman who has given him joy.

But Renoir's natural masters – parents one would say if a man could have more than two – were Fragonard, Boucher, and Watteau.

* * *

The purest of painters becomes historical by accident. He expresses the unalloyed sensibility of an artist in terms of delicious contemporary life and gives us, adventitiously, romance. A fascinating period, but not the great one.

Towards the end of 1881 Renoir set out on a tour in Italy, and, as if to show how little he was affected by what he found there, painted at Naples a large and important *Baigneuse* (now in the Durand-Ruel collection) in which I can discover not the slightest trace of Italian influence. He is too thorough a Frenchman to be much of anything else. The emphatic statement and counter-statement of the great Primitives is not in his way. He prefers to insinuate. Even in his most glorious moments he is discreet and tactful, fonder of a transition than an opposition, never passionate. The new thing that came into his art about this time, and was to affect it for the next twenty years, was not Italy but Ingres.

COLORPLATE 77

The influence was at first an unhappy one. During three or four years, unable, it seems, to match the new conception of form with his intensely personal reaction, Renoir produced a certain number of unconvincing and

uncharacteristic pictures (eg, the dance series, *Danse à la Ville,* etc.). There is an uneasy harshness about the contours, the forms are imperfectly felt, they are wooden even, and in their placing one misses the old inevitability. Signed with another name these essays might by a dashing critic be called doctrinaire. Then in 1885 came the first *Baigneuses* (collection J. E. Blanche), whereby Renoir put himself a good head above all contemporaries save Cézanne. If this picture were hung in a public gallery, and the numerous drawings made for it ranged alongside, how finely discredited would be those knowing ones who, in their desire to emphasize the difference between form and that of which form is composed, are in the habit of calling Renoir a great colourist and then pausing impressively. I suppose it is because he rarely uses a lead pencil that the wiseacres are able to fulfil their destiny. Drawing in charcoal or pastel need not be taken seriously; while drawing with the brush is apparently not drawing at all. That Renoir is a great draughtsman may be inferred from almost everything he has ever done. But (though that amazing *Boy with a Cat* was achieved as early as 1868) it is the work of this period – and *Les Baigneuses,* with its attendant studies, are capital examples – that makes patent his mastery and entitles him obviously to a place between Ingres and Daumier.

That it should be difficult to find a date for the beginning of Renoir's last period does not much trouble me; but I am sorry that it is quite impossible to indicate in words its character. One can say confidently that the new conception was being elaborated between 1895 and 1900; one can suppose that its final character was to some extent imposed on the master by his growing infirmities. A painter who can hardly move arm or fingers will neither sweep nor niggle. He must paint, if he is to paint at all, in blobs and smears and patches and soft strokes; and it is out of these that Renoir's latest works are built up. "Built up" – the expression is absurd. Rather, it is as though forms had been melted down to their component colours, and the pool of iridescent loveliness thus created fixed by a touch of the master's magic – lightly frozen over by an enchanting frost. Only ice is cold. At any rate, what happens to the spectator is that first he perceives a tangle of rather hot and apparently inharmonious tones; gradually he becomes aware of a subtle, astonishing, and unlooked-for harmony; finally, from this harmony emerge completely realized and exquisitely related forms. After which, if he has any sense of art, he remains spellbound and uncritical, and ceases to bother about how the thing was done. That, at least is my impression of Renoir's latest style. . . .

COLORPLATES 82, 83, 84

COLORPLATE 97

(Daulte 42)

ROGER FRY

VISION AND DESIGN

"Renoir"

Roger Fry (1866–1934), English painter, critic, theorist, whose two exhibitions of post-Impressionist painting in London, 1910–12, were a key vehicle for increasing awareness of modern French art among British artists.

1920

What a lover of the commonplace Renoir was! It is a rare quality among artists. . . .

Something odd or exotic in their taste for life seems to be normal for artists. The few artists or writers who have shared the tastes of the average man have, as a rule, been like Dickens – to take an obvious case – very imperfect and very impure artists however great their genius. Among great artists one thinks at once of Rubens as the most remarkable example of a man of common tastes, a lover of all that was rich, exuberant, and even florid. Titian too, comes nearly up to the same standard. . . . Renoir, in the frankness of his colour harmonies, in his feeling for design and even in the quality of his pigment, constantly reminds us of these two. Now it is easier to see how an artist of the sixteenth or seventeenth century could develop commonplace tastes than one of our own times. For with the nineteenth century came in a gradual process of differentiation of the artist from the average man. The modern artist finds himself so little understood by the crowd, in his aims and methods, that he tends to become distinct in his whole attitude to life.

What, then, is so peculiar about Renoir is that he has this perfectly ordinary taste in things and yet remains so intensely, so purely, an artist. The fact is perhaps that he was so much an artist that he never had to go round the corner to get his inspiration; the immediate, obvious, front view of everything was more than sufficient to start the creative impulse. He enjoyed instinctively, almost animally, all the common good things of life, and yet he always kept just enough detachment to feel his delight aesthetically – he kept, as it were, just out of reach of appetite.

More than any other great modern artist, Renoir trusted implicitly to his own sensibility; he imposed no barrier between his own delight in certain things and the delight which he communicates. He liked passionately the obviously good things of life, the young human animal, sunshine, sky, trees, water, fruit; the things that everyone likes; only he liked them at just the right distance with just enough detachment to replace appetite by emotion. He could rely on this detachment so thoroughly that he could dare, what hardly any other genuine modern has dared, to say how much he liked even a pretty sight. But what gives his art so immediate, so universal an appeal is that his detachment went no further than was just necessary. His sensibility is kept at the exact point where it is transmuted into emotion. And the emotion, though it has of course the generalised aesthetic feeling, keeps something of the fullness and immediacy of the simpler attitude. Not that Renoir was either naive or stupid. When he chose he showed that he was capable of logical construction and vigorous design. But for his own pleasure he would, as he himself said, have been satisfied to make little isolated records of his delight in the detail of a flower or a lock of hair. With the exception of *"Les Parapluies"* at the National Gallery we have rarely seen his more deliberate compositions in England. But in all his work alike, Renoir remains the man who could trust recklessly his instinctive reaction to life.

COLORPLATE 90

Let me confess that these characteristics – this way of keeping, as it were, just out of reach of appetite – make Renoir to me, personally, a peculiarly difficult artist. . . . I am sometimes in danger of not doing Renoir justice, because at the first approach to one of his pictures I miss the purely accessory delight of an unexpected attitude. The first approach

At the Concert (In the Box). 1880.
39 × 31¾″ (99 × 81 cm). Sterling
and Francine Clark Art Institute,
Williamstown, Mass.

to one of his pictures may indeed remind one of pictures that would be the delight of the servants' hall, so unaffectedly simple is his acceptance of rosy-cheeked girls, of pretty posies, and dappled sunlight. And yet one knows well enough that Renoir was as "artful" as one could wish. Though he had not the biting wit of a Degas, he had a peculiar love of mischievous humour; he was anything but a harmless or innocent character. All his simplicity is on the surface only. The longer one looks, the deeper does Renoir retire behind veil after veil of subtlety. And yet, compared with some modern artists, he was, after all, easy and instinctively simple. Even his plastic unity was arrived at by what seems a more natural method than, say Cézanne's. Whereas Cézanne undertook his indefatigable research for the perspective of the receding planes, Renoir seems to have accepted a very simple general plastic formula. Whatever Cézanne may have meant by his celebrated saying about cones and cylinders, Renoir seems to have thought the sphere and cylinder sufficient for his purpose. The figure presents itself to his eye as an arrangement of more or less hemispherical bosses and cylinders, and he appears to arrange the light so that the most prominent part of each boss receives the highest light. From this the planes recede by insensible gradations towards the contour, which generally remains the vaguest, least ascertained part of the modelling.

Whatever lies immediately behind the contour tends to become drawn into its sphere of influence, to form an undefined recession enveloping and receiving the receding planes. As the eye passes away from the contour, new but less marked bosses form themselves and fill the background with repetitions of the general theme. The picture tends thus to take the form of a bas-relief in which the recessions are not into the profound distances of pictorial space, but only back, as it were, to the block out of which the bossed reliefs emerge, though of course, by means of atmospheric colour the eye may interpret these recessions as distance. This is clearly in marked contrast to Cézanne's method. . . .

Renoir's drawing takes on the same fundamental simplicity. An Ingres arrived at the simplified statement necessary for great design by a process of gradual elimination of all the superfluous sinuosities which his hand had recorded in the first drawing from nature. Renoir seems never to have allowed his eye to accept more than the larger elements of mass and direction. His full, rounded curves embrace the form in its most general aspect. With advancing years and continually growing science he was able, at last, to state his essential synthesis with amazing breadth and ease. He continually increased the amplitude of his forms until, in his latest nudes, the whole design is filled with a few perfectly related bosses. Like Titian's, Renoir's power of design increased up to the very end of his life. True he was capable at all periods of conceiving large and finely coordinated compositions, such as *"Les Parapluies"* and the *"*Charpentier family;" but at the end even the smallest studies have structural completeness.

Maurice Denis, *Renoir*.
Watercolor. 1913. Private
Collection (Photo Lauros-
Giraudon, Paris). © DACS 1987.

MAURICE DENIS

LA VIE

"Renoir"

February 1, 1920

The funeral oration for Renoir delivered by the Curé of Cagnes is the finest tribute that has been paid to his memory. Emile Wéry, who sent it to *La Vie*, and the periodical itself in publishing it, have thereby associated themselves with a very touching demonstration of admiration and sympathy which Renoir would have appreciated for its sincerity and simplicity. The picture which it gives of Renoir sitting riveted in his invalid chair, his face turned towards a beautiful sunset, drinking in this splendor with his eyes and saying: "Imagine the beauty of the God who made that!," is a noble, true and moving picture that will live on.

This speech excells on more than one count. But those who believe in the resurrection of the flesh, a doctrine which is widely overlooked, will have been particularly happy to read the eulogy of a poet of the flesh given by a priest during a Catholic ceremony. The flesh is entitled to some consideration. The idolatrous world, with its fanatical cult of vice and immorality, is foolish to criticize Catholicism for ignoring life's joys and the beauty of created things. This is wholly to misunderstand its nature and the glories of its artistic past. Of course religion will not deify passions or confuse the unequal values of the different orders of human activity. Moreover, Catholics in general have an unhealthy fear of nudity; they are shocked to see the *Three Graces* in the sacristy in Siena and cannot tolerate the liberties taken by Renaissance artists in Italian churches. Art conflicts with caution. I would bring the case of Renoir to the attention of M Jacques Maritain, the author of *Art et Scolastique:* it might help to elucidate

(see pp. 276–77.)
Emile Wéry (1868–1935), French landscape painter, friend of Matisse

282

this difficult problem. Why is there nothing shocking about his nudes? First of all because they are so healthy. Secondly, because they have been transformed by lyricism, Renoir's plastic sense. They are not idealized, thank God! They have become forms and colors. The world in which they expose their plump, pearly flesh is the world of painting; the magic of the art is such that they are no more than a pink light, relieved by pearl gray, lilac and green and sustained by harmonious volumes and balanced masses. They are signs, symbols, images of Renoir's optimistic sensibility and retain from nature only what the painter has wished to keep for amusement and for delectation, as it used to be said in Poussin's day; and nothing for the baser passions.

Besides, the healthiness of the human species made in this mold, the health of these beautiful bodies, the robustness of these carnal creations, marked with classical serenity, is free from perverseness. *Sana sancta.* Their expression of innocent bestiality assimilates them into the natural order of magnificent flowers or fruit. Antiquity has never better translated this instinct, this ingenuousness of instinct, nor in a more sensual or more chaste way.

If Renoir is to be reproached with anything, it is for lacking a sense of sin, of original corruption. And yet these beautiful faces have a certain melancholy: the melancholy of antiquity. It is Rubens who might seem to be the pagan. When the good Renoir thundered against the protestant mind, which we also call Jansenist, and when he contrasted the heavy Jordaens with the divine Rubens, did he know that Rubens observed religious practices throughout his life, which he himself did not, with daily Mass and meditation, not to mention the edifying readings that he insisted on while he was working? Pagan or not, the figures by Rubens or Renoir are sanctified by painting: good painting is religious in itself, as Michelangelo said.

The Curé of Cagnes has told us about Renoir's inner feelings. All those who had the honor and pleasure of getting close to him know that he was loyal and good. They know too that his sayings, collected by Vollard – the paradoxes and fantasies of an aging *scamp* of the Second Empire – are in any case less vicious than the sayings of Degas or Clemenceau, and conceal an undaunted optimism and a rare shyness. His natural malice was his only defence. But behind this mask of benign irony there was solid good sense, and respect and love for all the good old French traditions, including religious tradition, a horror of novelty and change, in short the mind of an *honnête homme* of the old regime, a sort of ironical Poussin who was nonetheless deeply spiritualistic.

Cézanne, a believer too, was I think more sensitive than Renoir to the idea of death. . . . But Cézanne was more of a thinker, more complicated and also more austere. There is in Cézanne a kind of asceticism which is also to be seen in his art; Renoir did not have such a rigid conception of life or painting.

These two men who lived, one of them his last years at least, in Provence, in the southern sunlight, are the undisputed masters among the young. In the eyes of the young, they represent the unalloyed purity of painting, unconcerned with imitating or imagining a subject.

* * *

Both of them age well: their color matures. Renoir's daring gamut, his harmonies of wine and brick colors calm down and take on a golden hue. Cézanne acquires solidity, like a wall. Renoir's painting becomes transparent like lacquer, shimmering like silk.

But Renoir admired Cézanne. . . . He liked to tell how he had got Choquet's first Cézanne in that important collection into his home.

Madame Choquet intensely disliked Cézanne's painting, so discretion was called for. It was agreed that Renoir would look after the picture that Choquet had just acquired and would keep praising Cézanne in Madame

Seated Bather Drying her Arm. Pen and pencil. c. 1885. 10¼ × 8½" (26 × 21.5 cm). Louvre, Paris.

The statesman, Georges Clemenceau (1841– 1929)

Victor Choquet (1821–91), a customs official, devoted collector of Cézanne and Renoir (see Colorplate 35).

Choquet's presence. "So, my dear Renoir, you are a great admirer of Cézanne's painting?" "I have a very fine one at home," replied Renoir. "There are a few faults but it is a beautiful thing." "Well bring it tomorrow so we can see it."

Renoir brought it several times only to take it away again. At the foot of the stairs Choquet would say to him: "No, Renoir, not today, my wife won't want to." At last it was shown, to Mme Choquet's great alarm. "But Marie, Marie! it isn't mine. You know perfectly well it belongs to M Renoir." But Renoir felt that the joke had gone on long enough. He took advantage of Choquet's absence to tell his wife everything. "Pretend you didn't know, you will make him so happy!" And Cézanne's picture was finally hung in the Choquets' home.

The aim of art is delectation. Since Cézanne our pleasure is above all intellectual. In the old esthetics there was no axis between intelligence and sensitivity nor between the concept of the picture itself and the imitation of nature. Let us hope for the return of those happy days and that Renoir's example will restore our taste for what is real and felt, for good sense and health. In the world of art:

> *There is nothing there but order and beauty,*
> *Luxury, calm and voluptuousness.*

Quoted from Baudelaire's Invitation au Voyage

I am in favor of order. But I think that by virtue of ordering polyhedra, pipes, women without heads and faces without noses, by harmonizing dissonant colors which have been made dirty and messy, the role of voluptuousness in painting tends to be forgotten rather too easily. And the luxury and the richness of the craft! The calm and continuity of effort! And above all voluptuousness! That is what Renoir teaches. That is what can be learned in the Louvre, in front of the fine portrait of Mme Charpentier, a new flower in the French garden, a new glory of that French school which Renoir loved above all other.

ANDRÉ LHÔTE

"Renoir and Impressionism"

1920

André Lhôte (1885–1962), French painter, writer on art and an influential teacher

Renoir's death has been lamented in newspapers and magazines the world over, as they have paid tribute to that admirable life which was wholly dedicated to work; but in their haste too many writers have extolled just the "Impressionist master," propagating an error with which the public are only too content. For in their eyes there is no basic difference between Monet, say, and Renoir: they are both "Impressionist masters." Now if there is one legend which it seems our duty to destroy it is the idea of these two being brothers. Renoir, like Cézanne, was an anti-Impressionist painter. If he was not at the outset, he was quick to become so at the time when this about-turn became necessary. Morever it was because of this that he collected rebuffs and courted unpopularity and ceased to be called the "heir to the Masters of the past," a title which he deserved more than ever. It is worth noting in this connection that it was the same with Impressionism as it was, is and evermore shall be with all artistic schools which only really stand out by virtue of the defections that they provoke from among their own faithful. A method reaches true greatness only when it inspires revolt. Born out of a reaction against the totally outworn formula of official academicism, the Impressionist School awoke a laudable desire for realism. But this desire immediately set itself the most unreasonable goal imaginable: it confused the real with the visible, presumed that sensation alone could determine consciousness and supposed that it was a valid artistic exercise to set down visual impressions without some device to determine their cohesion and rhythm. The pure Impressionist ideal is, essentially, very naive. The way it inflamed the hearts of the most gifted artists of the time can only be explained if it is viewed as an instinctive manifestation of that higher and, so to speak, immanent necessity of reversing pictorial values, which was here somehow acknowledged for the first time. . . . To forget everything and to demand everything from nature was the attitude of those whose sensitivity survived intact: a simplistic solution, which might have compromised the fate of painting had it not been for the appearance of renegade heroes, who, weary of searching visually, finally decided to search it intellectually. Heretics within the bosom of Heresy, they deserted the realm of the senses, which was the delight of the "purists" of the new school, in order to return gradually to the realms of intelligence. Cézanne, Seurat and Renoir all understood, from their own standpoints, that the scientific or spontaneous reproduction of some material facts does not constitute a "worthy" language and that it is good to come back to earth, not to get bogged down there but, like Antaeus, to bounce back up.

"In my view the main cause of the decline of the crafts is the lack of an ideal. The most adept hand is only ever the servant of thought." Those are the *authentic* words of Renoir which throw more light on the painter of *The Bathers* than the puerile sayings that everybody prides themselves on quoting. It is important to draw attention to the meticulous care with which most commentators choose to praise Renoir only as an instinctive artist, as one lacking in self-control and hostile to anything calculated; they believe in all good faith that in this they are glorifying their hero and increasing his stature, and it is by mocking young "intellectuals" that they extoll the perfect unconsciousness and total irresponsibility of the old man. Ignoring Renoir's other comments they choose to dwell on the principle of *"plein air"* painting, quoting admiringly this joke of his: "I have neither rules nor methods," which the speaker intended to be lost in the wind since he then wrote: "Painting is a craft like joinery or ironwork and subject to the same rules."

COLORPLATE 97

The truth is that Renoir, with his extreme acuteness, appreciated how ridiculous these "coffee house" theories were, with metaphysics all too often taking up more room than painting, and he feared above all the interpretations which were mostly put on artists' comments by literary hacks. Hiding his preoccupations behind an attitude of spiritual detachment, he silently created for himself an amazingly precise discipline, to judge by the continuity of his effort and the unity of his work, free from those contradictions which, with often very talented painters, indicate the lack of any inner direction. Renoir's wit lay in understanding that a discipline is made not only out of words and that a theory is void unless it leads straight to practice where there is a place for instinct. The Word has to be made flesh. Giving direction to ideas, incorporating them into one's own substance, making the purely cerebral organic, this is the work that genius must perform. It is a hard and arduous task, requiring "close-lipped patience," which is rewarded by freedom in execution, fruitfulness and serenity.

If the Impressionists' reality was above all illusory, their technique in some way compensates for this deficiency in its complexity and material richness. It is understandable that the day Renoir became interested in what is permanent, his formula changed: it naturally went back to classical, unchangeable sources. It was in his voluntary adoption of an attitude equivalent to that of the Masters of the Renaissance – if not in appropriating their technique like Delacroix – that Renoir rediscovered their fine convictions and created forms to *last*. For the pure Impressionists, Monet Sisley, Berthe Morisot, etc, the painter's attitude is localized on the sun's brightness, the incidental play of a prism on the surface of objects. The *effect* becomes the motif; it absorbs the objects which are now merely secondary and which fade away once they no longer have to tolerate the terrible "lighting." The color perspective, the credo of painters of the new school, leads objects towards their disintegration, inciting them to total destruction in the bosom of the all-devouring sun. *Pure Impressionism is a death-wish; Monet's Nymphéas illustrate the suicide of genius.*

Renoir, who is interested in light only to the extent that it reveals deep qualities of the subject he observes, thinks, in his love for all things, that no one object is worthy to receive it. For him it is no longer the unique monarch whose least signs are orders; it is his helper; he has it in his hand like a tool and, no longer projecting it on to one form rather than another, he spreads it on all the focal points of his picture; it highlights the culminating part of objects which, far from fading way, flow towards the eye and are shaped with equality. The visual space of the Impressionists space is abolished and the artist's spiritual space is reinstated. Renoir's beautifully smooth curves are not spread out in measurable depth, but roll

Bather. c. 1903. 36¼ × 28¾″ (92 × 73 cm). Kunsthistorisches Museum, Vienna.

on top of one another, balanced and superimposed like luminous globes. Having sought the secret of nature's stability, *causes,* which for him follow *effects,* have become the only motif. Like Cézanne he discovered the divine laws of equilibrium which he uses to control the economy of this reduced universe: the picture, which he creates after the fashion of God, if such a God exists, who smiles on his genius. . . . While Monet, the archetypal Impressionist, pushing his speculations to the absurd, gives up portraying not only man but also everything in the landscape that could be articulated like human limbs. All that attract his attention are the phenomena bringing about the dissolution of objects: smoke, fog, wind and water; fluidity and mobility, to which his *Thames* series are the drained poems.

There is an essentially French virtue which we may no longer have much opportunity to mention. That is the good humor – sister of guilelessness and mother of fantasy – that Renoir possessed more than any other painter of his generation. It is that delightful gift which compelled the great man to mislead the hacks around him with many jokes and which has given us that legend of the nightingale-painter, on whose creation he smiled benevolently, although he was laughing up his sleeve, thinking that his works were weighty enough to allow him to leave to posterity only a slight, almost diminished image of himself. Cézanne too (and this gave rise to some misleading legends) had this tendency to present himself as a "dauber" which is so displeasing in the unsuccessful, but enchanting in the great talents. For the benefit of an over-respectful audience, certain artists are moved to utter these paradoxes which are taken literally, spread around and commented on, and serve to create false pictures of great men. The letter which Renoir wrote to Henry Mottez, as a preface for the new edition of Cennino Cennini's *Il Libro dell'Arte,* proves *(see pp. 241–42.)* not only that he thought and wrote well, as any authentic artist can do, but also that he set great store by these thousand everyday assertions which all together go to make up the technical and intellectual equipment of every creative artist. Let us mention just one of the false things written about him: Renoir was not an austere teacher or pedantic esthetician, nor an ideologist: he was a craftsman. There is no finer claim to fame for a painter. When you portray French sculptors or painters at a distance, you can do no more than show them humble before their work, pleasant, straightforward, furnished with a small number of essential truths, going about their daily task happily, indefatigable, calm and without excessive romantic tension.

In society Renoir was an amusing companion, but in the studio he would become a silent thinker. To us he looks like a popular painter intent on the faithful description of the beauties whom the supreme "Master craftsman" lines up before us. If that conclusion suits the art critics whose interpretations we have found unacceptable, we ask no more than to elevate with them the pure finger of Renoir stripped of all pride, unpretentiously learned, a meditator but not an ideologist, his trivial, frivolous remarks masking the seriousness of his thought.

GIORGIO DE CHIRICO

IL CONVEGNO I

"Augosto Renoir"

1920

Giorgio de Chirico (1888–1978), Italian, founder of the Scuola Metafisica, *one of the major figurative painters of the early 20th century*

By subjecting himself to the influence of the Impressionists, Renoir showed that he was neither spiritually profound nor intellectually strong; being only a *painter* he inevitably underwent the influence of almost all the other Impressionists. . . . When this period was over, Renoir found his way. He returned to large figure paintings, the portrait and the nude. But the solidity of his early years, the profoundly pictorial sense of his first works, was gone. The Impressionist period left an indelible mark on all his subsequent paintings. He began to neglect drawing; violet and orange are his predominant colors. He later eliminates, or, rather, reduces the use of these two colors so characteristic of Impressionism, and uses more reds and ochres. In this period he treats the figure in an exaggerated manner which often lends his pictures a fascinating psychological and caricature-like aspect.

COLORPLATE 76

The Luncheon of the Boating Party, full of melancholy and deep *ennui.* . . . The boredom of a Sunday afternoon, of a trip to the country, of the minor daily tragedies, are fixed in the gestures and expressions of his modest characters. This boredom and melancholy is not devoid of certain metaphysical implications, of the subtle, inexplicable feeling which always accompanies a true work of art. . . .

The type of woman whom Renoir left us is the petit bourgeois, the housewife, the mother, the maid, or the young girl; she may be at a piano, in the backyard, or in the garden, but always in a somewhat stifling setting. These women, when indoors, always seem to be in somewhat low-ceilinged rooms. When outdoors, they are portrayed in the still, sultry heat of a summer evening, or in one of those heavy, oppressive late spring afternoons like that in which Flaubert makes the unhappy husband of Madame Bovary die, with the solemn pathos of a Greek tragedy.

GUSTAVE GEFFROY

MONET, SA VIE, SON OEUVRE

"Memories of Renoir"

1924

The great painter of Montmartre has died at Cagnes, the village on the Mediterranean. His life and work were prolonged in this land of blue skies and sunshine. There he was able to breathe and paint, to contemplate its greenness and flowers, its sky and water. There on his doorstep or at the bottom of his garden was all that is beautiful and smiling in nature for Renoir's own use. In spite of his state of health which deteriorated year by year, he was able to live out of doors, hold his brush in his hand deformed by disease and still transcribe on to canvas the colored visions which his eyes admired and which became more highly colored in passing through his brain, that marvelous repository of living forms and luminous harmonies.

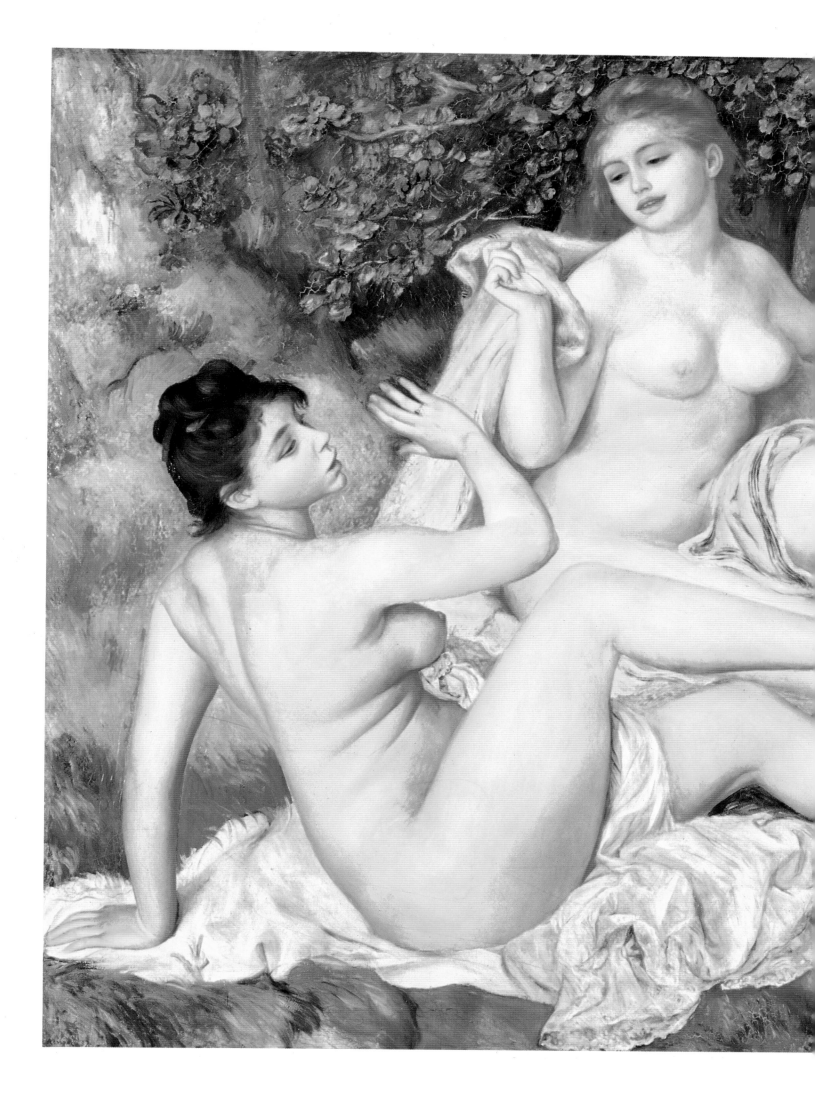

COLORPLATE 98. *Return from the Fields*. 1886. 21¼ × 25⅝″ (54 × 65 cm).
Reproduced by Permission of the Syndics of the Fitzwilliam Museum, Cambridge.

COLORPLATE 97. *The Bathers ("Grandes Baigneuses")*. 1885-7.
46⅜ × 67¼″ (118 × 170.5 cm). Philadelphia Museum of Art
(Mr. & Mrs. Carroll S. Tyson Collection).

Gabrielle Arising (Le Lever).
c. 1910. 24¾ × 20⅞″
(63 × 53 cm). © The Barnes
Foundation, Merion, Pa.

In this homely sunlit paradise, glistening with light, he dedicated his art to all the goddesses who were his life's religion: the fertile earth enriched by summer foliage, the dying richness of autumn and the renewal of spring; the flowers of every season, their remarkable faces swaying on their stems, with inquisitive looks, magic perfumes and mysterious grace; the flowing waters of the rivers which carry the landscape adrift from its course; and finally, woman who rules over this kingdom of painting, herself like a product of the nourishing earth, the flower garden and the water sparkling in the sun.

Right up until the end Renoir summoned out of nature, like an eternally new creation, the female form chosen by his instinct and perfected by his own taste, a mature woman, with round, plump shoulders, small breasts, not very tall but with long thighs, sturdy hands and feet and an eternally childish face. I am not surprised that he ended up making her into a Venus, with that extraordinary statue that he conceived and whose execution he supervized; it is indeed a Renoir among Renoirs, a surprising and bold summary of his work as a painter of women. Perhaps this familiar little model, if she gave a thought to anything other than living and blossoming, would be surprised to find herself raised up among the gods like this. But after all, why not? Venus has many forms and this one, the product of peasantry and suburbia, coming after the sea goddesses of Greece and the great ladies of Renaissance castles and forests,

PAGE 244

has no less its places of naturist nobility that is brought out by her admirable ingenuousness and the resolute way in which her nudity is exposed to the broad daylight and man's approval. Moreover she is always chosen, and the shepherd to whom it falls to give the symbolic apple has once again this time preferred Renoir's little Venus to the haughty Juno and thoughtful Minerva.

The artist who is thus characterized as a landscape painter, the painter of flowers and flowerbeds, and the worshipper of female flesh, leaves some even more varied and extended work. He was a charming portrait-painter, a trifle inclined in the second half of his life to modify all of the faces to the type of features he liked best. But there too, earlier, how many breathing, joyful faces, delightful in their refinement or splendid in their exaltation, has he not faithfully portrayed from the little Durand-Ruel girls, the Bérard family and the tender dreamer of the Choquet collection, to this astonishing Mme de Galéa, in whom he has also seen a modern goddess, silky, satiny, velvety and with clothes and ribbons adding splashes of color, which could well serve as the multi-colored insignia of his oeuvre.

COLORPLATES 91, 3
(*1912, private collection*)

Renoir possessed to a rare degree that sense of the modern which is the mark of original artists of all times. He looked at life very directly: people at parties, lovers talking, pleasure scenes and elegant entertainments, and he has been the painter of the free life through which he paraded the fantasy of his youth and the apparent capriciousness of his studious art, scrupulous and searching. This is the Renoir of suburban holidays; young people embark for the Cytheras of Bougival, Chatou and Nogent; Parisian women whose malicious smiles and dreamy looks made them the boat-men's Mona Lisas; open-air picnics where the sparkling atmosphere of fine days, the colors of eyes and outlines of smiles dissolve delightfully amidst the cigarette smoke and light intoxication of the conversation; formal evenings where handsome society characters are set in the red velvet framework of theatre boxes; and finally, to complete this list, the Renoir of *Dancing at the Moulin de la Galette*, donated by Caillebotte to the Luxembourg museum, where it waits to enter the Louvre, a masterpiece of naive animation, completely given over to the joy of the moment, depicting the flower of life, the whirling dances of carefree girls who lack both wisdom and foresight, their pink cheeks lit by blue eyes or black eyes, their mouths half open to exude happiness and to hum a love song; it is an afternoon in Montmartre captured for posterity, its immediate truth instantly changed to synthesis, a demonstration of all that goes by the name of Impressionism, but really that timeless art that has no need of theory or label.

COLORPLATE 53

The group of painters to which Renoir belonged has nonetheless had to gather behind a campaign banner, at the time when the output of all these artists was challenged and when the struggle to make a living was made worse for them by their exclusion from the Salons and by the gibes of the press. This was their heroic period, the time when they would sell their marvelous canvases for a crust of bread, one can truly say, or for a fifty-franc note which would enable them to buy tubes of color to go on painting. Renoir and Monet lived together for a whole season off a field of potatoes that they had sown and grown themselves. It was also, of course, a good time, a time when their whole future lay before them.

I also knew a Renoir who was calmer than he appeared when dining with the Impressionists, Renoir at home in Montmartre, at lunch with Stéphane Mallarmé who was a great peacemaker and imposed his calm on all the subjects under debate around him.

Then he left for Cagnes, returning to Paris less and less frequently, where I saw him again, still painting, hard at work in front of his model. Then he died, and that some day I received from Monet a letter which recounted his sorrow at the loss of the companion-in-arms whom he loved dearly. It is a farewell to Renoir to which with emotion I add my own signature.

Photograph of Renoir and Mallarmé, by Degas. 1895. Bibliothèque Littéraire Jacques Doucet, Paris.

WALTER SICKERT

THE BURLINGTON MAGAZINE

"French Art of the Nineteenth Century"

June 1922

Walter Richard Sickert (1860–1942), British post-Impressionist painter, friend of Whistler and Degas

Renoir is a classic example of the great painter who has achieved a series of masterpieces by the methods of the sketcher. . . . He had the good luck to enter upon the painting of easel-pictures after the finest education conceivable, that of a painter on *biscuit*. . . . Instead of being demoralised in his youth by the *gran' commodita* of oil painting, he earned his living at the age of thirteen in a medium which imposes, with every touch, decisions that are irrevocable. Painting on *biscuit* imposes also a certain order on the operations, which happens to be the ideal order for the formation of a painter. You are obliged to paint first and draw afterwards. The china painter, therefore, instead of beginning by staining drawings with paint, enters his world, as he should, head foremost, literally a "born painter." I have named two forms of discipline that are imposed on the potter's servant, but there is a third. The painter on *biscuit* knows that the lamp behind his purple jar is the white ground of the *biscuit* itself. Thus triply armed, not in theory only, but in training, Renoir passed, by way of the fan and the painted blind, on to canvas.

i.e. a decorator of porcelain

And so this perfect painter proceeds, for the rest of his brilliant life, to improvise from nature, subject to immediate revision at home, his astounding array of impeccable masterpieces in terms of the flowers of the vetch. As much, and no more, of drawing as was needed for his feast of colour. In a dry-point by Renoir you may see the arms and hands of his little girls hardly carried much further than to what they have in common with the paws of a rabbit, and the eyes, out of tone, like twinkling cherries off a Staffordshire teapot. . . . Renoir was a great intellect, in nothing greater than this, that his august critical faculty retained him from all digression. His comprehension was universal. He understood himself, as he understood everything, with the complete detachment that belongs to the highest intelligence. So he stuck to his last.

CLIVE BELL

NATION AND ATHENAEUM

"The Rediscovery of Paganism"

October 20, 1923

Bell comments on the newly-acquired taste of the English rich for Impressionist painting. The article was illustrated by Renoir's Bathers of 1885–87. (Colorplate 97).

The cultivated rich seem at last to have discovered in the Impressionists what the Impressionists themselves rediscovered half by accident. They rediscovered paganism – real paganism, I mean – something real enough to be the inspiration and content of supreme works of art. Paganism, I take it, is the acceptance of life as something good and satisfying in itself. To enjoy life the pagan need not make himself believe that it is a means to something else – to a better life in another world, for instance, or a juster organization of society, or complete self-development: he does not regard it as a brief span or portion in which to do something for his own soul, or for his fellow-creatures, or for the future. He takes the world as it is, and enjoys to the utmost what he finds in it. . . . Your true pagan neither regrets nor idealizes: and while Swinburne was yearning nostalgically for "the breasts of the nymph in the brake," Renoir was finding inspiration for a glorious work of art in the petticoats of the shopgirls at the Moulin de la Galette.

Algernon Charles Swinburne (1837–1909)

I am talking about art and artists, mind you. There have always been plenty of people to delight in shopgirls' legs; but only an artist can get far enough away from, without losing hold of, this agreeable theme to transmute it into a thing of beauty. The common man when he tries to handle it is merely prurient or pornographic. In Renoir's pictures or Manet's there is no taint of anecdote or reminiscence, nothing of Félicien Rops or Van Dongen. They make you feel surely enough that the scene – be it dance or picnic, promenade or bar – is joyous, that "the atmosphere" is delightful; but both are far too much artists to hint at any particular feeling of their own for the model, considered not as a form but as a particular human being, or, worse still, to invite you to share it. All they have to express comes in to them through form and colour, and through form and colour goes out. If you want to mark for yourself the difference between the feeling of an artist for the gaiety and romance of Montmartre in the latter part of last century and that of some one who was not, you need only turn first to a picture by Renoir (e.g., *Le Moulin de la Galette*). . . .

Félicien Rops (1833–98)
Kees van Dongen (1877–1968)

I said that the Impressionists rediscovered paganism half by accident. They came at it through, of all things in the world, a doctrine – the pleinairiste doctrine. One hardly realizes how contrary to all the rules it was – I don't say it never was done – for a painter, before the Impressionists, to take his canvas out of doors and there complete his picture. Corot himself never made more than sketches *sur le motif,* and I think the same is true of Constable and Courbet. Daumier, to be sure, went into the street; but to seek, not its beauty and movement, but its tragic significance: if any precursor of Impressionist paganism there be, assuredly he is not Daumier. Still less is he that occasionally admirable painter Monticelli, who had no sense of actuality at all; but perhaps there is something to be said for the claims of Constantin Guys. The Impress-ionists at any rate, in search of *le motif,* took their easels out with them; took them into the streets and public gardens, into the country, into railway stations, down the river; and in the *motif* itself had to find an inspiration to fill their canvases to the brim. For another impressionist doctrine – dogma, one might almost say – which made for the rediscovery of paganism was what contemporaries of Claude Monet were pleased to call the doctrine of scientific representation. Claude Monet insisted that the artist should paint only what he saw; he was to put nothing into his picture but what was visible in the object. . . .

COLORPLATE 53

Honoré Daumier (1808–79), Adolph Monticelli (1824–96), Constantin Guys (1805–92)

The consequence of these pleinairiste and pseudo-scientific theories was that the Impressionists gave a vision of life at one remove – transformed by a temperament, that is to say – instead of giving it at two, as the artist must who works from studies and adds sentiments in a carefully arranged north light. Compare any picnic or garden scene by Renoir with some picture of a fête by Watteau, and you will see in a moment what I am driving at. The Impressionist painter is so much closer to reality – not in representation, of course, but in sentiment – that by comparison Watteau seems almost to be giving us the picture of a picnic on the stage. I am not suggesting that there is any superiority in the impressionist method – I do not think there is: but I am suggesting that it led directly to the rediscovery of paganism. The impressionist painters had to extract all the beauty and significance they required from their

surroundings: they could depend neither on the intellectual additions and transformations nor on the traditional technical enrichments of the studio; nor were they permitted to eke out an artistic living by drawing on the dignity or picturesqueness of their theme. History and exoticism were taboo. In contemporary life they had to find all that they required, and contemporary life was lavish beyond their needs; so naturally they fell in love with it, and made the most exquisitely civilized of their generation and ours share their emotion.

* * *

The impressionist painter was in love with his world. He was in love with the absurd little horse-cab that took him to the gare St. Lazare, with its yellow body and its driver's shiny white hat. He was in love with the streets and the passers-by and the garish shop windows and the architecture of the boulevards even. He was in love with the station when he got there, with the bookstalls and the piles of luggage and the tall carriages and the puffing locomotives. He was in love with the cuttings and embankments and bridges, and the ridiculous little villas seen from the window, with their palisades and vegetable plots. . . .

Watteau, *Interior of a Park*. c. 1720? 50¼ × 76″ (127.6 × 193 cm). Wallace Collection, London.

WALTER SICKERT

THE SOUTHPORT VISITOR

Late Renoir

May 24, 1924

It is not surprising that speculators in Renoir should have been to the last unanimous in asserting that Renoir's latest works were better than ever. That any critic should have been found innocent enough to echo this two-edged politeness has always astonished me. It may not be necessary to tell an old man, stricken with mortal malady, that his work can never again be what it was. He certainly knows this better than anyone else. The transparent flattery combines derision of his intelligence with obvious insult to his masterpieces.

Messrs Lefèvre & Son and Mr Alexander Reid have now at their galleries in King Street, St James's, one of the most brilliant Renoirs in existence, a flower painting of roses and honeysuckle. With the recent memory of the flower pieces by Fantin sold at Christie's, this canvas by Renoir brings sharply before us the gulf that separates the painter of genius from one of respectable achievement.

AMBROISE VOLLARD

RENOIR, AN INTIMATE RECORD

1925

All the excerpts in quotation marks are spoken by Renoir himself, unless indicated otherwise.

"Some of our serving maids have had admirable figures and have posed like angels. But I must admit I'm not hard to please. I had just as rather paint the first old crone that comes along, so long as she has a skin that takes the light. I don't see how artists can paint those over-bred females they call society women! Have you ever seen a society woman whose hands are worth painting? A woman's hands are lovely – if they are accustomed to housework. At the Farnesina in Rome there is a *Venus supplicating Jupiter* by Raphael. What marvellous hands and arms! She looks like a great healthy housewife snatched for a moment from her kitchen to pose for Venus!"

* * *

After a pause he [the painter Laporte] went on: "Renoir's weak point is his drawing, don't you think? Heaven knows I begged him often enough to guard against it! I have always had a great weakness for David. There's a painter who doesn't trifle when it comes to line! If Renoir had listened to me and had paid as much attention to drawing as to colour, who knows if he might not have become another David. . . . I once said to Renoir: 'you must *make* yourself draw!' and do you know what he replied? 'I am like a cork thrown into a stream and tossed about on the current. When I paint, I just let myself go completely.'"

Jacques-Louis David (1748–1825)

* * *

"When I've painted a woman's behind so that I want to touch it, then it's finished."

* * *

Portrait of Ambroise Vollard. 1908.
32 × 25½″ (81.5 × 65 cm).
Courtauld Institute Galleries,
London.

"There is no doubt that Manet was surer of himself with black and white than with high-keyed colours. . . .

He was the first to establish a simple formula such as we were all trying to find.

Everyone knows how easily Manet could be influenced. He has been called "an imitator with genius." But when he really let himself go. . . . I saw in a window in the Rue Lafitte one of those little sketches of a woman's legs that Manet used to dash off in the street. . . . It was unique."

* * *

"Japanese prints are certainly most interesting, as Japanese prints . . . that is to say, on condition that they stay in Japan. No people should appreciate what does not belong to their own race, if they don't want to make themselves ridiculous. If they do, they produce nothing but a kind of bastard art, with no real character. Certain critics are beginning to claim me as a true member of the French school. I am glad of that, not because I think that that school is superior, but because – being a Frenchman – I ought to represent my own country."

* * *

Manet, *At the Café, Study of Legs.*
c. 1880. 7¼ × 4¾″ (18.5 × 12 cm).
Cabinet des Dessins du Louvre,
Paris.

[Renoir responds to a comparison of Degas with Toulouse-Lautrec.] "Ridiculous! Lautrec did some very fine posters, but that's about all. . . . Just compare their paintings of *cocottes* . . . why, they're worlds apart! Lautrec just painted a prostitute, while Degas painted all prostitutes rolled into one. Lautrec's prostitutes are vicious – Degas's never. Have you ever seen *The Patronne's Birthday?* It's superb!

"When others paint a brothel, the result is usually pornographic – always sad to the point of despair. Degas is the only painter who can combine a certain joyousness and the rhythm of an Egyptian bas-relief in a subject of that kind. That chaste, half-religious side, which makes his work so great, is at its best when he paints those poor girls. . . ."

The Patronne's Birthday, *(c. 1876/85), a monotype*

* * *

"I recently saw a drawing by Degas in a dealer's window – a simple charcoal outline in a gold frame which would have killed anything else. But it held its own superbly. I've never seen a finer drawing.

". . . Look at his pastels. Just to think that with a medium so very disagreeable to handle, he was able to obtain the freshness of a fresco! When he had that extraordinary exhibition of his in 1885 at Durand-Ruel's, I was right in the middle of my experiments with frescoes in oil. I was completely bowled over by that show. . . .

"Degas is the greatest living sculptor! You should have seen a bas-relief of his . . . he just let it crumble into pieces . . . it was as beautiful as an antique. And that ballet dancer in wax! . . . the mouth . . . just a suggestion, but what drawing!"

* * *

"Ah yes, *petit point*. Mirbeau took me one day to see an exhibition of that. But the worst of it was that on entering, you were informed that to be able to tell what the pictures represented, you must stand a metre away from them. You know how I love to walk close to a picture, and even take it in my hands! You remember the large picture by Seurat, *Les Poseuses*, that we saw together – a canvas painted in *petit point*, the last word in science! Lord! that picture was ugly in tone! . . .

"Can you imagine Veronese's *Last Supper* being painted in *petit point?*

"But when Seurat paints without tricks! . . . you know those little canvases of his, unpretentious, no "pure tones;" how beautifully they are preserved.

"The truth is that in painting, as in the other arts, there is not a single process, no matter how insignificant, which can reasonably be made into a formula. . . . The "scientific" artists thought they had discovered a truth once they had learned that the juxtaposition of yellow and blue gives violet shadows. But even when you know that, you still don't know anything. There is something in painting which cannot be explained, and that something is the essential. You come to Nature with your theories, and she knocks them all flat."

* * *

[Vollard asked: "Corot painted all his life in the open, didn't he?" Renoir replied as follows:] "His studies, yes, but his compositions were done in the studio. He *corrected* Nature. Everybody used to say that he was wrong to work his sketches over indoors. I had the good fortune to meet Corot once and I told him of the difficulty I had in working out of doors. He replied: 'That's because you can never be sure of what you're doing. You must always repaint in the studio.' But that did not prevent Corot from interpreting Nature with a realism that no Impressionist painter has ever been able to equal!"

* * *

"What I love so much is that aristocratic quality that you find over and over again in Velasquez, in the smallest detail, the simplest ribbon. The whole of painting is in the little pink bow of the *Infanta Margherita* in the Louvre! How lovely the eyes are and the skin in the hollow of the eyes! There is not the slightest shadow of sentimentality, either.

"I know that the critics find fault with Velasquez for his excessive facility. But what better proof that Velasquez knew his craft to perfection? Only the painter who knows his business thoroughly can create the impression that a picture was done at one stroke. His work looks so easy, but think of the experiments it must have involved. His blacks are magnificent. The older I grow, the more I love black!

"The workmanship in these pictures is so superb! He gives you thick and heavy embroideries with a simple rubbing of black and white. I know nothing more beautiful than *The Spinners*. The background of that picture is sheer gold and diamonds.

"Wasn't it Charles Blanc who said that Velasquez is too matter-of-fact? Why do people always look for ideas in painting? When I look at a masterpiece, I am satisfied simply to enjoy it. . . .

"There is another thing in Velasquez that delights me: his painting radiates with the joy the artist had in doing it."

* * *

"My friendship with her has been one of the finest I have ever had . . . what a curious thing Fate is! A painter with such a definite temperament born into the most austerely bourgeois milieu that ever was, and at a time when a child who wanted to be an artist was considered little short of a dishonour to the family! And what an anomaly too, in our age of realism, to find a painter so impregnated with the grace and delicacy of the eighteenth century; she was the last elegant and "feminine" artist that we have had since Fragonard, not to mention that "virginal" something that she had to such a high degree in her painting."

* * *

I used to go and see Renoir as a rule on Sunday morning. About eleven-o-clock Madame Renoir would say: "Is there anything you want, Renoir? I'm going to Mass."

"It is marvellous how you manage everything!" I said. I had found her shelling peas, with little Jean on her lap. He was teething and therefore not behaving very well. "To think that you even find time to go to Mass!"

Madame Renoir got up brusquely.

"Oh dear, the brushes haven't been cleaned!" And, dropping the peas and little Jean, . . . Madame Renoir flew into the next room. She came back with a handful of brushes.

"Renoir says that I clean his brushes better than Gabrielle. . . ."

* * *

"I don't know anything as awful as his *Oedipus and the Sphinx*. It has one good bit, however, a beautifully painted ear. His Napoleon seated on the throne is exceedingly beautiful too. What majesty it has! But Ingres' masterpiece is *Madame de Senonnes*: the colour is superb. . . . It is painted like a Titian. You must go to Nantes to see it. . . .

"It is a curious thing that when Ingres is carried away by his passion, he seems to run to imbecility. Look at the *Francesca da Rimini*: he tried to express so much passion in the attitude of the young man, that he made the neck twice as long as it should be; and Lord knows he knew how to draw a neck! The neck of *Madame Rivière*, in the Louvre, is another example! And the neck of the woman in *Roger and Angélique*. . . . People usually think she has a goitre! That is because Ingres, in making her bend her head back so far to show pain, threw the muscles of the neck out of position. And yet people will tell you he painted without passion."

* * *

Velasquez, *Infanta Margharita*. 1656/57. 27⅝ × 23¼" (70 × 59 cm). Louvre, Paris.

PAGE 162

307

"There isn't a finer picture in the world than the *Algerian Woman*. How really Oriental those women are – the one who has a little rose in her hair for instance! And the gait of the negress is absolutely right. You can almost smell the incense; it takes me back at once to Algeria."

PAGE 334

* * *

"Progress in painting? No, I cannot see any. No progress in ideas, nor any in technique, either. I once tried to change the yellow on my palette; the result was that I floundered about for ten years and then came back to the same one I used before . . . On the whole, the modern palette is the same as one used by the artists of Pompeii . . . down to Poussin, Corot and Cézanne; I mean that it has not been enriched. The ancients used earths, ochres and ivory black – you can do anything with that palette. Other tones have been added of course, but we could easily do without them. I have told you, haven't I, about the great discovery people thought they had made by substituting blue and red for black? But it doesn't come anywhere near giving you the richness of ivory black!"

CHARLES FOGDAL

ESSAIS CRITIQUES SUR L'ART MODERNE

"One Hundred and Sixty Renoirs"

1927

The critic Charles Fogdal writes about a prolific Renoir collector of the later years, the retired engineer Maurice Gangnat (1856–1924).

It is never a good idea to speak ill of chance: there is at times something divine in its hidden aims and distant benefits.

When the great industrialist Maurice Gangnat retired from business, it was not so that he could lead the glittering but empty life of socialites and snobs nor to indulge despicably in an upstart's delights.

At the clever prompting of his wife he decided to seek the finest, purest and fullest of joys in the arts. He began by frequenting museums; he would spend whole days at the Louvre, he visited the Salons and, in particular, the galleries and special collections. His fine, moderate taste quickly took him in preference to places where he could see and enjoy works by living artists.

One day in 1905 Maurice Gangnat was with Paul Gallimard; they had a heated conversation about the Impressionist masters, and mainly about Renoir; so much so that Paul Gallimard promised to put M Gangnat in touch with the great artist.

Paul Gallimard (1850–1929), owner of the Théâtre de Variétés, Paris. Friend and patron of Renoir from 1891; traveled with him to Spain in 1892.

He soon paid his first visit to Renoir who had moved to Cagnes in the South of France in 1900. On that occasion the amateur enthusiast took twelve canvases home with him. Gradually real bonds of understanding, then of friendship grew up between them. Renoir never let more than a year go by without leaving six, eight, even ten canvases for M Maurice Gangnat chosen from his work of the past twelve months. But after five years Renoir suddenly said to his purchaser, half seriously, half joking, in a friendly but determined voice:

"My friend, I am not going to sell you any more canvases! No, it's over; you have too many of my canvases! Your home must be terrible, with them piling up like that! The same painter on all the walls of one apartment!"

Portrait of Maurice Gangnat. 1916.
18½ × 15″ (47 × 38 cm). Private
Collection, Paris (Photo Studio
Lourmel).

"Come and see them," was all that M Gangnat would say.

When he left the collector, his friend Renoir was convinced: the faultless display of each of his many canvases made him retract his capricious threat.

The richness of the Gangnat collection continued to grow, with new works by Renoir being added up until the end.

I have just seen this "piling up" that Renoir referred to, in all the rooms of the huge apartment in the Avenue Friedland.

It is a color spectacular, an extravaganza of light, a wonder of art. There are one hundred and sixty Renoirs and four Cézannes. The canvases have been framed, positioned, mounted and shown to their best advantage with unusually expert taste, logic and perception, which leads one to the inescapable conclusion that many collectors, and many of our museum directors, not to mention artists, could learn a clear and useful lesson here.

There should have been crowds of them there at the exhibition, at the sale of those French treasures, now broken up, treasures which were as pure as they were sensual, with Renoir, infinitely varying the reds, pinks and ochers, appearing not as an Impressionist – he hated the word and described himself as a direct descendant of the eighteenth century – but simply, in humility, as a painter, a painter who was crazy about color in the golden light of Provence!

Of course it cannot be forgotten that Renoir at the end of his life, when he was a martyr to gout, had his brush fastened to his hand and his terribly twisted wrist. Of course people remember his suffering and his courage. For himself he thought only of the joy in painting and he never tired of repeating to his visitors: "If I hadn't survived beyond seventy I wouldn't exist!"

That was another whim; but it has to be remembered, with some ten years' difference, because Renoir's period after 1900 will perhaps prove to be the most significant. It is the period which, by virtue of the opulent fullness of his craft, with the materials ranging from a liquid lightness to carefully spread volume, will in time take on an incomparable vigor and a velvet quality.

In Mme Gangnat's main lounge beside the *Portrait of Mlle Bérard* (1887) the *Woman in the Grass* (1895), and the *Bois de la Chaise à Noirmoutiers* with its purple shadows, there is the *Woman with a Bouquet* (1917) with a beautifully modulated background, where Renoir has had fun drawing a comparison between the artificial flower in the woman's hair and the real flowers in a vase.

Turning round I can see a Cézanne without equal; it is *The Tall Pine,* a canvas of considerable size in which the background sky is so astonishing, where the cadence of colors is intensely felt and expressed and where the sun and the atmosphere seem to breathe life into this ancient landscape of Aix, loved and understood, and here in miniature.

On one side hangs *Le Canet,* a Renoir landscape which has to balance it on the other side Cézanne's *Banks of the Oise.* We shall soon see two more Cézannes, one a picture of the mountain behind Aix entitled *Mont Sainte Victoire,* and the other a water-color, *Climbing Geranium,* whose precision and finish are so deliberate and stubborn that you cannot help but think of the trouble which Cézanne must have chosen to give himself.

Soon again we shall see in a corridor a Vuillard, *Interior* with its deeply sensitive details; but that will be all and from now on our attention and admiration will be reserved for the Renoirs alone. They are everywhere, pre-eminent even in the library where there are small studies leaning against books. . . .

I go past the *Girl Reading* (1909); *The Post Office at Cagnes* (1908); and *Coco* (1905), a charming portrait of a baby copied by Renoir from Renoir, depicting the child's very soul in its freshness and tenderness.

COLORPLATE 109

In a small salon where the hangings, furniture and objects form a very eighteenth-century harmony, Renoir is reminiscent of Watteau with a *Seated Nude* with its soft, delicate grace; he brings to mind Fragonard with this other *Coco* – called, what is more, by Renoir himself *Coco Frago;* he is also reminiscent of a marquis of days gone by with a passionate interest in antiquity with his *Ode to the Flowers* inspired by Anacreon. And these *Flowers* are so alive with the dampness of sap and dew! And the nudes are so generalized, so symbolic, typical "Renoir women!" Nudes from the years 1905-12 which never spill over into debauchery or equivocation. How well here Renoir's art is seen as it really is, pictorially sensual, clear, harmonious and intoxicated with healthy beauty!

In the dining-room there are the two big ornamental panels of dancers: *Dancer with Tamborine, Dancer with Castanets,* there is the *Women with Hats* and a key work: *Wounded Bather.* This last canvas, originally entitled simply *Bather,* Renoir who signed a picture only after it was sold, had decided was incomplete; he looked at it for a long time, then in sudden inspiration seized his brush and palette; he added the red stain, the color of blood, and signed it. The *Wounded Bather* was finished.

COLORPLATES 112, 113

In a little boudoir beside the *Woman in a Pink Dress,* the *Peasant Girl Drying her Foot,* and *Little Maria Reading,* there are some landscapes: *La Poudrerie de La Rochelle* (1875), two representations of the south (1909), and *The Seaside Walk* (1910). And soon, coming to these other canvases where, full of a secret and penetrating poetry, there bursts forth the life of trees and vibrant skies and pulsating atmosphere, the life of the sun and moving shadows – such as: *The Farm of les Collettes* (1908), *Tall Tree* (1909), *Landscape with Woman and Dog* (1917), *The Rose Garden, Young Girl in a Vineyard*, – and similarly that little canvas which is so fervent, pious and enthusiastic a copy from Corot – soon I begin to think that perhaps Renoir does not yet have the place among the great landscape painters that he deserves. No one else, while remaining himself, has been able to vary his craft according to the time, light, motif, transitory vision or fleeting emotion as he has done; no one else has been able still to be "one" while being so "varied," always the painter of this fair Provence captured brilliantly because it is loved to excess.

Love! that is the secret of art. Love of color, that is the true secret of Renoir's art, a love that seems to be without restraint or limit, a passionate love that transfigures everything he uses as an excuse for painting. Look at Renoir's still life paintings! There are certainly more than twenty of them here that are unparalleled in savor and stunningly lyrical: material, objects, fruit; they seem to have hidden in them an indefinable, unexpected soul, with something of a wonder in its presence.

And so, yesterday, in the big Salon amidst the Renoirs and in front of the large Cézanne landscape, Mme Gangnat showed me mock-ups of the catalog for the forthcoming sale.

One hundred and sixty Renoirs! . . . The catalog, a work of art in itself, seemed to me – putting myself in the place of the amateur whose collection is to be broken up – a swansong of long and faithful affection. . . . I cast a farewell glance at the pictures hung here in this apartment of such refined and elevated taste; I looked at them and was overwhelmed by immense feelings of joy and melancholy.

CHRISTIAN ZERVOS

CAHIERS D'ART

"Is a Return to Subject Matter Likely?"

1931

This article by the art historian Christian Zervos, a Picasso scholar, considered which past painters of the figure may be relevant to young artists of the 1930s.

. . . With Renoir it is the sensual element in art that predominates: the wholly spontaneous invention of color that weaves its threads of dazzling light into bodies and faces and which endows the work of his second period with an almost physical quality hitherto unknown and charming.

Yet these are just qualities fit to delight only the senses, as sensually and directly as nature herself may delight them. We are unaware that behind this sensual delight Renoir has managed to conceal poetry or intelligence. In his representations that more mysterious, more refined element is missing, which is more subtle and moving than anything that a formal view of the world might produce and that Renoir was never able to elevate as far as the soul's intimacy and solemnity.

With form and construction having become for him ends in themselves and the feeling of sensuality being the very essence and the whole of his work, Renoir often managed to give new expression to things which, on their own, were devoid of character. All these spontaneous qualities created in Renoir's works a kind of musical principle and it is through this secondary feeling of music that I think Renoir touches the viewer much more than by the powerful sensuality of his temperament.

I am not trying to deny the plastic qualities of this artist whose creative force appears in his treatment of color (I am deliberately avoiding the

*Seated Bather in a Landscape, called
Eurydice.* 1895/1900. 45⅝ × 35″
(116 × 89 cm). Musée Picasso,
Paris.

Picasso, *The Spring*. Crayon on
canvas. 1921. 39⅜ × 78¾″
(100 × 200 cm). Musée Picasso,
Paris, © DACS 1987.

question of line), but yet these are only the effects of his temperament which lead him to permeate matter with a strong, burning sensuality. I have never come across a work where Renoir has risen to heights of perception, overcoming his subservience to physical matter. That is why he has never been influential in painting: he has never put anything into his work other than the sensual element of art, which can do no more than create a series of minor impressions.

It is Cézanne's work which has had the greatest influence on the painting of modern times, where all the constituent elements are welded together so well that "the form is no longer directed solely at the eye, but form and matter in their union and identity aim simply at one and the same effect which touches our *imaginative reason,* that complex faculty where every thought and feeling comes into being at the same time as its material analog or symbol."

Cézanne's work, which is indisputably the most lyrical of the nineteenth century, brings with it a mystery which reaches us simultaneously by the least familiar routes of our senses and reason. It is this work which, for the first time in the modern period, has sought to attain the very principle of art and rid it of everything superfluous. The genius of Cézanne has instinctively brought together and expressed the purest conditions of the art of painting better than any other painter of the last century. No one has stated so definitively the problem that preoccupies us and no other work could shed as much light on it.

HERBERT READ

THE MEANING OF ART

1931

Sir Herbert Read (1893–1968), British philosopher, art historian and critic who played a major role in the advancement of modern art in Britain from the 1930s.

But there is Renoir. Renoir is almost banal. No artist of the last hundred years was so free from self-conscious reflection on his activity as Renoir. He even disliked the word "artist" and preferred to be called a painter. His characteristic sayings reflect his modesty and lack of pretence in all that concerned his craft. "I have spent my life amusing myself by putting colours on canvas," he would say. Or "I think that perhaps I have not done badly because I have worked so hard." . . . no artist can be so certainly identified without a signature. And yet he was the most traditional of the great artists of his time. . . . Renoir is the final representative of a tradition which runs directly from Rubens to Watteau.

And yet Renoir is also one of our conquerors. . . . Merely in the commercial sense, he is probably the most appreciated of all nineteenth century artists. In 1878 some of his pictures are known to have been sold for forty or fifty francs; in 1928 one of them passed to America for the amazing sum of 125,000 dollars. But these figures should not intimidate us; they bear no relation to aesthetic values. Indeed there is no doubt that certain adventitious aspects of Renoir's art – the fact that more often than not he painted women, the "prettiness" of his palette, the simplicity of his subjects – tell more in his favour than those aspects of form and feeling which constitute the real strength of his art.

But in Renoir's case, it would be a mistake to emphasise the formal element. Some of his pictures, and the "Umbrellas" in the Tate Gallery is one of them, are no doubt marvellously composed, but others have no composition at all . . . generally in his paintings one is aware not of structure, but of surface. Renoir had an extraordinary sensibility for the surface of things, and particularly the surface of delicate flesh and of the

A Couple in the Street. Pen and black chalk. Illustration for *La Vie Moderne.* 17¾ × 11⅜" (45 × 29 cm). Fogg Art Museum, Cambridge, Mass.

petals of flowers. Flowers and the flower-like flesh-tones of a woman's or a child's body – Renoir hardly ever painted anything else; and it is said that he would turn away from a half-finished painting of a nude to paint roses, many roses, until he had learnt from this exercise how to render the subtle sheen on the model's skin.

Renoir led a quiet and retired life. He was content with his garden and the company of his family. And yet scarcely any other painter of the last century so faithfully reflects the life and spirit of his period. When the curious student of the future turns to the paintings of this period to learn something of the visual aspects of its life, he will find scarcely anything of significance in Cézanne, or Gauguin, or Van Gogh; he will find many curious sidelights in Monet, Manet and Toulouse-Lautrec; but only in Renoir will he find the colour and gaiety and the character of everyday life. In that sense Renoir is the most representative painter of his age.

ROBERT REY

LA RENAISSANCE DU SENTIMENT CLASSIQUE

"Renoir"

1931

Robert Rey, art historian, was concerned like Zervos (pp. 311–333) to draw contemporary attention to the great figure painters of post-Impressionism.

With Renoir we come to a very different personality. He is far removed from that mental tension and self-surveillance which in Degas soon becomes painfully uneasy; his whole work breathes serenity. And if his hazardous beginnings and then the meditations of his riper years built up a more austere character towards the end, we never see in his work any changes in the striking contentment that it exudes.

With Degas it was possible for the classical sensibility to develop helped by a high degree of culture along with an atavism which preserved in him some quite decidedly conservative traditions. These even formed his opinions which were much in contrast with what was to be called, in ecclesiastical language, modernism.

This same classical feeling had different origins in Renoir's case.

He came from a modest background. His parents were artists, or rather artisans. They enjoyed, and consciously or not Renoir enjoyed with them, the prestige of masters, living or dead, whose extensive work, with its recognized technical merit, invested them with a certain glory.

During the years when he was influenced by Courbet and also close to Manet, Renoir naturally adopted a language and attitudes which were intensely hostile to academicism. And as his cultural awareness had not yet pointed him towards museums, and as he was not a great reader and was not much given to reflection, there are occasional remarks of his about various great masters of the past – Chardin for example – which reveal opinions which were not only insensitive but surprisingly brutal. It would be wrong to take them literally. Just the sight of his own works gives the lie to the sincerity of any remarks of this kind that he might have made. Less bent on systematic independence than Pissarro or Sisley . . . he was concerned to learn the elements of his craft as a painter from an artist whose official standing seemed well founded: Gleyre. Of course Sisley and Bazille also came to Gleyre's studio. It was there that Renoir got to know them. The friendship of which we find such interesting traces in Renoir's work dates from that time.

COLORPLATE 101. *Beach at Pornic.* 1892. 26 × 32″ (65.5 × 81.5 cm).
Private Collection (Photo M. Knoedler & Co., New York).

COLORPLATE 102. *Girl with a Basket of Fish.* c. 1889. 51½ × 16½"
(130.7 × 41.8 cm).
National Gallery of Art, Washington D.C.
(Gift of William Robertson Coe).

COLORPLATE 103. *Girl with a Basket of Oranges*. c. 1889. 51½ × 16½"
(130.7 × 42 cm).
National Gallery of Art, Washington D.C.
(Gift of William Robertson Coe).

COLORPLATE 104. *Apples and Pears.* c. 1885/90. 12½ × 16⅛″ (32 × 41 cm).
Musée de l'Orangerie, Paris (Collection Jean Walter and Paul Guillaume).

COLORPLATE 107. *Bather Drying her Leg*. 1895. 20 × 15¾″ (51 × 40 cm).
Musée de l'Orangerie, Paris (Collection Jean Walter and Paul Guillaume).

COLORPLATE 108. *Place de la Trinité.* c. 1892. 21½ × 25¾″ (54.5 × 65 cm).
Private Collection.

COLORPLATE III. *Judgement of Paris*. Sanguine and white drawing. 1908. 18½ × 24″ (46.9 × 60.9 cm).
Phillips Collection, Washington D.C.

COLORPLATE 112. *Dancer with Tambourine.* 1909.
61 × 25½″ (155 × 65 cm).
National Gallery, London.

COLORPLATE 115. *Gabrielle with Jewelry*. c. 1910. 32 × 25½″ (81.3 × 64.8 cm).
Private Collection (Photo courtesy Acquavella Galleries, New York).

COLORPLATE 116. *Peaches on a Plate.* 1902/5. 8¾ × 14″ (22.2 × 35.6 cm).
National Gallery of Art, Washington D.C. (Ailsa Mellon Bruce Collection).

At first Renoir's existence was spent in hard-working obscurity. In order to make a living he was obliged to undertake artisans', almost workmen's, jobs. But he was no less assiduous in attending sessions with Gleyre.

Gleyre is now barely remembered. Virtually all that is well known is his *Lost Illusions*, where his poetry proves to be delicate but facile, expressed through rather dry drawing and links its creator with the short-lived group of *Pompeians*. But instead of sculptural strength, we find in Gleyre a certain elevation of thought, a fairly acute but not vulgar sensuality, and especially concern for modeling forms while retaining their luminosity. Some of his nymphs and bathers present a kind of smooth majesty in their outlines, where there may perhaps be found a very distant echo of the ideal of Ingres.

When Renoir was with Gleyre in 1862, the young . . . all favored Courbet's realism, a realism which as we have said was more theoretical than actual, a realism in the style of Caravaggio, a realism drawn from museums and including ostentatious relief, from which Gleyre, on the other hand, distanced himself.

Did Renoir have any feelings of gratitude towards Gleyre? We have seen that in his early life, when he was less given to cerebral activity than Degas, it is his works which count rather than his words. These seem to show that Renoir did indeed feel a certain gratitude towards the master of the *Lost Illusions*, the proof of which is to be found in the catalog of the salons where Renoir appeared between 1864 and 1870:

1864 Salon. Renoir (Pierre-Auguste), born at Limoges. Pupil of M. Gleyre, rue d'Argenteuil, 23. 1618. *Esmeralda.*

1865 Salon. Renoir (Pierre-Auguste), pupil of M. Gleyre, avenue d'Eylau, 43. 1802. Portrait of Mme W.S. – 1803. *Summer Evening.*

1868 Salon. Renoir (Pierre-Auguste), rue de la Paix, 9, Batignolles.

Charles Gleyre, *Evening (Lost Illusions)*. 1843. 62⅝ × 92¼″ (159 × 242cm). Louvre, Paris.

2113 – *Lise* (the reference: pupil of M. Gleyre does not appear).

1869 Salon. Renoir (Pierre-Auguste). Same address. Pupil of M. Gleyre. – 2021. *In Summer, Study.*

1870 Salon. Renoir (Pierre-Auguste). Pupil of M. Gleyre. c/o M. Bazille, rue des Beaux-Arts, 8. – 2405. *Bather, Woman of Algiers.*

Was he, in doing this, trying to win favor with the jury? All that has been said about his character leads us to reject such an explanation. Neither Renoir nor his fellow disciples were so far-sighted. Sisley, when he had a showing at the Salon in 1867, called himself a pupil of Corot before mentioning Gleyre; and even in 1867 Corot was not considered to be a very effective reference.

In Renoir's loyalty we are led rather to see a tribute to the man whose teaching he did not think to have been without its uses.

* * *

In 1865 Manet, a rich Parisian dandy, enjoyed a considerable reputation although one built on scandal, and must have seemed to them to be a successful, if fairly distant, contemporary.

But while his boulevard education and frame of mind and his "Café Tortoni" appearance might have attracted a Degas or a Bazille who could argue with him, they did not give much confidence to Pissarro – who was three years older than Manet – whose tastes, both rustic and meditative, were ill-suited to an eloquence which appeared to him rather disconcerting; or Cézanne, a provincial with a strong accent; Renoir, accustomed to the simple customs of the art workshop, or even Claude Monet, snatched from the vicissitudes of an impecunious and fairly rough Bohemian existence.

All these did not attend without a certain embarrassment the glittering café meetings at the Café de Bade and then the Café Guerbois, where the witty Manet was to be seen at times trenchant, at times casual, surrounded by writers, poets and well-known critics, full of pointed remarks and abounding in subversive paradox.

For a long time they kept themselves at a distance. We should not be misled by the well-known *Studio in the Batignolles Quarter*, where Fantin-Latour in 1870 grouped Renoir, Monet and Bazille around Manet. In a letter to Edward Edwins, Fantin-Latour makes it sufficiently clear that these were young men of talent and goodwill, but of no importance, and that the painter is using them as motifs at least as much as models.

At least until 1865 we can understand how Courbet could have seemed to them a more expensive and more accessible personality, as the triumphant prince of rebellious daubers and how they were able to reconcile their admiration for the master of the *Fight between Stags* with academic teaching, which was the first and only stage that could be envisaged by a young man with no money or contacts.

In any case Renoir's modesty in seeking to learn the grammar of his art at the Beaux-Arts, and his constant citing of Gleyre's name, means that he was less resolved than others systematically to adopt realism.

The first work that he had accepted by the Salon, in 1864, was an *Esmeralda*, a picture of academic romanticism that he subsequently destroyed. To depict the victim of Phoebus was not to betray Courbet. Courbet, in his naive, truculent narcissism had not hesitated in the past, like all the students of his generation, to appear in the guise of a bearded, brightly dressed guitar player, looking vaguely Florentine. Later in the *Wounded Man,* he painted himself at the foot of a tree, covered in blood like a dying assassin. Even better, this great advocate of realism had shown his own self-portrait in the Salon of 1849, laden with echoes of Tintoretto, and with the title *Study of a Venetian.* It was Delacroix and not Courbet who wrote: "We are sick of imitations of old pictures."

Nonetheless, when the scandal of Manet's *Luncheon on the Grass* was already a year old and when every day in Martinet's window the painter of

COLORPLATE 7

COLORPLATE 6

COLORPLATE 54

Café Tortoni was a fashionable meeting place for Manet and his circle.

PAGE 353

Lola de Valence was showing canvases where the play of natural light produced such abrupt and unforeseen effects, how could such romantic illusions as the *Esmeralda* be perpetuated?

Renoir was able to remain faithful to Courbet as far as the technique of the picture in question was concerned, but he was bound to follow the example of the master with the Assyrian beard more closely. He was back in the Salon again in 1865 with a *Portrait of Madame W.S.* and a *Summer Evening*. Thus Renoir was already working as a portrait-painter. As with Degas the human face and body were to become his main source of inspiration. While Sisley, Pissarro and Monet especially were increasingly eliminating character in favour of pure landscape, Renoir followed a completely opposite path and his last human figures almost filled the canvas.

This should read Monsieur W.S., a portrait of Sisley's father (Daulte 11)

* * *

We have seen that Renoir's work did not figure at the Salon in 1867. The picture that he sent was refused. It portrayed *Diana the Huntress*. . . . In this same picture there are many details to show that Edouard Manet also haunted him: the way in which the eyes, the eyebrows are indicated just by plain, dark accents, and the way the shadows of the contours are grouped at the outline, along the left arm, in contrast to the outer profile of the right forearm, so as to interfere as little as possible with the essential volume of the body. Renoir was perfectly well aware of Edouard Manet's esthetics and technique. He had done a drawing based on Manet's *Fife player* which the Salon had rejected in 1866: it is an interpretation more than anything; in the monochrome sketch the simplified architecture of the figure (particularly the left arm) comes over with unusual vigor. From the careful study of a document like this, moreover, we can see the great difference that lies between him and Edouard Manet.

COLORPLATE 10

Drawing after Manet's *The Fifer*. 1883.

* * *

If we compare Renoir's *Lise* shown in 1869 and Claude Monet's *Luncheon on the Grass* painted in 1867, we can see how Claude Monet is content with sights captured from life in their full vigor and with the surprise of the unexpected, while Renoir is very concerned with poetic perception, with making perceptible the essential architecture of a form and finally and particularly giving to that form a fullness that is both robust and gentle, and an almost superhuman serenity corresponding to his inner dream. But while geniuses like Ingres and Degas could, instinctively, do without the resources provided by light and the symphony of colors, Renoir's painting, on the other hand, is constantly thirsting for the sun. We have seen how the great classical painters are always on common ground when setting out their esthetic ideas, but they do not remain any the less committed to their own particular temperaments when it comes to the means by which they convey their dreams through art. . . .

* * *

As the years passed, during which we have seen him modestly submitting to academic disciplines, and as his maturity gradually set him free from Courbet's charisma and the proximity of Edouard Manet, he discovered the master in whom we can recognize his direct forerunner: Delacroix. And, through Delacroix, Rubens.

In 1870 he showed at the Salon a model dressed as a *Woman of Algiers*. Let us be clear that this was not one of those works inspired by documentary romanticism such as those produced some twenty years earlier by Decamps, Belly or Marilhat.

On the contrary, in treating this subject, Renoir was freeing himself from fashionable realism and simply using the excuse of the brilliant

COLORPLATE 54

materials which decked his model to give free rein to his need both to create joyous symphonies of color and to use some of Delacroix's range. He wanted to soak in his luminous power. He studied his works passionately; he made a copy of the *Women of Algiers*, just as Delacroix himself had made a copy of Rubens' *Christ before Pilate*, a copy which today hangs next to the original.

In 1872 Renoir sent to the Salon his famous *Harem*, whose real title was *Parisian Women Dressed as Algerians*.

PAGE 335

Everywhere in this picture there are echoes of Delacroix. The young Algerian girl at the bottom left of the canvas holding out a mirror is of a design that closely follows the crouching concubine of the *Women of Algiers*. At the back, there is the rear view of a woman sitting on a sort of coffer whose bright ornaments exactly evoke the scarlets which Delacroix used to embellish the furniture in *Women of Algiers*. The arms, size of the bust and the deliberately relaxed drawing of the forearms and hands with the fingers spread out are taken from, indeed are almost traced from, certain of Delacroix's characters. In his powerful ingenuousness Renoir tries to give, in the sultana in the center, an impression of lavish, ornamented beauty which is quite independent of the subject. Like all the great classical poets of the brush, he resorts to the most naive means of expression that a more cultured but less fervently inspired mind would have shunned as being too simplistic.

He paints metaphors. You say "dazzling beauty" and he establishes his main character with a gamut of whites, pinks, crimsons and lacquer so that the whole achieves the greatest possible luminosity in painting. If you say "golden hair" there are, indeed, gold lights crowning the sultana's fine forehead. If you say of tulle draping a body that it is as "light as a mist," then it is not cloth but sumptuous mist that covers the model's shoulders and girds her waist.

This strength in quite simply displaying an entity represented by the character painted, which is not provided by the model's appearance alone, is what makes Renoir's great portraits, especially those dating from the period 1870 and 1880, unique of their kind.

Being of humble birth and having grown up among laborers, he is amazed at luxury. He conveys it with an ingenuousness which magnifies

Delacroix, *Women of Algiers*. 1834. 70⅞ × 90⅛" (180 × 229 cm). Louvre, Paris.

transitory details and raises them to the level of lasting beauty. The most famous and most characteristic of the many portraits he painted is that of Mme Charpentier and her two daughters, a picture now in the proud possession of the Metropolitan Museum in New York.

Mme Charpentier's luxurious dress spreads out over a sofa of oriental material and flows on to the floor revealing the lace of her petticoat, like foam on the crest of a wave. In the background a still life (fruit, a ewer) has an opulent glow. One of the two little girls is sitting on the sofa, the other on a gigantic St Bernard. The children's bodies and limbs with their rounded contours, especially the younger one, enable the artist to create a strange kind of melody in the line. He has done more than a child's portrait, he has created a delightful unconscious mask; one can guess that he was less concerned to depict a particular child with a name, than "childhood." His young models are clad in all the luxury of blues and silky whites. He does not hesitate to accentuate the complex richness of current fashion. The huge, gentle dog, lying in the foreground, is of unlikely proportions; he is more like a bear with enormous paws; his black and white fur is mannered, like an heraldic ornament. The animal's power contrasts with the youth and slenderness of the little girl with chestnut hair, who is using his wide shaggy flanks as a seat.

Such a picture would be ridiculous in anyone else's hands. One even wonders how, miraculously, it not only does not make you want to laugh but induces that kind of happy contemplation that some of Veronese's canvases can also create.

COLORPLATE 75

Parisian Women in Algerian Dress. 1872. 61⅜ × 50¾" (156 × 129 cm). National Museum of Western Art, Tokyo (Matsukata Collection).

It is precisely because, with a serenity and responsiveness equal to that of Veronese, Renoir sees these details, and these signs of richness simply as elements of form and color, and with a kind of passion he expresses their forms with the maximum harmony and their color with the maximum brilliance.

Ten years earlier at Marlotte he had painted *Mother Antony's Inn*. He had also portrayed the vigorous boatmen of Chatou and their laughing female companions. And at more or less the same time as Mme Charpentier's portrait he began that of the actress Jeanne Samary. In all these works we can see his astonishing ability to force the spectator to move from the idea of a portrait to that of a symbol.

COLORPLATE 3
COLORPLATE 76

COLORPLATE 69

* * *

There is no doubt that Renoir underwent a sort of crisis at that point in his life (early 1880s). Had he before then thought very much about Ingres' esthetics? One of his more thoughtful biographers thinks so.

Towards the end of his life a friend asked him whether he felt any affinity with Ingres. Renoir replied: "I should very much like to" (François Fosca).

François Fosca, Renoir, *Paris 1923*

The nudes with big curves and full, broad seats (like the nude in the Stchukin collection in Moscow) took on a different appearance when, from 1875 onwards, he looked beyond the model and turned them into beings analogous to Rubens' nymphs. His discoveries on his Italian journey took an order and organization and completely modified his art. . . .

We have seen Renoir like Ingres before him admiring the ceramic paintings in the Naples museum. The Pompeian frescoes disturbed him deeply.

As his life drew to a close Renoir entrusted his memories to Ambroise Vollard, a conscientious listener who has faithfully passed on to us those conversations. There, in a lively and colloquial form, we have the painter's very thoughts, confirmed by the facts themselves.

(see p. 55.)

"In about 1883 there came a break in my work. I had gone right to the limits of Impressionism and had come to the conclusion that I could neither paint nor draw. Put simply, I had reached a dead end."

So he had to revise all his pictural beliefs and all the details of his art. An example that speaks of greatness. Renoir was still known only to a limited group of amateurs. His financial situation remained precarious. Yet he sacrificed his bright palette to his inner needs, of which he became more conscious with this reversal, in order to raise himself still further above realism.

First he restrained his love for the bright sunlight. Of course he did not deny the splendors of the open air. But they were fraught with danger, obliterating contours and changing forms. They were experienced by the eye without there being any channeling of thought. Renoir accurately observed: "You are captivated by the light and have no time to think about composition; then, out of doors, you cannot see what you are doing."

Composition! The word sums up a whole aspect of classical art which Renoir's so-called "Impressionist" colleagues pretended hardly to care about.

The Pompeian figures had surprised and charmed him by their simplicity and evocative power. "Those priestesses in their silver gray tunics look exactly like Corot's nymphs," he said. Now they are painted free from any preoccupation with atmosphere. They stand out in the crystal-clear air, like Ingres' nudes or M Bertin's portrait. Their conception and in particular their execution was the reverse of what Renoir had done hitherto.

Until then he had indicated "depth" by means of the variations in color that we have been talking about. He now forced himself to model forms in terms of relations between light and dark. When he was in Naples again in 1881 he painted a large nude with hardly any shadow at all at the drawn outline, dispensing with that atmospheric haze in which he had hitherto loved to bathe them. Soon he was experimenting with painting only in red ocher, yellow ocher and earth green. "Happy the ancients," he would say, "who could use only ochers and browns."

He wanted to strip his composition of all the extravagant color that had saturated it until then. At Rome he had seen murals painted in oils, by Raphael, presumably in the Vatican loggie. He tried to recapture the luminous matt of those frescos which he had described in a letter to Mme Charpentier as being full of sun. To achieve this he "imagined," as he himself said later, "removing the oil from the color." He did not manage to obtain the effects he wanted. "I did not know then that elementary truth that oil painting must be done with oil. And, of course, none of those who had drawn up the rules of the 'new' painting had thought to give us that vital clue. . . ."

He admired the precise technique, devoid of gloss, of Degas' portraits. He pursued his idea of painting if not exactly a fresco at least in the style of a fresco and tried painting on cement.

He attempted a real retreat; he wanted to free his painting from all flashiness and it was with that in mind that he began in 1882 the famous picture of the *Bathers* in the Jacques-Emile Blanche collection. It cost him three years' sustained effort, according to his biographers, to work out this picture. The composition was reworked several times during that time. A naked woman sits on a river bank drawing back the draperies which had covered her; to her left another woman leans half over backwards to avoid water being thrown at her by a third nymph, who is in the water up to the middle of her thighs. In the background two more figures can be seen, one standing up and tying back her hair, the other swimming.

COLORPLATE 97

Even a reproduction shows the difference between the atmosphere and the relief of the figures; how concern for composition and for simplicity must have preoccupied the painter.

Certain gestures, such as that of the bather on the left bending back her foot at an acute angle, are reminiscent of some of the attitudes found in Japanese prints that Renoir would have known. But rather than a search for style, it is far more a quasi-mythological interpretation of summer that is expressed by the contour of this great pink form, rendered in a smooth, thick paste that is variously compared to lacquer, kaolin and polished marble.

These bathers recall the most elegant and idealist works of the Fontainebleau School or Girardon's delightful bas-reliefs "which were the artist's inspiration" (François Fosca).

Confronted with the reproduction of such a work one can understand how sincere Renoir must have been when he said: "The lesson of the museum is the only one for the artist."

* * *

When in about 1888 Renoir freed himself from these memories of formal classicism, he returned to all the variegated effects of his earlier pictures. He had withdrawn to spend years alone with those he recognized as masters. He had paid devout homage to them. He no longer owed them anything. However it feels now as though the forms he invented like pagan prayers (yet innocent of anything written!) were of more importance to him than the almost kaleidoscopic extravaganzas, contemporary with his great canvases of 1872 to 1875.

Then came the period that later generations will perhaps see as the most complete in Renoir's work. From his palette there arose a race of goddesses with low foreheads, stretched out on celestial lawns, full of that luxuriant happiness that befits heavenly beings. His career blossomed with portraits of women and children amid beautiful flowers until 1900, when gout forced him to seek the warmth of southern climes.

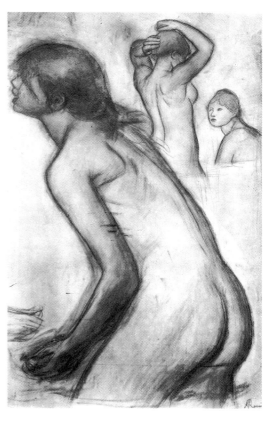

Study for *The Bathers*. Pencil.
1884/5. 41 × 64"
(104 × 162.5 cm). Louvre, Paris
(Photo Durand-Ruel).

Strengthened by the knowledge he had acquired during the crisis described above, he came back to the sun and sought its enchantment once again. But he had acquired a meticulous respect for form and the brilliance of the light no longer hid its power from him. Renoir no longer referred to Impressionism except to condemn more strongly than ever the Realist fallacy of which that so-called school was the ultimate consequence. . . .

To a lady who told him that her son, a young man of fifteen who wanted to be a painter, was true to nature, Renoir replied severely: "So young and already true to nature! Well, Madame, he is lost."

This last period of his life is that of the great nudes in the open air.

The model is of little importance to him, her presence in the sun is needed only for passing reference; it enables him to be reassured that his invention is not moving improbably far from the truth. Yet he wanted his models to be strong and rounded, and above all for their flesh to take the light well. Like Gauguin he had no place for tiny ankles and slender wrists.

The idea of the divine began to grow in him. That idea became more obsessive as Renoir approached death, and particularly pervasive in his last figures, where the tones have an extraordinary range and the torsos are as powerfully articulated as in Michelangelo's *Night*.

* * *

Renoir thought continually of antiquity. As a child he had spent many hours in the department of antiquities at the Louvre; and the mystical germ that those visits had planted in his mind now bore fruit. His large nudes retained from nature what the painter wanted to keep for his amusement and for "delectation" as Poussin said; nothing for the lower thoughts. Besides he now talked of art as Ingres had done before him. While admiring the work he disapproved of the *Dance* by Carpeaux remaining on its pedestal; he even went so far as to say "Let these drunken women be taken somewhere else. . . . The dance taught at the Opéra has a tradition and it is a noble thing."

At his home in Cagnes he embarked on real allegories such as *The Rhône* and *The Saône;* he roughed out a *Chloë* and a *Judgment of Paris;* he did numerous sketches for an *Oedipus Rex*. And, through natural inclination, he tackled sculpture. He tackled it at the highest point where Degas had left off. And he added that sense of the divine with which he was more and more deeply imbued. Together with a young sculptor, Guino, he did a bas-relief, the *Judgment of Paris*, and modeled a large Venus, closely related in the scope and serenity of its forms to the *Venus Anadyomene* that Chassériau had painted in 1839.

Many years before, in 1883, during his long retreat, one of his friends had discovered on a stall on the embankment the little *Treatise on Painting* by Cennino Cennini. Renoir had been struck by a meticulous good faith and naively elevated thought which dominated the text, which offered instruction in grinding mortar suitable for a fresco as well as in pure living in order to conceive fine works.

Mottez, Ingres' favourite pupil, who had done the frescoes at Saint-Sulpice and Saint-Germain l'Auxerrois, had produced an edition of it. And Mottez' son, who was on the point of bringing out a revised edition of the *Libro dell'Arte*, had asked Renoir to write the preface. We might see this preface as Renoir's testament. On every page his faith in the classical tradition is affirmed. . . .

* * *

From a future vantage point, when external differences are no longer apparent, people will come to see Renoir's last great nymphs on the same superhuman level as the *Grand Odalisque d'Ingres* of 1814 or the *Diane d'Anet;* both of them are no less arbitrary in form, no less immunized against the evils of thought and of the flesh to which mortals are prone.

COLORPLATE III

PAGE 244

Victor Louis Mottez (1809–97)

(see pp. 241–42.)

More consistently than Degas and impelled by a desire which was by nature much more spontaneous, he was a great representative of classical feeling at a time apparently so lacking a sense of order.

Renoir's physical weakness has often been stressed, his frail, withered hand which could hold a brush only with the help of an unpleasant looking contrivance.

But in this final period where his will was growing weak without there being any change in his astonishing lucidity, did he not say himself that every day he felt freer and more in command? And he rose continuously towards an ever higher conception of both discipline and tradition.

ALBERT C. BARNES AND VIOLETTE DE MAZIA

THE ART OF RENOIR

1935

Albert C. Barnes (1872–1951), American research chemist who became a prodigious collector; founder of the Barnes Foundation, Merion, Pa., which opened in 1924, including a very considerable holding of Renoirs. Violette de Mazia is Vice-President of the Foundation and Director of Education.

The vital importance in art of a constantly increasing capital of aesthetic meanings, may be illustrated by a comparison of Monet's work with Renoir's. Because Monet's sensitivity and interest were practically restricted to the field of out-of-door light-and-colour effects, each new impact upon his senses called forth a type of reaction similar to previous reactions; selection and interpretation took place each time according to the monotonous dictates of his fixed set habits and limited background, and correspondingly, failed to enrich the latter by expanding the boundaries of his vision.

Renoir too was interested in the impressionistic interpretation of nature and in Monet's technical method of expressing it; but the impact upon his senses, and his interpretation of what was being done by his contemporaries, instead of limiting his field of vision, quickened his sense of perception and broadened his insight. Thus the impressionistic form itself, in Renoir's hands, acquired a richer meaning because his keener perception and greater freedom of receptivity had discovered in it fuller possibilities than were ever suspected by its originators.

A set of landscapes by Monet offers great variety in subject-matter – especially in their character of illumination at different times of the day; but the essential quality expressive of the interaction of the scene with the man's personality is monotonously alike in all. Monet, in other words, was awake to only certain phases of life, beyond which his specialised vision seldom reached; Renoir, on the other hand, was continuously unfolding in his perception of Nature. He consistently inquired for, discovered, selected, established, organised and expressed new pictorial effects, connections, relationships, values and meanings, all reflecting a wide field of life activities, and a profound assimilation of the great traditions of painting. In contrast to Monet, Renoir could paint the very same spot of landscape a number of times and each version would reveal an essentially different ramification of his spirit and feelings.

JOHN REWALD

RENOIR DRAWINGS

1946

Among those who turned to Delacroix in the decisive years of their apprenticeship was Auguste Renoir. Like Manet and Cézanne – and later Gauguin and Van Gogh – he copied the master's work. However, his admiration for Delacroix by no means blinded him to Ingres' merits. In fact, Renoir was the only painter of the second half of the nineteenth century who frankly acknowledged his debt to both Delacroix and Ingres. Whereas the former guided his early steps and assisted him in establishing a link with the past, with Rubens and Watteau, the latter helped to extricate him from the complex difficulties when he felt, many years later, the need for structure and line. But at the time when he turned to Ingres, Renoir already possessed the one quality whose development he owed to Delacroix – spontaneity – and this rescued him from dangerous submission to linear proficiency. Ingres delivered him only after Delacroix had saved him. Thus Renoir combined two heritages and reconciled the two poles, colour and line. . . .

Portrait of Paul Cézanne. Pastel. 1880. 21¼ × 17″ (54 × 43 cm). Private Collection (Photo Durand-Ruel).

Turning towards line as a means of discipline, Renoir applied himself to simplifying forms at the expense of colour. Like Ingres – whom he understood better after having admired Raphael – he tried to imprison breathing forms in rigorous contours, sometimes simple, sometimes even elegant, but occasionally also reminiscent of that linear "straightjacket" of which Baudelaire wrote. So complete was the change in his work that many friends viewed Renoir's evolution with alarm, while others hailed in him the true inheritor of a great tradition. The rumours which spread about his new style are reflected in an article by George Moore, who asserted that for two years Renoir had "laboured in the life class, working on an average from seven to ten hours a day, and in two years he had utterly destroyed every trace of the charming and delightful art which had taken him twenty years to build up." And Moore added, somewhat patronisingly: "I know of no more tragic story."

There was, however, nothing tragic in Renoir's development. With admirable lucidity and will-power he fought against his spontaneity, and what he lost in charm, he gained in grandeur. When he eventually became aware of the fact that he would never completely defeat his spontaneity – the most precious of his gifts – he decided to abandon his one-sided emphasis on line. "Honour to you Renoir, for not having feared to commit an error!" Rouault later exclaimed. Indeed, Renoir might have erred in allowing himself to be inspired by Raphael and Ingres; but an error admitted is no longer an error – it may even become a virtue.

When Renoir abandoned what has been called his "Ingresque" period, he was not only richer in experience, he was ready to be himself. Far from returning to where he had left off when he first went to Italy, he found himself on a new threshold, ready to combine his colourist's instinct with his draughtsman's knowledge. Of impressionism he retained merely the glistening textures, the technique of small strokes, with which he now endeavoured to create voluminous forms. He modelled with colour, and though he did not rely on line, neither did he ignore it. Like Delacroix he achieved the perfect unity of colour and line. But while the former's concern had been with movement, Renoir's was with plasticity.

Having found a way to unite colour and line, Renoir discovered the whole range of possibilities offered by each.

PATRICK HERON

THE CHANGING FORMS OF ART

"Pierre Bonnard and Abstraction"

1947

His [Bonnard's] paintings have a visual alloverness, an evenness of emphasis and handling which are more reminiscent, as isolated qualities, of the vision of the perceptual Monet than of the more conceptual Renoir. But these qualities in Bonnard are not isolated; and altogether he is far nearer Renoir than Monet. On the whole we cannot class Bonnard as a conceptual. . . . He forged a conceptual imagery out of perceptions. His form is very powerful; but it is distinct from the form of Renoir in that it is developed entirely in terms of this "alloverness." Renoir developed the forms of the various objects in his composition more or less separately: that is, sculpturally. The beauty of form of a head, a breast or an arm, or of tree trunks, or fruit, in a Renoir picture, is something we can contemplate in ignorance of the rest of the canvas: each object has its own self-centred perfection of form – which is a sculptural form. But the form of the objects

Pierre Bonnard (1867-1947), *Renoir*. Etching. 1916. 10⅝ × 7⅞" (27 × 20 cm). Bibliothèque Nationale, Paris. © ADAGP 1987.

in a picture by Bonnard hardly exists in isolation from the total configuration. . . . Form in Bonnard is more essentially pictorial than it is even in Renoir, for whom a picture was an arrangement of solid, rotund, sculptural, separate forms. Indeed, Bonnard's forms have an apparent flatness: the masses of his forms seem flattened so as to display the largest area or plane to the spectator. But this flattening is somehow itself the very agent of spatial realisation. . . .

CLEMENT GREENBERG

ART AND CULTURE

"Renoir"

1950

Clement Greenberg (b. 1909), American critic who propounded in the 1950s and 60s an influential hierarchy of formal values for modern art.

My reactions to Renoir keep changing. One day I find him almost powerful, another day almost weak; one moment brilliant, the next merely flashy; one day quite firm and the next merely soft. The extraordinary sensitivity of his pictures – even, and sometimes especially, the late ones – to the lighting under which they are seen has, I feel sure, something to do with this. Supposedly, the Impressionist aesthetic made lighting and distance all-important factors in the viewing of a picture – but only supposedly. None of the Impressionists themselves seems actually to have made any more of a case about viewing conditions than artists usually do, and successful Impressionist pictures will generally declare their success under the same conditions as other successful pictures. That Renoir's should form such an exception would seem to be due to Renoir himself rather than to Impressionism.

I think part of the explanation may lie in the very special way in which he handled light and dark, making their contrasts seem just barely to coincide with contrasts of pure color; it may be for this reason that his contrasts tend to fade under a direct or bright light or when seen too near. But the un-Impressionist variety of Renoir's subject matter may also help to explain the fluctuations in one's response to the quality of his art. Landscape, still life, portrait, figure, group and even anecdote – he went from one to another easily and often, if not always with success. Even the best of his landscapes, which came around 1880, lack a certain finality, and so do the famous group scenes of earlier date. With the single figure, the still life and the flower piece – things he could see with an un-Impressionist closeness – he could at the same time succeed more consistently. On the other hand, some of the best pictures of his old age – and thus some of the very best of all his pictures – are group compositions.

Twenty years ago there was less question among professionals about Renoir's standing. Simplification, broadness, directness, as perceived in the later Monet, and in Matisse too, are what excite us at the moment, and we begin to feel that Renoir and even Cézanne can often be a little niggling. Renoir could execute broadly and directly; but in conceiving he was guided by the ordinary, self-evident, anecdotal complicatedness of nature, which he acknowledged as much in his later as in his earlier works. The main difference towards the end was that he rid himself of the picturesque, which had entered his art in the late 1870s, and let his Impressionist technique arrive at ends more consonant with itself.

The picturesque means the picture as a result and as little else but a result – a sure-fire effect. The picturesque means all that is viable, transmittable, liftable without risk, in the ingredients of proven art. In Renoir's case it meant eighteenth century French and early Romantic

342

painting, but also the popular art that was so speedily fashioned from these sources.

He was not alone among the advanced artists of his time in his susceptibility to the popular. . . . But Renoir was the only one with whom the picturesque – if not exactly the popular – settled down for a long stay, to bring him relatively early financial success as well as to contribute to the genuine felicity of more than a few of his pre-1900 pictures. The Impressionist slice of nature, unmanipulated by "human interest" and uniform in emphasis from edge to edge of the canvas, was in Renoir's art given a sweeter but also a crisper unity. Without that, his lushness might have spilled over into a suffocating kind of decorativeness, given that he had even less appetite in the beginning for sculptural definition than Monet and was never quite sure of himself in articulating an illusion of really deep space. Always, after the middle 1870s, he tended to half-identify broad planes with the picture plane itself and to deal with them in terms of color texture rather than spatial function, dissolving large surfaces into dappled, swirling iridescences. But he would preserve enough of the motif's actuality to keep the eye from questioning the picture as a representation of three-dimensional forms; here the picturesque, with its manipulation of the motif in terms of anecdotal interest and set patterns of design, could serve to firm up the whole and impose coherence. The

Judgement of Paris. c. 1913/14.
28¾ × 36¼″ (73 × 92 cm).
Hiroshima Museum of Art
(Photo Archives Durand-Ruel).

result often verged on prettiness, but it is perhaps the most valid prettiness ever seen in modernist art. In the last decades of his life Renoir won through to a new handling of three-dimensional form. He achieved this in two ways: by throwing the entire emphasis of his color on warmth – his adherence to a bas-relief organisation of the picture, in which solid forms were lined up on a single frontal, therefore advancing plane (as in Titian), permitted him to do this with plausibility – and by modeling throughout with white highlights and correspondingly light and translucent coppery reds and silvery grays. It is above all to this high-keyed aerated modeling that Renoir owes the triumphs of his later nudes, portraits and figure compositions. Paradoxically, it was by dint of becoming more sculptural, after having at last tried his hand at actual sculpture, that he joined the Venetians and Rubens on the heights of painterly painting. But wherever he went into deeper space, the outcome still remained doubtful. His later landscapes often tend to be sketchy in a bad sense, and in these alone does his increasing addiction to madders and alizarin really become a mannerism.

Perhaps we are still too close to Renoir fully to appreciate his uniqueness. The current notion of what constitutes paint quality and highly finished painting derives very largely from his art, which in his own time was reproached, like that of the other Impressionists, for crudeness of *facture* and lack of finish; and this notion is a compromising one. At the same time, his method of high-keyed modeling has become a staple of academic modernism. What perhaps we still do not appreciate correctly is the essential vision that animates Renoir's technique, the vision behind his vision of the aims of art. There is a disjunction here which he just succeeded in overcoming late in life, with the fading of the desire to please, and with the abandonment of preconceptions about "good" or even polite painting. The less Renoir tried to conceal what I can only call his coarseness, the less there remained in it to be ashamed of.

KEITH VAUGHAN

JOURNAL

January 18, 1953

Keith Vaughan (1912–77), British painter

Renoir. He indulged a purely personal delight which happened to be shared by others. He painted in the same way as one might outline in one's memory recollections and fantasies of pleasure. Because he was utterly unconcerned with any other aspect of painting beyond manufacturing mementoes, his mementoes acquire a compelling power, and he is rated a great painter. But it really is not very difficult to paint this way. No struggle or search is required, no reaching out, no surpassing. Just the caressing brush, over and over again – the same beloved, longed-for forms. And like Brahms, the same lushness, the same apparent profundity and richness which in the end leaves only a feeling of indigestion and smell of cigar smoke (the F minor piano quintet, but not the songs). It is not enough that he did it supremely well. There must be some quality measured in the ambition.

KENNETH CLARK

THE NUDE

"Venus II"

1960

Sir Kenneth Clark (1903–83) (Lord Clark of Saltwood), art historian, Director of the National Gallery, London, 1934–45, was also a collector and patron of modern British artists.

Everyone who writes about Renoir refers to his adoration of the female body, and quotes one of his sayings to the effect that without it he would scarcely have become a painter. The reader must therefore be reminded that until his fortieth year his pictures of the nude are few and far between. The first to achieve celebrity was the *Bather with the Griffon*, now in the Museum of São Paulo. It was exhibited in the Salon of 1870 and won for Renoir the only popular success he was to enjoy for twenty years. With his usual simplicity he took no pains to conceal the origins of his composition. The pose is taken from an engraving of the Cnidian Venus, the lighting and the way of seeing are derived from Courbet. These contrary sources indicate the problems which were to occupy him for half his life; how to give the female body that character of wholeness and order which was the discovery of the Greeks and combine such order with a feeling for its warm reality. In the *Bather with the Griffon*, admirable as it is, the two components are not yet united. The antique pose is too obvious and the earthiness of Courbet's style does not express Renoir's own sunny temperament.

We may suppose that Renoir would have corrected these inconsistencies immediately had it not been that during the next ten years he became absorbed in the theories of Impressionism. Now Impressionism in its first, doctrinaire condition could not easily accept a subject which was both artificial and formal. The nude being a kind of ideal art is closely connected with that first projection of an idea, the outline; and during the 70s the Impressionists, Renoir among them, were at pains to demonstrate that the outline does not exist. When he painted the figure, he broke up its contours by dappling them with patches of light and shadow. But even in these years his instinctive understanding of the European tradition showed him how the great Venetians had rendered form through colour and he painted two nudes, the Anna in Moscow and the Torso in the Barnes Collection, which might almost be details from Titian's *Diana and Actaeon*. In these the outline is minimised by overlapping forms and the broken tones of the background, but the modelling is solid, and there seems to be no reason why Renoir should not have continued to paint a series of masterpieces in this manner. However, it did not satisfy his conviction that the nude must be simple and sculptural, like a column or an egg, and by 1881, when he had exhausted the possibilities of Impressionism, he began to look for an example on which such a conception of the nude would be based. He found it in Raphael's frescoes in the Farnesina and in the antique decorations from Pompeii and Herculaneum. The immediate result was a picture of his wife as the *Baigneuse blonde*, painted at Sorrento towards the end of the year, in which her body, pale and simple as a pearl, stands out against her apricot hair and the dark Mediterranean sea as firmly as in a painting of antiquity.

Like Raphael's Galatea and Titian's Venus Anadyomene, the *Baigneuse blonde* gives us the illusion that we are looking through some magic glass at one of the lost masterpieces extolled by Pliny, and we realise once more that classicism is not achieved by following rules – for young Madame Renoir's measurements are far removed from those of the Cnidian – but by acceptance of the physical life as capable of its own tranquil nobility.

Bertall, Caricature of the *Bather with the Griffon*. 1870. *Le Journal Amusant*, Paris, June 18, 1870. (Photo Bibliothèque Nationale.)

COLORPLATE 56; *Daulte 144(?)*

COLORPLATE 77

PAGE 346

The moment of revelation which inspired the *Baigneuse blonde* did not survive Renoir's return to France, and for the next three years he continued to struggle with the problems which he had solved by instinct beside the bay of Naples. To concentrate his forces he undertook a masterpiece, a composition of girls bathing, which should have all the qualities of classic French art from Goujon to Ingres. The general movement and some of the poses were inspired by a relief on Girardon's Fountain of the Nymphs at Versailles and throughout the many studies for the finished picture this sculptural conception persists. It is most marked in a large drawing, a cartoon worthy of the Renaissance, where the sense of relief and the flow of the line are so perfectly satisfying that I cannot conceive why Renoir should have altered them; yet in the finished picture every interval is worked out afresh. The execution is equally deliberate and although the tonality recalls Boucher, the use of paint has none of his decorative ease. In certain lights it almost seems as if the painstaking enamel of the surface has killed the first sensation of delight; but a passing cloud of an unexpected reflection will soften those dry transitions so that the whole picture flatters the eye like a Gobelins tapestry.

PAGE 254

Titian, *Venus Anadyomene.* 1525. 29⅞ × 22½″ (76 × 57.3 cm). Duke of Sutherland Collection, on Loan to the National Gallery of Scotland.

The *Grandes Baigneuses* occupied Renoir from 1885 to 1887, and whether we consider it a masterpiece or a prodigious exercise of will, it liberated him from his anxieties. In the next twenty years his nudes still show to the perceptive eye evidence of labour and calculation, but it is artfully concealed. These charming creatures sit by the banks of streams, dry themselves or splash each other with an appearance of perfect naturalness and spontaneity. They are somewhat plumper than the classical norm and have an air of Arcadian health. Unlike the models of Rubens, their skin never has the creases and puckers of a body that is normally clothed, but fits them closely, like an animal's coat. In the unselfconscious acceptance of their nudity they are perhaps more Greek than any nudes painted since the Renaissance and come closest to attaining the antique balance between truth and the ideal.

We know that Renoir, like Praxiteles, was dependent on his models. Madame Renoir complained that the maids had to be chosen because "their skin took the light well," and at the end of his life, crippled and bereaved, it was the sight of a new model that gave him the impetus to start painting again. But to write of Renoir's nudes as if they were ripe peaches which he had only to stretch out a hand and pluck from the wall is to forget his long struggle with the classic style, a struggle which continued long after the victory of 1887. Not only Boucher and Clodion, but Raphael and even Michelangelo are drawn upon; and above all he studied ancient

COLORPLATE 97

Clodion i.e. Claude Michel (1738–1814), French sculptor

Bather. 1892. 31½ × 25⅛″ (80 × 64 cm). Private Collection, Paris (Photo Durand-Ruel).

Greece. Memories of Pompeii and the occasional sight of bronzes and terra cottas in the Louvre lead him away from the official classicism of the cast room to the long pear-shaped body of Alexandrian Hellenism. In these minor arts the nude, although still achieving the oneness of antiquity, had not been deadened by centuries of imitation, and no doubt their flavour of popular naturalism – their touch of Vegetable Venus – also appealed to him. . . .

PAGE 244

. . . it is as a piece of sculpture that Renoir's Venus achieves her most complete form, and by a strange paradox this master of oil paint has had little influence on subsequent painting, but a decisive influence on modern sculpture.

The sculpture of nudes produced by Renoir between 1885 and his death in 1919, one of the most satisfying tributes ever paid to Venus by a great artist, knits together all the threads in this long chapter. Praxiteles and Giorgione, Rubens and Ingres, different as they are from one another, would all have recognised him as their successor. Like him they would probably have spoken about their works as if they were simply the skilled representation of beautiful individuals. That is the way that artists should speak. But in fact all of them were looking for something which had grown up in their minds from a confluence of memories, needs and beliefs: the memories of earlier works of art, the needs of their personal sensibilities and the belief that the female body was the token of a harmonious order. They looked with such eagerness at *Venus Naturalis* because they had caught a glimpse of her inaccessible twin sister.

JEAN RENOIR

RENOIR, MY FATHER

1958

Jean Renoir's admittedly biased biography is nevertheless the major single source of biographical information on his father.

Renoir, an Intimate Record (see p. 55)

I have the greatest admiration for Vollard's biography, but it would be a mistake to take his word as gospel truth – partly because Renoir sometimes liked to "lead on" picture dealers, and especially because Vollard was a visionary as well as a businessman, who lived in a dream and "heard only what he wanted to hear." My father once said, in commenting on the work, "Not bad, Vollard's book on Vollard." Besides he always thought any book about himself a sort of childish undertaking. "If it amuses him, I can't see any harm in it" – he added, "especially as nobody will read it."

To him the beauty of an athlete was at its best when the young man was lifting only a light weight. He did not like a *tour de force*. He maintained that harmony was in general the product of facility.

* * *

Renoir began by putting incomprehensible little touches on the white background, without even a suggestion of form. At times the paint, diluted with linseed oil and turpentine, was so liquid that it ran down the canvas. Renoir called it "juice." Thanks to the juice, he could, with several brushstrokes, establish the general tonality he was trying for. It almost covered the whole surface of the canvas – or rather, the surface of the eventual picture, for Renoir often left part of the background blank. These "open" spots represented indispensable values to him. The background had to be clear and smooth. I often prepared my father's canvases with flake white mixed with one third linseed oil and two thirds turpentine. It was then left to dry for several days.

Jean Renoir Drawing. 1901.
17¾ × 21½" (45 × 54.5 cm).
Virginia Museum, Richmond,
Va. (Gift of Mr. and Mrs. Paul
Mellon).

He would begin with little pink or blue strokes, which would then be intermingled with burnt sienna, all perfectly balanced. As a rule, Naples yellow and red madder were applied in the later stages. Ivory black came last of all. He never proceeded by direct or angular strokes. His method was round so to speak, and in curves, as if he were following the contour of a young breast. "There is no such thing as a straight line in Nature. . . ."

He succeeded in taking complete possession of his subject only after a struggle. . . . The anxious rapidity of his brushstrokes, which were urgent, precise, flashing extensions of his acute sight, made me think of the zigzag flight of a swallow catching insects. . . . The description would be incomplete if I failed to point out that Renoir in the act of painting had a wild side to him which startled me several times when I was small.

Sometimes the forms and colours were still indefinite at the end of the first session. Only on the following day was it possible to sense what would come. For the onlooker, the overwhelming impression was that the subject, defeated, was disappearing and the picture was coming out of Renoir himself. Towards the end of his life, Renoir had so perfected his method that he eliminated "little details" more quickly and got down at once to what was essential. But to the day of his death, he continued to "caress and touch the motif" the way one caresses and touches a woman so that she can express all her love. For this is what Renoir needed: that state of abandon on the part of the model, which would allow him to touch the depths of human nature, freed of all cares and prejudices of the moment. He painted bodies devoid of clothing and landscapes devoid of the picturesque. The spirit inherent in the girls and boys, the children and trees, which filled the world he created, is as purely naked as Gabrielle's nude body. And, last of all, in this nakedness Renoir disclosed his own self.

* * *

Renoir nearly always travelled by easy stages. He could not understand the frantic haste of his contemporaries. "The more we save, the less we get done, it seems to me. I heard of an author who because he had a typewriter was able to complete a book in three years. Molière or Shakespeare could turn out a play in a week with just a quill pen. . . ."

. . . though he accepted the methods of modern art-dealers, he could not help regretting that there were no longer any Medicis. "It's not a picture you hang up on the wall these days, but an investment. Why not frame some Suez Canal shares? . . .

"A bank is not a very cheerful institution, but the modern world is arranged in such a way that you can't do without them. It's all of a piece with railways, sewers, gas and electricity operations."

* * *

I never saw my father kiss his wife in public, or even in front of us children. . . . A married couple or a pair of lovers showing their feelings too openly in public made Renoir feel uncomfortable. "It won't last long," he would say, "they're waving it around too much."

* * *

My father had something of an old Arab about him, and a great deal of the French countryman – apart from the fact that his skin had remained as fair as that of an adolescent because it was constantly protected from the rays of the sun. . . . What struck strangers most at first meeting him were his eyes and his hands. His eyes were light brown, bordering on amber, and they were sharp and penetrating. . . . As for their expression, they had

Photograph of Renoir in Wheelchair with Dédée. 1915. (Photo Archives Durand-Ruel.)

Photograph of Renoir painting, Cagnes. c.1915. (© BBC Hulton Picture Library.)

a look of tenderness mixed with irony, of merriment and sensuousness. They always seemed to be laughing, perceiving the odd side of things. But it was a gentle, loving laughter. Perhaps it also served as a mask. For Renoir was also extremely shy about his feelings. . . . His hands were terribly deformed. His rheumatism had made the joints stiff, and caused the thumbs to turn inwards towards the palms and his fingers to bend towards the wrists. Visitors who were unprepared for this could not take their eyes off his deformity. . . .

His hair, which had once been light brown, had turned white but was still quite thick at the back of his head. On top, however, he was completely bald. . . . His nose was aquiline and gave him an air of authority. He had a beautiful white beard, and one of us always kept it trimmed to a point. . . . As a rule he dressed in a jacket with a buttoned-up collar and long, baggy trousers, both of striped grey cloth. His Lavallière cravat, royal blue with white polka-dots, was carefully knotted round the collar of his flannel shirt. . . . In the evening, except in summer, a little cape was put round his shoulders. He wore high grey-checked carpet slippers, or else plain dark brown ones with a metal clasp. Out of doors he was shielded from the sun by a white linen hat. In the house he preferred a cloth cap with ear-flaps of a type advertised at the beginning of the century as "chauffeurs' caps." He did not look much like a man of our times. . . .

* * *

There are several photographs of Renoir taken at the end of his life: portraits disturbingly true to life, by Albert André; a bust, made on the day of his death, by Gimond. They give an idea of his physical appearance, of his frightening emaciation. His body became more and more petrified. His hands with the fingers curled inwards could no longer pick up anything. It has been said and written, that his brush was fastened to his hand. That is not entirely accurate. The truth is that his skin had become so tender that contact with the wooden handle of the brush injured it. To avoid this, he had a little piece of cloth inserted in the hollow of his hand. His twisted fingers trapped rather than held the brush. But until his last breath his arm remained as steady as that of a young man and his eyesight as keen as ever. I can still see him applying a point of white, no larger than a pin-head, to his canvas to indicate a reflection in the eye of a model. Unhesitatingly, the brush started off like the shot of a good marksman, and hit the bull's-eye. . . . He sometimes wore glasses for reading. . . . When he was in a hurry or mislaid his glasses, he managed quite well without them.

JEAN RENOIR

RENOIR, MY FATHER

Renoir on Art and Artists

1958

DEGAS

Since the days of the cathedrals we have had but one sculptor. Sculpture is hard. You can still find a few painters and bucketsful of writers and musicians, but to be a sculptor you have to be a saint, and have the strength to escape the snare of cleverness. . . . Since Chartres there has only been one sculptor, in my view and that is Degas. . . .

Those who worked on the cathedrals succeeded in giving us an idea of eternity. That was the greatest preoccupation of their time. Degas has found a way of expressing the malady of our contemporaries: I mean movement. Nowadays we all have the itch to move. Even Degas's jockeys and horses "move." Before he came along, only the Chinese had discovered the secret of movement. That is Degas's greatness: movement in a French style.

* * *

MODELS

Those picture dealing scoundrels [a sale at Sotheby's] know perfectly well that the public is sentimental. They stuck a blasted title on my poor girl who can do no more about it than I can. They call her *La Pensée*. My models don't think at all.

COLORPLATE 60

* * *

COROT AND THE SCHOOL OF FONTAINEBLEAU

Rousseau amazed me, and Daubigny as well; but I realized immediately that the really great painter was Corot. His work is for all time. . . . I loathed Millet. His sentimental peasants made me think of actors dressed up like peasants. I loved Diaz. He was someone I could grasp and I said to myself that if I were a painter, I would have liked to paint the way he did.

* * *

Fantin-Latour, *The Studio of the Batignolles*. 1870. 80¼ × 106¼″ (204 × 270 cm). Musée d'Orsay, Paris. (Renoir, third from left wearing a hat is among the artists paying homage to Manet.)

MANET

Manet is as important to us as Cimabue or Giotto were to the Quattrocento; and as The Renaissance is beginning again, we must be part of it. . . .

* * *

THE PROFESSION

I, for instance, believe that it would be better for a painter to grind his own pigments or else to have them ground by an apprentice. But there are no apprentices any more, and as I prefer to paint rather than prepare my own pigments I buy them from my old friend Mullard, the artists' supplier in the Rue Pigalle, because he grinds them for me. If I wasted my time preparing pigments I would be as much of an idiot as if when I wanted to paint, I dressed up like Andrea del Sarto . . . [who] lived in the days when people had plenty of time and he had apprentices who worked without pay, so grinding pigments was economical. That is why I am willing to get my paint in tubes. It is the business of behaving like a cork again, but this passive attitude has brought its reward. Paints in tubes, being easy to carry, allowed us to work from Nature, and Nature alone. Without paint in tubes, there would have been no Cézanne, no Monet, no Sisley or Pissarro, nothing of what the journalists were later to call Impressionism. Nevertheless, I am sorry there are no apprentices any longer. . . .

Andrea del Sarto (1486–1530).

The discipline of having to copy the same anatomical model ten times is excellent. It's boring and if you weren't paying for it, you wouldn't bother to do it. But the Louvre is the only place to learn really.

* * *

LANDSCAPE PAINTING

A picture is meant to be looked at inside a house, where the windows let in a false light. So a little work must be done in the studio as well as what one has done out of doors. You should get away from the intoxication of real light and digest your impressions in the real light of the room. Then you can get drunk on sunlight again. You go out and work; you come back and work. That way your painting begins to get somewhere.

JEAN RENOIR

RENOIR, MY FATHER

Renoir's Advice to his Son

1958

"Before marriage you do whatever you please. You owe nothing to anybody. . . . But afterwards, when you've given your word to a life-companion, that sort of behaviour is treason. And it always ends badly. . . ."

"Get away from your wife often, but not for long at a time. After you've been away you'll be glad to get back to her. If you stay away too long you may think she's ugly when you return, and she'll think the same about you. When you grow old together, neither of you notices how the other looks. You don't see the surplus fat or the wrinkles. Love is made up of a great many things and I'm not clever enough to explain them. But I know it is also habit. . . ."

It's not much fun to spend the night with a whore. The best part is what leads up to it. . . . It's the risk that adds spice to the affair. . . .

"Women don't question anything. With them the world becomes something quite simple. They put the right value on things and they know that their washing is just as important as the constitution of the German Empire. You feel reassured when you're with them."

He had no difficulty in conveying to me the atmosphere created by women. Our house was full of women. My mother, Gabrielle, and all the young girls, servants and models who moved around the house, gave it a distinctly anti-masculine tone. The tables were strewn with odds and ends for sewing and dressmaking.

* * *

Renoir repeated, "I can't stand having anybody around me but women." And women returned his affection. . . .

Renoir bloomed both physically and spiritually when in the company of women. Men's voices tired him, women's voices soothed him. He wanted all the female servants to sing, laugh and feel at ease when working around him. The more naive and even stupid their songs were, the more pleased he was. . . .

. . . he would punctuate his statement about the superiority of women by a few jibes at their newly-acquired desire for independence and education. When someone mentioned a woman lawyer, he shook his head and remarked, "I can't see myself getting into bed with a lawyer. . . . I like women best when they don't know how to read. . . ."

"Why teach women such boring occupations as law, medicine, science and journalism, which men excel in, when women are so fitted for a task which men can never dream of attempting, and that is to make life bearable. . . . What women may gain by education they lose in other fields. I am afraid that future generations won't know how to make love well, and that would be most unfortunate for those who haven't got painting."

His misgivings, though casually voiced, were very real to him. He contended that the lack of physical exercise – "and the best exercise for a woman is to kneel down and scrub the floor, light fires or do the washing: their bellies need that sort of movement" – was going to produce girls incapable of enjoying sexual intercourse to the full.

"You'll find fewer and fewer of those pretty tarts who lose their heads when they give themselves completely. There's a risk that love-making, even the most normal, may become a kind of masturbation. . . .

"When women were slaves, they were really mistresses. Now that they have begun to have rights, they are losing their importance. When they become men's equals, they will be really slaves. . . ."

* * *

To return to the subject of women, Renoir was fully aware of their faults. One thing that annoyed him was their slavish devotion to fashion. The vogue for the slender figure had just begun at the time he was starting out in life. Berthe undoubtedly asked him on occasion to help her lace up her corset. In order to perform the operation properly it was necessary for the husband or lover to place his knee against the victim's backside so that she could brace herself while he pulled the laces. Renoir protested against this brand of torture.

"Their ribs are squeezed together and gradually get deformed," he said. "And when they become pregnant. . . . I pity the poor brat inside. . . . But when it comes to fashion, they go completely out of their minds. And it's all to fill the pockets of the corset-makers, who ought to be put in prison."

Narrow shoes and high heels also displeased him. On the other hand, lace pantelettes and a plethora of petticoats amused him, and he sometimes compared a woman undressing to one of those circus numbers in which the clown takes off half a dozen vests. "They cover up their behinds as if they were at the North Pole, but above they strip down to the navel."

* * *

My father once said to me: "There's nothing underhand about your mother. She is never sentimental."

He discovered in her the same dignity he so admired in his mother, "with the difference that your mother was fond of good food." This weakness delighted him. An abstemious man himself, he hated diets, and considered such self-imposed sacrifice as a sign of egotism. Though he did not mind being deprived of good things, he could nevertheless appreciate them. . . .

My earliest recollection of my mother is that she was already well filled out. I can imagine her at twenty with lovely curves and a "wasp waist." The pictures in which she appears are of some help in forming a clearer perception of her. I have mentioned earlier how Renoir was attracted to the "cat" type of woman. Aline Charigot was the perfect example of the species. "You wanted to tickle her under the chin." My father's reserve about that period of his life leads me to suppose that a great love existed between them. According to Rivière: "There were times when he would put down his palette and gaze at her instead of painting, asking himself why he toiled, since what he was trying to achieve was there already." But this little crisis passed quickly enough. For after all, my mother is to be seen in any number of his pictures.

It would seem that the lovers spent most of their time on the banks of the Seine. The Fournaise restaurant was their favourite meeting place. . . . At the Fournaises' the pair formed a group of friends who seemed to watch over their idyll with tender interest. The painter Caillebotte looked after Aline Charigot like a young sister. Ellen André and Mlle Henriot adopted her; they decided to take her in hand, and try "to polish up this sweet country girl." Aline was very touched by their friendliness. She listened to them, but went on doing as she pleased. "I didn't want to lose my accent and become an imitation Parisian. . . ."

I should like to give an idea of the physical proportions which Renoir considered ideal in a face: the eyes should be half-way between the top of the head and the tip of the chin. If the upper half of the head was too big, in his view it was the sign of an enlarged brain – "the brain of a megalomaniac or, more simply, an intellectual; not to mention water on the brain." If the top half of the face was too small, it signified good, honest stupidity. If the lower part of the face was too pronounced, it meant stubbornness. "Never marry a woman with a large chin. She'd rather be torn to pieces than admit she was in the wrong."

He liked women who had a tendency to grow fat, whereas men, he thought, should be lean. He liked small noses better than large ones, and

Photograph of Renoir, Aline and Coco. 1912.

356

he made no secret of his preference for wide mouths, with full, but not thick, lips; small teeth; fair complexions and blonde hair. "Pouting lips indicate affectation; thin lips, suspicion." Once he had drawn up these rules, emphasising the importance of dividing up the face at the line of the eyes, my father would add: "After that you have to follow your own instinct. With rules you're sometimes apt to go wrong. I've known exquisite girls with a slipper chin, and unbearable bitches with perfectly-proportioned features. It so happened that Aline Charigot was not unbearable; that the proportions of her features and body accorded with the canons Renoir had formulated; that her slightly almond-shaped eyes sent the impressions they received to a well-balanced brain; that she had a light step – "she could walk on grass without hurting it;" that she kept the vigour of the sharp little winds that sweep over her native hillsides; and that she knew how to twist her unruly hair into a simple chignon, sweeping it with a slow curling movement that Renoir liked to watch because it was "truly round. . . ."

. . . from the moment he took up a brush to paint, perhaps even earlier, perhaps even in his childhood dreams, thirty years before he ever knew her, Renoir was painting the portrait of Aline Charigot . . . whenever he painted subjects of his own choosing, he returned to the physical characteristics which were essentially those of his future wife.

* * *

As far back as I can remember, my parents always slept apart. They nearly always had separate, but adjoining rooms. "You have to be very young to be able to live in close contact continually without getting on each other's nerves." On the other hand, Renoir was very much against long separations. I am almost certain that he never deceived his wife. "In the first place it's pointless. In general, the second woman is like the first, without being accustomed to your whims." He maintained that, apart from certain queer fish afflicted with a peculiar make-up, like his friend Lhote, who sometimes had to go to the nearest brothel to satisfy a desire as urgent as thirst, most men pursue their one ideal of a woman, which doesn't change. Their different adventures are only a reflection of that ideal. Hence the resemblance between legitimate wives and mistresses. In his youth he once made a dreadful mistake. One of his friends had a mistress whom he often took to the Moulin de la Galette. He had introduced her to Renoir. One day my father met the same woman on the street – or so he thought – and complimented her on the graceful way she danced. But it was his friend's wife!

During Gabrielle's last years . . . she and I got into the way of discussing everything quite openly. Sometimes we talked about the sexual relations between my father and mother. We both thought that their love life had been very active and affectionate and that their physical relations had only ended after illness had riveted Renoir to his invalid's chair once and for all. I hope my parents will forgive me for not respecting the intimacy which meant so much to them, but I think it is of sufficient importance to justify my taking this liberty, if only to stress how normal Renoir was in everything, including sex.

Photograph of Renoir and Gabrielle at Les Collettes, Cagnes.
© BBC Hulton Picture Library.

357

JOHN BERGER

PERMANENT RED

"Renoir and the Aftermath"

1960

John Berger (b. 1926), British novelist and writer on art

Renoir was the last great bourgeois artist. That is to say he was the last painter who was able to accept frankly bourgeois values of security, domesticity and leisure and to make from these a confident art. The other Impressionists retreated from such concepts to emphasise the ephemeral and the casual. Bonnard, who in a different way tried to produce an art based on similar values to Renoir's, was forced to camouflage his intentions under cover of pure colour and pattern. Everything merges in nostalgic light. Bonnard is a sort of urban Claude: a lost Arcadia lies beyond his french windows.

Look, for instance, at Renoir's "Woman seated at a stove" or at his portrait of his small son Jean drawing at a table. For all their difference of temperament and technique, these two pictures evoke an atmosphere essentially the same as that evoked by a Chardin. And Chardin was perhaps the first great bourgeois artist, reacting in his time against what had become the nostalgic aimlessness of aristocratic art. Nor does one argue like this simply to prove a Marxist point. It leads one through a host of current illusions to a truer understanding of the art in question. Because Renoir painted and so obviously enjoyed the female nude, it is often said that he is the sensuous, sexual artist *par excellence*. But this is only a half-truth. Certainly in every one of his pictures, even in his landscapes and flower-pieces, there is a voluptuous sexual awareness. But their mood is always – almost without exception – languid and drowsy. It is the aftermath of love that he paints – just as it is the dreamy aftermath of a secure culture of material comfort and private property that he represents historically. Think, for example, of the concept of love and security in the films that his son Jean was to make. In one generation one can see how the climate had to change.

Renoir's greatness lies in the fact that he so completely and honestly derived from actual subjects and images, symbols to correspond to his view of life: thus, the solid truth he discovered in them will remain meaningful long after the values imposed upon him by his class and time have come to seem one-sided. This brings us to an understanding of Renoir's development as an artist. One can see why he had to discard his early Courbet-like style which implied an austerity alien to his ideal of ease; how impressionism first offered him a way of communicating his sensuous delight but later began to destroy the substance of it; how Raphael, Cézanne and the draughtsman's discipline of Ingres showed him that only by the careful, patient study of Nature could he find the equilibrium, the peacefulness that could express his belief in sensuous comfort; how finally he was able to achieve – perhaps without realising the significance of it himself – a true synthesis of the inevitable contradictions of his attitude – how in his later paintings he literally dissolved the outlines of the world in order to extend and make timeless the brief moment of physical contentment, of well-being without further desire.

PAGE 349

Jean-Baptiste Chardin (1699–1779)

HENRY MOORE

A Statement

1961

Henry Moore (1898–1986), British sculptor. A statement written in support of the Director of the National Gallery, Sir Philip Hendy, when two Renoirs, Dancer with Tambourine, Dancer with Castanets, *(Colorplates 112, 113) were purchased by the Gallery, 1961. They were painted originally for the dining room of Renoir's patron, Maurice Gangnat.*

Whoever doesn't like those girls doesn't understand what Renoir was trying to do. The two pictures must represent at least three or four months of continuous work at the best period of Renoir's life. A tremendous amount of application went into the painting of them, a great deal of real ambition; they represent a big effort to produce something worthy of the museums.

If you copy nature as it is, as Renoir was mainly doing during his earlier impressionist period, you can't really show the form that underlies appearances. Nature is too complicated, and to make a work of art out of it you have to simplify, to invent a system of vision. In painting, where you have to reduce everything to a flat surface with only colour and texture, you have above all, to simplify the lighting. Renoir hit on this method of lighting the model, as it were, simply from his own eyes; so that all his surfaces are subject to a logical system of lighting which explains the form. In these pictures he has learned to fit his forms into space. The shapes of these two girls are melted into the background; so that what you see and feel about them comes from inside the forms, not just from the outlines, as it did earlier, in his hard-edge paintings.

And yet these rounded forms have a marvellous supple rhythm, such as people are apt to associate only with outlines. What one likes about them is that, though they are so monumental, yet, if you compare them, for instance, with Maillol's sculptures, they have none of the stiffness which these are apt to have. They make me realise that Renoir was really a much greater sculptor than Maillol. And, in addition, what lovely passages there are of delicious painting and wonderful colour! There are so many subtleties in the painting of them which one goes on discovering that I never know which I like the better of the two. One day it's one, another day it's the other.

Aristide Maillol (1861–1944)

One could say most of these things if these were "abstract" pictures. But they are anything but that; Renoir tried to put into them all that he felt about women. The way he dressed them up is a key to this. For me their costumes only emphasise the sculptural grandeur of them, as Rembrandt wanted to do when he dressed up Saskia. Renoir didn't just paint these girls as he saw them about the house, as he did in so many of his smaller, more everyday pictures. When they came into his studio in the morning to pose, they didn't just take their clothes off either. The whole ceremony of getting dressed up would help to make the occasion important.

The pictures represent, I'm sure, a significant episode in Renoir's career, a special effort; that's why I think they are not just ordinary pictures for private collectors, why I believe they are the kind of pictures we should have in the National Gallery.

KENNETH CLARK

CIVILISATION

"Heroic Materialism"

1969

Never before in history have artists been so isolated from society and from official sources of patronage as were the so-called Impressionists. . . . But one of them, Renoir, continued for a time to live in Paris, and to represent the life around him. He was poor, and the people he painted were neither grand nor rich. But they were happy. Before one makes gloomy generalisations about the late nineteenth century – the miseries of the poor, the oppressive luxury of the rich and so forth – it's as well to remember that two of the most beautiful pictures of the period are Renoir's *Boating Party* and his *Moulin de la Galette*. No awakened conscience, and no heroic materialism. No Nietzsche, no Marx, no Freud. Just a group of ordinary human beings enjoying themselves.

COLORPLATE 76
COLORPLATE 53

JOEL ISAACSON

THE CRISIS OF IMPRESSIONISM *1878-1882*

"The Exhibition of 1882: Changing Styles"

1979

Joel Isaacson (b. 1930), American art historian

. . . Renoir's absence from the Impressionist exhibitions and his courting of wealthy clients, portrait commissions, and Salon acceptability have served to obscure a facet of his work that he had been developing throughout the second half of the 1870s but which had not been exhibited and was left unresolved as he pushed further into his classical phase. I have in mind a distinctly unclassical, experimental body of work in which Renoir was closer to Degas than to any other Impressionist.

During the later '70s Renoir had pursued intermittently his fascination with the urban setting, with the variety, pace and intimacy of the city that claimed his attention and served as his home and studio throughout the period. In these works, among which the *Moulin de la Galette* and *The Swing*, both exhibited in 1877, are possibly the best known, he concentrated upon figures informally grouped at the café, the dinner table, in the street, at the theatre, in the intimacy of their apartments. In approaching these subjects he elaborated a fragmentary, close-up unexpected view of the world that suggested not the "distance" of a painted framed composition but the immediacy and flux of actual vision and experience. In this effort he took the same exploratory stance, emphasising surprise, accident and intimacy, as did Degas. In composition, he placed his figures close to the surface, cut them off at the edges, investigated the contrasts between near and far, between focused and peripheral vision, and in the process participated excitedly in the reorientation of traditional perspective that Courbet and

COLORPLATES 53, 49

Manet had begun in the 1850s and 1860s and which Degas, above all, along with Caillebotte, continued to pursue in the 1870s.

In numerous works dating from 1876 into the early 1880s, Renoir developed an informal, close-range examination of his subject, often painted in sketchy fashion and so cropped as to suggest a vignette or fragment rather than a balanced or centralised composition. Among the earliest of these paintings is *Dans l'atelier de la rue Saint-Georges*, 1876, which in its depiction of an informal group of artist friends including Pissarro, is a private work done for other painters; two paintings titled *Au Café*, 1877, which may be compared closely to Manet's café scenes of the second half of the 1870s but also to Degas's *Women in front of the café*, 1877, in the Louvre; *Chez la Modiste*, c.1878, (. . .) extremely sketchy especially in the depiction of the flanking figures and comparable to such extreme close-up views by Degas as *At the Races*, c.1878, and in general sharing Degas's favored device of a diagonal entry into the composition. . . .

In other works, Renoir explored the contrast between focused figures set close to the frame and peripheral and distant elements seen out of focus and somewhat randomly dispersed within the composition. One example is *The First Outing*, which offers an abrupt relationship between near and

Girl in a Boat. 1877.
28¾ × 36⅜″ (73 × 92.5 cm).
Private Collection, New York
(Photo Archives Durand-Ruel).

COLORPLATE 58

(*Daulte 238, 239.*)

COLORPLATE 59

(*Daulte 182.*)

far that may be seen again in Degas's works. . . . In the masterful *Place Clichy* of about 1880, Renoir seems to experiment with the photographic phenomena of depth of field and snapshot framing, as well as with the capturing of the sense of motion and energy, a combined effort comparable to Degas's great *Place de la Concorde* of c.1875 and Manet's *Rue de Berne* . . . of 1878.

Another painting by Renoir, *Girl in a Boat* of 1887, in its juxtaposition of near and far also seems to relate to Degas's *Place de la Concorde* and other works. . . . *Girl in a Boat* offers, however, another quality that derives from the disparate size relationships within the picture, the suddenness of the jump from foreground to middleground, and the discontinuity of the setting seen in a different perspective to either side of the foreground woman. The effect is comparable to a collage, to a pasting together of separately observed and recorded parts, and in this painting seems to hark back to the problematic experiments of Manet . . . an attempt on Manet's part to challenge the authority of three-dimensional perspective coherence. The collage-like, the additive, resulting in a disruption of spatial unity and the conventions of pictorial homogeneity, was an intermittent and important concern of Renoir's. We see it again in one of the first paintings from his Venetian trip, the *Gondola in Venice*, 1881, in which the size and spatial relationship between the foreground woman and the gondola defy perspective, while the gondola seems to be plastered against the area of water.

One sees in these works from the late 1870s and early '80s the evidences of an experimental effort that runs counter to Renoir's more formal commissioned portraits and Salon paintings and to his increasing concern for classical probity during the first half of the 1880s. The problematic character of these paintings suggests that Renoir's classical reaction to Impressionism was directed against something more than the movement's plein-air and colouristic emphasis. He was, to some, extent, reacting against his infatuation with the work and attitudes of Degas. His experiments of the late '70s may now have seemed to him particularly uncertain and threatening for they involved, even more than did his atmospheric plein-airism, a free, random approach to the character of experience and, in the translation, to a form of painting that seemed formless, that amounted to an abandonment of the traditional concept of a painting as artful, distanced, homogeneous, as a composition the function of which was to frame and unify and establish order. These paintings were, nevertheless, as we confirm through our experience of the art of the time, an intelligent and innovative effort to expand the possibilities of a new painting, one that would, in accord with the oft-repeated imperative of the time, provide a viable integration of a modern iconography with a modern experimental style.

Renoir did not exhibit these works at the Salon nor at the Impressionist exhibitions during the years of our concern (1878-1882). His Salon effort was geared towards acceptance, towards the relatively large or finished work that, in order to attain admission, had to have the rough edges smoothed out. He acted as Monet did in 1880 on the occasion of his return to the Salon; at that time Monet deliberately submitted what he called the more "discreet and bourgeois" of his works, holding back the more personal and, he makes it clear, more highly prized and explorative of his efforts. . . . When Renoir returned to the group show (1882) he, unlike Monet, remained relatively aloof from the enterprise and designated as his agent Durand-Ruel, who selected most of the paintings from those already belonging to his storehouse. The experimental works we have been considering either stayed with Renoir or were acquired by minor sympathetic collectors.

Renoir's downplaying of these works and their relative neglect in the literature on the artist may be in part the result of his decision to follow the path of the Salon. Had he remained loyal to the Impressionists, to the

COLORPLATE 71

PAGE 361

The Bathers. 1886/7. Detail of Colorplate 97. 46⅜ × 67¼" (117.8 × 170.8 cm). Philadelphia Museum of Art (Mr. and Mrs. Carroll S. Tyson Collection).

potential of their shows as a vehicle for exposing new works to the public, he might have pursued the possibilities of these paintings more fully, joined more closely with Degas, as did Pissarro, in furthering their spirit of experimentation.

Even without Renoir's most innovative works however, the seventh group show, as those that preceded it provided an arena for the exhibition of change. Renoir's entries, as gathered by Durand-Ruel, revealed his mastery of the Impressionist coloristic aesthetic and, in the *Luncheon of the Boating Party*, indications of the new solidity, firmness and cohesion that he was to stress increasingly in the years to come. . . .

Renoir's most experimental works of the late 1870s formed no part of the history of the Impressionist exhibitions, but their very absence may tell us something of importance about the movement itself. Their absence points up, by indirection, the role that the shows did play as well as the more complete role they might have played for the display of the most innovative work being done in France at the time. The Salon could not permit such exposure, and it was in recognition of that fact that the group was initially formed. The potential of the exhibitions was seriously compromised, however by the gradual loss of group solidarity.

Without the record at the exhibitions themselves of Renoir's most innovative works, we are prone to be less aware of them and to overemphasise his links to the colourists and landscapists while all but disregarding his affinities to the vision of Degas. . . .

COLORPLATE 76

ROSZIKA PARKER AND GRISELDA POLLOCK

OLD MISTRESSES: WOMEN, ART AND IDEOLOGY

1981

Roszika Parker (b. 1945) and Griselda Pollock (b. 1949), British art historians

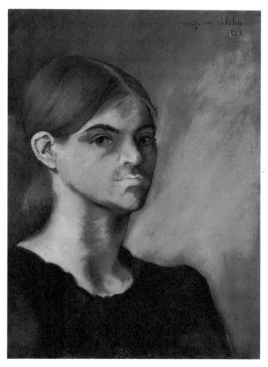

(Suzanne) Valadon was working class, daughter of a laundress, one-time trapeze artist, and came initially into contact with painting through working as an artist's model. She earned her living "selling" her body and face to artists for their transformation into their own images of women. In Renoir's *The Bathers* Valadon was the model for the figure on the right hand side. In this idyllic version of modern nymphs bathing, the conception of the female nude – a boneless, well-fed body, a smooth expanse of palpable flesh displayed for the viewer's pleasure – is combined with a whimsical vision of the modern Parisienne, all pouting mouth and retroussé nose. In a *Self-Portrait* by Valadon, painted only shortly before Renoir's composition, a radically different conception of Valadon is displayed. Admittedly it is a portrait, and not a subject picture. The artist depicts herself clothed and it is not a nude. In her concentration upon the face, she underlines the heavy jawline, the dark eyebrows, the indifferent but nonetheless assertive gaze turned upon herself and thus the spectator. The comparison is not intended to suggest that in the *Self-Portrait* we see a truer picture of Valadon. It is as much an image, a constructed representation, as Renoir's. But its choice of emphasis and its effect as an image of a woman dispute those that have operated in Renoir's picture.

Suzanne Valadon, *Self-Portrait*. Pastel. 1883. 17¾ × 12⅝″ (45 × 32 cm). Musée d'Art Moderne, Paris. © DACS 1987.

TAMAR GARB

Tamar Garb (b. 1946), British art historian

THE OXFORD ART JOURNAL

"Renoir and the Natural Woman"

1985

By obscuring the real relationships between people, classes and genders, Renoir gives form to a fin-de-siecle fantasy which still has currency today.

Renoir's evasion of reality produced an idealised, timeless and therefore mythic vision of women. Such a construction rather than operating as a hymn of praise as is so often assumed, must ultimately be oppressive because of its inability to engage with the reality of women's lives. . . .

Although robbed of her status as goddess or nymph because of the absence of specific anecdotal referents in the Renoir images, the mythic image of woman remains intact so that while there is indeed no "story" in these paintings, they form part of a deeper level of narrative, produced around the image of woman. . . . Resting or playing, animal-like in the vegetation, woman exists without thought, conflict or even self-consciousness. There is in these paintings no confronting gaze – at most we feel a coquettish awareness of being surveyed – there is no command of the space occupied. Rarely have women been more available. Content in a state of original innocence, woman is powerless, she exists only for her flesh. Her nakedness is an expression of her submission to the viewer, her body is often twisted to reveal her breasts or thighs and her passivity or harmless playfulness reassures the viewer of his mastery over her.

In Renoir's images of the nude the very painterliness of his technique, with its lack of differentiation of texture, fuses the body of woman with the vegetation that surrounds her. The female body dissolves into the landscape, becoming yet another natural phenomenon in a natural paradise. As a being fused with nature, the naked woman provides writers with a symbol of all that is good and wholesome. . . . For Jean Renoir and many of Renoir's critics, his nudes function as a reassuring reminder of the stability of the universe, an assurance that all is well despite the horrors of twentieth century reality. . . .

The retreat to Arcadian nature worship with its nostalgic overtones and the positioning of women within a fantastic natural paradise functions as a resistance to the political and social demands which were being made by feminists, both male and female, during the French Third Republic with unprecedented intensity. . . . Renoir's position on feminism was clear. His frequent allusions to it indicate his awareness of women's growing aspirations.

There is no doubt that Renoir came into contact with independent and powerful women and that he was aware of current debates on the "woman question." Madame Ada, whom he so denigrated, was one of France's foremost political journalists and a regular frequenter of the republican Salon of Madame Charpentier. . . .

Renoir's close friendship with Berthe Morisot belies his vehement antagonism towards the woman artist. It is interesting though, that when he painted Morisot, it was in her role of mother and not artist. Renoir's relationship with Morisot was complicated by her own consciousness of the class differences which separated them. Proud as he was of his artisan origins and contemptuous as he remained of bourgeois customs, he was nevertheless reluctant to let Morisot know of his association with a peasant woman, Aline Charigot. When he showed her the drawings of Aline and their son Pierre, he did not tell her that these were of his common-law wife and child. It is possible therefore, that Renoir's narrow prescriptions for women's sphere were suspended in relation to certain women of the haute-bourgeoisie on whom he depended for patronage and support. . . .

Renoir's image of woman can therefore be seen in the context of the most pervasive, dominant and reactionary nineteenth century constructions of womanhood. As part of the debates around the "woman question," so heated during his lifetime, his paintings can be seen to reinforce the dominant Proudhonian construct with which, we know, he felt most comfortable. His paintings operate, not as a reflection of social attitudes, but as a powerful non-verbal promoter of an identifiable political position.

Pierre-Joseph Proudhon (1809–65), socialist writer

LAWRENCE GOWING

RENOIR

"Renoir's Sense and Sentiment"

1985

Sir Lawrence Gowing (b. 1918), British painter and art historian

Renoir's art cannot claim that base in sensation and logic which, as Cézanne remarked with reason, makes an artist impregnable. Renoir's vision and imagining were at the service rather of sensuality and impulse. They are thus vulnerable to criticism. Renoir makes his own kind of sense, but the meaning communicated by sensuousness and sensuality in themselves are no longer acceptable as they were in Renoir's time.

Yet the recent neglect of Renoir overlooks qualities that we can hardly spare from the repertory that painting affords us. We can recognise their rarity yet still hardly describe what they consist of. Is there another respected modern painter whose work is so full of charming people and attractive sentiment? And all in the best possible taste. Yet what lingers is not cloying sweetness but a freshness that is not entirely explicable. It is like a scent or the bloom on a grape. The self-management was impeccably natural and effortless, as if Renoir relied on what was innate. His son compared it to the sense of direction in a migrating bird. The assumptions that he took for granted are no longer unquestioned.

Renoir possessed, it seems from the beginning, an awareness that the other future impressionists had no idea of. He had a sense of the image trade and retained that sense through the period in which painting and drawing were changing utterly, changing in the skills they could command, the formulations they supplied and the clientèle they served, the period in which artists transformed the craft and lost the trade. . . .

Renoir was a tradesman not only by upbringing, but by nature, and he never forgot it. So far from unfaithful, he always preserved an intelligent understanding of what the image tradition consisted in. The eighteenth century remained very present and imaginatively important to him all his life. For him a good Louis Quinze frame, which his patron had ready, was a positive reason for painting a portrait (and lowering his price). Renoir was acutely aware, as no one else, of the tragedy of the age which seemed until the very *fin de siècle* to lack a decorative style of its own. . . .

None of his friends experimented so widely and inconsistently. None would have cared to embark on so many different styles, or to imitate them so closely. None was inspired by such unblushing hedonism. What gave Renoir's point of departure a commanding advantage was without doubt his capacity and determination from the first to please himself. It might not commend itself to the high-minded. Indeed, as we can read, it still does not. But his motivation certainly offered a compelling and, despite its traditionalism (or because of it), original blend of painterly and sexual greed. . . .

The idea of painting as a quite physical indulgence dictated the philosophy and the coherent strategy of life that were entirely his own. It was itself a kind of originality and it was entirely conscious; questioned about it Renoir would answer with an unaffected and unforced coarseness. He was neither modest nor boastful about the phallic role in which he imagined his brush. An artist's brush had hardly ever been so completely an organ of physical pleasure and so little of anything else as it was in Renoir's hand. Its sensate tip, an inseparable part of him, seemed positively to please itself. In the forms it caressed it awakened the life of feeling and it led them not to climactic fulfilment but to prolonged and undemanding play without any particular reserve or restraint – or commitment. If the brush defines and records, it is for pleasure, and the shapes it makes, quivering in their pearly veil, discover satisfaction and completeness. One feels the surface of his paint itself as living skin: Renoir's aesthetic was wholly physical and sensuous, and it was unclouded. In essence his art had no other matter; human identity and character were seen entirely in terms of it. His ethos was ideal for an art that must express physical things in physical terms, and there was no great part in it for theory or thought or reflection, nor perhaps at root even for generosity, open-hearted though he was. His love distributed its favours at random, decorating the visible scene with its capricious indifference. The fruits of his sentiment are abundant – in every sense voluminous: few, I think, look at them unmoved. . . .

Such explicitly illustrative pictures, especially of subjects so plainly pleasurable and enjoyed, have not attracted advanced support in the hundred years since they were painted. Serious critics do not take them seriously, unless to question their social enlightenment. These interactions of real people fulfilling natural drives with well-adjusted enjoyment remain the popular masterpieces of modern art (as it used to be called), and the fact that they are not fraught and tragic, without the slightest social unrest in view, or even much sign of the spatial and communal disjunction which some persist in seeking, is far from removing their interests.

If we look at Renoir as an illustrator of human interaction he has satisfying surprises to offer in these best known pictures. In picture after picture, for example, a woman (Ellen André in *Luncheon of the Boating Party*, Suzanne Valadon in *Dance at Bougival*) lets the concentrated admiration of a bearded young man, who is oblivious of anyone else or of us, rest steadily upon her; the intentness is almost palpable. She receives it; it bathes her; she luxuriates in it, smiles a little to herself. Presently an inward look and something in her bearing admit complicity. The two are at one; their state is blessed. Eventually, in *Dance in the Country* she laughs with open irrepressible delight as the dance whirls her away. . . .

Ellen André (b. c. 1860), actress; Suzanne Valadon (1867–1938)

They are images of what is mutual, tender and ardent, which returned to the stillness of painting the satisfaction that the painter had plundered and would again. They show the painting of love and the love of painting to be intimately linked and treasured resources and lastingly add them to the richness of art. We find ourselves treating this, which we had taken for makeshift picture-making, as great painting and notice that in this special dimension, which is Renoir's own and no one else's, there is no contradiction.

FRED ORTON

Fred Orton (b. 1945), British art historian

THE OXFORD ART JOURNAL

"Reactions to Renoir keep Changing"

1985

Modernist criticism and history has found Renoir's production problematic. We might say that of all the Artists we read about in the History of Impressionism it's Renoir who causes the Modernist most problems in terms of the value to be placed on his paintings and hence the value of those paintings, and of Renoir, to Modernism. . . .

How then to value Renoir? That's still the problem for art history and criticism in 1985.

It's plain to me that the concepts that helped determine the dominant theory or description of Modernist painting and which determine Renoir's paintings of the late 1860s through (to) the mid 1880s do not – unfortunately for the Modernist – reappear as sufficiently or regularly regulative in his work between c. 1886–1919. The conceptual importance of the dominant theory's technical features and concerns don't seem to have determined his paintings as much as they do some others', Monet's or Cézanne's for example. This occasions a kind of crisis of evaluation. The concepts of the dominant description cannot be used in the dominant critical and historical discourse except with an unease and a doubt about quality. But the dominant discourse is constrained to use the dominant theory even when it doesn't fit.

The putative evolution of Modernist painting according to the dominant theory has been characterised as the gradual "victory" of *surface* over *subject*. For a painter, like Renoir, in whose practice this contrast was raised as a real issue – as an antinomy – it seems that all decisions which had to be taken when making a painting could at some point be indexed to be one or other of these concerns: *vivid surface* or *vivid subject*.

Clearly vivid surface and vivid subject aren't always seen as antinomic in practice. I'm sure they weren't for Monet or Cézanne, or Braque for example – that, I would suggest, is what makes their stock in Modernism secure. Neither surface nor subject predominates. . . . In Renoir's production one finds surface and subject held in tension from *La Grenouillère* (1869) until the latter rather than the former is emphasised in *The Bathers* (1887). And when subject is reasserted in this manifesto-like painting it is one which is almost impossible to celebrate under the dominant theory.

COLORPLATE 13
COLORPLATE 97

The 'nude' is a difficult subject for an artist wanting to achieve with the dominant theory of modern art. The problem is one of how to reconcile the vivid emphatic subject and its vivid emphatic plasticity with the conceptual and practical insistence that the surface of the painting be used to insist on its surfaceness as the surface of a painting. How does the nude suffer under this description? It's discredited, even disintegrated. With Renoir painting to the telos of the dominant theory, the "nude" almost disappears (*Study*, known as *Nude in the Sunlight* of 1875), or else the dominant theory is jettisoned (the *Bathers* of 1887, 1892-5, and 1918-19; the reclining nudes of 1905-7; and the *Judgement of Paris* of 1908 and 1913-14). It's very difficult for Modernist criticism and history to value these post-1887 "nudes" especially when they're placed against the valued achievements of Modernist painting contemporaneous with them, for example Picasso's *Demoiselles d'Avignon* (1907); Braque's *Big Nude* (1907); Matisse's *Blue Nude* and *Le Luxe* (1907) . . . or *Bathers by a River* (completed in 1916); and Duchamp's *Nude Descending a Staircase* (1912) . . . or *The Bride*

COLORPLATE 44
COLORPLATES 97, 124
PAGE 343

Stripped Bare by her Bachelors even (The Large Glass) (1915-23). . . . How does management go about valuing Renoir's problematic production next to that body of paintings? The answer is, of course, that it doesn't. . . .

House also talked about class – or rather, he didn't talk about class, that's my point. He talked about the bourgeoisie and with reference for example to *The Apple Seller* (c. 1890, The Cleveland Museum of Art) about a commercial transaction between a peasant woman and a *bourgeoise* and her children. In his catalogue note he points out how "the pyramidal arrangement which encompasses all four figures draws them into a single harmonious ensemble." I'd say that here House was raising the problem of representing class and even, maybe, of the Renoir family's relation to the *classe ouvrière* and the *bourgeoisie*. It doesn't really matter if the seated woman isn't Mme Renoir and the children aren't Pierre and nephew Edmond, Jnr., Renoir, it seems to me, is painting himself, Aline and the kids into the *bourgeoisie*. . . . *The Apple Seller* has to be seen as an ideological representation of changing social circumstances . . . and as of Renoir as a producer working for specific audiences and publics.

This refers to the writings of John House, organizer of the Renoir *exhibition, Hayward Gallery, London, 1985, in the catalog to that exhibition and elsewhere.*

The Apple-Seller. 1890.
25⅞ × 21⁵/₁₆″ (66 × 54 cm). The Cleveland Museum of Art (Bequest of Leonard C. Hanna Jnr.).

BRIDGET RILEY, HOWARD HODGKIN AND DAVID SYLVESTER

"Renoir. What is Painting for Anyway?"
1985

Three personal views at the time of the 1985 Renoir exhibition at the Hayward Gallery, London. The British painters Bridget Riley (b. 1931) and Howard Hodgkin (b. 1932) and the critic David Sylvester (b. 1924) in excerpts from a BBC television film "Renoir. What is painting for, anyway?" produced by Ann Turner. (This material is a transcript of the three interviews.)

BRIDGET RILEY

I was giving a lecture on colour and I had already covered two what you might call moderately provocative Renoir's and I'd been able to carry the audience with me, in that they had followed the points I was able to make about Renoir with no violent reaction. But when I showed the "Great Bathers" (1918-19), there was a sharp intake of breath. And I was sad to hear it. I think the prejudice against him was the one that was levelled at Rubens for years, that it was acres of flesh.

COLORPLATE 124

I love his children paintings. I think he has the same feeling as Rubens for children, that they are a source of light. They nearly always glow in the paintings. They radiate freshness and youth. They're like little butterflies or small flowers. They're so unbelievably delicate.

I think one of his qualities is prettiness and prettiness is something that we think is "pretty-pretty." But true prettiness is an aristocratic quality. It requires a certain leisure, a certain withdrawal to, as it were, permit prettiness.

I think his roots are very old and very deep and stretch way back and I think he was very aware of this. And I think his search for monumentality was not only an anxiety about the painting slipping around and trying to get a unity for it, to make it solid, I think it was also to paint eternal images, to reach into the very core of humanity.

It seems to me that *The Swing* is one of the clearest, literal demonstrations of his type of structure. This dappling in which the whole scene is enveloped allows him to suppress forms, pull them forward, modulate them – independently of what they actually are – and I think that as he goes on in his life and develops, this becomes a firm anchor for the way that he organises pictorial unity. In the end he's binding his paintings together by what you might call a kind of permanent dappling which embraces everything.

COLORPLATE 49

Renoir seems to me to have been overlooked in the type of structure that he builds, which is this caressing, rising-and-falling of the picture plane, the dissolving of forms into one another, and the emerging of other forms. So that you have an entire, softly breathing, airy, strokable structure.

I think much more of a painting like the *Grandes Baigneuses* (1918-19) in which the sky and its clouds turn into the mountain, turn into the foothills, turn into the shrubs, turn into the water, turn into the hats, the flowers and finally into the women lying in the middle: that continuum of using colour and his beautiful, circling, clustering brushstrokes to weld a complete form out of an entire landscape and what it contains.

To find someone whose work is tender, loving, happy, full of all benign virtues, to find this unacceptable is a very curious situation.

HOWARD HODGKIN

I've always wondered whether I really like his work or not. He's a very difficult artist to get near, compared to most. . . . I have extraordinarily mixed feelings about him.

I think the reason why he's still an enormously celebrated artist – it's obviously difficult for me to know too much about this, being a painter –

but I think people who are not painters and not involved and so on, like him because he's immediately warm. His pictures are very rich and they look like real oil paintings in a way that so few other artists do. One sees brilliantly coloured brushstrokes, immensely attractive.

I think it's interesting the idea of there being a marshmallow quality in Renoir, but I wonder how much we put in there as compared to it being there already. I think we put it there. He painted lots of pictures of children, lots of pictures of soft, voluptuous nudes, which, because of his technique as much as anything and the actual way he applied paint to canvas, has a kind of softness – of soft focus, almost – which I think is nothing to do with his sentiment, his own thoughts and feelings. So that when we look at them, we make them sentimental.

He worked very hard at this picture [The *Grandes Baigneuses* of 1883-7] and it's a tremendous success. I would say that it was undoubtedly one of the truly great classical paintings produced in the history of French painting. It's certainly on a par with Seurat on one hand and Poussin on the other. But it seems to have taken almost too much out of him, so that though he painted further, they don't so much fall short as somehow by-pass the intensity and commitment of that painting. One of the very strange things about it is that the colour of the flesh of the girls is not what one would expect of Renoir. It's very cold, tonally very close: almost the antithesis of the hot, warm embracing flesh which we see in so many of his later compositions with nude figures. Partly to flatten them out, partly to make them lie parallel with the picture plane, but I think also to draw attention to the movements of the forms rather than the movement of the surface of the forms which you find in his later pictures, the colours are very close in tone, very flat. And the pose of the nearest figures is, of course, completely insane in terms of what the real human body could do. The longer one looks at it, the more one realises it's really an assemblage of different gestures . . . they're movements that would be very difficult to do at the same time.

[*The Luncheon of the Boating Party*.] The artificiality of his pictures is something we forget very easily. They are artificial in the way that all great painting is artificial. There are extraordinary discrepancies in scale and the most obvious one is in the standing male figure on the left, with his tiny girl friend in front of him. She's much nearer the spectator than he, as she's sitting in front, but their scale is completely reversed. . . . This was necessary for obvious pictorial reasons: these two figures anchor the whole painting, because after that the forms sort of disappear like a bunch of flowers that's been thrown down on the table.

[*Grandes Baigneuses*, 1918-19.] It was as if, right at the end of his life, he was using this tiny aspect of the way Rubens painted flesh for painting everything – the sky, the sea, the hair – which is generalising and often quite ugly. It's a sort of Michelin-man series of forms applied to everything.

COLORPLATE 97

COLORPLATE 76

COLORPLATE 124

DAVID SYLVESTER

I enjoy Renoir's paintings the way I enjoy Hollywood musicals – the way I enjoy a Minelli musical. It's very charming but at the same time I know that someone's trying to charm me. And that's never totally seductive, is it?

* * *

For me, Renoir becomes a really great artist in the late nudes, above all in *Les Grandes Baigneuses*. It's an absolutely unique and very extraordinary and very profoundly moving perception of their bodies and I think it has a kind of enveloping feeling – as enveloping as Monet's waterlilies – which makes you feel really as if you imagine you are back in the womb. I don't think it's especially sexy; it's extremely maternal – the only expression that

378

I can think of in art of a sensation that is the sense of the return to the comfortable, consoling paradise that we were pulled out of.

* * *

I think normally with great artists we have a certain constancy of feeling about them, even if it's ambivalent. One might feel very ambivalent about giants like Rembrandt and Michelangelo, one may have a very love/hate relationship with them, but still it's a constant. . . . With Renoir, I really feel that he's one of those artists where one is somewhat influenced by the last work of his one happens to have seen.

* * *

I don't know whether it's fair to say this, but his son quotes the story of Renoir saying . . . "Of course I'm not a genius – I haven't got syphillis, I'm not a pederast, I don't take drugs" – in other words putting his money on the notion of being an ordinary man, with an ordinary view of the world, behaving in ordinary ways. But I'm not saying he chose that . . . he was like that. And people like Cézanne, Degas and Monet, they are much madder and at the same time much grander. Like gods, not like chaps. And Renoir was a chap.

Picasso, *Renoir* (drawing after a photograph, cf. p. 258). Charcoal and graphite. 1919. 24⅛ × 19¼″ (Photo Giraudon).
© DACS 1987.

INDEX

(Numbers in italics refer to the page numbers of the illustrations)